QUEER FAMILIES, QUEER POLITICS

Challenging Culture
and the State

*Edited by Mary Bernstein
and Renate Reimann*

COLUMBIA UNIVERSITY PRESS
NEW YORK

COLUMBIA UNIVERSITY PRESS
NEW YORK

Columbia University Press
Publishers Since 1893
New York   Chichester, West Sussex
Copyright © 2001 Columbia University Press
All rights reserved

Library of Congress Cataloging-in-Publication Data
Queer families, queer politics : challenging culture and the state / edited by Mary
Bernstein and Renate Reimann
p. cm. — (Between men—between women)
Includes bibliographical references and index.
ISBN 0–231—11690–X (cloth) — ISBN 0–231–11691–8 (paper)
1. Gay and lesbian studies. 2. Bisexuality. 3. Gay men—Family relationships. 4. Lesbians—
Family relationships. I. Bernstein, Mary. II. Reimann, Renate. III. Series.

HQ75.15 .Q44   2001
306.76'6—dc21   00–052340

Casebound editions of Columbia University Press books are printed on
permanent and durable acid-free paper.
Printed in the United States of America
Designed by Lisa Hamm
c 10 9 8 7 6 5 4 3 2 1
p 10 9 8 7 6 5 4 3 2 1

QUEER FAMILIES,
QUEER POLITICS

BETWEEN MEN ~ BETWEEN WOMEN
Lesbian and Gay Studies
Lillian Faderman and Larry Gross, Editors

BETWEEN MEN ~ BETWEEN WOMEN
Lesbian and Gay Studies
Lillian Faderman and Larry Gross, Editors

Advisory Board of Editors

Claudia Card
Terry Castle
John D'Emilio
Esther Newton
Anne Peplau
Eugene Rice
Kendall Thomas
Jeffrey Weeks

BETWEEN MEN ~ BETWEEN WOMEN is a forum for current lesbian and gay scholarship in the humanities and social sciences. The series includes both books that rest within specific traditional disciplines and are substantially about gay men, bisexuals, or lesbians and books that are interdisciplinary in ways that reveal new insights into gay, bisexual, or lesbian experience, transform traditional disciplinary methods in consequence of the perspectives that experience provides, or begin to establish lesbian and gay studies as a freestanding inquiry. Established to contribute to an increased understanding of lesbians, bisexuals, and gay men, the series also aims to provide through that understanding a wider comprehension of culture in general.

Contents

PART 2 Parenthood

Acknowledgments

Mary and Renate would both like to give special thanks to David Greenberg for his critical advice on the content of the book as well as on the publishing process. Mary would like to thank Rose Weitz for her thoughtful direction at the early stages of this project. Nancy Jurik and Marjorie Zatz deserve special credit for their feedback on this volume. Without the tireless efforts of Mary Fran Draisker in formatting, and checking references and grammar, this book would not have been possible. We wish her all the best in her own battle.

Mary would also like to acknowledge the contributions of Emily Gaarder, Kristi Wimmer, and Bin Liang for their able research assistance and for helping with much of the tedious work that goes into compiling such a volume. Special thanks go to Malea Chavez, who reviewed several chapters and shared her energy.

Nancy Naples's contributions to this volume deserve acknowledgment on two levels. Intellectually, Nancy provided critical insight on whatever was placed in front of her. Personally, she helped Mary to create a new family. Nancy's emotional support and love continue to enrich Mary's life. Mary would also like to thank Roma, Bruce, and Joan Bernstein for their love.

Many wonderful colleagues and mentors have supported Renate along the way. Cynthia Fuchs Epstein and Barbara Katz Rothman pointed her in just the right direction on several occasions. Paul Attewell and William Kornblum offered some crucial insights into publishing. The encouraging words of Dan Chambliss, Mitchell Stevens, and Kerry Mullins always fell onto eager ears. And, as always, Julia Wrigley has been an inspiring presence. Her sense of humor carried Renate through many rough spots and made bearable those heavy moments of happiness and success.

Renate's friends deserve an unmeasurable amount of acknowledgment. Renate would have accomplished nothing without the love and care of Angela Bauer, Pam Donovan, Stephanie Foster, Manuel Guzmàn, Linda Horwitz, Hilke Kayser, Irma Levecque, Jack Levinson, Matthew Lindholm, Liz Randolph, Kerstin Söderblom, Randi Solberg, Sylvia de Swan, Selena Whang, and many others who stood by her side throughout this process.

Renate would also like to thank her family for their tireless support, particularly her mother who empowered Renate to do the things that are important to her. Her mother's boundless love never ceases to amaze.

Last but by no means least, Renate would like to credit the two women whose commitment to creating new ways of living and loving has enabled her to work miracles. Venice Fouchard brought her wonderful sense of elegance and style into Renate's life when she most needed to be surrounded by beauty. And Margarita Zambrano continues to inspire Renate with her leaps of faith and logic.

Mary and Renate would both like to thank the contributors as well as all the participants in "Relatively Speaking: A Conference on Lesbian, Gay, Bisexual, and Transgendered Families," which took place in 1997 at New York University, where many of these chapters were originally presented. We would particularly like to thank the Center for Lesbian and Gay Studies at the Graduate Center of the City University of New York for giving us the initial seed money for the conference, as well as the Humanities Council at New York University for their generosity. Many people made the conference a success, including, Juan Battle, Terry Boggis, Paula Ettelbrick, Tina Fetner, Arnold Grossman, Manolo Guzman, Eszter Hargitai, Lynne Huffer, Howard Maurer, and Selena Whang. Special thanks also go to Gilda Zwerman who's initial guidance helped make this book possible.

QUEER FAMILIES,
QUEER POLITICS

1 | Queer Families and the Politics of Visibility

Mary Bernstein and Renate Reimann

"Vermont's High Court Avoids the M-Word and Makes History" proclaims a recent *Boston Globe* headline (Graff 2000). Struggles over same-sex marriage, grandmothers suing their lesbian daughters for custody of their grandchildren (*Bottoms v. Bottoms*), battles over gays as foster parents, and queer teenagers organizing in schools are all topics making the front pages of national, regional, and local newspapers. Talk-show hosts cannot get enough of the queer invasion of American cultural life and news-magazine shows scramble to locate the next same-sex poster couple for the "homosexual" issue of the day.

Widespread visibility, however, has not translated into unequivocal improvements in the lives of lesbian, gay, bisexual, and transgendered (LGBT) individuals and families. Forceful opposition to acceptance of queer families comes from conservatives who view the very existence of queers as an immoral threat to the sanctity of the heterosexual order and to society itself. At the other end of the spectrum, many LGBTs strive desperately for acceptance and understanding from mainstream society. Still other LGBTs believe that queers *are* different and rightly challenge society's cherished norms about gender and the privatized heterosexual-nuclear family.

The chapters in this book examine the political and cultural impact of queers and their families as they struggle for the right to exist. Just over half of the chapters in this anthology were originally presented at a conference we chaired, entitled "Relatively Speaking: A Conference on Lesbian, Gay,

Bisexual, and Transgender Families," sponsored primarily by the Center for Lesbian and Gay Studies of the Graduate Center at the City University of New York and by the Humanities Council of New York University. All but two chapters are original works. The contributors to this volume are political activists, LGBT parents, as well as academics coming from a range of disciplines including sociology, political science, communication, and the law. This anthology, as did the conference, seeks to connect the microdynamics of family, gender, and sexuality with the macrodynamics of politics and the law.

The book is divided into three sections: in part I, "Relationships," the creation of intimate relationships among queer adults and relationships with families of origin is considered. Part II, "Parenthood," examines queer parents' disparate access to institutions that support families and discusses the ways in which children force issues of visibility. Finally, part III, "Political Activism," explores the links between the visibility of queer families, political and legal change, and the aspirations of queer families. The book examines the themes of visibility, transgression and resistance, and the intersection between the personal and political in the different contexts of relationships, children, and political activism. In it, we argue that queer families not only challenge culture and the state but also, because of their diversity, complicate lesbian and gay politics. This chapter begins with a discussion of what queer families are and how they pose a distinctive challenge to the primacy of the privatized heterosexual–nuclear family.

QUEER FAMILIES

THE TERM "FAMILY" CARRIES great emotional and cultural force. Yet few agree on what constitutes a family. Official and legal definitions of "family" range from groups of individuals who cohabit and are related by blood in the first degree, marriage, or adoption (U.S. Census Bureau) to definitions that include grandparents or nonmarried cohabiting couples (Minow 1998). In everyday terms, family can be any two or more people who feel emotionally committed to each other.

Although lawyers, sociologists, and psychologists all mean different things by the term "family," the privatized–nuclear family holds a sacred place in the American psyche and is embedded in most major social and legal institutions. As an ideal type, *The Family* consists of a legally married (biologically male) husband and a (biologically female) wife, approximately two children, and the obligatory dog or cat. Although a wife may work, her primary responsibility remains taking care of the home, husband, and children; the husband's main task is breadwinning, though he may, on occasion, deign to "help out" around the house. Although clearly not representative of the majority of American families,[1] this view of *The Family* is hegemonic and has been called an "ideological code" (Smith 1999:159) or a "privileged construct" (Weston 1991:6). Heteronormative assumptions about appropriate gender roles underpin the hegemonic view of family.

Historically, "the traditional family"—or the "modern family" as Stacey (1996) terms it—is a recent and, in light of demographic trends, a rather short-lived phenomenon (Coontz 1992, 1997). Industrialization and urbanization prompted massive changes in family life throughout the nineteenth and twentieth centuries worldwide. The material need for extended families diminished, children lost in economic but gained in emotional value (Zelizer 1985), nuclear families became smaller, and, as the life span lengthened and economic dependencies decreased, marriages for life were no longer the reality for an increasing number of couples. As a result, families come in all shapes and colors ranging from "traditional" families to couples without children, single-parent families, stepfamilies, and families of choice whose members are not always related by marriage, blood, or law (Coontz 1999; Stacey 1996; Weston 1991).

So, what is a "queer family?" Although some of the authors in this book prefer the terms "gay," "lesbian," "bisexual," or "transgender," we employ the term "queer" families here to signify the diverse family structures formed by those with nonnormative gender behaviors or sexual orientations. The term "family" refers to groups of individuals who define each other as family and share a strong emotional and/or financial commitment to each other, whether or not they cohabit, are related by blood, law, or adoption, have children, or are recognized by the law.

As reclaimed by lesbian, gay, bisexual, and transgender activists, the word "queer," and queer politics more generally, seeks to destabilize categories of identity, such as gay/lesbian, man/woman (Gamson 1995). According to Phelan (1997), "queer theory's ultimate target is identity itself" (56–57). Thus "queer" implies a self-conscious deconstruction of heteronormativity and a breaking down of arbitrary boundaries based on sex, gender, and sexual orientation. By destabilizing categories and focusing on a politics of inclusion rather than exclusion, "queer" helps to build coalitions among disparate groups and to break down barriers that demarcate identities such as transgendered, lesbian, or bisexual. Theoretically, the concept "queer" can be marshaled to mean anything that challenges heteronormativity. "For both academics and activists, 'queer' gets a critical edge by defining itself against the normal rather than the heterosexual" (Warner 1993:xxvi).

Queer families are part of the historical move toward family as a site of emotional and sexual gratification (D'Emilio and Freedman 1988). In recent years the increasing divorce of sexuality from reproduction has opened new opportunities for same-sex couples to procreate, resulting in the dissociation of reproduction from heterosexuality. Although same-sex erotic communities have existed throughout history in times and places where individuals could live outside the nuclear family or where one member of a same-sex couple adopted the gender role of the opposite sex (Eskridge 1993; Greenberg 1988), both developments—sexuality for pleasure rather than reproduction, and pro-creation independent of heterosexual intercourse—have revolutionized the possibilities of organizing family life based on same-sex erotic choices.

Despite the heterogeneity of contemporary family forms, families that deviate from the ideal type of the "modern family" are judged inadequate. For example, immigrant and poor families and families of color have drawn criticism from conservatives and liberals alike for their diverse, noncon-forming family organizations. Their difference from the ideal of the white, bourgeois, native-born family was and continues to be interpreted as the primary source of each group's social problems and society's ills in general (Coontz 1992; Rubin 1994).

Daniel Patrick Moynihan's report (1965), for example, sparked a decades-long debate about the relationship between African American family struc-tures and the plight of blacks in America. Many commentators attribute poverty within the black community to African American family structures. In response, other researchers see the low incidence of two-parent married African American couples as a result of racism and poor economic oppor-tunities (Wilson 1987). In either view, African American families are com-pared to white middle-class families and seen as deviant. The main differ-ence between conservative and liberal critics lies in whether they blame such families for their "deviation" or attribute these "deviations" to struc-tural factors.

Alternatively, some commentators have stressed the adaptive strength of African American families in the face of great economic and social pressure (McAdoo 1998; Stack 1974). For example, Collins (1990), hooks (1984), and Sudarkasa (1998) stress that mainstream society can learn much from the long tradition of shared economic responsibility among spouses and the support of extended and fictive kin for (single) parents in black communi-ties. Although there are few studies of family forms among white ethnic and working-class families, existing studies suggest that they have many positive benefits—such as extended kinship structures that promote family well-being (Rubin 1994; Sennett and Cobb 1972).

Heterosexual families that fall outside the "traditional" family structure challenge patriarchal assumptions about the proper roles women and men should play within the family as well as American ideals of individualism. The notion that each privatized-nuclear family should be a self-sufficient unit, with the man responsible for the family's economic well-being and the woman responsible for the family's emotional health is contested by the family forms of immigrants, poor families, and families of color.

Queer families present new challenges to the privatized-nuclear family, contradicting the sexual dimorphism upon which the ideal family is based. Such families challenge dominant notions of not only gender but also sexuality. Queers of color, low-income LGBTs, resistance to dyadic coupled bliss, preference for nonmonogamy, same-sex couples wanting children, lesbians not wanting children—all confound heteronormativity, contest the hegemonic family ideal, *and* complicate lesbian and gay politics.

THE PRIVILEGE AND POLITICS OF BEING OUT

BECAUSE LESBIANS, GAY MEN, and bisexuals have the option, however unpleasant and damaging to the soul it may be, of remaining invisible, presentation of self becomes central to gay and lesbian politics. Whether we present ourselves as bull daggers, dykes on bikes, nelly queens, or as ordinary as the boy or girl next door (save for our choice of romantic partners) has implications for the challenge lesbians, gay men, and bisexuals present to the dominant heteronormative culture and to the state. Thus, not surprisingly, gay and lesbian politics as well as politics said to be "queer" center around issues of visibility.

The lesbian and gay movement regulates internally who are the acceptable queers and who are the queers better left in the closet (Gamson 1997; Seidman 1993). Over time, the movement has veered between deploying identities that emphasize similarities to the majority, striving to be a "model minority," and deploying identities that stress differences from the heteronormative mainstream, seeking to transgress (Bernstein 1997a, 1997b). LGB people often embrace white, middle-class, straight, suburban American norms in the ongoing quest for acceptance. Racial- and ethnic-minority queers, working-class queers, and all who would challenge dominant beliefs about gender, including transgendered people, fall outside acceptable norms, and their presence in the movement is often minimized (Bull and Gallagher 1996). While coming out has been a privileged movement strategy, uneasiness remains when the "wrong people" claim visibility. Thus, *how* we present ourselves is as important as *that* we present ourselves. "Queer" families, then, force issues of visibility and invisibility in distinctive ways.

"Coming out" is often considered the most important political step that a lesbian, gay, or bisexual person can take. Lesbian and gay activists exhort people to come out of the closet, with the assumption that to know us is to love us. This seemingly democratic strategy is often subverted in the practice of actual political campaigns when those who transgress the dominant norms of femininity or masculinity, the working class, and people of color, are expected to remain in the closet, because of the potentially negative effect their presence could have on political outcomes (Bernstein 1997a, 1997b, chapter 24; Bull and Gallagher 1996). Even sexuality itself is ignored in, for example, campaigns to decriminalize consensual sex acts between adults that stress the issue of privacy but avoid referring to actual physical acts (see Bernstein, chapter 24).

Decisions about whether or not to come out to one's family or about one's queer family members have both private and public dimensions that are often ignored by the discourse of the dominant gay and lesbian rights movement. In more "private" contexts, the institution of the family forces individuals to make decisions about whether or not to come out of the closet to relatives and the person(s) who raised them.

The chapters in part I show that coming out to one's family has disparate meanings depending on the class and race locations of the actors as well as on their sexual identity. In Asian American (see chapter 10) and American Indian families (see chapter 6), for example, not only does homosexuality violate cultural taboos that are specific to these racial/ethnic groups, but discussion of sexuality (and particularly homosexuality) with one's family violates culturally cherished notions of respect and interconnectedness. In cultures that do not place the same values on individualism as mainstream American culture does, expectations of being out are culturally inappropriate and carry greater risk to those who depend on their families and communities for refuge from an often hostile and racist outside world. The white middle-class gay/lesbian expectation that one should be out to one's family neglects the ways in which this "choice" is in fact a privilege, one that carries greater sanctions for some than for others. But as the chapters by Margaret Waller and Roland McAllen-Walker (chapter 6) and Gustavo Yep,

Karen Lovaas, and Philip Ho (chapter 10) suggest, not coming out to one's family also carries a price.

Class influences family relationships and the meaning of coming out in complex ways. As Lionel Cantú illustrates (see chapter 8), upper-class Mexican gay men have more freedom to express their sexuality because of their economic privilege, while poor Mexican men gain acceptance for their sexuality as they become better economic providers. The narrow construction of gender promulgated in the family constrains these Mexican men and serves as an impetus to migrate. Nonetheless, maintaining ties with their families of origin remains important. In a white working-class Irish-Catholic family, where the family boundaries are strictly drawn, the gulf between achieved social status as well as nonnormative sexuality strains family ties, as Nancy Naples illustrates (see chapter 2).

As society appears to become more tolerant, lesbians and gay men as well as heterosexuals redraw the lines between tolerance and rejection. For example, Jeffrey Ringer discusses the challenge of constructing happy non-monagamous relationships (see chapter 9). Similarly, Elizabeth Randolph recounts how her Southern, conservative African American family *as well as* her more progressive lesbian and gay friends refuse to accept her bisexuality, wanting her to choose one "team" or the other (see chapter 7). In much the same way, Naples's history of relationships with men made it easier for her family to deny the existence of her lesbian relationships (see chapter 2).

Just as lesbians and gay men go through a coming-out process, which is considered necessary for healthy identity development (Cass 1984; Walters 1997), the families of lesbians and gays must also decide whether or not to come out about their own queer family members. Once again, family forces the issue of visibility. However, this issue takes on different tones within various racial/ethnic communities. As Bennett and Battle argue (see chapter 4), for African Americans to come out about their queer family members means airing laundry considered by many to be "dirty." Just as the moniker "lesbian" is used to discredit feminists, acknowledgment of queer family members makes African Americans vulnerable to more claims that their families are inadequate.

The flip side of discreditation is romanticization. As Waller and McAllen-Walker argue (see chapter 6), American Indians who are out in culturally diverse queer communities are often sought out for the perceived acceptance they receive from their families and communities. Since their experience often contradicts these romanticized visions, queer American Indians are left with no place to be entirely safe. The strategy of being out, in short, stems from a privileged location, as a discussion of queer families and communities of color illustrates.

When queers decide to come out in the context of their relationships, how they present themselves has implications for political and cultural change. For example, as Ellen Lewin argues (see chapter 3), commitment ceremonies by members of the same sex may blend elements of assimilation and transgression. By declaring commitments publicly, same-sex couples force onlookers to acknowledge the nature of their relationships, allowing friends and family no room to deny the sexual and emotional dimensions of their gay/lesbian or queer identities.

Queer family issues play out dramatically on daytime talk TV. Gender radicals and working-class queers, who are among the mainstays of this genre, help redefine cultural levels of tolerance and complicate lesbian and gay politics. In the expressive world of talk shows, the middle-class, predominantly white lesbian and gay rights movement has lost control over the presentation of the movement. Over the airwaves of daytime talk TV, the model minority seems to have run amok as queer-family dramas construct new norms for inclusion and exclusion. As Joshua Gamson points out (see chapter 5), the public, happily devouring their daily dose of queerness, draws the line at gender radicals, particularly those who are transgendered, and at bisexuals for the potential threat they pose to the traditional monogamous family.

Whether or not to include transgendered people and bisexuals in the lesbian and gay rights movement has been a debate within the lesbian and gay movement for decades (Bernstein 1997a, 1997b; see Halle, chapter 22; Marotta 1981). Similarly, the political and legal fight for gay marriage grew out of grassroots organizing and was spearheaded by individuals independent of and often against the advice of queer political leaders. In fact, early resistance to same-sex marriage on the part of professional queer organizers alienated many individuals at the grassroots level (see Javors, chapter 18). Thus, in the context of family, movement leaders have lost control of the discourse on many levels.

Academia also serves as a site where political and cultural gatekeeping takes place. Publishing norms as well as modernist understandings of what constitutes "science" privilege certain ways of knowing over others (Harding 1987). In the second half of chapter 2, Naples lays out a feminist theoretical framework for understanding the importance of self-reflectivity and personal experience as a valuable method of inquiry that can serve as both personal and political interventions. In analyzing the challenges queer American Indians face from within and outside their communities, Waller and McAllen-Walker (see chapter 6) also allow the narrative to speak for itself, consistent with the Navajo tradition of teaching through stories. Thus we have chosen to begin each section of this book with personal testimonials from lesbian and gay activists, parents, and children in order to give voice to different types of knowledge that can further understanding of queer family politics and increase the volume of hitherto silenced voices.

CHILDREN, PRIVACY, AND THE CONTRADICTIONS OF VISIBILITY

"WHAT WOULD YOU DO if your child were gay?" is a question often leveled at homophobes in a thinly disguised plea for tolerance. But what happens when it is the parents who are queer instead? With respect to children, the family is anything but a private realm. In order to become a parent, as a queer person, or to maintain contact with one's children from a former heterosexual relationship, issues of class, race, and visibility once again interact in complex ways. It is perhaps here that heteronormativity is at its strongest. After setting aside the myth that lesbians and gay men will molest their children (Herek 1991), society fears that queer parents will produce gay children or children with "inappropriate" gender roles. As Bernstein argues (see chapter 24), lesbians and gay men are successful in maintaining custody of their children, at becoming foster parents, or at obtaining second-parent adoptions only to the extent that they can show that their parenting will not threaten the heteronormative order by producing children with nontraditional gender behavior or children who are gay or lesbian.

In general, queers who want to be parents have limited choices. Put simply, the more money one has, the more options one has. Terry Boggis, director of Center Kids at the Gay and Lesbian Community Services Center in New York City, argues that the creation of the model minority, particularly by the lesbian and gay parenting movement, increases the marginalization and invisibility of poor queer parents. As a result, the needs and interests of poor queers who are or want to become parents are disregarded. For example, the lesbian and gay parenting movement ignores issues of social support and public services for poor queers, focusing instead on issues such as access to artificial insemination (see Murphy, chapter 12) or second-parent adoption (see Dalton, chapter 13), services only the well-to-do can afford.

Similarly, in chapter 13, Susan Dalton illustrates the level of intrusion that lesbian and gay couples are subjected to by the state in order to establish a legal relationship with their children. In order to be granted second-parent adoptions, queer parents must not only prove their "model-minority" status but often become educators for uninformed and prejudiced social workers. Both the monetary cost and the requirement to be a "model minority" create disparate access for queers who wish to become parents, depending on race/ethnicity and class.

Having children forces queers to make important decisions about whether or not to come out, and if so, how to manage their self-presentation. As Maureen Sullivan argues (see chapter 15), being a parent in public places forces comothers to confront new situations where they must either disclose to acquaintances and strangers their relationship to the child, and hence their sexuality, or lie. For example, when a child and his/her two mothers are in public settings such as department stores or play groups, the role of the "second" mother becomes unintelligible to most strangers and thus requires legitimation and explanation. Moreover, assimilation and transgression are not simply about choice for lesbian mothers and comothers but are about safety and taking care of their children.

In chapter 16 Renate Reimann discusses issues of self-disclosure of mothers in the work place. Invisibility and heteronormative assumptions play out differently for birthmothers and comothers. Birthmothers must come out when they want their lesbian romantic choices to be acknowledged in the workplace. Comothers, in addition to being recognized as lesbians, need to come out to claim parental benefits in the workplace. Only if they are willing to disclose their queer family life are they able to demand the employer support granted to heterosexual parents as a matter of course. In either case they face difficult decisions about coming out at work. As Sullivan and Reimann argue, others play a significant role in the coming-out process. That is, visibility is not simply an act performed by queers but the result of complex interactions and exercises of power between queers and their interlocutors.

FULL CIRCLE: THE IMPLICATIONS OF INVISIBILITY

AS WE HAVE ALREADY discussed, being out is a privileged position that is complicated by issues of race, class, and children. But what happens when queer families remain in the closet? Janet Wright (see chapter 17) argues that children of lesbians and gays are not worried about their own gender development or sexual orientation, but are deathly afraid of being teased for the tiny little way in which their families differ from heteronormative families. The solution, argues Wright, is increased visibility for queers generally, and for lesbian and gay families specifically. It is only through a plethora of positive and realistic images that we can help children of queers not to live in fear.

However, if we are to resist heteronormativity and engage in more democratic queer politics, a variety of family structures must be visible, so that we can choose family forms that will suit our diverse interests and needs. For example, hegemonic notions of masculinity and the nuclear family limit gay men's family choices in specific ways. Gay men have long had a tradition of sexual liberation (Weeks 1989) that challenges the monogamous dyadic family form. With the onset of AIDS, however, many gay men have abandoned the sexually free, nonmonogamous lifestyle of the 1970s out of fear of disease (Shilts 1987). Others, nonetheless, continue to defy the rule of monogamy. Jeffrey Ringer's research asserts (see chapter 9) that there are multiple ways of constructing healthy and happy nonmonogamous relationships. As Ringer demonstrates, we construct and maintain our families through communication, especially when our relational choices contradict social expectations and norms. Without visible role models, however, anyone seeking to live such a lifestyle, must constantly reinvent the wheel.

Gay men who wish to raise children also face a lack of visible role models, particularly because dominant constructions of masculinity and male sexuality deem children to be the province of women (making it understandable within a heteronormative order why lesbians would want to parent). Additionally, as John Miller argues (see chapter 14), the gay-male role has often been inconsistent with the role of father. Whether gay men create families that coincide with or challenge dominant notions of masculinity, they require support from both queer and straight communities and must have visible role models from which to choose. Yet for many LGBTs, particularly queers of color, the dilemma between visibility and respecting cultural norms about sexuality and sexual orientation places them in an untenable position so that they often lead double lives—being "gay" in one setting and a "person of color" in another.

ACCEPTANCE, TRANSGRESSION, AND THE POLITICS OF QUEER FAMILIES

THE THIRD PART OF this book focuses on the politics and cultural implications of same-sex marriage as well as on the relationship between visibility, gender transgression, and the extent to which the law can meet the needs of queers. The lesbian and gay movement has historically been split between those who seek to transform dominant gender norms and visions about sexuality—in other words those who seek to transform the heteronormative order—and those who view homosexuality as a difference as benign as left-handedness, which would have no meaning in the absence of discrimination (Bernstein 1997a, 1997b; Cruikshank 1992; Vaid 1995). The arena of the family is particularly charged for both sides of the debate further inflaming the politics of visibility. Who may be present in queer political campaigns organized around the issue of family?

Critical race and feminist legal theorists (e.g., Delgado 1995; Fineman 1995; Smart 1989; Williams 1991) recognize that the law is a limited vehicle for social change because it channels groups into making rights-based claims on the basis of narrow identities based on race, gender, or sexual orientation. Nonetheless, they also contend that the law is potentially a useful tool that can be used by oppressed groups in the quest for social change (see also McCann 1991). Can the law be marshaled by LGBT people either to gain acceptance or to transform dominant cultural narms?

Feminist legal scholars (e.g., Fineman 1995; Smart 1989) bring the question of similarity and difference to bear on the relationship between law and social change. For example, in discussing divorce law, feminists ask should the law treat men and women equally, when in fact they are not similarly situated? Gender inequality in the workplace as well as norms for who should raise children, position men and women differently in these debates. Thus many argue that women have been badly hurt by divorce-law reform that purports to treat men and women equally while failing to recognize how they are differently positioned (Fineman 1995; Weitzman 1985). Building on the feminist analysis of similarity and difference, we must ask, can laws designed to suit the needs of (white male) heterosexuals meet the needs of LGBT people?

Julien Murphy, for example, asks whether or not the patriarchal rules that govern access to artificial insemination services suit the needs of lesbians (see chapter 12). Such rules often require that a woman be married before being allowed access to donor sperm, a condition that negatively affects single heterosexual women as well. Alternatively, women who are married to infertile men are considered "relationally" infertile, another categorization that does not translate well for lesbians. Rather than being forced into these patriarchal and heteronormative categories, lesbians would benefit from a revisioning of reproduction that emphasizes choice within a variety of family forms.

In light of the conflicts between the desire for social acceptance and the resistance to being pigeonholed into dominant cultural patterns, David Chambers (see chapter 19) and Suzanna Walters (see chapter 20) consider whether same-sex marriage would in fact meet the needs of lesbians and gay men. Chambers classifies the laws relating to married couples and assesses whether they fill the real needs expressed by lesbians and gay men. His answer is a resounding "yes." Walters, on the other hand, offers a radical feminist critique of marriage, arguing that marriage privileges certain kinds of relationships and simply redraws the boundaries of who are the acceptable queers. As Gamson shows (see chapter 5), the public seems willing to accept monogamous lesbians and gay men but draws the line at what Nan Hunter (1991) has called "gender dissent."

The issue of visibility, and who can be visible, is intimately linked to whether family politics are tied to acceptance or transformation. In a personal testimonial, activist Irene Javors argues (see chapter 18) that what the queer public really wants is acceptance and that marriage is the way to achieve the acceptance so deeply craved, particularly by closeted queers. As Donald Haider-Markel maintains (see chapter 21), the ability to frame the issue of marriage will determine whether or not it even gets on the political agenda. The extent to which queers are willing (or able) to make the concessions necessary to win the right to marry remains open to debate.

But what of the gender radicals—the queers who conservatives within the movement see as giving "virtually normal" (Eskridge 1996; Sullivan 1995) queers a bad name? Mary Coombs takes the issue of same-sex marriage a step further (see chapter 23) by examining the relationship between transgenderism and sexual orientation, and between gender and sexual orientation. In all likelihood, according to Coombs, the first challenge to anti-same-sex marriage laws may well come from transgendered people. Randall Halle's case study of organizing around same-sex marriage and queer families in Cambridge, Massachusetts (see chapter 22) illustrates the tensions between activists' goals of challenging cultural values and gaining concessions from the state. Halle finds that critiquing gender roles often makes obtaining legal reform more difficult, creating dilemmas for activists. Bernstein argues (see chapter 24) that in order to win legal change, activists must often "sanitize" homosexuality to the point where erotic desire for a person of the same sex, engaging in sexual acts, and taking on nontraditional gender roles disappears. Although the law may provide protection from harm and grant rights to queers, legal change in and of itself neither creates acceptance for queers nor transforms heteronormativity.

Queer families create multiple sites where presumably private and personal decisions regarding visibility are made. Such decisions have an indelible impact on American culture and politics and often take place beyond the reach of professional lesbian and gay activists. By connecting the microdynamics of gender, sexuality, and family with the macrodynamics of politics and law, we hope that this book will contribute to an increased understanding of queer families and queer politics—in particular the ways in which the issue of visibility is informed by race, class, and gender dynamics. Visibility for queers and their families is about more than just the playful irony usually associated with queer politics (Butler 1990; Ferguson 1993); it is a function of power and context, often propelled by the realities of family life, such as, for example, sick children who need one of their two daddies to stay home from work with them.

Heteronormativity constrains queers and their families in multiple ways. Access to institutions is predicated on fitting into dominant categories that often make no sense for queers. Regardless of whether queers are seeking acceptance or transformation, the categories and tools of mainstream society will not easily meet their needs.

The law, in particular, holds promise as well as danger for LGBT families. Although the law provides some protection from harm, and choice is important, we must be cautious when pursuing legal change that privileges some relationships while excluding others. It would be a mistake to simply redraw the boundaries of acceptable families to include just a few lesbian and gay couples. In the words of Martha Fineman (1995):

> To be a "just" society, we must treat "all" families with respect and concern at the same time that we realize that the traditional family is not a panacea for the problems society faces. . . . The family can no longer be an assumed institution in policy discussions, but must be an explicitly self-conscious, constantly reconsidered configuration that reflects both existing reality and collective responsibility. (236)

It is our hope that this book will contribute to an understanding of the interplay between queer families, politics, and culture.

NOTE

1. In 1998, only 6.7 percent of all households fit the "traditional" nuclear-family model. Even among married couples with children under eighteen years of age only about 27 percent of the husbands were the sole breadwinners.

This number increases to a mere 35 percent in married couples with children under six years old (U.S. Census Bureau 1998). At the same time, about 10 percent of adults were "currently divorced," 35 percent of twenty-five to thirty-four-year-olds had never been married, and 28 percent of children under eighteen years of age lived with just one parent, primarily their mother (84 percent) (U.S. Census Bureau 1999).

REFERENCES

Bernstein, Mary. 1997a. "Celebration and Suppression: The Strategic Uses of Identity by the Lesbian and Gay Movement." *American Journal of Sociology* 103 (3): 531–65.

———. 1997b. "Sexual Orientation Policy, Protest, and the State." Ph.D. diss., New York University.

Bull, Chris and John Gallagher. 1996. *Perfect Enemies: The Religious Right, the Gay Movement, and the Politics of the 1990s.* New York: Crown.

Cass, V. 1984. "Homosexual Identity Formation: Testing a Theoretical Model." *Journal of Sex Research* 20: 143–67.

Collins, Patricia Hill. 1990. *Black Feminist Thought: Knowledge, Consciousness, and the Politics of Empowerment.* Boston: Unwin Hyman.

Coontz, Stephanie. 1992. *The Way We Never Were: American Families and the Nostalgia Trip.* New York: Basic Books.

———. 1997. *The Way We Really Are: Coming to Terms with America's Changing Families.* New York: Basic Books.

Coontz, Stephanie, with Maya Parson and Gabrielle Raley, eds. 1999. *American Families: A Multicultural Reader.* New York: Routledge.

Cruikshank, Margaret. 1992. *The Gay and Lesbian Liberation Movement.* New York: Routledge.

Delgado, Richard (ed.). 1995. *Critical Race Theory: The Cutting Edge.* Philadelphia, PA: Temple University Press.

D'Emilio, John. 1983. "Capitalism and Gay Identity." In Ann Snitow, Christine Stansell, and Sharon Thompson, eds., *Powers of Desire: The Politics of Sexuality*, pp. 100–13. New York: Monthly Review Press.

D'Emilio, John and Estelle Freedman. 1998. *Intimate Matters: A History of Sexuality in America.* 2d. ed. New York: Harper & Row.

Eskridge, William N. Jr. 1993. "A History of Same-Sex Marriage." *Virginia Law Review* 79: 1419–1514.

———. 1996. *The Case for Same-Sex Marriage.* New York: Free Press.

Ferguson, Kathy E. 1993. *The Man Question: Visions of Subjectivity in Feminist Theory.*
　　Berkeley: University of California Press.

Fineman, Martha Albertson. 1995. *The Neutered Mother, the Sexual Family, and Other*
　　Twentieth-Century Tragedies. New York: Routledge.

Gamson, Joshua. 1995. "Must Identity Movements Self-Destruct: A Queer
　　Dilemma." *Social Problems* 42 (3): 390–407.

——. 1997. "Messages of Exclusion: Gender, Movements, and Symbolic Bound-
　　aries." *Gender & Society* 11 (2): 178–99.

Graff, E. J. 2000. "Vermont's High Court Avoids the M–Word and Makes History."
　　The Boston Globe, January 2, 2000, p. C7.

Greenberg, David F. 1988. *The Construction of Homosexuality.* Chicago: University of
　　Chicago Press.

Harding Sandra. 1987. *Feminism and Methodology: Social Science Issues.* Bloomington:
　　Indiana University Press

Herek, Gregory M. 1991. "Myths About Sexual Orientation: A Lawyer's Guide to
　　Social Science Research." *Law & Sexuality* 1 (Summer): 133–72.

hooks, bell. 1984. *Feminist Theory: From Margin to Center.* Boston: South End Press.

Hunter, Nan D. 1991. "Marriage, Law, and Gender: A Feminist Inquiry." *Law & Sex-*
　　uality 1 (Summer): 9–30.

Marotta, Toby. 1981. *The Politics of Homosexuality.* Boston: Houghton Mifflin.

McAdoo, Harriette P. 1998. "African-American Families." In Charles H. Mindel,
　　Robert W. Haberstein, and Roosevelt Wright, Jr., eds., *Ethnic Families in America:*
　　Patterns and Variations, pp. 361–81. Upper Saddle River, N.J.: Prentice-Hall.

McCann, Michael W. 1991. "Legal Mobilization and Social Reform Movements:
　　Notes on Theory and its Application." In *Studies in Law, Politics, and Society*
　　11:225–254. Greenwich, Conn.: JAI Press.

Minow, Martha. 1998. "Redefining Families: Who's In and Who's Out?" In Karen V.
　　Hansen and Anita Ilta Garey, eds., *Families in the U.S.: Kinship and Domestic Poli-*
　　tics, pp. 7–19. Philadelphia: Temple University Press.

Moynihan, Daniel Patrick. 1965. *The Negro Family: The Case for National Action.* Wash-
　　ington, D.C.: Office of Policy Planning and Research, U.S. Department of
　　Labor.

Phelan, Shane. 1997. "The Shape of Queer: Assimilation and Articulation." *Women*
　　and Politics 18 (2): 55–73.

Rubin, Lillian. 1994. *Families on the Fault Line: America's Working Class Speaks about the*
　　Family, the Economy, Race, and Ethnicity. New York: HarperCollins.

Seidman, Steven. 1993. "Identity and Politics in a 'Postmodern' Gay Culture: Some
　　Historical and Conceptual Notes." In Michael Warner, ed., *Fear of a Queer Planet:*
　　Queer Politics and Social Theory, pp. 105–42. Minneapolis: University of Minnesota
　　Press.

Sennett, Richard and Jonathan Cobb, 1972. *Hidden Injuries of Class*. New York: Vintage.

Shilts, Randy. 1987. *And the Band Played On: Politics, People, and the AIDS Epidemic*. New York: Penguin.

Smart, Carol. 1989. *Feminism and the Power of Law*. London: Routledge.

Smith, Dorothy E. 1999. *Writing the Social: Critique, Theory, and Investigations*. Toronto: University of Toronto Press.

Stacey, Judith. 1996. *In the Name of the Family: Rethinking Family Values in the Postmodern Age*. Boston: Beacon Press.

Stack, Carol. 1974. *All Our Kin: Strategies for Survival in a Black Community*. New York: Harper & Row.

Sudarkasa, Niara. 1998. "Interpreting the African Heritage in Afro-American Family Organization." In Karen V. Hansen and Anita Ilta Garey, eds., *Families in the U.S.: Kinship and Domestic Politics*, pp. 91–104. Philadelphia: Temple University Press.

Sullivan, Andrew. 1995. *Virtually Normal: An Argument About Homosexuality*. New York: Knopf.

U.S. Census Bureau, 1999, http://www.census.gov/Press-Release/www/1999/cb99–03.html

U.S. Census Bureau, 1998, Internet release date: 12/11/98, http://www.census.gov/population/socdemo/hh-fam/htabMC-1.txt

Vaid, Urvashi. 1995. *Virtual Equality: The Mainstreaming of Gay and Lesbian Liberation*. New York: Anchor Books.

Walters, Kath. 1997. "Urban Lesbian and Gay American Indian Identity: Implications for Mental Health Service Delivery." In Lester B. Brown, ed., *Two-Spirit People: American Indian Lesbian Women and Gay Men*, pp. 43–65. New York: Haworth.

Warner, Michael, ed. 1993. *Fear of a Queer Planet: Queer Politics and Social Theory*. Minneapolis: University of Minnesota Press.

Weeks, Jeffrey. 1989. *Sexuality and Its Discontents: Meanings, Myths, & Modern Sexualities*. London: Routledge.

Weitzman, Lenore J. 1985. *The Divorce Revolution: The Unexpected Social and Economic Consequences for Women in America*. New York: The Free Press.

Weston, Kath. 1991. *Families We Choose: Lesbians, Gays, Kinship*. New York: Columbia University Press.

Williams, Patricia J. 1991. *The Alchemy of Race and Rights*. Cambridge: Harvard University Press.

Wilson, William Julius. 1987. *The Truly Disadvantaged: The Inner City, the Underclass, and Public Policy*. Chicago: University of Chicago Press.

Zelizer, Viviana A. 1985. *Pricing the Priceless Child: The Changing Social Value of Children*. New York: Basic Books.

PART 1 | *Relationships*

2 A Member of the Funeral:
An Introspective Ethnography

Nancy A. Naples

S tanding at my father's freshly dug grave holding the American flag the funeral director had just handed to me, I had
the feeling I was in a bad made-for-TV movie. Since my
mother was too sick with Alzheimer's to attend and I was the oldest of the
six siblings, I was given the "honor." I thought it was especially odd since,
given my left-leaning politics, I would be the least likely member of my
family to fly the flag on the major military and other national holidays. As I
watched my three sisters, two brothers, their spouses, and my fifteen nieces
and nephews slowly make their way back to the cars with other members
of my large "heteronormal" extended family, I at once ached to be accepted
as a part of their world and longed for my "real" family.

I flashed back to the last time I stood by this graveside. It was also a somewhat dreary fall day. My brother Donald, who was the nearest in age to me
(born less than a year and a half after me) and who was closest to me in other
ways as well, had died in a car crash. At this time, my father decided to buy
a plot in the local cemetery in their suburban community just north of New
York City that would fit eight family members—less than needed if all of
us wanted to be buried there, more if everyone else was buried with their
own nuclear family. So now two of the plots are inhabited. I wondered who
besides my mother would join them. I presumed that all the other siblings
would be buried with their nuclear families. Maybe my father thought that
since I was "single," namely had no "family" of my own, it would make sense
for me to join them when the time came.

The significance of my singleness in the context of all the two-parent male and female families who made up the funeral procession was not lost on my two aunts. Earlier at the funeral parlor I overheard one of my aunts say to another aunt, "You know, the one I feel the most sorry for is Nancy. She has nobody." Their hushed and worried exchange amused me somewhat, although I also felt a great deal of sadness since, as many gays and lesbians, I am rich with loving and intimate friends whom I consider my "real" family. Yet in fact I was indeed alone at my father's funeral. Where was everybody?

When my brother Donald died in 1985, two of my most treasured "real" family were there for me. My lover Nina, who died in 1987 of breast cancer, and Peter, my brother-in-spirit who died of AIDS in 1996, were with me and were important witnesses over the years to the difficulties I had negotiating relationships with my family. Nina and Peter most assuredly would have been by my side had they been alive. Yet since neither Nina nor Peter were my legal nor biological relations, their presence would have done little to shake the perception of my aloneness in the heteronormative world of my family.

Nina was my first female lover. We met in graduate school and I fell madly in love with her. When I "came out" to a lesbian friend about our relationship, she expressed great pleasure at my "coming to consciousness" or something to that effect. She made me feel that my more than fifteen years as a practicing heterosexual was something akin to false sexual consciousness. I resisted the revised grand narrative she attempted to impose on my sexual identity. I asserted that my relationships with men, as troubled as they were, were authentic expressions of my sexual desire. However, as I made this statement I remember feeling uncomfortable about laying claim to some authentic self.

Maybe my long heterosexual history has made it difficult for my siblings to accept my claim to a lesbian identity. Nina was incorporated into my family as my "best friend." No questions were asked about why I was no longer seeing my boyfriend Mark, nor did anyone ever ask why I never had another boyfriend after him. This seemed like an obvious question since I had dated boys since eighth grade, been married once, and lived with another man for several years. Nor did I take the initiative to explain. I just believed deep in my bones that coming out to my parents and siblings at the time would only strain my already conflict-ridden relationship with them. I did not feel that I had anything to gain from doing so and had much more to lose. I remember having drinks with Donald one Christmas eve. When he said he wanted to ask me something important about Nina, I held my breath for what I thought would be the inevitable question: Are you and Nina lovers? I remember how perversely relieved I was when he asked me a very different question: Had I ever thought about her dying?—she was in the first of several rounds of chemotherapy treatment for breast cancer.

Not surprisingly, the unspoken but palpable homophobia I felt from my family was deeply woven into my own psyche. I colluded in the silence about it while Nina was alive. However, after she died I desperately wanted them to acknowledge who she was in my life and what her loss meant for me. I remember my mother commenting on what a good friend and social worker (my previous career) I was, given my central role in Nina's care, which included taking her to doctors' appointments and chemo treatments, sleeping over at the hospital during the last months of her life, and acting as executor of her will. Not even the fact that she left me all her worldly possessions, the money from the successful lawsuit against the breast surgeon who misdiagnosed the cancer, and her precious dog, Lucy, could shake my family's construction of my "friendship" with Nina.

Given the diversity among my siblings, coming out to them was much easier as well as much harder than I anticipated. The reactions ranged from downright hostility and rejection to ambivalent acceptance (the subtle message was that as long as I did not speak too much about my life as a lesbian, they could accept it). My brother John, the most hostile one, was violently angry and said in an attacking tone that having a sister who was a lesbian was a great embarrassment for him and that he would surely lose friends because of it. My brother Paul refused to hear it at all. Lisa and Melissa, the youngest of the clan, were mildly accepting, although over the years it became clear that, as Lisa put it, they would rather "not think about it." Karen, the remaining sister, was the most profoundly disturbed by it. Karen became a born-again Christian in her early twenties and was very invested in the antihomosexual position her church promulgated. Her comments about how homosexuality was a sin against God and that gays were sexually promiscuous, carriers of diseases, and a basic threat to the moral fabric of society greatly distressed me even though I was well versed in the religious right's view of what they disparagingly call the "homosexual lifestyle." Once, I tried to explain the epidemiology of the AIDS virus to her. I dispassionately noted that the majority of those infected throughout the world are practicing heterosexuals and that lesbians are not at especially high risk of HIV. Karen responded, "Well you have your opinion and I have mine." I realized in this brief attempt to present another view that I was forced to sell

out gay men who did have AIDS. I knew better. After all, I teach about
homosexuality, compulsory heterosexuality, and the social construction of
gender to large classes of undergraduates and have had to find that careful
balance between encouraging a critical consciousness and directly challenging their worldviews.

Religion also served as a main wedge between my other siblings and me.
We were brought up by a devout Catholic mother, and all of my siblings—
with the exception of my sister Karen, who became a member of a conservative Christian church—continued to attend mass regularly and participate
in all the Catholic sacraments. They baptized each of their children in the
Catholic Church. I attended most of the baptisms but became increasingly
pained by the way this ritual further marginalized me in the family. My lack
of religious affiliation and unmarried status made me unfit, in my siblings'
eyes, to be godparent to any of my fifteen nieces and nephews.

Regardless of their individual responses to my coming out as a lesbian,
each sibling strongly warned me against telling my parents. I think they all
firmly believed that, as my brother John said, "it would kill daddy"—a pro-
jection of their own fears and a threat that is frequently used to keep gays
and lesbians in the closet. Of course I did not really believe that the simple
statement about my sexual orientation would kill my father or mother.
However, on one level I felt I had nothing to gain by taking the risk and, on
another level, I figured my father already knew. After all, he was a firefighter
in the West Village for twenty-five years, even helping to put out the fires of
Stonewall. I rationalized that if he wanted to deal with my lesbian identity,
he would bring it up himself. So we developed an unspoken contract. I
would not name my relationships with women as lesbian and he would
accept my girlfriends into his home, no questions asked. I thought that was
fair for the most part. In retrospect, I realize that I somehow bought into the
fear that my lesbian self was a shameful secret that might have the power if
not to kill, at least to deeply harm others.

Over the more than ten years since I came out as a lesbian to my siblings,
I tried to find a way to be a part of the family while also trying to protect
myself from their rejection of my lesbian self. I maintained normalized relationships with all but my brother John and related to the other brother Paul
through my sister-in-law, who seemed to be more open. I stopped celebrating Christmas and Thanksgiving with them. I would limit my visits to one
or two days, staying over no more than one or two nights. Since my parents
had moved from my childhood home on Staten Island to a small town just
an hour and a half north of Manhattan, I could stay with my friends and

drive up for the day. I did not discuss my relationships with my family and showed up unaccompanied, even when in a relationship, for most events such as christenings, weddings, baby showers, and physical and mental health crises. I sent money or gifts for birthdays and Christmas, but generally kept my worlds separate. When I moved to California, just forty miles south of my sister Lisa, I expected some challenge in balancing the different worlds, but she happened to be one of the two supportive sisters so I was not too concerned about it.

Yet in some ways the geographic closeness did pose some additional dilemmas. I recall the Christmas of 1994 right after my nephew James was born. Wanting to be helpful, I offered to make Christmas dinner for Lisa and her husband, Michael. But Melinda, my lover at the time, did not want to do the holiday thing in this way. What she wanted was a quiet dinner with me at home. Caught between my different families, I decided to make dinner for us at home and later to bring dinner to Lisa and Michael. This seemed doable at the time. The first snag, however, occurred after I described the Sante-Fe-inspired meal I planned to make. Lisa explained that her husband would not eat what Melinda and I had decided on for the main course and that since she was breast-feeding James, she would have to pass on the jalapeno corn bread. Okay, I thought, I need a fall-back plan. I decided to make two dinners, one for Melinda and me, plus one for Lisa and Michael. I made two corn breads, one with and one without the jalapenos. After completing our main course, I put a chicken in the oven to roast. Naturally, all of this took extra time so Melinda and I sat down to eat later than I intended. With the fireplace burning brightly and the candles nicely lit on the table, Melinda was anticipating a very relaxed meal. I, on the other hand, was anxious that we were running late so I could not really enjoy the meal, which was also interrupted several times while I checked the chicken. Then the phone rang. It was my sister wondering where we were. She told me that Michael loved my cooking so that he skipped lunch and was starving. I explained that things were taking a bit longer but that I would be there soon. Melinda, however, did not want to join me on the trip up to my sister's and I struggled with her for a while until the phone rang.

It was Peter wishing me a Merry Christmas. I explained the dilemma to him and complained that Melinda would not come with me to my sister's. Having met many of my family members, he not-so-diplomatically said, "Why should she? Let her stay home if she wants." It did seem such an obvious solution but I now realized how much I wanted to merge my different worlds for that holiday. So out the door I went, telling Melinda I would be back as soon as I could to share desert with her. Arriving at my sister's, I went into a flurry of activity heating up and then serving the food. I felt like a volunteer for Meals-on-Wheels. And, of course, I could not relax with them much since I felt I needed to get back home or Melinda would start feeling abandoned. I can laugh at the scene now, but it more than symbolized the absurdity and frustration in my attempts to navigate between different family forms.

So, for the most part, my siblings did not have to see me in a relationship with a woman. My long history as a practicing heterosexual was enough to negate my claims to a lesbian identity. How could someone who was involved with men for so long really be a lesbian? I fit none of their stereotypes. My sister Karen rationalized my claim to a lesbian identity as follows: "Well, after all you had such bad relationships with men." The obvious implication was that if I met the right man, I would change my mind. Again I was faced with proving my authentic identity, this time foregrounding my lesbian self. Another cliché I recognized in my family's response was the one that links having a career with my not needing men. Here the traditional gender division of labor, which assigns women to the private sphere of the home and men to the public breadwinner, role was upset by the fact that I had a career and therefore did not need the male breadwinner. Of course, what logically follows that particular assumption is that women's full-time employment is a basic threat to the heterosexual family form—an old but persistent concern.

My family is more traditional than many, I suppose. During the 1950s and 1960s, we even had a girl's side and a boy's side of the dinner table. If you tried to cross over to the wrong side, you suffered great insults. The boys were taught auto mechanics and electronics among other technical skills. The girls learned child care and cooking among other homemaking skills. I always resisted. Fortunately my sister Karen, who was three years younger than me, took to these activities, and I put up such a stink about performing them that I was off the hook.

My siblings have all followed the traditional route. The women have taken their husbands' names and have, for the most part, placed their own careers on hold until all their children are in school. My life as an unmarried college professor of sociology and women's studies was so far from their own lives that they could hardly comprehend it except that they knew I attended a lot of conferences. Furthermore, they never wanted to learn more about it so I rarely discuss what I do with them. I do not think my experience here differs much from other academics who come from the working class. However, I fear that part of my family's reluctance to ask more about my life's work is that for them women's studies equals feminist equals lesbian—and therefore something about my lesbian world might come up. So it is best not to even start down that road.

I continued to keep my worlds relatively separate with a few moments of overlap until 1997 when my mother's Alzheimer's escalated and we had to put her in a nursing home. This precipitated more intense and regular contact with my family. This difficult event overlapped with the start of a new relationship with Sharon, a woman who said that she would not mind being integrated into my family. In fact, she said, "I'm good with lover's families. They like me." I was so pleased to finally have the opportunity to merge my worlds. I neglected to warn her, however, that I had never successfully done so before. She did wonder why I became increasingly anxious as we drove closer to my father's house a week before Christmas. I even passed the turnoff and drove her around the town and several of the surrounding towns before returning to complete the drive to the house. When we arrived at my father's home, my sister Melisssa with her son and my hostile brother, John, were there.

My plan was to spend the night and go visit my other brother, Paul's family before making the four-hour drive to Sharon's home the next afternoon. However, shortly after our arrival, as I was wrapping presents in one of the bedrooms, John comes in and asks me in a very accusatory tone: "You're not going to make some big announcement that we should know about? Paul is afraid to come over because he thinks you are planning some big surprise." I was speechless with fury. I now wish I had thought of some clever rejoinder such as: "Oh, you must be watching too many episodes of *Ellen*. If so, you'd know I would only do it in an airport over a loudspeaker." But instead, I was paralyzed with anger and fear. I emerged from the room, didn't say a word to Sharon, went to play with my nephew, and left her to interact with my father and brothers—the second of whom had shown up by this time. Paul proceeded to glare at her from the kitchen. He never spoke to her. It was as though Sharon had a neon sign on her chest that read in bold scarlet letters: BEWARE, LESBIAN IN THE HOUSE. Later she explained that she felt I had taken her to some anonymous suburban family and dropped her off where she had to introduce herself and be subjected to the critical gaze of the residents. I disappeared emotionally under the homophobic gaze of my brothers. Sharon was angry that I had left her with these "strangers." I tried to explain that I could not have anticipated my reaction since it was the first time I ever really allowed the two worlds to collide so directly. She said that

I should have at least warned her that she was the first female lover that I had introduced into the family. I had mistakenly assumed that Nina was the first lover they had met. Since I came out to them after she died, I had wishfully thought that would count and so my introducing them to Sharon should be no big deal.

The Christmas visit would send me on a very difficult soul-searching journey to confront and effectively eject much of the self-hate I had internalized. This was indeed a very good thing for me in the long run. Unfortunately, in the short run, I was to face a series of painful internal and external crises before I felt purged of some of my own internalized homophobia.

So now fast forward to the week of my father's death, which was quite unexpected. He had problems with his lungs, emphysema, a series of bouts with pneumonia, but until this last week or so no one thought his illness was life-threatening. I won't go into the unfortunate series of medical events that contributed to his death but state simply that I did not have much time to prepare for how I would balance my conflicting worlds while all this was going on.

As a consequence of the previous Christmas I had decided not to stay over with my family if I could avoid it. When I got the call from my youngest sister, Melissa, that I better get "home," I did not even think about what it would be like to stay with my siblings during the emotionally painful days leading up to my father's death. Since it involved coming to a collective decision about removing the breathing tube, I assumed it best to stay with them. I also thought I would be criticized harshly if I chose to stay in Manhattan with my friends Jen and Terry, whose apartment was in fact closer to the hospital. I rented a car at the airport and drove to Melissa's home in New Jersey.

The first couple of days were difficult but manageable. All six of us seemed to be getting along pretty well. I remember calling one of my aunts to give her an update and saying how good our communication was as we were debating the pros and cons of removing the ventilator. Each day I spoke to my soon-to-be ex-lover, Sharon (we were in the process of breaking up), who was trying to be supportive. She had initiated the break-up a few weeks earlier. I was resisting vehemently. I had some crazy idea in the back of my mind that this crisis might bring us closer together. Little did I know how wrong I was. Each day Sharon offered to come. I so wanted to take her up on her offer. After all, my siblings all had their spouses and children with them. I had neither lover nor friend. But I also knew, given the view of homosexuality held by my sister Karen, that it would be difficult to have my ex-lover with me, although I had no idea how messy it would become.

When Karen and her children began discussing the possibility of moving up to my father's house so they could be closer to the other cousins, I finally saw an opportunity to invite Sharon to join me. When I mentioned that she was coming, Karen threw a fit. She ranted, "How could you bring this into the family at such a time? What about the children? This is a time for the family to be together. It's not a time for us to have to deal with this." I tried to explain that Sharon was my family and that I needed the support. And, further, I was a lesbian whether my lover was with me or not. She refused to calm down and, in a huff, went up to pack hers and her children's bags.

Melissa, the youngest sibling, came to me pleading, "Nancy, do something!" So I took a deep breath, went to my sister Karen and said, "Fine, I'll tell my lover not to come." I thought that this was the only way we could get through the next couple of days. I felt defeated and so alone but I was, after all, the older sister, a role that I performed uncritically for much of my life. After this incident, I could no longer stay with them. I quietly packed my bags and said that I would go stay with my friends in Manhattan. I drove away thinking what a fool I was for forgetting where I really belonged. When I arrived at the airport, I should have gone directly to Jen and Terry's apartment for they were part of my "real" family. How could I have gotten it so wrong?

To make matters worse, Sharon was profoundly offended by my decision to acquiesce to Karen's tantrum. She resented that I placed my need to keep peace in the family over our relationship and told me that if I had discussed my fear of merging the two worlds with her, she might have helped me come up with the solution that eventually I had to turn to anyway—staying with my friends in the city. Further, she painfully exclaimed, how did I think this made her feel as the one defined as a dreaded threat to the moral integrity of my family? I could not find the words to explain what it had been like for me the day before with my sisters.

This conversation took place over the phone. I had just left my father's bed in intensive care when I called her. When I asked her if she would be willing to come after my father died, she initially said, "Why should I? After all, one goes to a funeral to be supportive of the family and your family doesn't want me there." Well, I was devastated to say the least. I called another dear friend and sobbed for an hour. When I returned to my father's bedside, he was dead. So you can see now why I increasingly felt as though the bad TV-movie kept getting worse. Here I was, the only family member left at the hospital, staying through the night to be with my father so that he wouldn't be alone when he died, only to get caught up in a competing drama down the hall. I hope the guilt I feel over this dreadful episode will diminish with time.

After my father died, the nurse contacted my other siblings and they all returned to the hospital. We each said goodbye in our own way and left. It was after 2 A.M. I drove back to Manhattan, exhausted and traumatized by what had just occurred, and I collapsed into bed.

The following day I spent a long time describing the events to Jen and Terry and called some of my other close friends. I also contacted Sharon and asked her once again if she would come to be with me. She finally agreed but we did not decide whether or not she would attend the wake and funeral. I felt a bit aimless that day and thought that, even though it would have been easier to avoid it, I should drive to my father's house and together with my siblings confront the reality of his death. I also resented letting Karen's fear of my lesbian existence keep me away. I did not want her to have that much power over my choices at this point. Anyway, very quickly after I arrived it became clear to me that my lesbianism and the fear that my lover would come to the wake and funeral was the central topic of conversation. I went into the living room and all but my brother Paul were sitting there. John turned to me and said, on behalf of my siblings, that they wanted to talk to me, that they wanted to know what it was going to be like. At first I did not understand what they wanted to know. I thought that maybe since I had experienced so much loss, they wanted me to explain what it would be like at the funeral or the wake. I asked what they meant.

My sister Lisa then turned to me and said, "We want to know what it is going to be like when your lover comes. Are you two going to be touching or whatever?" At this point, I chose not to let them know that Sharon was, in fact, my ex-lover. I thought if I said, "Oh, you don't have to worry. We broke up," it would only feed into their self-righteousness and belief that there was something dangerous about lesbian love. As John and my two youngest sisters tried to explain their concerns, I painfully noted the smug look on my sister Karen's face. Now she was not the sole voice, the religious fanatic with some extreme view, but, rather, just another of my siblings, who all felt that it was an awful thing for me to be a lesbian. I wondered what they thought Sharon and I would do at the funeral parlor. Everyone but Karen had met her the previous Christmas, but paranoia had overtaken them and they clearly were not thinking rationally.

I, of course, felt attacked, horrified and desperately alone in my father's house. I knew that my siblings only felt free to express their hatred and fear of my lesbian self because he was dead. It made me miss him even more. I got up and started packing my things to leave. Lisa came in and tried to explain why she thought it was a good thing for us to have this discussion, that my lesbianism was no longer a taboo subject, that she loved me, and that my lover would always be welcome in her house. I was appalled at the thought that there should have to be any question about this. I replied that they should deal with their own irrational fears about my sexuality but to leave me out of their conversations in the future. How unloving and hateful could a group of people be—people who are supposed to love me and want the best for me! I understood then that I was tolerated as part of the family as long as they thought I was alone, had no one to love me, to hold me, to comfort me. As I drove back to Manhattan, I understood even more deeply that the precious intimate friendships I had constructed over the years were truer expressions of "real" family than my biological family ever had been.

I missed Nina and Peter more than ever. How different the energy that surrounded Nina's last weeks and her memorial service. Right after Nina died, Peter told me that he had asked her what he was supposed to do with me—since we weren't really "friends," not like he was with Nina. I inherited Peter from Nina, and, I guess, he inherited me as well. He replaced Donald as the brother I could talk to. There was so much I couldn't tell Donald. His own homophobia made him less than the best confident for me when Nina was first diagnosed with cancer. I am so grateful to Nina for leaving Peter to me and me to him. We were "real" family for each other, Peter with no other kinfolk, me with lots of related kin but none I felt close to or who loved me as freely. Peter was there for me from the time Nina died until his own untimely death.

I so much prefer the version of family I learned from Nina and Peter to the one my biological family embraces. For my biological family, the effort to "do family" takes the form of boundary maintenance—controlling who and what can enter for fear that the family constellation is so fragile any slight disruption will cause permanent damage. Ironically, in their efforts to patrol the borders, the illusive ties that kept me linked to my family have been irrevocably severed.

I don't expect to have any future contact with my two brothers or my sister Karen. For Karen, I would have to confess my "sin," repent, and renounce my "homosexual lifestyle." Equally unlikely, she would have to forsake the treasured religious beliefs that have provided an anchor for her since her early twenties. Recently her ten-year-old son sent a letter to all his aunts and uncles seeking money for a bike-athon to support a missionary for his church. I could no longer ignore my negative feelings about this church in order to fulfill my familial obligations as his aunt. And I do not expect to have any meaningful contact with Sharon. This also saddens me greatly for despite the fact that we could not negotiate my family nor build toward our own version of family, we did love each other.

Yet despite all the loses I have suffered over the years in both my families, I am an incurable romantic. I deeply long to create daily life with someone—to swap stories of the day, to perform mundane household tasks together, to share meals, and to regularly experience the pleasures of physical touch. Fortunately, I find myself in a new relationship, this time with someone who wants to "do" family in much the same way I envision. The process of negotiating my two families continues, however. My new lover is coming to visit soon. In order to miss the Los Angeles traffic the morning she returns home, it would be most convenient for us to stay with my sister Lisa, who lives ten minutes from the airport. Recall that she was the one who said that my lover would always be welcome in her home. Yet does this offer extend to an overnight stay? I fear calling her on it and bumping up once again against the razor-sharp boundary of my biological family. I also want to protect my new lover from any hurt or rejection, to do a better job than I did for Sharon. I am torn. Should I just give up my desire to merge my worlds and book a room in a hotel by the airport or should I give my sister a chance to show up for me. It is a hard call.

Well, after my father's funeral everyone returned to his house for a luncheon. I returned with them, flag in hand, and spent my remaining hours in his house talking to my aunts and several of my favorite cousins. After they left, I wasn't sure what to do. I wandered from room to room, looked in closets, found the hardcover copy of my book that I had recently given my father, and took one of his flannel shirts off a hanger. I decided to call my ex-lover. But she was neither at her home nor her work phone. She and my friend Jen had, in fact, made it to the first night of the wake. Need I add that, not surprisingly, nothing dramatic happened. None of my siblings' fears about how our presence together might disrupt the dignified nature of the wake were realized. I did feel compelled to keep my physical distance from her. Sharon decided to leave the next morning. We both agreed that was best. But I was glad she came, even for the one night. The only surprising and touching moment occurred when my sister Melissa introduced herself to Jen and thanked her for taking care of me, her big sister.

When I decided I needed to leave my father's house after the funeral luncheon and return to my "real" family in Manhattan, I put on the flannel shirt and went looking for my brother John, who had been so outraged by my lesbian self. I gave him the flag and my book and told him I didn't expect him to read it but he could have it if he wanted. I drove away while he stood motionless in the driveway. I knew he would miss my father more than anyone since he lived the closest and had followed closely in his footsteps as a New York City firefighter. The house was recently sold and even though I never lived there, I felt the loss of the "family homestead." I also mourned the fantasy that one day I would be an accepted member of my biological family. Yet letting go of the need to keep my heteronormal self alive, I have come to more fully embrace and gain sustenance from my "real" family who have been there all along.

The process of writing the story of my father's funeral involved analyzing the complex and changing relationships I have with members of both my so-called family of origin and my family of choice. Telling the story, writing the essay, and discussing the narrative I produced involved retelling and revising the story as well as reexperiencing many of the painful feelings I had while the story was unfolding for the first time. I was struck by the ways in which my relationship to the story and to the essay changed with each interaction with friends as readers and reviewers, with the story as text, and with myself as author. The purpose of this telling is simultaneously personal, political, and pedagogical. The questions I address in analyzing both the process of narrative construction and the narrative product include: How do we achieve visibility in our families? How do we resist reproducing patterns of exclusion in our families of choice? How do personal narratives function as tools for these interrelated goals?

The story I tell about my father's funeral emphasizes the emotional work involved in "doing family."[1] Family is not merely a natural constellation of individuals connected by biology and the state with some set of behaviors that everyone knows and willingly performs. Family must be achieved and constructed on a daily basis. Bisexuals, gays, lesbians, and all of us who do not fit into the normative heterosexual-family model understand this well. But all of us, regardless of the family form we inherit or create, must work to sustain these relationships.

I draw on the symbolic-constructionist perspective for my analysis of "doing family." Candice West and Don Zimmerman (1987) argue that "gender is fundamental, institutionalized, and enduring; yet, because members of social groups must constantly (whether they realize it or not) 'do' gender to maintain their proper status, the seeds of change are ever present" (Lorber 1987:124; also see Fishman 1978). As Barrie Thorne (1995:498) points out, " 'Doing gender' is a compelling concept because it jolts the assumption of gender as an innate condition and replaces it with a sense of ongoing process and activity." Yet gender, and family, are more than performances. They are structured in ways that are not always visible to the performers. As Thorne (1995:499) argues, "gender extends beyond daily cultural performance, and it will take much more than doing drag and mocking naturalized conceptions to transform it. Gender—and race, class, and compulsory heterosexuality—extend deep into the unconscious and the shaping of emotions . . . and outward into social structure and material interests." In much the same way, I argue, how we perform "family" is shaped by material as well as cultural practices that are often invisible to us as we interact with family, friends, lovers, coworkers. However, the practice of ongoing self-reflection provides one strategy to make visible how daily interactions are shaped by dominant constructions and structures of family. Self-reflective practice is a collective activity that involves ongoing dialogue, behaviors, and political activities that serve to challenge the more oppressive features of patriarchal families.

We first learn to do family and relationships more generally in the families in which we grow up, whether biological, adopted, or otherwise constituted. Since many of these families adhere to some version of compulsory heterosexuality (Rich 1980), our models for performing family are constrained by prescriptions of the "family ethic."[2] Consequently, developing alternative models of "doing family" forms a central task for gays and lesbians and others who do not fit into the normative heterosexual-family form (see Lewin 1993; Weston 1991). We are also challenged by the complex negotiations and contradictions between the performance of family, gender, and sexuality expected by our families and the relationships we form as lesbians, gay men, bisexuals, or transgendered people. Unfortunately, we often find ourselves repeating behaviors and imposing expectations that were developed through our early family experiences, thus limiting relational expression to patriarchal patterns of interaction. The process of telling, retelling, writing, and rewriting this story provided me with the distance to see how my attempts to construct my own family form were circumscribed by the limited vision of family I brought into this activity.

The essay about my father's funeral can thus be read as an introspective ethnography (see Timmermans 1994; Ellis 1991). With this formulation, it is possible to view the process of its production through the lens of a family ethnography concerning the struggle of a white lesbian with a heterosexual history to become visible and accepted in her working-class family. The self-reflective process I employ includes feedback from friends, some of whom appear in the story. This dialogic strategy provided me with an analytic distance from the experiences described. However, I also recognize the limitations of my angle of vision and how my positionality[3] in the story privileges my version.

I utilize the biographical narrative approach in much of my scholarship on women's community activism and therefore value this methodology for exploring the development of and shifts in political consciousness and diverse political practices over time without artificially foregrounding any one dimension or influence (see Naples 1998). However, such narratives cannot be taken up unproblematically. For, as the Personal Narratives Group (1989:4) emphasize:

> The act of constructing a life narrative forces the author to move from accounts of discrete experiences to an account of why and how the life took the shape it did. The why and how—the interpretive acts that shape a life, and a life narrative—need to take as high a place on the feminist agenda as the recording of women's experiences.

Yet as both interpreter and subject of the interpretation, I find myself in a complicated relationship to the narrative I have produced. In fact, in attempting to present the story of how the events surrounding my father's funeral helped me reflect on the dilemmas of doing family, I was often amazed at how many different versions I could tell, depending on which aspects of the story I chose to emphasize or how I combined different facets of my self-presentation (Abu-Lughod 1993; Behar 1993; Wolf 1992; also see Naples 1998).

There are many who critique this form of storytelling, namely, the privileging of one particular account over the multiple stories that could be told about the same phenomenon or set of experiences (see, e.g., Patai 1994). Self-disclosure or "going public" (Naples with Clark 1996) with painful life events, emotional difficulties, and personal failures has been criticized within and outside feminism, within and outside the academy, and in multiple arenas from the arts to literature to academic research. Anthropologist Ruth Behar (1995:12–13) notes that: "No one objects to autobiography, as such, as a genre in its own right. What bothers critics is the insertion of personal stories into what we have been taught to think of as the analysis of impersonal social facts."

Defined by some as "confessional modes of self-representation" (Bernstein 1992), taking the first person and centering one's own experiences as a basis for knowledge claims—once a privileged strategy for the production of feminist scholarship—is now viewed with suspicion by many (see, e.g., Armstrong 1990 cited in Alcoff and Gray 1993; Kaminer 1995). Those theorists critical of this move to discredit experiential theorizing argue that the decentering of women's experiences in feminist scholarship is a consequence of the growing acceptance of certain feminist projects within the academy and other institutions, thus diminishing the necessity of taking an oppositional stance with regard to knowledge production in the academy (see Naples 2001). Some fear that by valorizing women's experiences over other ways of knowing, women's studies classrooms do not measure up to academic standards of "excellence" (see Patai and Koertge 1994).

In contrast, I believe that experiential theorizing, and the process of critical self-reflection it entails, offers a way to uncover and render visible the complex dynamics of doing family. This process illustrates the theoretical insights of feminist-standpoint epistemologies (see Collins 1990; Hartsock 1983; Lugones 1992; Naples 1999; Sandoval 1991; Smith 1987). Donna Haraway (1988:584), in her now classic article, "Situated Knowledges: The Science Question in Feminism and the Privilege of the Partial Perspective," argues that those subjugated by forces of oppression "are knowledgeable of modes of denial through repression, forgetting, and disappearing acts." In the midst of my family's exaggerated performance of heteronormativity, I often felt my lesbian self rendered invisible despite "coming out" to all my siblings. For much of my adult life I could not break through their denial. The events leading up to and surrounding my father's death served to thrust my lesbian self into the center of their consciousness in such a way that it symbolized a threat to the integrity of the family unit. Of course, it was my father's death that fundamentally unraveled the tightly bound net that held us together. In many ways, I was unprepared for the rejection; in other ways, I had been preparing for it most of my conscious life. The crisis led to a reevaluation of my relationship to my family as well as an opportunity to develop a new interpretive framework through which I might be able to construct a family that does not replicate the negative aspects of the earlier formation. However, I recognize the challenge posed by the legacy of doing family unreflectively for so many years,

The construction of this new interpretative framework involved a process of politicization whereby I began to attribute my discontent to structural, cultural, or systemic causes rather than to my personal failings or individual deviance (Taylor and Whittier 1992:114). For, despite my political and academic education and my own research on the development of "oppositional consciousness"[4] (Sandoval 1991), I had not achieved the angle of vision that permitted me to understand my own agency in reproducing the family dynamics I found so painful. Fortunately, as Nancy Hartsock (1996:271) explains: "the development of situated knowledges can constitute alternatives: they open possibilities that may or may not be realized. To the extent that these knowledges become self-conscious about their assumptions, they make available new epistemologies and political options."

While I expect that I will gain more from this exercise than my readers, I hope that I have demonstrated the challenges we all face and the benefits that ensue when we do family self-reflectively, rather than treat family as a taken-for-granted institution outside of our own making. This lesson is one I have learned from my many lesbian, gay, bisexual, and heterosexual family and friends. The family form I recommend is one built on respect for differences and openness to the diversity of expressions of intimacy.

Since I start and end with my own perspective on doing family, I must acknowledge that others mentioned in my story, including former lovers and siblings, will have different stories to tell about the relational activities I describe. While we were all confronted with the emotional and structural dilemmas associated with my attempt to negotiate different approaches to family, the experiences and analyses of what this all means for doing family will necessarily differ. Furthermore, the narrative I have constructed is one that glosses over the complexities of the interpersonal negotiations between former lovers and family members. As Melinda emphasized, following her reading of an early draft of the essay,

> through the selective reporting of one event [Christmas 1994], the reader is offered a universalized picture of my relationship to your family as distanced, unwilling to interface with their community and you in it. . . . [T]he problem for me is that this nice vignette for the sake of argument doesn't match the reality for many, many times I interfaced with your siblings at holidays as well as with your parents so it just is not the "real" story."

Melinda and I were together for almost five years. Over that period of time there were many opportunities for her to visit with members of my family. One of my favorite pictures of her shows her holding my sister Lisa's newborn baby, Max, shortly after Christmas Day, 1994. Obviously, then, this story as I tell it takes on meaning not as an incontestable sequence of events—namely, as what really happened or as true in some objective way—but in the emotional and interpretative framing that shaped my interactions with different families and individual family members.

While the story I tell is particular to my own coming to consciousness about the dilemmas of doing family, I believe it illustrates some of the conflicts between different constructions of family that many of us encounter. The features of my own story include the ways in which religion, class differences, as well as gender and sexuality increasingly widened the emotional and physical divide that ultimately severed me from my family as a complex unitary form. The struggle to negotiate my lived experiences as a lesbian within my family has helped me differentiate among the family members, distancing me from some siblings while drawing me closer to others. In this way, I can now integrate these particular members of my childhood family as chosen members of my family of choice, creating a much more affirming and flexible relational structure. For me, the challenge of doing family had always meant choosing between one form or the other, rather than finding a way to include different family members from my different families together. Given the very bounded way my family did familial relationships, however, it is not surprising that I encountered such difficulty. In her response to my essay, Melinda asked an obvious question about my family, one that I take up somewhat in the narrative, namely, "Do they/did they ever do much to include anyone?" She noted how they never asked about her or made an effort to get to know her when she did interact with them.

My introspective ethnography of doing family brought home to me how much I had privileged my childhood family's version, at times marginalizing my relationships with lovers and friends in order to show up for the family in a way they could handle and I would feel safe from their criticisms. This highlighted a point raised by my friend Jen who asked: "What are your responsibilities to past lovers and how has your participation in your family drama let them down?" And a question from another friend: "How do we create family without expecting our family of choice to fill in the emotional holes left from childhood?" Attempts to answer these poignant questions would require further self-reflection and dialogue and still would remain a work-in-progress. However, experiential theorizing and the self-reflective process it entails may offer a strategy to address questions such as the ones these friends have posed.

The dilemmas of bisexuality also complicated my relationships with my family. Despite the postmodern critiques of essentialized identities and futile searches for some ultimate truth about a mythical unfractured self, I remember the satisfaction I felt when I read Ann Ferguson's (1991) conceptualization of her own bisexual lesbian identity. The category worked for me as a shortcut to describe my sexual history, although I have been lesbian-identified since 1980. Categories, as misguided as they may be to a postmodern sensibility, can be quite comforting and useful at times. Yet I also realize that while I adopt the term "bisexual lesbian" to make sense of my personal history, it serves only as a fleeting comfort. It fails to capture the processes of negotiation and redefinition embedded in my ongoing identity construction. And, furthermore, it had little meaning for my siblings, who really did not know how to make sense of my shift in sexual partners.

In reviewing this essay, Jen asked why my family had such significance for me. Others might have distanced themselves more quickly than I did in response to the homophobia I encountered from it. I believe in retrospect that part of the answer can be found in the intense emotional and practical hold that my large working-class family had over me. As the oldest child in an Irish-Catholic working-class family, the pressure I felt to show up for the family in a variety of ways formed part of my earliest memories. As we grew older, I listened to my parents' great disappointment when one sibling, then a second, moved away. (I was the third to "leave.") We were expected to stay close, to be there for each other, in what was a fairly tightly bounded family constellation (see Cantú, chapter 8)

My long history as a practicing heterosexual provided a convenient backdrop for my family's denial of my lesbian existence. But today I can also see how internalized homophobia played a role in my willingness to remain silent and to continue to perform a version of my heteronormative self into my forties. My need to maintain this role within my family had particular consequences for my women lovers, who were not as invested in performing such roles. Although it took me many years and the death of my father to fully acknowledge the shame that kept me silent, I also gained much strength from my lovers and others in my family of choice who taught me how to trust my heart, find my voice, and construct a new vision for doing family. I dedicate this essay to them.[5]

NOTES

1. The names of all but those who have died have been changed.
2. Mimi Abramovitz (1988:2) defines the "family ethic" as a "preoccupation with the nuclear family unit featuring a male breadwinner and an economically dependent female homemaker." The family ethic also privileges the white middle-class family over working-class and nonwhite racial-ethnic families.
3. Linda Alcoff (1988:433) uses the concept "positionality" to describe "the subject as nonessentialized and emergent from a historical experience."
4. Aldon Morris (1992:363) defines "oppositional consciousness" with "hegemonic consciousness" as: "that set of insurgent ideas and beliefs constructed and developed by an oppressed group for the purposes of guiding its struggle to undermine, reform, or overthrow a system of domination." The power of "oppositional consciousness" lies in its ability "to strip away the garments of universality from hegemonic consciousness, revealing its essentialist characteristics" (370).
5. My heartfelt thanks to Mary Bernstein, Lauren Cruz, Dawn Esposito, Maya Hostettler, Val Jenness, Kate Kinney, Theresa Montini, Nancy Rose, Bettina Soestwohner, Cindy Truelove, and Gilda Zwerman, for their insightful comments on earlier drafts of this chapter.

REFERENCES

Abramovitz, Mimi. 1988. *Regulating the Lives of Women: Social Welfare Policy from Colonial Times to the Present.* Boston: South End Press.

Alcoff, Linda. 1988. "Cultural Feminism Versus Post-Structuralism: The Identity Crisis in Feminist Theory." *Signs* 13 (3): 405–36.

Alcoff, Linda, and Laura Gray. 1993. "Survivor Discourse: Transgression or Recuperation?" *Signs* 18 (2): 260–90.

Anzaldúa, Gloria. 1987. *Borderlands/La Frontera: The New Mestiza.* San Francisco: Spinsters/Aunt Lute.

Armstrong, Louise. 1990. "The Personal Is Apolitical." *Women's Review of Books* (March): 1–44.

Behar, Ruth. 1993. *Translated Woman: Crossing the Border with Esperanza's Story.* Boston: Beacon Press.

———. 1995. *The Vulnerable Observer: Anthropology That Breaks Your Heart.* Boston: Beacon Press.

Bernstein, Susan David. 1992. "Confessing Feminist Theory: What's 'I' Got to Do with It?" *Hypatia* 7 (2): 120–47.

Cantú, Lionel. 1999. "Border Crossings: Mexican Men and the Sexuality of Migration." Ph.D. diss., University of California, Irvine.

Chodorow, Nancy. 1978. *The Reproduction of Mothering.* Berkeley: University of California Press.

Collins, Patricia Hill. 1990. *Black Feminist Thought.* Boston: Unwin Hyman.

Collins, Patricia Hill. 1991. "Learning from the Outsider Within: The Sociological Significance of Black Feminist Thought." In Mary Margaret Fonow and Judith A. Cook, eds., *Beyond Methodology,* pp. 35–59. Bloomington: Indiana University Press.

Ellis, Carolyn. 1991. "Sociological Introspection and Emotional Experience." *Symbolic Interaction* 14 (1): 23–40.

Ferguson, Ann. 1989. *Blood at the Root: Motherhood, Sexuality and Male Dominance.* Boston: Unwin Hyman.

Ferguson, Ann. 1991. *Sexual Democracy: Women, Oppression, and Revolution.* Boulder: Westview.

Haraway, Donna. 1988. "Situated Knowledges: The Science Question in Feminism and the Privilege of Partial Perspective." *Feminist Studies* 14 (3): 575–99.

Hartsock, Nancy. 1983. *Money, Sex, and Power.* Boston: Northeastern University Press.

Hundleby, Catherine. 1997. "Where Standpoint Stands Now." In Sally J. Kenney and Helen Kinsella, eds., *Politics and Feminist Standpoint Theories,* pp. 25–43. New York, Haworth.

Kaminer, Wendy. 1995. "Review of *Voices from the Next Feminist Generation.*" *New York Times Review of Books* June 4.

Lewin, Ellen. 1993. "Lesbian and Gay Kinship: Kath Weston's *Families We Choose* and Contemporary Anthropology." *Signs* 18 (4): 974–89.

Lorber, Judith. 1987. "From the Editor." *Gender & Society* 1 (2): 123–24.

Lugones, María. 1992. "On *Borderlands/La Frontera*: An Interpretive Essay." *Hypatia* 7 (4): 31–7.

Morris, Aldon D. 1992. "Political Consciousness and Collective Action." In Aldon D. Morris and Carol McClurg Mueller, eds., *Frontiers in Social Movement Theory,* pp. 351–73. New Haven: Yale University Press.

Naples, Nancy A. 1996. "A Feminist Revisiting of the Insider/Outsider Debate: The 'Outsider Phenomenon' in Rural Iowa." *Qualitative Sociology* 19 (1): 83–106.

Naples, Nancy A. 1998. *Grassroots Warriors: Activist Mothering, Community Work, and the War on Poverty.* New York: Routledge.

———. 2001. "Negotiating the Politics of Experiential Learning in Women's Studies."

In Robyn Weigman, ed., *Locating Feminism.* Durham, N.C.: Duke University Press.

Naples, Nancy A., with Emily Clark. 1996. "Feminist Participatory Research and Empowerment: Going Public as Survivors of Childhood Sexual Abuse." In Heidi Gottfried, ed., *Feminism and Social Change: Bridging Theory and Practice*, pp. 160–83. Champagne-Urbana: Illinois University Press.

Naples, Nancy A., with Carolyn Sachs. 2000. "Standpoint Epistemology and the Uses of Self-Reflection in Feminist Ethnography: Lessons for Rural Sociology." *Rural Sociology* 65 (2): 194–214.

Patai, Daphne. 1994. "Sick and Tired of Nouveau Solipsism." *The Chronicle of Higher Education*, February 23, Point of View essay.

Patai, Daphne, and Noretta Koertge. 1994. *Professing Feminism: Cautionary Tales from the Strange World of Women's Studies.* New York: Basic Books.

Phelan, Shane. 1989. *Identity Politics: Lesbian-Feminism and the Limits of Community.* Philadelphia: Temple University Press.

Phelan, Shane. 1993. "(Be)Coming Out: Lesbian Identity and Politics." *Signs* 18 (4): 765–90.

Richardson, Laurel. 1990. "Trash on the Corner: Ethics and Technography." *Journal of Contemporary Ethnography* 21 (1): 103–19.

Rich, Adrienne. 1980. "Compulsory Heterosexuality and Lesbian Existence," *Signs* 5: 631–60.

Ronai, Carol Rambo. 1995. "Multiple Reflections of Child Sex Abuse: An Argument for a Layered Account." *Journal of Contemporary Ethnography* 23 (4): 395–426.

Sandoval, Chela. 1991. "U.S. Third World Feminism: The Theory and Method of Oppositional Consciousness in the Postmodern World." *Genders* 10: 1–24.

Spelman, Elizabeth V. 1988. "Gender in the Context of Race and Class: Notes on Chodorow's *Reproduction of Mothering*. In Elizabeth V. Spelman, ed., *Inessential Woman: Problems of Exclusion in Feminist Thought*, pp. 80–113. Boston: Beacon Press.

Taylor, Verta, and Nancy E. Whittier. 1992. "Collective Identity in Social Movement Communities: Lesbian Feminist Mobilization." In Aldon D. Morris and Carol McClurg Mueller, eds., *Frontiers of Social Movement Theory*, pp. 104–29. New Haven: Yale University Press.

Thorne, Barrie. 1995. "Symposium: On West and Fenstermaker's 'Doing Difference.' " *Gender & Society* 9 (4): 497–99.

Timmermans, Stefan. 1994. "Dying of Awareness: The Theory of Awareness Contexts Revisited." *Journal of Health and Illness* 16 (3): 322–39.

West, Candice, and Sarah Fenstermaker. 1995. "Doing Difference." *Gender & Society* 9: 8–37.

West, Candice, and Don H. Zimmerman. 1987. "Doing Gender." *Gender & Society* 1: 125–51.

Weston, Kath. 1991. *Families We Choose: Lesbians, Gays, Kinship*. New York: Columbia University Press.

Wolf, Margery. 1992. *A Thrice-Told Tale*. Stanford: Stanford University Press.

3

Weddings Without Marriage: Making Sense of Lesbian and Gay Commitment Rituals

Ellen Lewin

The rise of lesbian/gay marriage as a civil rights issue and the emerging cultural prominence of a variety of ceremonial forms aimed at solemnizing lesbian/gay relationships in public and religious contexts pose vexing questions for the project of constituting gay/lesbian/queer existence as a phenomenon bearing distinct cultural or national insignia. "Marriage" is uncomfortably familiar to lesbians and gay men from our experience in the mainstream; our failure to marry is for many of us the very thing that has marked our difference from our heterosexual contemporaries. Many of us recall weddings as excruciating exercises in invisibility, events that required us to listen politely as heterosexual relationships were glorified while we knew that our own commitments would never be recognized as worthy of such celebration.

So gay/lesbian marriage can be perplexing both for the gay or lesbian individual and for the scholar of gender and sexuality. Does it constitute courageous repudiation of the notion that only persons of different sexes may marry, and as such can it be construed as outright resistance to heterosexism? Or does it represent instead simple accommodation to the norms of the straight world, a calculated effort to win acceptance by somehow fitting in?

Not all lesbians and gays see same-sex marriage as a welcome development. In fact, the debate over the legal status of relationships has in some ways galvanized a wider debate over the embrace or repudiation of difference that has been raised with regularity since the start of the gay liberation movement. Lesbian activist Urvashi Vaid characterizes this opposition as the central strain in queer politics, and she traces virtually every strategic misstep in our history to a dispute grounded in the resistance-accommodation dichotomy, usually faulting those she considers accommodationists with a failure of resolve (Vaid 1995). An early opinion piece by lesbian civil rights attorney Paula Ettelbrick, for instance, argues that gays and lesbians are not in fact similar to heterosexuals in all but civil rights, but that they are "fundamentally different." She situates difference, not assimilation, at the heart of gay liberation, explaining that "marriage runs contrary to two of the primary goals of the lesbian and gay movement: the affirmation of gay identity and culture; and the validation of many forms of relationships.' Being queer," Ettelbrick continues, "is more than setting up house, sleeping with a person of the same gender, and seeking state approval for doing so. It is an identity, a culture with many variations." Drawing on a broader feminist critique of the family, Ettelbrick claims that gay marriage will not challenge existing privileges for the few or affect the "systematic abuses" of society.[1] Ettelbrick not only calls for a feminist critique of the family[2] but argues for adoption of a queer oppositional stance toward mainstream cultural institutions, invoking the notion of queer community as an intrinsically subversive configuration.

Nancy Polikoff continues this discussion, questioning the need to parody this most unappealing of patriarchal institutions. Her concern is that "an effort to legalize lesbian and gay marriage would make public critique of the institution of marriage impossible"; since marriage is a social form historically based in gender inequality, seeking access to its privileges would make a mockery of efforts to value other forms of relationships (Polikoff 1993:1546).

In contrast, conservative gay authors such as Andrew Sullivan and Bruce Bawer focus on the legitimation of marriage as a key index of progress toward the achievement of equal treatment (Bawer 1993; Sullivan 1995). Sullivan goes so far as to espouse "equal access to civil marriage" as "the centerpiece" of the new politics he hopes to see emerge from the lesbian and gay community. Taking the position that marriage is a bond that demonstrates fundamental similarities between heterosexuals and homosexuals, legal gay marriage "could bring the essence of gay life—a gay couple—into the heart of the traditional family in a way the family can most understand and the gay offspring can most easily acknowledge. It could do more to heal the gay-straight rift than any amount of gay rights legislation." Sullivan argues, therefore, that "gay marriage is not a radical step; it is a profoundly humanizing, traditionalizing step. . . . It is ultimately the only reform that truly matters" (Sullivan 1995:178, 183–84, 185).

But other advocates of legalizing same-sex marriage locate their support in arguments that such legitimacy will radically alter the shape of conventional social arrangements. Like-gender marriage, attorney Nan Hunter explains, is a social construction that has no natural existence outside of legal regulations; it may be ancient, but its form has changed throughout history. She argues that legalizing same-sex marriage "would radically denaturalize the social construction of male/female differentness." Further, marriage offers the least expensive mechanism for allocating property and thus would provide particular advantages to less affluent gay and lesbian couples. Along similar lines, political philosopher Morris Kaplan proposes that same-sex marriage would serve as a type of civil disobedience and would thus further the potential transformation of public understandings of basic institutions.

While much of the discussion of same-sex marriage has revolved around the complex legal issues that the Hawaii case (*Baehr v. Miike*) presents and related struggles over the federal Defense of Marriage Act (DOMA) and efforts in many states to invalidate same-sex marriages,[3] the issue for many lesbians and gay men around the country is less a legal matter than a personal, spiritual concern. As attorney Evan Wolfson, a member of the legal team arguing the Hawaii case, points out, same-sex couples feel entitled to more than a limited package of benefits included in most domestic partner arrangements. "Domestic partnership," he explains, "fails to resonate with the emotional, declarative, and often religious power most people feel inheres in marriage" (Wolfson 1994–95:607).

This chapter directly speaks to Wolfson's point, arguing that the legal and political debates that surround the question of same-sex marriage are largely irrelevant to the lived experience of couples who choose to enact such ritual celebrations of their unions. Despite the fact that lesbian and gay marriage remains outside the realm of legal possibility, despite the fact that lesbian and gay couples who make their relationships public never receive benefits and rewards equivalent to those available to the legally married, increasing numbers of lesbians and gay men are choosing to stage ceremonies in which they publicly proclaim and solemnize their relationships. Whether these occasions are called "commitment ceremonies," "holy unions," or "weddings," they enshrine couples' demands for recognition and involve friends (what many, along with Kath Weston, call "chosen families"; see Weston 1991), relatives (either in person or represented symbolically), and often coworkers, neighbors, and children as members of a varied cast of not necessarily gay witnesses. These events are nearly always imbued with spiritual, if not outright religious content and generally use other markers of ritual separation from ordinary time—formal invitations, special cloth-ing, rings or other gifts, the use of symbolic foods (e.g., wedding cakes), and music, among other components of celebration.

This chapter also responds to the debate over accommodation and resist-ance I have outlined above, arguing that interpretations of lesbian and gay commitment ceremonies that locate their meaning at one of the poles of this debate in fact miss the subtle interplay of the two strands in constitut-ing one another as ritual dimensions. That is, at the same time that the explicit messages conveyed in these rituals are often about acceptance and conformity to wider community values—seemingly the opposite of any-thing we could easily recognize as "queer"—they also incorporate messages of "queerness" at vital points. First, the event itself focuses on the couple and their (presumptively sexual) bond, calling attention to the very thing that sets the lesbian and gay couple apart from heterosexual norms. Second, many ceremonies, by foregrounding the incongruities between the same-gender couple and the deployment of powerful symbols of conventional hetero-sexuality—the white bridal dress and veil, tuxedos, white multitiered cakes, diamond rings, elaborate floral decorations, and, most notably, the use of wedding liturgies from various religious traditions—highlight contradiction and irony even as they shun parody. And third, some couples deliberately bring elements they consider to be "queer" into the construction of their ceremonies, explaining their wish to mark the occasion as gay or lesbian or to highlight the difference between these occasions and ordinary weddings.

When I asked Mike Rubin and Duane Thomas, two gay men who had their wedding in San Francisco in the early 1990s, why they felt it was essen-tial that their ceremony be organized as a "theme wedding," Duane said emphatically, "Because we're *queer!*" He went on to explain that it was important to him that their ceremony, which combined predominantly Jew-ish liturgical elements with a country-western theme, would never be con-fused with a "straight wedding." Defying Jewish tradition, they incorporated the Jewish mourning prayer, the *kaddish*, into the ceremony, using it to make what they considered an essential statement about the AIDS epidemic and its impact on their lives. But they also saw other elements of the wedding's Jewish content as representing a tie to Mike's Jewish past. Mike unearthed the *talis* (prayer shawl) that his grandfather had given him for his bar mitz-vah and used it to cover the *chuppah* (wedding canopy). He particularly liked the symbolism of the canopy as a representation of the home, its sides open to evoke hospitality and connection to the wider community. And while their theme wedding recalled the classic gay idiom of the theme party

(Newton 1993), Mike and Duane took pride as they showed me their wedding video in pointing out the diversity of their guests—gay and straight, young and old, men and women, friends and family.

Mike and Duane's desire for public recognition also led them to register as domestic partners on February 14, 1991, the day the ordinance offering such registration went into effect in San Francisco. Roaring up to City Hall on their motorcycles, the two men joined more than two hundred other couples signing up for certificates that day and had their picture taken descending the grand staircase in the rotunda. Domestic partnership registration offers no actual benefits (unless one of the parties works for the city and county of San Francisco), but Mike explained that they wanted to be "part of history." A news crew followed them as they went through the various procedures of registering, and they later volunteered to be interviewed for a TV show about gay couples, explaining that they saw their situation as one that could validate other couples' desire for commitment and stability.

Eileen Brennan and Carmen Rodríguez, whose union, presided over by a Presbyterian minister, was attended by over a hundred family and friends, cited many elements of the ceremony as indicators of the "gayness" of the event. Not wanting to "mimic" the style of a traditional wedding, they wore dark formal clothing that suggested a night at the opera more than a marriage ceremony. Along with a succession of attendants that included a ring bearer and a flower girl, two men dressed in matching floral-pattern vests carried baskets of flowers, which they tossed into the crowd. They were the "flower fairies," according to Eileen and Carmen. The music that accompanied the procession was "Chapel of Love" sung by the Dixie Cups; the couple and their attendants literally danced down the aisle to the cheers and laughter of the spectators. At a key moment in the ceremony the congregation was asked not only to swear to uphold and support the marriage in the years to come, a common feature of Protestant weddings, but also to rise and vow to oppose homophobia wherever it might be encountered. At the same time, family members were seated at the front, wearing boutonnieres to distinguish them from other guests. Time was taken during the ceremony to mark the attendance of both brides' relatives, noteworthy in Carmen's case because of the large, multigenerational Mexican-American contingent who appeared and in Eileen's case because several of her Irish-American relatives had come all the way from the East Coast after earlier turning down her invitation. Immediately after the ceremony, while the guests were sipping champagne and nibbling hors d'oeuvres, the couple spent nearly an hour posing for formal photographs with their families.

Other ceremonies place greater emphasis on their resemblance to heterosexual weddings. Margaret Barnes and Lisa Howard held their wedding in a luxurious outdoor setting, a historic Victorian inn in California's wine country. The springtime ceremony was held on a veranda overlooking a formal garden, with both women wearing subdued pastel dresses in delicate shades of pink and green. Margaret and Lisa had begun their relationship nearly ten years earlier when they were graduate students in business school. They share similar backgrounds, coming from well-off families on the East Coast, and both had attended elite colleges and graduate schools. Now working for conservative investment firms, the two women seem anything but "queer." Their comfortable San Francisco home is far from the gay ghetto, and their demanding work schedules leave little time for participation in gay community events. But as they approached the tenth anniversary of their relationship, they wanted to celebrate their having endured many challenges to its survival, particularly those posed by years of conflicting professional obligations. Their conception of their wedding was both as an occasion for their families and their large circle of friends to support and celebrate their relationship, and as an opportunity for all of the important people in their lives to get to know each other and perhaps form lasting connections.

Margaret's family had had a difficult time accepting her lesbianism when she had revealed it to them some years earlier, and she was concerned that they might decide not to participate. Long before plans had been finalized or formal invitations sent out, she wrote them a letter describing the kind of event that they were planning and why her family's involvement was essential. In an effort to acknowledge the problems she felt they would have with the ceremony, Margaret said:

> I know that it has been hard for you to become comfortable with my being gay and not following the path you had always expected for me. But I also know that you are fond of Lisa, and I believe that at some level you realize that our path is not really so very different from yours, or from that of my sister and brothers. A year from now Lisa and I will have been together for 10 years, and our lives are pretty much like that of our married friends—we work hard, we pay lots of taxes, we entertain some, we give as much time as we can to volunteer work, we're faithful to each other, and we take care of each other. Under the circumstances it is sometimes amazing to us to think that we can't be married legally; who could object to such a boring and conventional life?

Their simple Protestant wedding was led by a Unitarian minister. Lisa and Margaret exchanged nonmatching rings, chosen specifically to not look like wedding rings that might stimulate questions about spouses. Though Margaret's firm offers an extra week of vacation to employees who get married, Margaret did not claim this benefit, instead taking regular vacation time for the wedding and honeymoon. In other words, everything about this wedding was calculated to be in good taste, discreet, and low-key. At the same time that they wanted very much to celebrate their relationship in a public manner, both Margaret and Lisa were apprehensive about drawing attention to themselves and about coming out to nongay colleagues. Only a few carefully selected coworkers were invited to the ceremony.

About a month after the ceremony, I settled into a lounge chair in Margaret and Lisa's garden. Over iced tea and cookies, they showed me their photo album, and with much laughter, recounted various odd happenings from the wedding weekend. Beyond the humor, however, their description was intense; they perceived the ceremony as having deepened their relationship in ways they had not anticipated. Even more startling, they had decided to come out at work and to become much more public than they ever had about being gay. When Margaret returned to work after her week off, she responded to her colleagues' casual questions about her vacation by announcing that she and her partner of ten years had gotten married. The responses she received seemed to be warm, for the most part, but she said that even if they weren't, she now felt it was her responsibility to let her coworkers and supervisors see that gay life is not only represented, as she put it, by the Sisters of Perpetual Indulgence, a local group of drag "nuns" noted for staging queer street theatre happenings. The wedding led her to see her relationship as the core of her life in a way that meant that disguising or refusing to acknowledge it would be betrayal. (Her assessment of her employer's response proved to be overly optimistic, however; about six months later she was laid off, despite her many years of outstanding performance in her job.)

A few months later I spoke with Margaret on the phone and she described an adventure she and Lisa had had at an elegant Peninsula restaurant with close friends, a straight married couple. This couple, who they knew from business school, count their anniversary from the same time that Margaret and Lisa do, and the two couples have celebrated the date together for many years. This year, for their joint tenth anniversary, they went out to dinner. During the dinner the waiters overheard talk of an "anniversary," and when they served dessert, they decorated a small cake with a candle and presented it, with much ceremony, to the straight couple. At that point the straight couple said, "But what about them?" pointing to Lisa and Margaret. When the confused waiter said, "But they're not married," Margaret and Lisa immediately answered, "Yes, we are," holding out their left hands and displaying the very nonmatching rings they had chosen so that they would not resemble wedding rings. A second cake arrived in minutes.

These brief examples suggest that lesbian and gay weddings often present complicated intersections between resistance and the quest for acceptance, intersections that cannot readily be teased apart, even within a single ceremony. On the one hand, the desire for public recognition would appear to be intrinsically accommodationist: couples almost uniformly express a desire to be seen as legitimate and visible, as being capable of the same degree of devotion, loyalty, and commitment attributed to heterosexual married couples. They elevate these values to center stage in the ceremonies, making "love" the star of the event even as "law" cannot be invoked (Schneider 1968).

But making this claim for legitimacy, accommodating the wider mainstream, necessarily demands elaboration of the images of difference, sometimes articulated as "queerness," that mark them as different. One cannot achieve visibility or legitimacy in the closet; the very demand for equality rests on confrontation even as it is staged at the altar or the bridal registry.

Most of these ceremonies play with both sets of meanings and overlap them constantly, offering a new twist on the camp aesthetic of incongruity and contradiction. While a desire for visibility may signal notions of community that compete with the whiff of subversion queerness seems to exude, visibility may be more disruptive than couples imagine—or intend. At the same time, ceremonies designed to foreground queerness often depend on symbols of family, community, and tradition to make intelligible their claims about love and commitment. Gay and lesbian weddings reorganize the meanings of being "out," merging Queer Nation's refrain, "We're here, we're queer, get used to it!" with a resilient nostalgia for the acceptance heterosexual couples can take for granted.

NOTES

1. Ettelbrick 1992. Since this essay was written, Ettelbrick's work with the Empire State Pride Agenda in New York seems to have led her to modify her position on same-sex marriage, becoming a persuasive advocate for its legalization. See also Browning 1996.

2. See, for example, Rubin 1975, for one classic statement of this position.

3.   See Wolfson 1994–95 for a detailed discussion of the legal debates that have arisen in connection with this case. See also Sullivan 1997 for a variety of perspectives on the issue.

REFERENCES

Bawer, Bruce. 1993. *A Place at the Table: The Gay Individual in American Society*. New York: Poseidon.

Browning, Frank. 1996. "Why Marry?" *New York Times*, April 17, sec. A, p. 17.

Ettelbrick, Paula. 1992. "Since When Is Marriage a Path to Liberation?" In S. Sherman, ed., *Lesbian and Gay Marriage*, pp. 20–26. Philadelphia: Temple University Press.

Newton, Esther. 1993. *Cherry Grove, Fire Island: Sixty Years in America's First Gay and Lesbian Town*. Boston: Beacon Press.

Polikoff, Nancy D. 1993. "Commentaries: We Will Get What We Ask For—Why Legalizing Gay and Lesbian Marriage Will Not 'Dismantle the Legal Structure of Gender in Every Marriage.' " *Virginia Law Review* 79 (7): 1535–50.

Rubin, Gayle. 1975. "The Traffic in Women: Notes on the 'Political Economy' of Sex." In Rayna R. Reiter, ed., *Toward an Anthropology of Women*, pp. 157–210. New York: Monthly Review.

Schneider, David. 1968. *American Kinship: A Cultural Account*. Englewood Cliffs, N.J.: Prentice-Hall.

Sullivan, Andrew. 1995. *Virtually Normal: An Argument About Homosexuality*. New York: Knopf.

Sullivan, Andrew, ed. 1997. *Same-Sex Marriage: Pro and Con, A Reader*. New York: Vintage.

Vaid, Urvashi. 1995. *Virtual Equality: The Mainstreaming of Gay and Lesbian Liberation*. New York: Anchor.

Weston, Kath. 1991. *Families We Choose: Lesbians, Gays, Kinship*. New York: Columbia University Press.

Wolfson, Evan. 1994–1995. "Crossing the Threshold: Equal Marriage Rights for Lesbians and Gay Men and the Intra-Community Critique." *New York Review of Law and Social Change* 21 (3): 567–615.

4 | "We Can See Them, But We Can't Hear Them": LGBT Members of African American Families

Michael Bennett and Juan Battle

In 1993, when Michael was a graduate student in English at the University of Virginia and Juan was a graduate student in sociology at the University of Michigan, we traveled together to Louisville, Kentucky, to attend the "The Twentieth Annual National Conference on the Black Family in America," where Juan delivered a paper entitled "The Invisible Black Family: An Analysis of Lesbian & Gay Issues within African-American Families." In that presentation, Juan stressed the importance for the black community to recognize its lesbian and gay family members and to support a variety of family structures. This message was delivered to a nearly empty room, populated largely by the spouses of the panelists, at a session that barely made it onto the program of a conference offering almost no visible support for analyses of "alternative" sexualities within black family structures. The irony of making a plea for inclusiveness at a session that was almost excluded and definitely marginalized was not lost on us. The words "gay and lesbian" appeared in only one session on the program of that large and lively conference. We were *seen* (especially when we attended the banquet as a couple, receiving more than a few odd looks), but we were most definitely not *heard*. We began to wonder, not for the first time, why this was the case.

We returned to this question a few years later when, now both professors in New York City and creating our own family of affinity, we collaborated on an essay on the legacy of the Moynihan report for African American families (Battle and Bennett 1997). While conducting our research, we once again encountered a silence where the voices of the Lesbian, Gay, Bisexual, and Transgender (LGBT) members of black families should have been.[1] This resounding silence was made all the more evident when Juan began to prepare to teach a course on the black family. He wanted to make sure that a diversity of experiences within the African American family was presented. But as we did our research and as Juan consulted the most widely used textbooks on the black family to construct his syllabus, we discovered that there were few if any references to LGBT members of African American families. As we discussed this problem, we had uncomfortable flashbacks to our experience at the Louisville conference, and we decided it was time to revisit our question about the reasons for such exclusions—this time in earnest.

Why this silence about LGBTs within black families in an era of our increasing visibility in U.S. popular culture and our more slowly established but still growing presence in academic research? As Kath Weston (1998) points out in the introduction to her brilliant book *Long Slow Burn*, the "sudden" appearance of sexuality as a "hot" issue—the numerous articles in the popular press, the rise of queer theory, *In & Out* and a host of gay-themed movies, *Ellen* and the now standard queer character in sitcoms—tends to obscure the "long slow burn" of issues of sexuality in social science research since mid-century—from Kinsey, Hooker, and Malinowski to their contemporary inheritors (1–2). In African American studies, however, the rise of sexuality as a hot topic in popular culture—the drag balls and voguing depicted in *Paris Is Burning* and Madonna videos, the resurgence of interest in Audre Lorde, the controversy surrounding the documentaries of Marlon Riggs, the phenomenon of Ru Paul—has been accompanied by a long slow silence in academic works on the black family. Why are LGBT members of black families increasingly seen but still not heard?

What follows is the result of our revisiting this question. We would like to examine why there is little or no representation of African American LGBTs within research on African American family structures. We will explore the ways in which normative family models influence the research of even the most well-intentioned investigators. Focusing in particular on the research we conducted for our previous collaboration (Battle and Bennett 1997) and on the most popular textbooks on black families,[2] we will stress the mechanisms of homophobia operative within the larger African American community, and within the black church specifically, as they are manifested within these texts. These mechanisms and models perpetuate the lack of support for research on this population. The dearth of research on LGBTs of color is not, of course, limited to the African American population. Indeed, it is quite probable that research is lacking on LGBTs within other communities of color for many of the same reasons as it is lacking within the African American community. However, we focus in particular on our experience of trying to find research on LGBT members of African American families and our efforts to understand and explain the silence that awaited our efforts.

Michel Foucault reminds us that the effort to fill this silence is not unproblematic—there is a danger involved when a group is inserted into the discourse of the social sciences. In *The History of Sexuality*, he demonstrates how the increasing visibility of LGBTs provided the material by which the "homosexual" came to be inscribed as a modern subject. This inscription has had both positive and negative effects; in short, as LGBTs become more visible, it becomes easier for them to be oppressed at the same time that it makes it easier for them to resist oppression. The same may be true of LGBT members within black families. Just as many LGBT members within mostly straight families remain closeted out of fear of the consequences of being open about their sexuality, so there may be negative consequences when LGBT family members emerge from the closet of social science research. At least when the role of LGBTs within black families is neglected, they cannot therefore be chastised or harassed. One of the unintended consequences of calling for the inclusion of LGBTs in constructions of the black family is that they may be included for the purpose of controlling or containing them.

Ultimately, however, the benefits of breaking this silence seem to outweigh the possible consequences. LGBT perspectives on the black family can both reveal the importance of creating a space for nonnormative self-representations and also scrutinize the effect of assumed heteronormativity in constructions of African American families. If these voices are not heeded—if the LGBT members of black families are only seen and not heard—then research on African American families will continue to be distorted by the omission of nonheterosexual family members or by viewing these members only through the lens of a heterosexual norm. As Halperin (1995) notes, this pattern has been repeated over and over in social science research: "By constituting homosexuality as an object of knowledge, heterosexuality also constitutes itself as a privileged stance of subjectivity—as the very condition of knowing—and thereby avoids becoming an object of knowledge itself, and the target of a possible critique" (47). To avoid the continual reproduction of this heteronormative position, it is necessary not only to hear the stories told by LGBT members of black families but also for researchers to reveal their own subjective positions and to allow their own subjectivities to be questioned by their research subjects.

In other words, the inclusion of LGBTs in research on the black family is not just a question of redressing an imbalance, it is a matter of resisting models of heteronormativity that distort our understanding of human subjectivity and oppress LGBT African Americans by excluding them from the category of human subjects. The ugly history of racist social theory and physical anthropology is replicated on the ground of sexuality. That is, just as all blacks were often defined outside the realm of the fully human, LGBT African Americans are similarly excluded from the domain of human subjectivity even today.

At least since the release of the Moynihan report in 1965, a great deal of the research devoted to black families has been focused on either supporting or refuting Moynihan's contention that the "Negro family" is subject to a "tangle of pathologies," most of which stem from its "matriarchal" structure. Long before Moynihan became the senior senator from New York, he prepared this report, entitled *The Negro Family: The Case for National Action*, as part of his duties in the Johnson administration's Department of Labor. Though meant as a well-intentioned contribution to the 1960s War on Poverty, the long shadow cast by the Moynihan report has ensured that the bulk of research devoted to sexuality and alternative structures within the black family is concerned primarily with the effects of single mothers and absent fathers on African American children.

By its nature, this model assumes that two cohabiting parents of different genders are best able to meet the needs of black children and that any deviations from this model must be accounted for and excused. So even research devoted to questioning Moynihan's depiction of the "Negro family" often does not interrogate the practice of using low rates of single parenthood and divorce as measures of "successful" families. This model fails to consider that many families, especially with LGBT parents or members, may be better off with nonmarried coparents of the same sex, or the divorce of parents who are not compatible, or various extended family structures. Swan (1974) and Miao (1974), for example, question the methodology of Moynihan's report by suggesting that economic factors rather than racial characteristics cause black fathers to be absent, without questioning the notion that it is always best for a black child to have a father present (even if, say, the father is abusive, or the mother is living with a female partner, or single parent or extended family models are simply a better option). More recently, Platt (1987) and Ruiz and Cumming (1993) have questioned what the latter calls the "cultural ideology" of the Moynihan report without sufficiently questioning their own ideologies about nonnormative family structures. Though providing admirable critiques of the Moynihan report, these researchers fail to give voice to those LGBT parents and children for whom the normativization of heterosexual family structures is oppressive.

Why this stunning lack of information on African American LGBT families and LGBT members of families? Of course, historical oppression plays a role. As Gutman (1976) was among the first to demonstrate, slavery and its aftermath created oppressive social circumstances that severely tested the "adaptive capacities" (xxi) of black families. This historical cause gave rise to a number of effects, not the least of which is that African Americans have needed to develop a common agenda to combat their shared predicament in American society. In order to relieve historical oppression based upon race, members of black communities have been called upon to rally around that common agenda. As a result, subcultures or minority groups within that oppressed group often have to suppress their own agenda because it is thought to detract from a politics based on race. The problem with this reasoning is that not only has the larger African American community been historically oppressed on the basis of race but so too have its LGBT members been assaulted on the basis of sexuality. The process by which oppression leads to internal suppression of differences based on sexuality reifies dominant models and keeps heteronormativity firmly in place. The compounding of one oppression in order to relieve another is an untenable price to pay in the name of racial solidarity.

And yet this process has a long history. The suppression of gender issues within the black community, especially in the years prior to the modern feminist and womanist movements, provides a clear example of the process by which internal divisions were ignored so as to project a united front against external threats. During the early civil rights era, while issues of race were being debated, issues of gender were quite often taken off the table. This was also the case with issues of sexuality. The treatment of Bayard Rustin, for example, shows how nonnormative sexualities are shunted aside when they are thought to detract from racial politics. Rustin's displacement during the 1963 March on Washington, which he took a leading role in organizing, was justified on the basis that bad publicity concerning his homosexuality might sully the image of the whole march. In the presence of a perceived common agenda, subcultures and issues not perceived as being directly related to achieving that overarching goal are considered expendable. So Rustin, one of the architects of the Civil Rights movement, was excluded from perhaps the most famous moment in the movement out of fear that his sexuality would detract from the legitimacy of the event. And those LGBTs who, like Rustin, are fearful of having their sexuality revealed—even those who don't dread exposure per se but who fear ostracism and harassment by the very ethnic community that promises refuge from the pressures and oppressions of the dominant culture—are sacrificed on the altar of heteronormativity.

These fears of the consequences of straying from normative models have only been magnified by the prominent role of the black church in African American communities. All LGBT members of ethnic communities have to deal with discrimination from within and from outside their particular population; however, the situation for LGBT members of African American families is uniquely affected by the role of the black church in promoting an uncommonly virulent strain of homophobia. Each ethnic group has its own expression of religion that is unique to that particular population, and many of these expressions are harshly critical of LGBTs, but the black church has taken an explicit stand on the issue of homosexuality. Reverend Irene Monroe (1997), an African American scholar at Harvard, notes:

> Our black churches, both denominational and storefront, are fertile soils for planting and cultivating homo hatred. Their evangelical-conservative theologies and biblical fundamentalism share pews with the Christian right. And like the Christian right, most believe in prescribed gender roles for men and women in order to maintain the traditional composition of the heterosexual family. Most believe that many of society's ills are traced to Jews, feminists, liberals, and queers. (9)

Given that the black church is so important to the African American community, the church's attitude toward sexuality becomes a unique and uniquely oppressive vessel for limiting the acknowledgment and openness of LGBT members of African American families, further enforcing a heteronormative model of black life.

This heteronormative model has been in part constructed and perpetuated by social science research, as evidenced in textbooks on the black family. A survey of various texts on the black family reveals that academics play an active role in circumscribing notions of black subjectivity to fit within this model. Though the twenty-two authors who contributed to Mindel, Habenstein, and Wright's anthology *Ethnic Families in America: Patterns and Variations* (1998) manage to discuss more than eighteen different racial and ethnic families, none make reference to any "variations" on the "pattern" of heterosexual family structures. The chapter specifically addressing the African American community has four subareas on the black family—the extended family, marital and family stability, marital structures of families, and parents and children. Unfortunately, within those broad categories, there is no "space" to mention LGBTs within the black family. The author clearly recognizes the heterogeneity within the black family:

> The diversity of histories and the pluralism of experiences within the African American community has [sic] resulted in a multitude of distinct individuals and subgroups and a quite heterogeneous population. Despite some obvious and not so obvious differences among individuals and subgroups, they have all had to, and still must to this day, face racism, discrimination, and oppression within our society. (376)

It is therefore all the more unfortunate that, by their exclusion, LGBTs must experience even more oppression from within the African American community.

The failure to allow space for LGBT African Americans in models of the black family forecloses otherwise laudable efforts to expand notions of black subjectivity. Even generally well-written and carefully edited volumes on a number of issues affecting black families nevertheless manage to avoid mentioning LGBT African Americans, including Taylor, Jackson, and Chatters's *Family Life in Black America* (1997) and Ronald Taylor's *Minority Families in the United States: A Multicultural Perspective* (1998). Both of these volumes should be applauded for their efforts not only to address the "standard" topics in the field but to also include more marginal, yet very important, black subjectivities. In *Family Life in Black America,* for example, an entire chapter is devoted to "Multiple Familial-Worker Role Strain and Psychological Well-Being: Moderating Effects of Coping Resources Among Black American Parents." Thus, both texts are careful to delineate the role of class, race, and gender in shaping black family structures; however, conspicuous by its absence in both volumes is any discussion of (homo)sexuality.

Another extremely popular textbook in this area that fails to create any space for LGBT subjectivities is McAdoo's *Black Families* (1997). The text contains over 360 pages, comprised of twenty chapters and with contributions by more than twenty authors, and not one line deals directly with LGBTs within black families. One contribution, by Rivers and Scanzoni, manages to highlight how the work of other researchers on varying formations of lesbian and gay families (for example Weston 1991) provides a model that might be applied to "social families among blacks" (339). In other words, without ever recognizing that a family might be both black AND non-heterosexual, Rivers and Scanzoni suggest that extended kinship models within African American families might share certain similarities with LGBT families.

A final example of the effect of heteronormative models on conceptions of black subjectivity is provided by Staples's book *The Black Family: Essays and Studies* (1994), which contains one abridged version of an article on gay men (Cochran and Mays 1994) that was originally printed in 1988. As the abstract states:

> This article reviews the literature on black gay and bisexual men. It reports on the development of a black gay identity, the integration of black gay men into the black heterosexual world, some of their sexual practices, behavior that places them at risk for AIDS and alcoholism, and their social networks. The authors caution that the experiences of black gay men cannot be interpreted in terms of a white gay male standard. (311)

One has to be particularly discouraged that, because of the dearth of research in the area, when an editor wishes to include issues concerning LGBTs within African American families, she or he is almost forced to select an article that excludes women and examines topics such as the prevalence of intravenous drug use and the role of alcohol as a cofactor of high-risk sexual behavior. Though these topics are important, when presented in a textbook entitled *The Black Family* and without any other representations of African American LGBTs, readers are being asked to severely circumscribe black subjectivity: (1) African American lesbians, bisexuals, and transgendered people don't exist, and (2) all African American gay males are likely to engage in high-risk behaviors.

No doubt many of these social scientists have shunted aside LGBT issues as part of their overarching agenda of defending the black family from external assaults. Admitting internal differences, particularly those that much of the dominant group finds offensive (e.g., nonnormative sexualities), is seen as politically risky. Given the long history of such assaults on African American families in both public policy and social science research, it is no wonder that there has been a tendency to circle the wagons and protect the family from external attacks without sufficiently accounting for internal differences.

We have seen how the legacy of the Moynihan report has engendered a body of research that, whether arguing for or against the report, takes as its founding assumption that a household headed by two heterosexual parents is the ideal situation. This assumption has so thoroughly permeated our culture that the popular press routinely runs stories decrying the fate of black children raised by single mothers, while scolding black fathers for being derelict in their duties. Witness syndicated columnist William Raspberry's claim (1993) that "children need both parents" or the conviction of cover stories by *Newsweek* and *Sports Illustrated* that, in the words of the former, "two parents living together are better than one" (Ingrassia 1993:21). As with the research and textbooks that we surveyed, members of the popular press were almost uniformly willing to exclude LGBT issues in their rush to preach the gospel of the heteronormative two-parent family.

Another reason for the lack of research on LGBT members of black families is the belief by many mainstream African American scholars and researchers that it's not their job to address the African American LGBT population if they themselves are not part of that population. "What," they might ask, "gives us the right to speak authoritatively on a subject position that we do not occupy?" This is a legitimate question, one that is related to other important questions about the role of subjectivity in social science research and the dangers of misappropriating the experience of research subjects. However, the implication that LGBTs should be the *only* ones held responsible for research in this area is erroneous. It acts as a way of dodging the hard work necessary to thoroughly research and fairly represent a research subject that is different from and perhaps even hostile to the researcher (a not unusual situation).

The experience of research on African American families offers a wonderful response to the line of reasoning that exonerates heterosexual scholars from studying LGBT issues. When there was a lack of research on black families in the larger (white) academy, African Americans did two things. First, they produced that research themselves, much as LGBTs are doing in a number of arenas. But, second, African Americans challenged the larger academy to produce research on African American populations and families and to incorporate such research in theoretical models and study designs concerning U.S. demographics and social structures. When it comes to challenging the larger (straight) academy to conduct research on LGBT family structures, however, there has been no meaningful response.

Contributors to Beverly Greene's book *Ethnic and Cultural Diversity Among Lesbians and Gay Men* (1997) highlight two additional problems with expecting African American LGBTs to be the sole contributors to research on this topic. In the opening pages of her preface, Greene addresses the difficulty she had in getting scholars to contribute to the book. First, they were concerned about how the information would be received by the larger academic community. Many scholars feared that they would be "airing their dirty laundry" before "outsiders" and they were concerned about perpetuating the further oppression of already oppressed groups:

> they voiced their concerns that discussing "family business"—matters that take place within their respective cultures that are not generally known to outsiders—with people who do not belong to the group would be perceived as being critical of ethnic communities that have already been historically victimized and then stigmatized. (xii)

Second, many of those asked to contribute to Greene's book were afraid of the professional repercussions. In describing scholars who are at "inhospitable" institutions, Greene found some who

> acknowledged feeling vulnerable about writing and conducting research on gay or lesbian issues, citing their concerns about potentially negative effects on their tenure, promotion, or candidacy. Lesbians and gay men of color in these situations reiterated their feelings of an even heightened vulnerability as well as a reluctance to take on yet another issue in addition to race. (xiv–xv)

So even those researchers who were very sympathetic to LGBT members of black families or who were themselves part of such families were reluctant to raise LGBT issues in their own research out of fear of what would be done to the research and/or out of fear of what would be done to them.

Given all of these cultural constraints—a history of oppression and the resulting desire to form a common agenda—and given the particular role of the black church, it should not be surprising that African American scholars who come from this culture would be less willing to do research on African American LGBTs. And as we have seen, this constraint is felt even by African American LGBTs themselves. Monroe (1997) argues that this heteronormative model is enforced by the black church through its role in promoting "compulsory heterosexuality" as the "Word of God" (9). It is difficult enough to go against social norms and challenge community solidarity; the added weight of violating the presumed word of God has proven to be too much for most African American scholars involved in researching the black family, thus creating a chilling effect on all research in the field.

But even with all these sociocultural constraints firmly in place, there are some whose research creates an opportunity for the discussion of LGBT issues by at least acknowledging a variety of black family forms. As discussed earlier, for example, McAdoo (1997) uses Kath Weston's formulations of voluntary family constructs in *Families We Choose* (1991)—a text primarily devoted to describing lesbians and gays who create different family forms—in developing her model of the different family forms that can be found in African American communities. However, McAdoo's willingness to talk about research on LGBTs as it impacts black family models without being willing to recognize that these categories sometimes overlap is astonishing. The willed blindness of presenting the lesbian- and gay-family model and the African American family model as though they are mutually exclusive prevents researchers from considering the possibility that the reason that the LGBT family model can be found in black families might be because African American LGBTs are creating those family forms. It's also interesting to note that these new forms benefit all African American families and not solely their LGBT members.

Even given all these factors that explain the dearth of research on LGBT members of African American families, there are reasons to be encouraged by the progress being made that should allow for greater future research. In the black church, for example, a number of African American congregations are becoming much more open and affirming of "alternative lifestyles" than they have been historically. Additionally, new churches "in the black tradition" are being formed to address the concerns of African American LGBTs of faith. Unity Fellowship Church, for example, was started primarily by African American LGBTs to address their concerns. Currently Unity Fellowship Church has grown to include some eight churches throughout the country. Balm in Gilead, located in New York City, is another organization doing impressive work in this area. Its main purpose is to educate black churches about issues concerning their LGBT members. Though such developments within the black church may have come about primarily as a result of the AIDS crisis, there is an ongoing infusion of inclusion taking place.

Another reason to be encouraged is that academic research is beginning to become more inclusive. Textbooks and research manuals are now being produced that deal with LGBT issues. Within many professional organizations, there are lesbian and gay caucuses and subcommittees. These outlets then become vessels for moving LGBT concerns from the margin closer to the center. And as LGBT activists build coalitions with activists from other oppressed groups, more voices join the choir exhorting us to combat oppression. Once scholars who have felt comfortable studying one form of oppression (e.g., on the basis of race) see that oppression can indeed take on many forms, they will then feel more comfortable simultaneously wrestling with racism, sexism, and homophobia. Beverly Greene's *Ethnic and Cultural Diversity Among Lesbians and Gay Men* is a wonderful example of progress being made in this area.

This progress should in no way, however, lead to the impression that the job is done. Though increasingly visible, the voices of LGBT members of black families are only faintly heard. And if, as we have come to learn, "Silence Equals Death," then the continuing silence concerning LGBT issues with the black family perpetuates the model of compulsory heterosexuality that sustains the oppression of LGBTs within the African American community. If indeed "my people are destroyed for lack of knowledge," then the African American community is made more vulnerable by not knowing more about such a significant part of its population. Further, the community is not utilizing to its fullest capacity a powerful portion of its population, one that is misunderstood, misrepresented, and mistreated.

A final important reason why textbooks on black families need to generate and incorporate research on LGBTs within the African American community is to help the authors better explain the heterogeneity within black families. Less than 10 percent of African American families look like the mythical American family prototype: a father working one full-time job, making enough money to sustain the family; a mother not working out of the home; no more than three children; a house in the suburbs, with no debt other than a mortgage; and everyone happily heterosexual (see Taylor, Jackson, and Chatters, 1997: chapter 2). One would assume that African American researchers would want to expand notions of the black family to prevent the ostracization of families that don't perfectly fit the prototype. Instead, by not addressing LGBT family structures as "normal" manifestations of African American family forms, these researchers are simultaneously perpetuating the constrictive norms they are trying to overcome. In other words, while trying to break down some stereotypes, they are building up others. An important step in empowering the individuals oppressed by these stereotypes is the presentation of their experiences and contributions in research generated by those who know the detrimental effects of oppression all too well. Only by ending the suppression of internal differences can social science research challenge the heteronormative order.

The two means of fighting homophobia that are outlined by Halperin (1995)—exposing the "operations of homophobic discourses" and creating "specific opportunities for the voices of the disempowered to be heard, recorded, published, and circulated" (52)—are the same means most likely to combat the homophobic exclusion of LGBTs from research and writing on African American families. This dual strategy is, as Halperin suggests, an attempt to "reverse the subject- and object-positions typically assigned by those apparatuses [of power/knowledge] to the empowered and the disempowered, respectively" (56). In other words, revealing the limitations of traditional scholarship while insisting that LGBTs be allowed to tell their own stories are the steps necessary in the effort to make LGBTs not merely the objects omitted from research models—or, alternately, objects of hostile scrutiny—but, rather, the subjects of informed research. Such research aimed at empowering LGBT members of black families by granting them subjectivity and exploring its parameters must be informed by the self-representations of LGBTs and it must carefully situate the researchers' own status. This has been the lesson of the new ethnography: the illusion of objectivity must give way to considerations of the interaction of the subjectivities of researchers and those they are researching. Otherwise, social science research simply reproduces the power relations that have silenced LGBTs in the first place by replicating their objectification at the expense of their self-definition and agency and by allowing heteronormativity to go unquestioned.

We hope to contribute to the ending of this silence—to not just seeing, but also hearing LGBT members of black families—because anyone who knows us knows that we, and especially Juan, do not like to be silenced. Least of all, do we wish to silence ourselves. But if we, and here "we" means all LGBT academics, only work within the traditional family models that we have inherited, then we will perpetuate our own exclusion. This is a lesson that we, Mike and Juan, have learned as we conduct our own research and build our own family. It is only in undertaking the retrospective analysis of research on the black family that we have noticed how even our own work (Battle and Bennett 1997) fails to adequately theorize how LGBT family members destabilize normative models of black families (when writing about the Moynihan report's fetishization of the dual-parent family, for instance, we failed to mention the role of LGBT family configurations in resisting this normativization). This creeping heteronormativity is especially ironic given the nature of our own family, with us (an interracial gay couple) at the core; various rotating housemates—black and white; gay, straight, and other—who have become members of our extended family; and plans for the foster care and adoption of children who will almost certainly (we live in Brooklyn) be of various ethnic backgrounds. Only by listening to our own voices and those of other LGBT members of black families can we (and here "we" includes Mike and Juan and other researchers on African American family structures) make sure that we do not become the objects of heteronormative models but, rather, the subjects of our own inclusive black family structures.

NOTES

1. When we refer to "LGBT members of black families," we envision a variety of family structures, including but not limited to mostly straight families with one or two LGBT members and LGBT families of affinity in which none of the members are heterosexual.
2. The dual focus of this essay, on the resources we encountered during our previous research on black families and public policy and on our analysis of textbooks on the black family, is meant to include both the most recent specialized research on black families and the ways in which that research is distilled and made available to students in the more generalized and generally available form of college textbooks.

REFERENCES

Battle, Juan and Michael Bennett. 1997. "African-American Families and Public Policy: The Legacy of the Moynihan Report." In Cedric Herring, ed., *African Americans and the Public Agenda: The Paradoxes of Public Policy*, pp. 150–67. Thousand Oaks, Cal.: Sage.

Cochran, S. and V. Mays. 1994. "Sociocultural Facets of the Black Gay Male Experience." In Robert Staples, ed., *The Black Family: Essays and Studies* (5th ed.), pp. 311–18. Belmont, Cal.: Wadsworth.

Foucault, Michel. 1978. *The History of Sexuality.* Vol. 1. *An Introduction.* Trans. Robert Hurley. New York: Pantheon.

Greene, Beverly, ed. 1997. *Ethnic and Cultural Diversity Among Lesbians and Gay Men.* Thousand Oaks, Cal.: Sage.

Gutman, Herbert G. 1976. *The Black Family in Slavery and Freedom, 1750–1925.* New York: Vintage.

Halperin, David M. 1995. *Saint Foucault: Towards a Gay Hagiography.* New York: Oxford University Press.

Ingrassia, Michele. 1993. "Endangered Family." *Newsweek* August 30, pp. 16–27.

McAdoo, Harriette Pipes, ed. 1997. *Black Families.* 3d ed. Thousand Oaks, Cal.: Sage.

Miao, G. 1974. "Marital Instability and Unemployment among Whites and Non-whites: The Moynihan Report Revisited—Again." *Journal of Marriage and the Family* 36 (February 1):77–86.

Mindel, Charles H., Robert Habenstein, and Roosevelt Wright Jr., eds. 1998. *Ethnic Families in America: Patterns and Variations.* 4th ed. Riverside, N.J.: Simon & Schuster.

Monroe, I. 1997. "A Garden of Homophobia." *The Advocate* 9 (December 9): 9.

Moynihan, Daniel Patrick. 1965. *The Negro Family: The Case for National Action.* Washington, D.C.: Office of Policy Planning and Research, U.S. Department of Labor.

Platt, T. 1987. "E. Franklin Frazier and Daniel Patrick Moynihan: Setting the Record Straight." *Contemporary Crises* 11 (3): 265–77.

Raspberry, W. 1993. "Nothing Beats Having Two Parents." *York Dispatch*, September 28, sec. A, p. 4.

Ruiz, D. S. and R. G. Cumming. 1993. "Cultural Ideology and the Moynihan Report." *Western Journal of Black Studies* 17 (2) (summer): 65–72.

Staples, Robert, ed. 1994. *The Black Family: Essays and Studies.* 5th ed. Belmont, Cal.: Wadsworth.

Swan, A. L. 1974. "A Methodological Critique of the Moynihan Report." *Black Scholar* 5 (June 9): 18–24.

Taylor, R., ed. 1998. *Minority Families in the United States: A Multicultural Perspective.* 2d ed. Riverside, N.J.: Simon & Schuster.

Taylor, Robert J., James S. Jackson, and Linda M. Chatters, eds. 1997. *Family Life in Black America.* Thousand Oaks, Cal.: Sage.

Weston, Kath. 1991. *Families We Choose: Lesbians, Gays, Kinship.* New York: Columbia University Press.

——. 1998. *Long Slow Burn: Sexuality and Social Science.* New York: Routledge.

5 | Talking Freaks: Lesbian, Gay, Bisexual, and Transgender Families on Daytime Talk TV

Joshua Gamson

The thing we constantly ask ourselves is, "Is this something our audience can relate to?" So whereas lesbian issues aren't something that maybe middle America, you know, maybe the housewife with three kids who's in Kansas City isn't that related to, but yet she can understand a mother-son relationship. I think that people can kind of relate to what it must be like to be going through something like that and have to deal with your children. Or like coming out to your parents and friends. It's not necessary that everyone can relate to being homosexual, but people can relate to having to reveal something to your parents, reveal something to your friends, that's going to potentially cause problems.

—*Leeza* executive producer Nancy Alspaugh[1]

Springer had a person who had a sex change, and they dragged his family on there. His two sons saying, "We ain't going to talk to him anymore." And his little eleven-year-old daughter stands up in the audience, says, "I don't want to ever see him again." And Springer stands up with his last five-minute little comment and says, "If you're thinking about having one of these things and you brought kids into the world, why don't you just keep your pants on until they're grown up and out of the house and then do what you're going to do." That was an outright attack on our community and we are desperately trying to dry up his supply of transgenders. They'll still find people. They're going to have to find an awful lot of rogue people, though, people that aren't connected, because anybody who's connected with anything, we're going to basically say, "This show is quarantined."

—transsexual activist and former talk-show guest Cheryl-Ann Costa

Queer parents, parents of lesbians, cross-dressing teen-agers and their mothers, married gay couples adopting children, drag queens and their sisters: queer family relationships, while emerging in a strained and limited way in the political arena, are all over daytime television. Family politics, in fact, are emerging not in an arena of cultural silence in daytime entertainment genres but in one of exploding cultural visibility, of ongoing chatter, testimony, and display. Now that Ellen's coming-out episode is already a distant memory, and drag queen Ru Paul holds court on *The Hollywood Squares*, and prime-time sitcom *Will and Grace* boasts the first gay male title character, and both gay-male "best-friend" characters and chic lesbian bars are becoming movie clichés, it is time to revisit the politics of visibility. We are clearly in the midst of an explosion of visibility for gay, lesbian, bisexual, and transgender people in commercial-media culture. Even though plenty of Hollywood stars remain closeted (Signorile 1993), much of what is happening seems to be right in line with what many of us have craved personally for years, and organizations such as the Gay and Lesbian Alliance Against Defamation (GLAAD) have pursued politically for years. It has been something of a sacred cow in gay-media studies and politics that more exposure is the goal (Fejes and Petrich 1993; Gross 1989; Russo 1987), and now we are getting that. But looking at representations of lesbian, gay, bisexual, and transgender families on daytime television talk shows complicates the question of visibility just a bit—and now is an especially important time to do so.

On a collective level, the desire for visibility is especially powerful for marginalized groups, whose public images are often minimal or wildly distorted. Since contemporary lesbian and gay identities began forming earlier in this century, cultural visibility has been a central concern for lesbian, gay, bisexual, and transgender people, who have been subject to the charge that they do not exist, and many of whom, since queerness is not marked on the body, can and do choose to be invisible. The positive effects of visibility are quite plain: "Cultural visibility can prepare the ground for gay civil rights protection," as Rosemary Hennessy sums it up, and "affirmative images of lesbians and gays in the mainstream media . . . can be empowering for those of us who have lived most of our lives with no validation at all from the dominant culture" (1994/95:31–32). In the case of political struggle for the recognition of a diversity of lesbian, gay, bisexual and transgender family forms, for instance, the fact that such families *exist* on their own terms, and the stories that get widely told about where sex- and gender-noncon-formists fit in "the family," are clearly important. The desire to be recognized, affirmed, validated, and to lay the cultural groundwork for political change, in fact, is so strong it has tended to inhibit careful analysis of the dynamics of becoming visible.

A number of things recommend talk shows as a place to look at visibility processes. For one, in a sense they paved the way for the kinds of publicity we are seeing now: they have been really the one place in commercial media where we, since the 1970s, have been consistently visible. It is no accident that Oprah Winfrey played Ellen-the-character's therapist in the famous 1996 coming-out episode, and that Ellen-the-star chose Winfrey's show as the one on which to first appear with then-girlfriend Anne Heche. On a certain level, "queers" rule these shows (Gamson 1998a; Shattuc 1997). More important, they offer a case in which transgendered people, lesbians, bisexuals, and gay men are, at least partially and potentially, *agents* in their own visibility. Beyond their obvious exploitative and sensationalist nature, that is the twist talk shows provide: people playing themselves. A close look appropriately messes up conventional thinking about visibility. What kinds of visibility does television provide, and for whom exactly, and on what terms? Might "positive" images also be "negative" ones? Just what kind of cultural environment underwrites the politics of the family?

It is with these more general questions in mind—what is, can, and should be going on with cultural visibility—that I turn to the representation of families in the talk-show genre. As anyone who has watched one of these shows knows, "family" is a topic of particular interest to talk shows. One dominant format, especially now, is programming that features families in conflict; more generally, producers, aiming primarily at women for whom everyday marriage and family relationships are central, routinely produce their programs by putting such family issues at the center. In the culture at large, put simply, sexual "deviants" have been seen as aliens within families or outcasts from them, biologically incapable of reproducing (Weston 1991); on talk shows, families with queers in them, and queer families, can usually be counted upon for a certain amount of conflict, and are thus constants.

In fact, "family" is the firm, beating heart of daytime talk TV. As a genre that is highly domestic, in which chattering people in pseudo-living rooms make their way into actual living rooms, and a genre targeting primarily women at home, there is a constant return to the concerns of family life. "In the end," as Jane Shattuc has argued, "the shows depend on the nuclear family as their mainstay. . . . Almost every show plays upon the fear and loss and the triumph and return of the nuclear family" (1997:45). That mainstay is and has been an opening for sexually nonconforming people—who are parts of families and make trouble for them—one major source of lesbian, gay, bisexual, and transgender visibility on these shows, a visibility that simultaneously gives voice and exploits. It is also the source of a major tension on the shows: between promoting "acceptance" and "tolerance" of different sorts of family members and protecting the underpinnings of the heterosexual, monogamous, nuclear family, in which people of "opposite" sexes make exclusive emotional and sexual commitments to one another, divide up tasks (at least loosely) along gender lines, and rear children together.

As I move into the details of this picture, I want to expand on this tension between "normalizing" and "freakifying" our families. Talk shows do this, I will argue, by on the one hand working with a loosely liberal ideology while on the other hand establishing a new, updated, culturally conservative version of "normal" families that includes gays and lesbians while programming transgendered and bisexual people as too selfish and monstrous for the family. This is another important reminder that our visibility is shot through with a politics of division (Gamson 1998b; Schacter 1997). The cultural visibility strategies to which family politics are attached must take these divisions carefully into account.

TALK SHOWS, CLASS, AND FAMILIES

The show was about people who can't accept their gay relatives, and my job was to sort through all of the things that had just been seen on the air and try to come to some sort of understanding. . . . So it's about five minutes into the show, and I realize that they have on a collection of the most incredibly dysfunctional people from rural parts of the United States. People who have never been on television before and are saying the most horrific, hateful things to each other. Mother to daughter, lesbian lover to the mother-in-law, half-brother to brother. And I'm watching this thinking, "How am I ever going to go out there and make any sense of any of this?" One guy yelled, "The only pussy you've ever seen is the cat that crawled across the floor in your house," and "my fucking daughter this and that." Every other word was "fuck." Then they introduced a mother and her straight daughter and they interviewed the lesbian daughter—they haven't seen each other in I don't know how long—and her lover. There was screaming back and forth. "You're not my child. They must have mixed up the babies at the hospital." And the sister says, "She's ruined her life. They took the children away because of the lover." Terrible things back and forth. Then they brought out a sister and brother, Hispanic sister and brother. And, "fucking this," and "fuck that," and "he borrows my clothes and I'm going to get AIDS from the clothes." And then Sally introduced two boys, sixteen and nineteen, straight kids from the mountains of Tennessee, who had the most horrible things to say about gay people. They were there because their brother was going to be on the show. Well, they introduced the brother and the lover. They came out holding hands, swish onto the stage, throw themselves in their chairs and tongue kiss. But they were worked up too, they were angry and they were told to do whatever, and they're not going on with any particular agendas. And I thought, "We're in great shape now."

—Writer and *Sally* guest Eric Marcus

The recent history of the TV-talk genre offers the first indicators of the kinds of divisions on which talk-show visibility depends. The talk-show genre has always combined the rational, "propriety"-oriented styles of public participation associated with the middle classes with the more emotional, "irreverent" public culture associated with American lower classes. There is nothing inherent in class background, of course, that dictates how one behaves in public, nothing inherently rational about middle-class people or inherently emotional about working-class ones. Yet historically, to boil it down to its simplest, class cultures developed—typically by defining themselves against one another—such that rationality became the more common middle-class public participatory strategy and emotionality became the stronger base of working-class public participation (see DiMaggio 1991; Habermas 1991; Levine 1988; Peiss 1986).

Talk shows joined the two, exaggerating each through various strategies and routines (guest and audience recruitment, programming frames, guest and audience coaching, host styles, and so on). In the earlier days of the genre, when the *Donahue* model dominated, and continuing in some programs today, primarily white, middle-class, highly educated, organizationally affiliated guests came on to talk "rationally" about issues, either in debate or testimonial format. More recently, beginning in the 1990s with *Ricki Lake*, *Jerry Springer*, and their imitators—who targeted a younger, more racially and socioeconomically diverse audience—primarily unaffiliated, working-class and poor people of many colors with little education come on TV mainly to argue emotionally about interpersonal relationships (Gamson 1998a; Grindstaff 1997; Shattuc 1997). The genre has thus more or less split into two subgenres: one dependent on an exaggerated middle-class "social controversy" and "service" culture, the other on an exaggerated working-class and underclass "interpersonal conflict" culture; one relatively polite and taking itself quite seriously, the other unapologetically and playfully rowdy.

"Class" takes its place on TV-talk shows not so much through explicit discussion—a rarity in American popular culture in general—but through its embodiment, often amplified by the programs, in both studio audiences and guests. Occupational markers may be provided (a guest presented and labeled as "lawyer" or "truck-lift operator"), but class backgrounds mostly come across through widely recognized markers such as their language use, levels of emotional effusiveness, gestures, the conditions of their bodies and teeth, and their clothing and hair styles. There may be occasional ambiguity, and we are not talking about class in any strict sociological sense, but for the most part it is safe to say that viewers know that on programs such as *Leeza* they are encountering middle-class people and discourses and on programs such as *Springer* they are encountering working-class or poverty-class people and discourses (Grindstaff 1997). These class-based divisions are the foundation on which talk-show representations of the family are constructed—and it is typically the "trashy" shows (read: the shows with guests and audiences who are not middle-class) that are criticized for giving lesbians, gay men, bisexuals, and transgendered people, among others, a bad name (Gamson 1998b).

For a taste of the differences, compare two 1995 programs on gay and lesbian parenting. The first, in the middle-class salon style, is hosted by former *Taxi* star Marilu Henner, whose guests—presumably recruited, as on this brand of shows they tend to be, through organizational networks—are various lesbians and gay men raising kids. No one is there to oppose them, no right-wing bigot to argue about recruitment and seduction and America's vulnerable children, and both host and audience are politely supportive. The guests are dressed in professional suitlike garb, the audience members are generally quiet, showing themselves through applause and asking informational questions; very little slang is used, and everyone speaks in the words and cadences of the college educated.

Everyone at this *Marilu* show pretty much agrees that loving families are a good thing. The implicit and sometimes explicit model of family offered, not surprisingly, is the one exemplified by the chosen guests: a liberal revision of the "normal" (and normative) mainstream, two-parent, middle-class nuclear family. Good parenting takes love, Henner suggests in her opening, and "it really shouldn't matter what color skin a parent has, or what religion they are, or even what their sexual orientation is, as long as a parent can raise a child with love and understanding." The rest of the show is structured to back up that thesis. Jeff, a white gay man in a suit and tie, an amiable cantor, talks about his adopted daughter ("a little Gemini," crows Marilu) and the women who help raise her and makes jokes about prejudice ("I don't make eggs in a gay way"). Debra, a blonde lesbian professional in a smart suit and pearls, talks about finding a "darling guy" in a Beverly Hills hair salon to donate sperm, quotes Thoreau, and praises her children's school ("the parents know we're gay, and nobody cares, and that's beautiful"), explaining that the "only negativity I feel is from Lou Sheldon and Newt Gingrich," and so on. The parents talk of spiritual paths and praying before dinner and "normal families" and "journeys of learning." Debra explains how when she began looking for "alternatives to how I could have children," it was still a pioneering area. "You probably made it easier for a lot of the people who were doing it," Marilu observes, to which Debra responds:

> Yes, I did. It was very scary to get into that, but one of the reasons I'm on this show twelve years later to discuss it is because it's worked out in such a positive way, and my children are wonderful and they're happy and they're thriving. So it was an experiment that's worked out in a very positive manner. So I think it's important that we share that with the world, when the radical right is trying to actually talk to us about family values and their family values.

"Mmm hmm," Marilu says, smiling and nodding. "Cause this looks like a family to me." There's a brief pause, and then the camera pans a calmly applauding audience—applauding, apparently, for the integration of lesbians into standard middle-class family forms, for a lesbian family that still "looks like a family to me" (Perpetual Notion 1995). This show, with its unthreatening, professional, woman-in-pearls/man-in-suit, clean-talking, articulate guests (and host, and audience) could have been scripted by GLAAD. But are these "positive" images?

The newer breed of shows, on the other hand, routinely recruits guests through toll-free numbers rather than through organizations, and attracts a crowd with little familiarity with a movement agenda; different kinds of queer families show up here. Consider, for instance, the class and ethnic markers in Eric Marcus's description, quoted in the epigraph to this section, of the rather typical *Sally* show on which he appeared as the middle-class, mainstream counterpoint: the bleeped-out swearing, the "Hispanic sister and brother," the "dysfunctional" guests from "the mountains of Tennessee," the public display of tongue kissing. Or consider a 1995 *Ricki Lake* show, which, despite the various markers announcing that the guests are not middle-class professionals (a straight-woman-versus-lesbian-mothers set from Arkansas, facing off in indelicate language about whether "a child of gay parents can grow up normal"), at first appears to be only a slight, personalized adaptation of the bigotry-is-bad programming of the *Donahue* years. When a panelist complains that the lesbians' kid will not know what is normal, Lake, in a sharp navy pants suit, gets a serious, slightly impatient look on her face, as though she is speaking to a small, somewhat bratty child. "But that's just it, what *is* normal, Lorraine?" Asked by Lake why straight couples can sit on the same sofa and hold hands at her house while the lesbians cannot, Lorraine says she is not ready to explain it to her kids. "What is the difference?" says Ricki. "They love each other. It's not like they're spewing hate everywhere. What *you're* doing is spewing hate telling them it's wrong to love someone." Applause from the audience. Bigots bad, lesbians good.

That is, until a "bad" lesbian mother shows up. Karen, a fifteen-year-old heterosexual African American, is there to tell her mother, Helen ("bartender, Illinois," says her caption) and her mother's Latina lover, Marie ("I'm a mechanic, I work in construction," she says to audience applause) that she thinks "being gay or lesbian is disgusting." Helen, in black leggings, big earrings, and a sparkly blazer, reports that she has seven kids, and speaks angrily, unapologetically, and colloquially—she is about as far as you can get from the middle-class lesbians on *Marilu*—about how this is "something Karen has to deal with," and how "her opinion doesn't matter to me, I'm happy, I made a choice to be with a woman and I'm not ashamed of it." The sympathy, not surprisingly, quickly moves toward the daughter, who confesses to Ricki that she was so bothered by her mother's lesbianism that she once tried to take her own life. The audience responds with cooing sympathy, and Helen becomes a lightning rod for audience hostility during the rest of the program, while various other guests do their shtick: a lesbian who doesn't think gay people should parent; a white gay man with discolored teeth who wants children bickering with a large straight woman who complains that he goes through his lovers like he changes his underwear; circuit-conservative Paul Cameron (a discredited psychologist from the right-wing Family Research Institute) who trades "facts" with certified homosexual Gabriel Rotello—the latter two, in professional outfits, clearly representing middle-class expertise. Helen spars with guests ("What society tell her to feel, I don't care"), with Lorraine ("How many daddies have your kids had?"), with her own daughter, and most of all with Cameron ("We up here to talk about *why* are peoples against it"). "Just because you got on a suit and tie and you got what they got a manhood down there," she spits at Cameron, "what make you so *normal?*"

One does not often see or hear from working-class lesbians of color raising children in American mass culture; on TV-talk shows, however, they make regular appearances. And Helen's arguments are not much different from those of white, college-educated gay activists—"normal" is often a synonym for "in power," homophobia not homosexuality is the social problem, lesbians and gays are as entitled to fulfillment as straight people, and so on—albeit in a different language, and in brief, hard-to-catch outbursts. Yet Helen herself is booed largely because of her presentational style, is not sympathetic, has a bad attitude, and most of all is a *"bad mother,"* (Paramount Pictures 1995a), lacking the "enlightened" parenting techniques advocated by middle-class experts. In the terms encouraged by the program, Helen lacks "class"; indeed, her status as a relatively poor, relatively uneducated woman of color makes it quite easy for class and racial hostilities to attach to hostilities toward nonnormative family forms, the whole package dismissed as selfish, unfair, inhumane.

Now, are these negative images? The newer, rowdier type of talk show, with its anyone-can-be-a-star recruitment strategies and its strategy of giving the stage to people from marginalized class and racial positions (in order to exploit them, of course), has meant, for instance, a tremendous diversification in the available images of families on these shows. It is no longer just white and middle-class people who are shown creating queer families or dealing with lesbian, gay, bisexual, or transgender family members. For another thing, it has meant that a much more aggressive, noisy, challenging, "in your face" approach to families of origin—*What makes you so normal?*—and to gay, bisexual, transgender, and lesbian people's roles in families and as parents has taken the stage. Activists interested in establishing the similarity of gay families to "normal" ones through their closeness to the middle-class mainstream, that is, have lost control of the discourse. The model of the lesbian or gay family that makes its way onto the screens on these kinds of shows thus includes, on the one hand, a much wider range of classes and races within it than one finds almost anywhere in American media culture, and these guests from marginalized class, ethnic, and racial statuses often present themselves with extraordinary strength, articulateness, and power; on the other hand, the lower status of the guests as poor, often not white, *and* queer, their heavily marked class positioning in a world where middle class is normative, their setting-off against representatives of middle-class family values, means that they and their families are easily dismissed as "dysfunctional" and not "respectable." The class division of talk shows has made the question of "positive" and "negative" family images harder to answer, in large part because it amplifies the question of just whose version of lesbian mother, or gay father, or transsexual daughter, or bisexual son is going to get air time. Whether one thinks the changes in the genre are good or not, they provide another important reminder of the divisions playing out as our visibility increases. Just whose families get to be seen as "ours"? Just whose "family values" get to be presented as ours? Any path to visibility must face down these questions.

THERAPEUTIC LIBERALISM AND THE VULNERABLE CHILD

These people are going to repeat the same thing, that if God wanted to create Adam and Steve he would have, blah blah blah. It's all been said and done before, so how are we going to advance it? You never get anywhere. You're never going to change the Bible thumpers. Never. No matter what you do. So why make that the issue of an hour show? It is one of those issues that people are so entrenched religiously, emotionally. How are we going to *maybe* change some of their minds? How are we going to *maybe* create tolerance? The only way you do it is not inherently make that the focus of the hour, not making it a right or wrong issue. It's not like it's right or wrong, it's more like, "Can this mother accept her son's gay lover?" It's like we're taking the assumption that the mother is accepting the son is gay. What you do is take real people that have real family concerns and they in particular want to try to get over it. Or they themselves within the two of them, the son and the mother, want to have some sort of peace. Like, "My mom kicked me out because I'm gay," okay. We're talking about individuals now. We're not talking about the issue of gayness. We're talking about an issue where a son wants to be able to go back into the house because he loves his mother. The mother can't accept the fact that he's gay. That goes beyond saying, "Is gay right or wrong?" We have a family in a crisis.

—Daytime talk show executive producer

Representations of gay, bisexual, lesbian, and transgender parents and family members are shaped not just by these two talk-show models but also by a more general ideological tension inherent in the genre: between a liberal-sexual ideology that eschews secrets and a conservative-gender ideology expressed in a concern for the creation of gender-normal boys and girls. On the one hand, talk shows—whether the older, more sedate Donahue-style or the newer, hipper Ricki style—are very receptive to the argument that family members must love and accept their homosexual children. This is in part because the shows operate with a loose ideology of liberal pluralism: we are all different, live and let live, tolerate and respect the rights of others to be who they are (Carbaugh 1989). This pluralist tone gets wedded, moreover, to therapeutic values—disseminated by hosts such as Oprah Winfrey—which give an extra push toward tolerance (White 1992). Speech and disclosure are cleansing and healthy, confession is good for the soul; at all costs, talk, you'll feel better. Given the profit-making strategies of the shows, this liberal, therapeutic ideology (once again, a feature of what can loosely be called bourgeois culture) makes good sense: for TV talk to work, everyone must be allowed to speak, or yell, regardless of their position; appeals in the name of tolerance, understanding, free speech, and mental health give this talk at least the appearance of a purpose.

Crass and cynical as it can be, this therapeutic-pluralism-turned-entertainment is much more sympathetic to liberal approaches to gay and lesbian families and family members (and sometimes to transgender and bisexual ones) than to conservative condemnations of it. The result, in fact, is often that the bigot who can't accept a family member becomes the pariah, and the accepting family member becomes the hero. *Donahue*, for instance, programmed a show on gay teens by bringing on a young man whose father tried to kill him after discovering his son was gay; a sixteen-year-old whose mother put him in a mental hospital because he's gay, along with the boy's mother and stepmother; and a nineteen-year-old lesbian and her mother. "We got to get rid of this closet," Donahue declares, typically. One boy, rejected by his biological family, talks about how he has "developed my own family," his surrogate parents, two men. The next tells how his mother called him a "little faggot" and then institutionalized him; she, contrite and ashamed, talks about how "I would say terrible things to him like that and I didn't realize the pressure he was going through," and the grandmother steps in to say "it's a matter of unconditional love." The young lesbian's mother, the last of the family guests, talks about how "you can either reject your child, you can tolerate your child, or you can accept your child," and gets in a plug for Parents and Friends of Lesbians and Gays (PFLAG) just before a brief interview with the associate executive director of Hetrick Martin, a New York City organization serving gay, lesbian, bisexual, and transgender youth. The audience is courteous and sympathetic. The show is quite explicitly programmed to model "acceptance" of gay and lesbian kids and even to give information about how to go about it (Multimedia Entertainment 1994).

Ricki Lake has taken this kind of show to its extreme, often by program-ming class-inflected lessons in tolerance. Writer and ACT UP veteran Michelangelo Signorile, for instance, took the role usually given to a thera-pist, holding forth from a thronelike chair on a show whose title, "I'm Gay, Get Over It!" even recalls Queer Nation's "We're here, we're queer, get used to it!" Various family members denounce their gay relatives, refusing, in Lake's terms, "to accept you for who you are": Tammy tells her sister Pam, a butch lift-truck operator from Georgia, that Pam doesn't know what she's missing ("I know what I'm missin', but I know what I'm a-gittin', too," Pam responds); a grandmother says she knew there was something wrong with her grandson when he was born ("Not wrong, just different," corrects Lake). "Michelangelo, can you educate her?" Lake says, turning to Signorile. "Michelangelo, enlighten us," which he does, telling this one to love her child and that one that there's nothing she can do about it. Not only was there no antigay, don't-accept-your-children "other side" but, in a twist that has some of the sweetness of just desserts, the militant gay activist had become the one dispensing advice to unloving family members, the gay son elevated to the therapist's throne (Paramount Pictures 1995c). "Remember," Lake says to the camera in her final word, sitting casually on the steps of the stooplike stage, after a series of people have been blasted by the audience and other panelists for objecting to gays coming near their kids, "children are not born to hate and fear, they are *taught* to hate and fear" (Paramount Pictures 1995b). Any moral condemnation of gayness that takes place within this kind of "love and accept your gay children" show is at a distinct disadvantage.

A general, self-interested constitutional hostility toward closets, toward secrets that are left unrevealed, leads many talk shows to tilt, regardless of their class compositions and class strategies, toward a welcoming of lesbian and gay family members. Yet, on the other hand, despite the repeated attacks the shows facilitate on the myth that homosexuals recruit children, or ruin them, or are never found in preadult forms, a ubiquitous concern for the fate of "the children" of gays and lesbians also continuously shows up and competes for primacy. Again, this is as much a production-driven concern as an ideo-logical one: the shows target primarily a female audience, often presumed to be mothers (middle-class or not), by programming from the point of view of a generic, heterosexual "mother." The arguments that queer kids should be accepted just like any other, and that children should not be taught to hate and fear gay people, are, in fact, just particular versions of the more general argument that children need parental protection and that families ought to provide safety rather than threat. Often, such a logic is turned against lesbians, gay men, bisexuals, and gender-crossers—especially when the issue of gay parenting comes up anywhere on the shows—triggering repeated expressions of worry by audiences for "the children." Significantly, although much of it is fueled by religiously based opposition to homosexuality in general, and in some cases simply repeats the charge that children of gay people will turn out to be gay themselves (and that such a fate is undesirable), the underlying worry seems to be how these children will learn to be "normal" *men and women*—that is, conventionally masculine or feminine.

So, for example, on a 1993 Oprah show on "The Lesbian and Gay Baby Boom," a mixed-race panel offers testimonials on the experience of being lesbian or gay and raising children, joined by expert testimony from lesbian researchers Charlotte Patterson and April Martin. Roberta and Jacqué, an African American couple, are joined by their kids Nabiway and Eqion, and John and Ron, a white gay couple who are both lawyers and parents, and another lesbian couple and their adult children. By the applause it seems the audience is on the side of tolerance, but when Oprah goes to the audience the program heats up. Hostile audience members object, some on the grounds that homosexuality is immoral and others on the grounds that subjecting children to the hardship and ridicule of having lesbian or gay parents is—as Paul Cameron, attacking Helen the bartender, would argue later on *Ricki*—"selfish." Oprah then hands the microphone to an African American man who seems dying to speak and who reveals the concern that often seems to underwrite the objection to lesbian and gay parenting. "How can these two gentlemen," he says, pointing at the lawyers, "going to teach a little girl to be a girl? And how can you people, how can you teach this boy to be a man, and he's a fruitcake?" (King World 1993). While TV-talk shows are often programmed to celebrate tolerance of lesbian and gay *children* by their straight parents, their "what about the children?" mantra also encourages attacks on lesbian and gay *parents* for undermining the life chances—the chance to be a "normal" man or woman, especially in terms of gender presentation—of their presumed-to-be-heterosexual children.

BISEXUALS, TRANSGENDERS, AND THE CONDITIONAL ACCEPTANCE OF QUEER FAMILIES

THIS CONCERN WITH "THE CHILDREN" is in part a knee-jerk habit, but the underlying concern with conformity to basic norms of gender and monogamy holds important clues. In many ways, bisexuals and transgendered people pay the price for daytime television's progay moral cheerleading. The push for accepting gay family members and gay families, in fact, is predicated upon the frequent dismissal of transgendered and bisexual people on TV talk. The ideology the talk-show field seems structured to protect is no longer so much the moral superiority of heterosexual families; rather, it is that of the moral inferiority of unconventional gender presentation and sexual nonmonogamy (see Ringer, chapter 9). This is an advance for *some* gay and lesbian families, but a severely compromised one.

To begin with, bisexuals appear much more rarely than homosexuals in family-focused talk-show formats in which their role as siblings or children or parents is central; instead, they are disproportionately programmed through the format of "relationship troubles." That is, they are positioned almost exclusively as those who make family life impossible, largely through the reliance on familiar, moldy stereotypes: as people who can't decide (caught in love triangles, or married bisexuals), who are sexually voracious (rarely do you find a monogamous bisexual), and so on (Hutchins and Ka'ahumanu 1990). Bisexuals are routinely attacked on these shows for their inability "to commit" and for wanting to "have their cake and eat it too." Although they sometimes get to talk about their families, bisexuals on talk shows for the most part appear as an external *threat* to monogamous family relationships taking place around them, be they heterosexual or homosexual. By comparison, monogamous homosexuals, in fact, look like relatively unthreatening, more easily accepted—more easily *absorbed*—family members. If homosexuals are often invited into the institution of the family on these programs, it is on the condition that they do not bring with them these stereotyped characteristics that TV-talk shows on bisexuals are structured to emphasize: multiple partnering, undisciplined sexuality, indecisiveness, and selfishness.

Transgendered people get much more air play, much of it in bikinis. But they are also very frequently programmed in "family conflict" dramas: confronting their own children, parents, and siblings. If they have children, they are routinely criticized for the gender "confusion" they are alleged to cause: "Do they call you mother or father?" is as standard a question as "Which bathroom do you use?," and both tend to elicit audience laughter. On the short-lived *Gabrielle* show, for example, activist and historian Susan Stryker is attacked by a young man asking her, "Do you think it's fair to your son that he calls you mother considering he has no father figure to play catch and teach him the manly things in life?" The audience explodes into applause and cheers (Twentieth Century Fox 1995). "When you bring a child into the world," Jerry Springer argues on another similar show, "until the child is grown, you have his or her life to live as well. And the trauma of having a young child see Dad become Mom is probably too much to lay on any kid. Until your kids are grown, let Mom wear the dress" (Multimedia Entertainment 1995a). What goes for gay families, obviously, does not go for transgendered ones here.

When they are dealing with their own parents, transgendered people fare a tiny bit better. For one thing, they get some sympathy for being "diseased": they should be accepted, Springer repeats on his many trans shows, just like you would accept a child born with a birth defect. For another thing, if their parents are particularly brutal, they get the same tolerance line offered lesbian and gay "victims." But they are still regularly attacked for disrupting their families with their "selfishness": if they would only act "normal," everything would be just fine. As one audience member put it to a cross-dressing teenager on *Sally*, "You don't think you're selfish to put your mother and brother on national TV looking like a freak?" (Multimedia Entertainment 1995c).

Gender-crossing, in fact, is often treated as homosexuality gone haywire, the nutty extreme of a sexual difference that is acceptable in gender-normative form. On a *Jerry Springer* show nicely titled "Please Act Straight!"— the coercive command phrased as a polite request—a series of transgendered kids are pelted with ridicule and attacks, mainly on the grounds that by cross-dressing they "flaunt" their homosexuality in ways that humiliate their families. They are unwilling, that is, to do *gender* the way others want them to do it, and thus they forfeit their place in the family. Springer asks a guest, the sister of a teenager waiting in the wings, what she thinks about his effeminacy. "I don't want my kids around that," she says. "I be wanting him to play football with them." When the young man emerges, deliberately and smilingly flouncing onto the stage wearing red high heels below an otherwise relatively conventional man's outfit, the crowd hoots and hollers its disapproval. "No," says his mother, simply, shaking her hand. "No way." Later, she flatly announces her plan of action should her son get a sex-change operation: "I'll kill him" (Multimedia Entertainment 1995b). The price for acceptance into the family, here, is gender conformity. With transgendered youth, or gay youth straying outside the bounds of gender norms, the repeated worry about children takes a different shape: it is the pained parent whose kid has "gone too far," who refuses to "*act* straight," who gets the sympathy of the victimized, not the child.

This is a rather stark contrast to the representation of lesbian and gay families, and a vivid, if somewhat unsurprising, example of the ideological barter going on here. An adjustment is made, as the family is shown to be open not just to heterosexuals but also to *certain* homosexuals. Unaccepting family members are vilified when their kids are run-of-the-mill, gender-normative gays and lesbians, but applauded when they cut off, publicly disown, or threaten to kill their transgendered kids. A new, postcloset kind of normalization pattern is at work here: the acceptability of lesbian and gay families, and of lesbian and gay people into their birth families, is predicated on their *not* exhibiting the "selfish" sexuality of bisexuals or the "freakish" gender of transgendered people.

FAMILIAL DIVISIONS

"AT THEIR WORST," Jane Shattuc suggests, daytime TV-talk shows "ostracize difference as antithetical to the morals of the familial structure. And at their best, they make difference permissible as the nation attempts to redefine the family in the late twentieth century" (1997:45). The lesson of talk-show visibility is thus perhaps not so much that we are faced with a choice between "positive" and "negative" imagery but that we are faced with a continual drawing of lines in and through the boom of cultural visibility for gay men, lesbians, transgendered people, and bisexuals in which we now find ourselves. TV-talk shows plant land mines in the ideological ground on which redefinitions of the family are taking shape. That is not of course something they do alone, but they are central to the process, partly because they help it along in such unintentional, entertaining ways and partly because they mix it so effectively with pleas for tolerance, enlightenment, and love.

The *kinds* of lines they emphasize, the kinds of differences that are allowed, in their protection of conventional family structures are telling: they set apart potentially powerful sets of political and cultural partners, helping to cut the threads linking various dissident family types and family members. They enact, in their profit-oriented attempt to capture audiences of various kinds through differing class-predicated programming formats, a class-based struggle over control of gay, lesbian, bisexual, and transgender family discourse. Activist guests seeking to establish the acceptable middle-classness of gay and lesbian families are set off against, and increasingly displaced by, working- and poverty-class guests (usually without an explicit political agenda), whose distance from middle-class acceptability offers a strikingly diverse, often more challenging, yet more easily dismissed, version of lesbian, gay, bisexual, and transgender family forms and values. The class lines cutting through queer family politics are exacerbated.

The alliance between those whose sexual object choice makes them "queer" and those whose gender nonconformity does so—always a tenuous alliance, and a longstanding fault line in sex and gender politics—is also aggravated. The talk show distaste for secrets, expressed routinely in calls for healing and tolerance, is undercut by the "what about the children?" refrain, but not so much, or at least not primarily, because of a worry that children are going to be raised gay. Healing and tolerance calls are instead rescinded primarily because of a concern for the "normal" *gender* future of the children; the temptation, often put into words, is for those gay people who can to emphasize gender normality, distancing themselves from gender-non-conforming "others." Moreover, the awkward, somewhat contorted steps taken on these programs toward the acceptance of lesbian and gay families (lesbian and gay children should be loved just like everyone else, lesbians and gay men have the right to raise their own children just like everyone else) are met by a heightened, quasi-systematic, often vicious treatment of trans-gendered and bisexual people as the more serious threats to the family structure. As gay and lesbian families move inside, that is, bisexual and transgen-dered ones move further toward the freaky; indeed, it is arguably through the positioning of transgenders and bisexuals as not-assimilable that homosexual families are rendered acceptable.

Here again, those who might share an interest in the transformation of the family structure are, through the process of talk-show visibility, pushed further and further apart. This line drawing, this exaggerated division of the "classy" from the "trashy" family, the "normal" from the "freaky" child, which conserves even as it revises the familial structure, is the biggest lesson for family politics from the weird world of daytime talk television.

NOTE

1. This chapter works from transcript, video, and interview data collected for a book-length study, *Freaks Talk Back* (Gamson 1998). Although only a small portion is discussed here, the data consist of the following: in-depth, semi-structured interview with twenty talk-show production staff and forty-four talk-show guests; quantitative and qualitative content analysis of the 160 available transcripts in which lesbian, gay, bisexual, and gender-crossing sub-

jects made a significant appearance, for the years 1984–86 and 1994–95; and interpretive analysis of about one hundred hours of talk-show videotapes. The data cover experiences on nearly every topic-driven daytime talk show that has had a life. Unless otherwise noted, quotations are from interviews conducted by the author in 1995 and 1996.

REFERENCES

Carbaugh, Donal. 1989. *Talking American: Cultural Discourses on Donahue*. Norwood, N.J.: Ablex.

DiMaggio, Paul. 1991. "Cultural Entrepreneurship in Nineteenth-Century Boston: The Creation of an Organizational Base for High Culture in America." In Chandra Mukerji and Michael Schudson, eds., *Rethinking Popular Culture: Contemporary Perspectives in Cultural Studies*, pp. 374–97. Berkeley: University of California Press.

Fejes, Fred, and Kevin Petrich. 1993. "Invisibility, Homophobia, and Heterosexism: Lesbians, Gays, and the Media." *Critical Studies in Mass Communication* 10 (December 4): 396–422.

Gamson, Joshua. 1998a. *Freaks Talk Back: Tabloid Talk Shows and Sexual Nonconformity*. Chicago: University of Chicago Press.

———. 1998b. "Publicity Traps: Television Talk Shows and Lesbian, Gay, Bisexual, and Transgender Visibility." *Sexualities* 1: 11–41.

Grindstaff, Laura. 1997. "Producing Trash, Class, and the Money Shot: A Behind the Scenes Account of Daytime TV Talkshows." In James Lull and Stephen Hinerman, eds., *Media Scandals*, pp. 164–202. New York: Columbia University Press.

Gross, Larry. 1989. "Out of the Mainstream: Sexual Minorities and the Mass Media." In Ellen Seiter, ed., *Remote Control: Television, Audiences, and Cultural Power*, pp. 130–49. New York: Routledge.

Habermas, Jurgen. 1991. *The Structural Transformation of the Public Sphere*. Cambridge: MIT Press.

Hennessy, Rosemary. 1994–95. "Queer Visibility in Commodity Culture." *Cultural Critique* (Winter): 31–75.

Hutchins, Loraine, and Lani Ka'ahumanu. 1990. *Bi Any Other Name: Bisexual People Speak Out*. Boston: Alyson.

King World. 1993. *Oprah* ("Lesbian and Gay Baby Boom"). Livingston, N.J.: Burrelle's Information Services. May 10.

Levine, Lawrence W. 1988. *Highbrow/Lowbrow: The Emergence of Cultural Hierarchy in America*. Cambridge: Harvard University Press.

Multimedia Entertainment. 1994. *Donahue* ("Gay Teens"). Denver, Col.: Journal Graphics, June 3.

——. 1995a. *The Jerry Springer Show* ("My Dad Is a Woman!"). Livingston, N.J.: Burrelle's Information Services. August 4.

——. 1995b. *The Jerry Springer Show* ("Please Act Straight!"). Livingston, N.J.: Burrelle's Information Services. October 23.

——. 1995c. *Sally Jessy Raphael* ("My Teen Son Wants to Be a Woman"). Livingston, N.J.: Burrelle's Information Services. June 27.

Paramount Pictures. 1995a. *Ricki Lake* ("You're Gay, How Dare You Raise a Child"). April 27.

——. 1995b. *Ricki Lake* ("Get It Straight: I Don't Want Gays Around My Kids"). June 15.

——. 1995c. *Ricki Lake* ("Listen, Family, I'm Gay . . . It's Not a Phase . . . Get Over It!"). November 20.

Peiss, Kathy. 1986. *Cheap Amusements: Working Women and Leisure in Turn-of-the-Century New York*. Philadelphia: Temple University Press.

Perpetual Notion Inc. 1995. *Marilu* ("Gay and Lesbian Parents"). April 4.

Russo, Vito. 1987. *The Celluloid Closet: Homosexuality in the Movies*. New York: Harper & Row.

Schacter, Jane S. 1997. "Skepticism, Culture, and the Gay Civil Rights Debate in Post-Civil-Rights Era." *Harvard Law Review* 110: 684–731.

Shattuc, Jane. 1997. *The Talking Cure: TV Talk Shows and Women*. New York: Routledge.

Signorile, Michelangelo. 1993. *Queer in America: Sex, the Media, and the Closets of Power*. New York: Anchor Books.

Twentieth Century Fox. 1995. *Gabrielle* ("Switching Sexes"). October 5.

Weston, Kath. 1991. *Families We Choose: Lesbians, Gays, Kinship*. New York: Columbia University Press.

White, Mimi. 1992. *Tele-Advising: Therapeutic Discourse in American Television*. Chapel Hill: University of North Carolina Press.

6 | One Man's Story of Being Gay and Diné (Navajo): A Study in Resiliency

Margaret Ann Waller and Roland McAllen-Walker

What is it to be gay in an American Indian family? We begin our discussion by emphasizing that the terms "Native American family" or "American Indian family" are misleading and obscure the truths about actual family realities. In the United States there are approximately 660 federally recognized tribes—360 located in the forty-eight (contiguous) states and another 300 in Alaska. These numbers do not include the 200 tribes still struggling with legal and governmental agenciess to gain federal recognition (Wright, Lopez, and Zumwalt 1997). Each tribe has its own beliefs, practices, ways of living, and language, including its own phenomenology with regard to family and sexual minorities (Roscoe 1987). As with any human group, there is also considerable diversity within any given tribe.

We asked Teles, a twenty-eight-year-old gay Navajo graduate student, if he would share his story with us so that we might situate our discussion of "two-spirit people" in American Indian families within the context of one person's lived experience and avoid inappropriate generalizations. This paper became a process of self-discovery for Teles as well as a learning experience for us, a nonnative lesbian social work practitioner/educator and a gay Diné educator. Consistent with contemporary narrative theory as well as with the Navajo tradition of teaching through stories, we present the text of Teles's story without the extensive paraphrasing and analysis that is customary in European American academic discussions of Native people's lives. We invite the reader to enjoy Teles's story and to allow the text to speak for itself.

Teles[1] travels (physically and psychologically) between Phoenix, Arizona, where he is a graduate student, and the Navajo Nation in Northern Arizona, where he spends time with his family. When at home, Teles thinks and speaks in Navajo and participates in traditional Navajo lifeways. His mother (of the Salt Clan), a longtime community activist, and his father (of the Bitter Water Clan), a native herbalist, raised Teles and his eleven siblings both on the reservation and in the adjacent bordertown. In so doing, they prepared their children both to embrace traditional lifeways and to navigate in the dominant society. Teles's Navajo and urban worlds converge in his relationships with his nieces who are college students in the city where he lives. Consistent with Navajo tradition, as their maternal uncle, Teles plays a major role in his nieces' lives. He maintains daily contact with them, providing nurturing and guidance as well as instrumental support.

FAMILY?

FAMILY HAS LONG BEEN seen as the main context for the development of personal identity. Nowadays, however, the term "family," has a postmodern ring to it, especially given that the idealized fifties model of the white, middle-class, intact nuclear family, headed by a breadwinner father and supported by a homemaker mother, is currently found in only 3 percent of households (Coontz 1997). One wonders, "Which family? Whose idea of family are you talking about?" In a recent volume on family resilience, family theorist Froma Walsh (1998) cautions, "our language and preconceptions about 'the normal family' can pathologize or distort family." She cites, for example, a case in which a judge denied a parental-rights request by a lesbian who had shared parenting for her partner's biological child, on the grounds that "it would be too confusing for a child to have two mothers" (29).

Sexual minority American Indians have another challenge. In addition to the usual heterosexual preconceptions, they run up against preconceived notions of "family" that exist within the dominant lesbian/gay community. The term "family," in the dominant lesbian/gay community is code for "one of us;" signifying "family of choice" in a community in which many individuals are disengaged from their families of origin. In this context the term "family" also suggests the existence of a network of social support. For American Indians, however, as with some other groups, the social support commonly associated with the word "family" in the dominant gay community is often not available (Font 1997; Marsiglia 1998). As a Navajo man in a large city, Teles must navigate within a hostile dominant culture. Rather than finding an oasis in the urban gay subculture, he finds another context of marginalization. Accordingly, he looks to his Navajo family as his most important source of social support. Teles describes a sense of closeness with his family of origin that far exceeds the closeness he experiences in his relationships in the city:

> I think that we are such a close family, I mean we've become actually closer, even though we don't see each other for quite some time, you know, a month, or two months. But still, I feel a connection to everybody back home in a sort of sense to where it will infiltrate my dreams, my thought processes, and sure enough, I'm right. If something's going on. Like for example, my sister is like, really, for some reason or another, I'll just pick up the phone to call, and it so happens that at that moment, you know, she will be trying to call me. We'll pick up the phone at the same time and we both get a busy signal. You know, that kind of thing. And so, and with my mom and dad it's that way too. And so in that sense, that I don't see them often but still feel this, I don't know, huge waves of something or another I feel like emanating from the North, and sure enough. And sure enough, when it's with me, I just know. It really kind of startled me for a while. It's, it's overwhelming. Especially with my mom and dad, and my sisters and brothers as well, it can be very overwhelming. But you know, you deal with it, you deal with it.

ROMANTICIZATION AND APPROPRIATION OF AMERICAN INDIAN SEXUALITIES

THE CURRENT FASCINATION WITH "two-spiritedness" in the dominant lesbian and gay community may be yet another instance of distortion, exotification, and exploitation of Native traditions by European Americans. European American travelers, missionaries, and anthropologists have long been fascinated with the sexual practices of Native Americans (see Jacobs 1997 and Wright, Lopez, and Zumwalt 1997 for more comprehensive discussion of discontinuities between Native and European American constructions of gender and sexualities). Thayer (1980), for example, illuminated the historical overemphasis on the sexual aspects of Native individuals classified as "berdache,"[2] "due, no doubt, to an obsession with primitive and sexual 'odd customs' " (293). Reductionistic Eurocentric classifications distort the wide diversity in Native American constructions of sexualities, as well as levels of acceptance of sexual diversity across tribes and over time. Little Crow, Wright, and Brown (1997), for example, contrast the Dakota *winkte* (not-woman) who was relegated to nonentity status, forbidden to interact with members of his family or tribe, and considered dead by the community; with the Lakota *wicassa wakan* (healer, performer, wizard) who was revered and considered an essential member of Lakota society.

Some researchers assert that more traditional American Indians tend to respect sexual minority individuals, whereas more acculturated American Indians tend to devalue and stigmatize them (Williams 1986). Teles's story paints a much more complicated picture. He has grown up in a Navajo family that continues to actively participate in traditional lifeways, yet he has heard nothing from his family conveying that being gay is acceptable. At the same time, he has heard "bits and pieces from here and there" that make him wonder if this has always been the case. Anything positive he has heard about homosexuality has come not from his family or elders in his tribe but from friends in the city or things he has read in books. As a Navajo gay man in the '90s, Teles is left to reconstruct the story of the meaning of being gay and Navajo from the words of outsiders.

> In the dominant gay community you see this sense of romanticism, that "you guys are indigenous, have the relationship with the land, and on top of all that, have the beauty of being two-spirited." It's like saying, "Oh, dancing with wolves." You know? And all this other stuff. All of that. Those are the kind of terms that are, you know, coined in such a way that, so that you know you have to think about individual people less. Like the [idea of the traditional] bisexuality of American Indians, I hear about that a lot in the dominant gay culture, but I have no response because I've never heard of it. In my family, as I was growing up I did not see any reverence toward Navajo individuals who were gay. I was aware of the opposite. I heard many derogatory references made to gay individuals, especially men. Gay men are seen as lesser than straight men. Not real different than the mainstream's misperception of mainstream gays.
>
> I have heard that when Navajo people would go out on their raiding parties, these people [effeminate men] would take on a domestic role for the warriors. They were risking their lives, because they weren't trained as warriors. It makes you wonder about how much they were valued.

They even serviced the warriors, you know, had sex with them. Today, I still do not know where gays fit into Navajo cultural life. As far as the language that's used for gay men, it's real derogatory. *Nádleehí* means "changing person." When it comes to an individual male, the way he's referred to is *Nádleehí* combined with a crude reference to his penis. I won't say the Navajo word. I can't say that.

Butch women in Navajo culture, from what I've seen, are seen in a different light than effeminate men. Butch women are valued on the reservation because they can work with cattle and things like that. They're economically useful. They are seen as well-rounded, accomplishing the tasks of men as well as the nurturing functions of women. Butch women are almost not seen as different than straight women. I don't even know of any Navajo word for lesbian women. They're often married too. I know many women who I perceive as being butch and they're married with children.

And it makes me even more curious about, you know, what is this thing about, um, religion and spirituality and being a homosexual? Were they really revered at one time? You know, and then I hear all these different stories. You know I've never heard that from my family. I have read contemporary pieces that talk about gays holding a special place in Native culture. Where? Have I missed something important while growing up? Nobody's ever made reference to that except my gay, my gay friends, gay Navajos, Navajos. I really don't know. I mean, for a lot of people it's totally different. I really can't speak for another tribe. I'm not too sure. I haven't read the literature. So, that's even more interesting. Like who knows, some of it might have been, like we've talked about, you know, whitewashed. Mainstream influence on Navajo life? Of course!

And of course they're generalizing. They always generalize when they talk about Indian people to begin with. But there might be some tribes—for example I've heard, just bits and pieces from other people, from some of my friends, just talking to people—about that tribe [Zuni] who had that person (We'Wha) who was dressed up as a woman and he even went to Washington D.C. as a part of a delegation to honor somebody, or something along those lines. A lot of people have gay people as part of their religion, you know, and all that, their origin stories, just like Estsá-natlehi (Changing Woman) for the Navajo, or Diné. I try to use Diné, because Navajo is a term that has been imposed upon us by Europeans. Navajo, for some reason or another that I've heard, has a derogatory meaning. I forget what it was, thieves, or something like that? Diné means

"the people." I just bounced totally off the subject. I would make a horrible native storyteller.[laughs] I remember, there's this one person who
I know who talked about some sort of island where they [gay men] separated themselves from the rest of the community and somehow they
were revered and played a religious role and all of that. Like some sort of
society of gay people living all alone.

Jacobs (1997) suggests that contemporary romanticization of Native
American sexuality and gender diversity may be an "adventure of white
homosexual males who are either appropriating cultural elements from
Native cultures or imputing to Native cultures characteristics that would
resolve their heartfelt desires to be recognized fully as productive and important members of their own society" (21). Of course, the same may be said
of white lesbian researchers.

There is deep, epistemological irony, for example, in the term, "two-spirit
people." The term was originally coined by Native American gay activists in
the early '90s who wished to distance themselves from white, gay male culture, but it was quickly appropriated by the white gay community as a symbol of freedom from oppression (Jacobs 1997). Whatever the motives driving the curiosity of nonnatives, the romanticization of Native sexualities
obscures the harsh realities experienced by contemporary sexual minority
American Indians. Gutierrez (1992) asks, for example, "How do we reconcile the ridicule and low status the berdaches had in Zuni society with the
high status and praise others [especially non-Indian gay males] lavish on
them?" (66). Jacobs (1997) captures this incongruity in the following quote,
"The irony is that as the 'bedarche' became an honored figure in the reconstructed romantic history of Native American cultures, lesbian, gay, two-
spirit, and transgender people of various American Indian heritages were
being beaten, disowned, and disavowed on their reservations" (22).

Eurocentric romanticization and appropriation of Native beliefs and
practices has become a psychological as well as physical health hazard to sexual minority American Indians—both on the reservation and in the city.
Wright, Lopez, and Zumwalt (1997) point out that the discontinuity
between Indian and dominant-culture worldviews creates a sense of disorientation for many urban-dwelling Indians that is further exacerbated by
deprivation of social support from family, clan, and tribe. Given these discontinuities, it is not surprising that many people report difficulty integrat-
ing their gay/lesbian and Indian identities (Chan 1989; Espin 1987; Garnets
and Kimmel 1991; Morales 1989) and forging a positive sense of self (Wal-

ters 1997). Some find that the stress associated with negotiating both gay and ethnic identity challenges their coping resources and psychological well-being (Jarvenpa 1985; Kemnitzer 1978). Teles describes this identity confusion as a "journey" that many gay American Indians find themselves taking:

> You see I think that it's a little bit more risky for people who are more impressionable, people who are younger, to be sucked up into all of that. Because I've come across really young people who have just really, who are, are just lost and who are, are searching, you know? And they're being led, you know, somewhere, and they find it an interesting, exciting journey but with all of that comes alcohol, drug abuse, and all this other stuff, and I see that, because I'm a little bit older than a lot of these young people in Phoenix now and those on the reservation. I see that a lot. Young Navajo people who are very impressionable. Of course, when you talk about role modeling, you know, they do attach themselves to people in the community. And here it means the bars and parties and drug abuse and all of that. And in the meantime, you know, they dress the part. They act the part and dress the part. As far as, you know, either, um, cross-dressing for example or um, certainly, people who dress a certain way, certain fetishes and that kind of thing. And you see that. And they go on that journey, you know.
>
> And those who choose to stay on the reservation are, of course, not as prevalent as far as being openly gay. I see them more or less as making their own community. A few years ago, some Navajo queens got together and had their own Navajo gay pride parade in a park on the rez. Some of my gay counterparts are the funniest people. I bet it would be a blast.

Romanticization of the "two-spirit" identity by the white, gay community is akin to the wider-scale appropriation of Native beliefs and practices by curious "New Agers," who may then derive a sense of identity, spiritual connectedness, and social status, and may even enjoy monetary gain from marketing distorted versions of traditional medicine ways such as the Sweat Lodge, "smudging" (burning sage), using ceremonial feathers and fans, assuming "Indian sounding" names, etc. Teles sees it this way:

> So back to spirituality and exploitation, so that's why I think all of that does a lot of damage. A lot of it has to do with the [dominant] value system changing. I see it more as an assault, appropriating American Indian values, practices, etc., and what exactly is that going to do? You know, I

mean, I think there are a lot of people who think that Indian people, Indian cultures, or Indian people in general, are like living saviors, you know. People have realized that we're all going to Hell anyway [laughs], you know, and try to slow down the process, you know, so let's see what the Indians are doing. I think people are searching, and when it comes to Indian people, we are now expected to be above all of this, you know? I think that that does damage as well.

Because I think that, so if people gear attention towards that, just like for example, um, spirituality, like with all these New Agers, it's just like it leaves a wide open space for exploitation, I mean, I mean, believe me, I see that. And I see people who are totally, you know, um, who shouldn't be doing that. You know they're messing with, you know, our, our universe . . . messing with our spirituality, our ceremonies, and all of that, you know. And people are making money off of it.

And what if a young gay person who's trying to find their place, you know, starts reading that? It's totally wrong, in most cases. So, I'm curious about all of this and then, when I pick up a book, I know if something, if it's, you know, real, um generalized, and you know, it's, and I, me, I pick up a lot of material and see a lot of materials as well, in my anthropology class, you know, and I can see that it's wrong, which is, which is good. And I can identify, you know, what's going on as far as, you know, talking about people. And we're all distinct cultures, very distinct. Everybody has their own view. Every tribe has their own views on different, different gender roles and all of that. So that's what I want to know. Capture all of that. You know, why can't somebody write about it rather than just talking about it, you know, lumping all of the tribes together. You know, this is what it's like to be gay and Indian! [laughs] You'll be accepted by everybody. [laughs] And you'll be considered a holy man or holy woman and all that kind of stuff. As if being gay had some sort of religious meaning. I think at one point in time you know, homosexuals may have been revered, that's why I think it's such an assault. It's so damaging, mainstream values regarding homosexuals and all of that, you know, and . . . and sort of romanticizing about it, you know?

Modoc novelist Michael Dorris (1987) explains the dynamics of this unrelenting (five hundred years and counting) process of exploitation:

For most people, the myth has become real and a preferred substitute for ethnographic reality. The Indian mystique was designed for mass consumption by a European audience . . . it is little wonder then, that many non-Indians literally would not know a real Native American if they fell over one, for they have been prepared for a well-defined, carefully honed legend. (99)

As well as being personally confusing, the Indian mystique is played out in cultural misunderstandings that range from the comical to the grotesque. For example, "An Indian who doesn't fit the stereotyped, romanticized image is often insulted with statements such as 'You're not really Indian, are you?' or, 'So, you're part Indian?'" (Wright, Lopez, and Zumwalt 1997:75). In her poem *Her Name is Helen*, Beth Brant (1988:177) illustrates how cultural misunderstandings occur in relationships between Indians and whites:

> When she was laid off from the factory
> she got a job in a bar, serving up shots and beer.
> Instead of tips, she gets presents from her customers.
> Little wooden statues of Indians in headdress.
> Naked pictures of squaws with braided hair.
> Feather roach clips in fuschia and chartreuse.
> Everybody loves Helen . . .
> She's had lots of girlfriends.
> White women who wanted to take care of her,
> who liked Indians,
> who think she's a tragedy . . .
> Her girlfriends took care of her.
> Told her what to say
> how to act more like an Indian.
> You should be proud of your Indian heritage.
> Wear more jewelry.
> Go to the Indian Center

Given the experience depicted in this poem, it should come as no surprise that one study (Grandbois and Schadt 1994) found a positive correlation between the number of years an Indian woman resides in an urban area and the degree of social isolation she experiences. Teles tells it this way:

> Sometimes when I go out with friends, somebody comes up to me and at first I think it's me they're interested in, and for once I feel like I'm being included. But as it turns out, what they're really interested in, curi-

ous about, is this whole romanticized thing about gay Native Americans having total acceptance in their communities. As if gay Native Americans live without experiencing discrimination in their lives! It's kind of embarrassing, because I think I'm being romanced, but they're really romancing my culture or whatever. This has happened to me many times.

Because of the intentional and unintentional racism Teles routinely experiences with urban gay friends and acquaintances, the dominant gay community doesn't feel like "family" to him.

DISCONTINUITY BETWEEN "COMING-OUT" THEORIES AND THE NAVAJO WORLDVIEW

A STRIKING PHENOMENOLOGICAL DISCONTINUITY appears when one juxtaposes "coming-out" models with a traditional Navajo worldview. It is said that stage theories are not necessarily linear (Grotevant 1987) and that individuals may spiral back through earlier stages at higher levels, or possess qualities of different stages simultaneously (Parham 1989). Nevertheless, stage theories suggest movement from a lower to a higher stage of development. The coming-out models of Cass (1984) and others, like all Eurocentric stage theories, are predicated on the assumption that autonomy and self-expression reflect a "higher" level of psychological development. Coming-out models are so named because they view being openly gay as necessary for healthy identity development (Cass 1984; Walters 1997). Coming out is the highest stage and, apparently, the endpoint, as none of these models addresses life after coming out, i.e., the continuing evolution of sexual identity during the course of adulthood (Walters 1997).

Stage theories have no place in the Navajo understanding of the world. In the Navajo worldview, development is a cyclical process with no endpoint, and human beings are neither autonomous nor distinct. Rather, human beings are inseparable from everything else in the cycle of the universe (Epple 1997). From this perspective, respect for and participation in the interconnectedness of all things is the hallmark of healthy human development. Maturity is the ability to nurture and maintain harmony within the complex web of family, clan, tribal, and universal roles and responsibilities. Given these diverging realities, declaration of one's gayness to one's family of origin signifies personal integrity in one meaning system and betrayal of responsibility to the group in another. Teles describes the reaction he might expect if he capitulated to the pressure of the dominant gay community and declared his gayness to his family:

> We've all heard stories about people coming out, you know, personal accounts, and I think it's a risk. And with Navajo people, with my family, you know, I just, I choose not to do that like, in your face thing, because they'll question my intentions. Why am I doing that. Why am I doing it, you know? Or bring a bunch of butch bikers home [laughs]. That Act Up and be out thing just doesn't wash with most Indian people I know. That kind of thing, and it just doesn't wash.

The same identity models that may be empowering and offer a sense of coherence to his European American counterparts discount Teles's reality. He seems to experience a sort of existential dissonance as he learns that success in the mainstream and, indeed, gaining status in the mainstream gay community, is predicated on self-assertion, whereas maintaining the integrity of his Navajo identity requires respect, deference, and the ability to engage in subtle social interplay rather than obvious self-expression.

> It's like there's a lot of respect going both ways and there's so much of it between myself and then my parents and my family, even my nieces, nobody will say anything about it [Teles's being gay] and I don't say anything because I have too much respect to just bring it out. I'm not taking that part of me home. I'm not sharing it. So that's what I mean about too much respect.
>
> In the Navajo context especially, I think if we [Navajos] talk about sexuality, or sex in general, I mean, that part of your life, I don't know what other people see, but this is the way I understand it, that part of your life, your sexuality, you know, that's just, that's very private and that's not to be shared with other family members, that's something that's so private, you know. You just don't do it. It's, it's taboo and there are repercussions. Major repercussions. I've heard this among other people as well. What repercussions? Um, insanity, um, that type of thing, if you talk about sex, even just jokingly. You just don't do that.

Morales (1989) attempted to integrate gay/lesbian and ethnic identity models with a five-stage ethnic gay and lesbian identity model. In this model an individual moves through denial of conflicts (I am not clear on what my gayness means to me and my ethnicity is no big deal); bisexual versus gay/lesbian (I prefer to identify as bisexual, even if my behavior and relationships are primarily homosexual); conflicts in allegiances (I identify as gay and not ethnic around gays and ethnic and not gay around other ethnics); establishing priorities in allegiances (I am ethnic and resent the racism in the gay community or I am gay and resent the homophobia in my ethnic community); and integration (I am both ethnic and gay). This model comes closer to describing Teles's experience, but still attributes feelings to Teles that he doesn't have.

BEING GAY AND DINÉ: ONE FAMILY'S CONSTRUCTION

THE DOMINANT GAY COMMUNITY in the city tells Teles one story about what it is to be gay. His traditional Navajo family tells another.

What's even more interesting in terms of our discussion is family dynamics. And that's what I'm interested in. The two-spirit people did have a very definite role in the community. You know I don't, I didn't see that in my family when I was growing up. I didn't see that. My family has like totally closed themselves off from the teachings about two-spirit people. They never shared it with me. It's a closed subject. And I still don't ask why. About all of that, because of that, you know, walking that fine line. I wonder how they are when I'm not around.

And of course, especially, for example, my grandmother and grandfather, especially my grandfather, was the funniest guy. Well, that's the way I thought cause, you know, he's the one who would tell me certain stories. I remember my grandfather told a very derogatory story about a group of men who had wanted tobacco. They had run out. So they had tricked a neighboring family into marrying off their very effeminate son for tobacco. The group of men decided that the bride price [the equivalent of a traditional dowry paid by a bride's family to the family of the groom] would be tobacco. It was very crude. His family didn't know. The groom didn't know until his wedding night. It was a story about trickery. Trickery is somehow tied in with being a homosexual.

And you know, it's like, where did he come up with this, you know? What was he thinking? You know? But it was all part of the humor. Our relationship with our maternal grandfather was wonderful, you know. My grandfather was kind of like . . . when we were on the reservation—

we grew up on the reservation basically on weekends and during the summer—so he was kind of the authority figure in the hogan and it's just interesting to me that, now reflecting on all of that, and thinking what he was talking about, you know?   ·

And then again, my parents use to call me Beezhee. You know Navajo parents have a way of revering someone they respect by giving their child that revered person's name, instilling the memory of that person in the child. This is especially true if their child reminds them of that revered person. My parents never told me why, but they used to call me this name, Beezhee, which was the nickname for my dad's uncle. Beezhee. That was the craziest name. My dad's uncle was such a character, very outgoing, and comical, and stuff. He was always joking with people. He was a boisterous kind of character. He wasn't effeminate in any way. A few years ago, my sister disclosed to me that he was gay.

I don't think I'm treated any differently than my siblings, but with my brothers they talk to them in that context, oh you know, "One day you'll have a family and that kind of thing." And with me it's kind of like, they never talk about that kind of thing. I should have picked up on that a long time ago. I don't think that they expect me to be in a relationship. I've brought Ramón [Teles's lover] home a few times and you know how goofy he is. He gets in with that Navajo humor and plays with everybody. But I don't know if my partner would ever become like part of my family, in that sense of an in-law, though. I guess that is a milestone that hasn't happened yet. Lord knows my parents probably don't want to think about their gay son having sex. It's like something they just wouldn't understand.

What they stress with me is that traditional role of maternal and paternal uncle with my nieces and nephews. There's that relationship that's expected because, really, kinship wise, and family wise, your paternal nieces and nephews are really considered your children. And as far as your maternal nieces and nephews, there is that relationship as well, but it's seen differently. It's a very special relationship. There's a lot of respect. You're sought out and revered more. Your maternal nieces and nephews defer to you as far as decision making, like as far as in a ceremony, or something like that. So my father and my mother stress the uncle role even more with me because they probably know that I'm not going to have a woman around or get married, or have children. Maybe that part also has to do with my being the one to pursue higher education and serving as a role model that way, and stuff like that.

So they've always told me, it's up to you what you want to do. It's always up to you. Like my brothers and sisters who have decided to stay on the reservation. Or when I decided to leave the reservation, they never were like, "Oh he's leaving the reservation and becoming white-washed," and that sort of thing. They just trust that you'll do the right thing. But that support and all that fuzzy stuff is always there whatever you decide to do.

The battle between the diverging realities of the dominant gay community and Teles's traditional Navajo family is enacted in Teles's struggle to compose a tricultural identity as a Navajo man, a gay man, and a participant in dominant society. Discontinuities routinely invade his thoughts, feelings, and relationships. Circular versus linear. Respect for the interconnectedness of all things versus Cartesian dualism. Family and tribe versus autonomy and self-assertion. The mythical versus the actual Indian. In his own homeland, Teles is an immigrant who can never go home. He faces homophobia within the Navajo community, and as an ethnic gay man, he faces racism (DeMarco 1983; Morales 1989) and loss of support (Chan 1989; Espin 1987) in the gay community. Conflicts in allegiances are routine (Garnets and Kimmel 1991; Loiacano 1989; Mays 1985; Morales 1989). He "walks in multiple worlds which requires a delicate balancing act that demands crossing many boundaries and enacting multiple social roles" (Walters 1997:54). As Morales (1989) puts it, "it requires constant effort to maintain oneself in three different social worlds, each of which fails to support significant aspects of a person's life" (217).

Romanticization and irrelevant identity models contribute to the lack of accurate understanding of American Indian sexualities. This lack of understanding, coupled with poverty, generally substandard health care, racism, and other forms of oppression imposed by the dominant society, along with homophobia within some Native communities (possibly a byproduct of interaction with European Americans), may help to explain the dismal statistics that put American Indians in a class of their own as regards human suffering. One example is the burgeoning of HIV-positive and AIDS cases in Indian communities. Unlike other populations, the distribution of Native American AIDS cases has hardly changed since reporting began. The majority of cases are among men (85 percent). Gay/bisexual men account for 79 percent of these cases (Rowell 1997).

We suggest that it is time for researchers to stop imposing European American models on Indian people and move beyond appropriating and

romanticizing American Indian sexualities as "symbols of potential liberation from gender identity construction, homophobia, and sexuality con-
tainment" (Jacobs 1997:36). We concur with Jacobs (1997), who proposes an
alternative motive for the study of Native sexualities, "If I can find answers
. . . maybe the young people will stop hurting; maybe they will stop killing
themselves, maybe they will be respected instead of denigrated and beaten
up in their communities" (26). In Teles's words:

> So, um, it's not, it's not like our lifeways are beautiful and traditional. We've
> changed. We have changed, you know. If you get meshing the two cul-
> tures together, um, Indian people have been changed, we've been condi-
> tioned, and all that, and some of that thinking [about sexual minority peo-
> ple] from way back is just lost, and you know you try to revitalize some
> of that, but you know, people change, all cultures change, you know, and
> we are changed, and we're headed in a new direction, and, and I think that
> people who are acculturated may be coming to terms in that sense.
>
> And you know with our history, our, you know, our connections
> with different aspects of Navajo life, you know hopefully I can make it
> all work. Somebody can make it work. Hopefully I can too, you know,
> that kind of thing. And, um, but you know everything's cool. Every-
> thing's cool. I think I'll reach that stage pretty soon. Maybe in the next
> couple of years. Being totally open and have actually found a strategy
> to, to maybe tackle this issue of creating dialogue within my family and
> to include my parents. To include them in. Well maybe, you know, not
> to include them in, in the sense, "accept it or else." Give them some
> space, as far as, you know, I'm not gonna bring in a string of, you know,
> transvestites [laughs], who are all flamboyant and stuff like that and take
> them to my mom's house, you know? Kind of let them deal with it.
> And if it's not appropriate, that's really fine, you know, we'll come to
> that point.

NOTES

1. Identifying information has been changed to protect Teles's right to come out
    at his own pace.
2. We put this term in quotation marks as it is "now considered to be an inap-
    propriate and insulting term by a number of Native Americans as well as by
    anthropologists" (Jacobs, Thomas, and Lang 1997:3).

REFERENCES

Brant, Beth. 1988. "Her Name Is Helen." In Will Roscoe, ed., *Living the Spirit: A Gay American Indian Anthology*, pp. 176–79. New York: St. Martin's Press.

Cass, V. 1984. "Homosexual Identity Formation: Testing a Theoretical Model." *Journal of Sex Research* 20: 143–67.

Chan, C. 1989. "Issues of Identity Development among Asian American Lesbians and Gay Men." *Journal of Counseling and Development* 68: 16–20.

Coontz, Stephanie. 1997. *The Way We Really Are. Coming to Terms with America's Changing Families*. New York: Basic Books.

DeMarco, J. 1983. "Gay Racism." In M. Smith, ed., *Black Men/White Men: A Gay Anthology*, pp. 109–18. San Francisco: Gay Sunshine Press.

Dorris, M. 1987. "Indians on the Shelf." In Calvin Martin, ed., *The American Indian and the Problem of History*, pp. 98–113. New York: Oxford University Press.

Epple, C. 1997. "A Navajo Worldview and Nádleehí: Implications for Western Categories." In Sue-Ellen Jacobs, Wesley Thomas, and Sabin Lang, eds., *Two-Spirit People: Native American Gender Identity, Sexuality, and Spirituality*, pp. 174–91. Chicago: University of Illinois Press.

Espin, O. 1987. "Issues of Identity in the Psychology of Latina Lesbians." In the Boston Lesbian Psychologies Collectives, eds., *Lesbian Psychologies: Explorations and Challenges*, pp. 35–51. Urbana-Champaign: University of Illinois Press.

Font, R. 1997. "Making Sense of Privilege and Pain." *In the Family* 3 (3): 9.

Garnets, Linda and Douglas Kimmel. 1991. "Lesbian and Gay Male Dimensions in the Psychological Study of Human Diversity." In Jacqueline D. Goodchilds, ed., *Psychological Perspectives on Human Diversity: Masters Lecturers*, pp. 143–89. Washington, D.C.: American Psychological Association.

Grandbois, G. and D. Schadt. 1994. "Indian Identification and Alienation in an Urban Community." *Psychological Reports* 74 (1): 211–16.

Grotevant, H. 1987. "Toward a Model of Identity Formation. *Journal of Adolescent Research* 2, 203–22.

Gutierrez, R. 1992. "Must We Deracinate Indians to Find Gay Roots?" In Wayne R. Dynes and Stephen Donaldson, eds., *Studies in Homosexuality*. Vol. 2. *Ethnographic Studies of Homosexuality*. New York: Garland.

Jacobs, Sue-Ellen. 1997. "Is the 'North American Berdache' Merely a Phantom in the Imagination of Western Social Scientists?" In Sue-Ellen Jacobs, Wesley Thomas, and Sabin Lang, eds., *Two-Spirit People: Native American Gender Identity, Sexuality, and Spirituality*, pp. 21–43. Chicago: University of Illinois Press.

Jacobs, Sue-Ellen, Wesley Thomas, and Sabine Lang, eds. 1997. *Two-Spirit People: Native American Gender Identity, Sexuality, and Spirituality*. Chicago: University of Illinois Press.

Jarvenpa, R. 1985. "The Political Economy and Political Ethnicity of American Indian Adaptations and Identities." *Ethnic and Racial Studies* 8: 29–48.

Kemnitzer, L. 1978. "Adjustment and Value Conflict in Urbanizing Dakota Indians Measured by Q-Sort Technique." *American Anthropologist* 75: 687–707.

Little Crow, J. Wright, and L. Brown. 1997. "Gender Selection in Two American Indian Tribes." In Lester B. Brown, ed., *Two-spirit People: American Indian Lesbian Women and Gay Men*, pp. 21–28. New York: Haworth.

Loiacano, D. 1989. "Gay Identity Issues among Black Americans: Racism, Homophobia, and the Need for Validation." *Journal of Counseling and Development* 68: 21–25.

Marsiglia, F. 1998. "Homosexuality and Latinos/as: Towards an Integration of Identities." *Journal of Gay and Lesbian Social Services* 8 (3): 113–25.

Mays, V. 1985. "Black Women Working Together: Diversity in Same Sex Relationships." *Women's Studies International Forum* 8: 67–71.

Morales, E. 1989. "Ethnic Minority Families and Minority Gays and Lesbians." *Marriage and Family Review* 14: 217–39.

Parham, T. 1989. "Cycles of Psychological Nigrescence." *The Counseling Psychologist* 17: 187–226.

Roscoe, W. 1987. "Bibliography of Berdache and Alternative Gender Roles among North American Indians." *Journal of Homosexuality* 14 (3/4): 81–171.

Rowell, R. 1997. "Developing AIDS Services for Native Americans: Rural and Urban Contrasts." In Lester B. Brown, ed., *Two-spirit People: American Indian Lesbian Women and Gay Men*, pp. 85–95. New York: Haworth.

Thayer, J. 1980. "The Berdache of the Northern Plains: A Socioreligious Perspective." *Journal of Anthropological Research* 36 (3): 287–93.

Williams, Walter L. 1986. *The Spirit and the Flesh: Sexual Diversity in American Indian Culture*. Boston: Beacon Press.

Walsh, Froma. 1998. *Strengthening Family Resilience*. New York: Guilford.

Walters, Kath. 1997. "Urban Lesbian and Gay American Indian Identity: Implications for Mental Health Service Delivery." In Lester B. Brown, ed., *Two-spirit People: American Indian Lesbian Women and Gay Men*, pp. 43–65. New York: Haworth.

Wright, J., M. Lopez, and L. Zumwalt. 1997. "That's What They Say: The Implications of American Gay and Lesbian Literature for Social Service Workers." In Lester B. Brown, ed., *Two-spirit People: American Indian Lesbian Women and Gay Men*, pp. 67–82. New York: Haworth.

7 Family Secrets, or . . . How to Become a Bisexual Alien Without Really Trying

Elizabeth Randolph

February, 1987

I sent my Mom a letter. Not the usual letter about landlord problems or how I'm thinking of going back to school, or what I did last weekend. No, this one read:

> *Dear Mom,*
>
> The last time we spoke, I felt there was a wall between us. I have always told you everything. Well, almost everything. I have made a stranger of you lately, editing my reports, whittling down my life to the most basic of components. New job. Got a cat. Need money. You must have felt that something was not the same with me, has not been for quite some time.
>
> You remember Diane[1] from the last time you visited. You liked her, as I recall. I hope you will still like her after what I have to say. I am a lesbian. We are lesbians together.
>
> Now, before your mind begins to reel with visions of what you think I am based on what you think "lesbians" are, let me say we are not "sick," we are not child molesters or freaks of nature. It feels quite natural to love her. If you want to know who I am now, let me remind you that you have known me all my life.
>
> You may think me a coward for telling you this way, but I've tried so many times to tell you over the phone. I'm afraid you won't even talk to me after this. The irony is I am telling you this because I miss you. The you I knew before I made a secret of my life.
>
> *Love you. Always will.*

I sent it and waited. Sunday—the day we usually call each other—went by. She didn't call. I didn't call. Three days later:

ME   Did you . . . get my letter?

MOM   I got it.

         [Silence]

ME   I—I tried to give you time to . . . process—

MOM   Take more than a week for that.

ME   Well, what did you think? About what I told you?

         [She sighs]

MOM   Well . . . I don't agree with that . . . lifestyle, but you're my daughter and I won't let that stop me from loving you.

I knew she had a less than sterling image of gay folk. To the homophobic mix of American culture add Southern, small-town, church-going, African American[2] culture. Stir. What do you get? Lots of misconceptions about queer folk in my family. So, I went on proactive mode. I sent Mom P-FLAG[3] materials. I gave her minilectures on how I really was a sane person, and yes, it was possible to be both well adjusted and lesbian. I was no more doomed to live an unhappy life than your garden-variety heterosexual. She seemed to take it all in stride, but never inquired about my lesbianism directly.

No matter. Mom loves me!

I'd come a long way. When I met my first girlfriend, I was quite aware of my attraction for men. I was also aware that my lingering attraction would make me a virtual pariah in the lesbian world, as well as an unacceptable entity in my own relationship. Under duress and threat of breakup, I renounced my bisexuality, admitted to Diane that my attraction to men *was* but a small flicker compared to the conflagration of my desire for women. I began to think, "Maybe I am a lesbian."

Mom was the only family member I "came out" to, not just because she'd asked me not to share this "information" with any of the other relatives.[4] It had not occurred to me to tell anyone else. My father had never been able to understand even the simplest thing about me. And I felt like an alien among my extended family who never ventured into psychological waters deeper than the weather forecast or the new stoplight on Highway 341.

I had "escaped" from that stifling small town to the therapized world of

New York City, where there was an imperative to speak your mind. And I liked it that way. In comparison, my family seemed ill equipped to deal with the complexity that was my life. Mom, I decided, was the person whose opinion I valued most in the world, thus the only person worth sharing this with.

Mom was politely Southern, inquiring about Diane from time to time, sending her cards on her birthday. And now that the cat was out of the bag, I was making up for lost time. I wanted to talk of nothing else except where Diane and I were going on vacation, how we couldn't decide on a color for the new couch. I couldn't have been happier.

One day, I complimented Mom on the way she was handling the news. "Why should I worry?" she said. "It's not your true nature. You'll go back to normal once you get this out of your system." Sinking heart.

She's humoring me.

Suddenly, I was cemented in lesbianism more than ever. The community was good to me, as long as I didn't mention my attraction to men.

Diane and I stayed together three years. She had an affair with her secretary. We broke up. I went to graduate school.

Andy from my gerontology class always asked me to dinner on Wednesday nights after class. It was February. Being from the South and rebellious by nature, I was chronically underdressed. He always let me wear his big warm gloves. I fell in love. I told him. He said, "Thanks, but no thanks. I'm gay."

Painful, but best not to tell Mom. I don't want to give her the "wrong" idea.

I was heavily allied and identified with the lesbian "community," even though I hadn't quite made it to the "homosexual" end of the Kinsey scale. I joined gay and lesbian organizations, attended marches, shouted at demonstrations, and organized committees. I gathered about me beloved lesbian and gay friends—a family of choice, a more satisfying version of family compared to the family I could not "tell."

Roni was my next big relationship. She was an activist and publisher of what she called a "lesbigaybitrans rag." She visited my parents' house twice. My mother liked her. My father thought she was pretty. What I liked most about her was that she had a good heart. And she could make me pee in my pants, she was so funny. We broke up after three years (my limit it seems), but we remain great friends.

Throughout the relationship, she had witnessed my transformation from a follower to a leader. In fact she'd encouraged me to take my activism to a higher level. I joined the board of a lesbian philanthropic organization. I eventually became board chairperson, speaking out about the organization on every stump I could find and meaning every word. I was "in." I was "Super Dyke." Right?

That's what I asked myself when, evaluating a gallery space for our next big fund-raiser, I found myself enthralled with Dmitri, a striking Bulgarian gallery assistant who brought me lattes. I left the gallery perturbed. I couldn't get him out of my mind and it was annoying the hell out of me. On a whim I called to invite him out for a drink. He was confused, recalling the organization I represented. After what seemed like minutes of silence, he finally relented: "Why not? I've learned to say yes in America."

Two days later we were in a jazz café playing footsies. Whereas Andy had been a sweet, puppy-dog love, this was lust. I wanted to screw Dmitri like a bottle cap.

Definitely can't tell Mom this!

Okay, so Dmitri turned out to be an opportunistic jerk who wanted a green card, but my intense attraction to him was a catalyst. Suddenly, I was examining the question: Can you repress a desire so much that it explodes like so much shaken seltzer?

Meanwhile, Roni and I continued to be "friends with benefits," occasionally having sex. One day, in a moment of postorgasmic honesty, she revealed her obsession with gay male porn. I confessed that I had been thinking about men a lot, too, but not gay men. I was nervous, expecting her to freak out on me, but she said she'd had a feeling.

Emboldened, I began to speak about it with other lesbian friends. Some were scandalized by the unapologetic way I now spoke of my attraction to men. Some admitted to their own attractions, but placed them in context. "I wouldn't turn down Denzel Washington" (or Ralph Fiennes . . . or Jacob Dylan, depending on the woman).

Most were relieved to hear that I hadn't actually slept with a man since I'd come out, and that I was interested in men as sexual partners, not boyfriends. Maybe I wasn't looking to change teams after all.

Interestingly, a few acquaintances admitted that they slept with men in secret but would never call themselves bisexual. What happened next made me understand their hesitation.

A controversy arose in the aforementioned lesbian organization—whether to open our grant-making process to bisexual artists and organizations seeking financial assistance. I listened stoically to arguments about how bisexuals couldn't be trusted.

"Why should we support them?" one women asked. "What have they done for us, except ride our coattails?" Someone else joked, "When would a bisexual have time to be politically active, anyway? They have too many dates." Another woman threw out the heterosexual privilege default: "Why don't their husbands just write them checks to fund their projects?"

Attempting to put things in perspective, a member of the staff reminded us that the organization had never had a bisexual woman serve on the board, that their contributions to the organization had been negligible, if not non-existent. I'd heard enough.

The fire of indignation that had erupted against all manner of bigots flared up against these women, who were supposed to be my comrades in arms. "Can't say that anymore," I blurted out. "Bisexual. Chair of the board." All around me eyes, waiting for me to announce it was all a joke. This time I didn't renounce anything.

Eventually my term ran out. I didn't renew. I had to finish graduate school. And frankly, I was pissed off. I was also struggling to negotiate my "factory-reconditioned" identity, and—get this—I was lonely.

Contrary to popular belief, I didn't date that often. Most lesbians wouldn't even consider me a potential partner, yet I'd been spoiled by the relatively easy intimacy found between women. Men, I observed, seemed wired to run away, and often their response to falling in love—terror followed by withdrawal—felt like the antithesis of loving. No Happily-Ever-Afters for yours truly.

February, 1997

I'd mostly been seeing men. Sex was easier to find with men but relationships scarce. Dealing with the mysterious "force" that is Male, I felt very much like an anthropologist studying a little-known culture. Still there were a couple of "meaningful" interludes thrown in for good measure. Like proverbial pellets of cheese intermittently released when the lab rat presses a bar, these relationships were frustrating, yet oddly addicting. At times I wondered whether I could ever affect the feeling of "family" with men, as intimacy with them had been fleeting at best.

I was still attracted to women, but hadn't had any luck. Even Roni had stopped having sex with me. The nerve of her new girlfriend putting a stop to it.

I got a phone call one night. Midnight. My aunt, the nurse. My mother was in the hospital. The doctors were having trouble stabilizing her blood pressure.

Something in the tone of her voice.

I was on the next flight to Georgia. By the time I got there, Mom was unconscious and never woke up. After she died, I held her hand, thinking I had made her a stranger after all.

Roni flew down. She wore pants to the funeral. Down south, especially in the black churches, women do *not* wear pants to church. A dyke cousin of mine told me later, there was quite a bit of gossip about it. One aunt said to another, "Who's that woman in the pants suit?" The other replied. "That's Liz's husband . . . so they say."

A few days later, I tried to have a heart-to-heart with the aunt who had inquired. She was the closest I had to a mother now. I wanted to tell her everything. I was helping her prepare for dinner. "Heard you were asking about my friend who came to the funeral."

"What friend?" She feigned amnesia, chopped her okra more forcefully.

"Because in case you were wondering, she's not my husband," I chuckled. "She's my *ex*-husband."

Silence. I grew serious, reassuring: "Mom knew about her. Mom liked her a lot."

My aunt closed her eyes tight and held up her hand. "Let's not talk about this, sweetheart. Just leave it be."

Dad had died nine months earlier, so I packed up Mom's house. Put it on the market and dragged myself back to New York. In the absence of both parents and my lesbian identity—things that had anchored, if not completely satisfied me—I had to reinvent myself.

The next few years were the hardest of my life. Depression. Prozac. Therapy. One day, my therapist encouraged me to list the positives. I had an apartment, two cats, a half-written thesis, and—thank God—my friends. My chosen family of lesbians (and one honorary boy-lesbian) gathered around, offered the support I needed to survive those years. For the first time, I allowed myself to depend on them, be vulnerable to them in a way I never allowed myself to be with my family of origin.

I shared my quest for love and sex, whether those adventures involved men or women. There was inevitably a period of adjustment in which my friends twitched and ticked every time I mentioned a man. They judged men more harshly than women. If a woman stood one of my friends up, she was forgiven because she was just disorganized or having a rough week. If a guy even showed up late without calling, they were yelling, "Dump him. He's a shmuck!"

After a breakup with a man, I had an unwelcome case of déja vu, when one friend declared, "You just need to work through this het phase and find yourself a woman."

Another concurred. "We know you have a choice. You can *be* with a woman. So why bother with these guys?" They were telling me, as my mother had, "Come back into the fold. We love you. We'll wait."

Obliquely, my friends questioned whether internalized homophobia had influenced my attraction to men—an understandable concern, as homophobia is hard to escape in this culture. But I couldn't remember feeling shame about my attraction to women, only fear of rejection. Coming out as a lesbian and surrounding myself with affirming influences had helped me to negotiate the waters of homophobia. My parents had never overtly pressured me to marry, but now that they were dead there wasn't even the concern that they may be silently suffering my "homosexuality." In fact, in my social sphere, the people whose opinions mattered most now were my circle of lesbian friends.

Which brings me to our most recent conflict. Three of my friends and I were stuck in a car together, heading for dinner. One was picking at me for buying a magazine expressly because there was an article with tips on how to give a man head. A little good-natured ribbing I can stand, but the conversation turned into a lesbian pep rally. Each taking turns talking about why they considered sleeping with men a waste of time.

When I objected, their camaraderie only increased. I looked around and biceps were *literally* flexing in solidarity all around me. They were so carried away that, for a moment, they ceased to remember that I was their friend, not a member of the rival team. It was then that I was reminded of the alienlike separation I had felt with my family of origin.

I had long been aware that identity can provide the glue that binds people together, but that it can also sever bonds. In adulthood, I had become an exile from my family of origin's straight, Christian, narrowly defined black identity. With my lesbian family, I was part of the "out group," too. They also hoped that I would recover from my "phase" and revert back to my "true essence," as they had defined it.

When we reached the restaurant, I pouted a bit and complained. They poured me a glass of wine and listened, really listened—a skill my family of origin had never mastered. A couple of them even promised to be more aware of their behavior. Afterward, I thought, maybe families are just like that. There are moments you fit and moments you don't. With this family, at least, there is progress. Thank God for therapy. Theirs and mine.

NOTES

1. Names have been changed to protect the identity and tender feelings of ex-lovers.
2. Some believed that homosexuality was an essentially "white invention" or due to white influence, not innate in African American culture.
3. A support group for the parents of gays and lesbians.
4. As PFLAG literature explains this phenomenon: when gay and lesbians come out, their parents are themselves forced to make a choice whether to come out and share this information with their friends and family members. Guilt and shame are often factors in their decision not to seek support from others. One of the goals of PFLAG is to alleviate this isolation.

8 | A Place Called Home: A Queer Political Economy of Mexican Immigrant Men's Family Experiences

Lionel Cantú

Driving the Interstate 5 Freeway, near San Diego and the San Onofre border checkpoint, there are large yellow signs graphically depicting a fleeing family (father leading, mother, and child—legs flailing behind). The almost surreal signs are meant to warn motorists of the danger of "illegal" immigrant families trying to cross the busy lanes. This image reveals not only the extreme risks that many immigrants are willing to take to get to the United States but also the way in which we imagine these immigrants. While most motorists probably do not think of a sexual message when they see the warning sign, it's there for us to see; if we only really look. The sign is symbolic at multiple levels: a nuclear family unit, heteronormative in definition, a threat to the racial social order by virtue of its reproductive potential. The sign is also symbolic of the current state of international migration studies: sexuality is an implicit part of migration that has been overlooked—ignored.

In this chapter I examine some of the ways in which sexuality, understood as a dimension of power, has shaped the lives, intimate relationships, and migratory processes of Mexican men who immigrate to the United States.[1] More specifically, I utilize ethnographic data to examine how traditional family relations and alternative support systems such as "chosen families" (Weston 1991) influence migration among Mexican immigrant men who have sex with men (MSMs). The men whom I interviewed and introduce in this essay had a variety of sexual identities both prior to and after migration. An important part of my research, therefore, is to examine from a queer materialist perspective dimensions that shape the social relations of families of origin and families of choice and thus, the intimate context by which identity itself is shaped. I argue for a theoretical move toward a *queer political economy* in order to understand the dynamics that shape "the sexuality of migration" and the fluidity of identities in a global context. In the first section of this chapter I briefly discuss how I conceptualize this theoretical framework (specific to the issues discussed here). I then discuss the ways in which these theoretical concepts are grounded in the everyday experiences of Mexican immigrant men.

QUEERING THE POLITICAL ECONOMY OF FAMILY AND MIGRATION

QUEER THEORY, A CONCEPTUAL framework that by its very logic resists definition and stability (Jagose 1996), has become both an area of growing influence and an entrenched resistance in the social sciences. These tensions and contradictions are due in part to an increased focus on issues of identity (including that of nation, race/ethnicity, gender, and sexuality) among scholars from a variety of disciplines with different theoretical perspectives and empirical concerns. Yet these tensions are rooted in queer theory itself, descended from the more modernist concerns of early gay- and lesbian-studies scholars and the postmodern influence of semiotics and the work of Foucault.

Queer theorists more closely aligned with the semiotic tradition have built upon Foucault's assertion that sexualities and identities can only be understood through discursive strategies and an "analytics of power" that examines the multiple sites where normalization occurs through discourse and knowledge production. (Cousins and Hussain 1984; Foucault 1990 [1978]; Martin 1988). However, an analytics of power restricted purely to an examination of textual discourse, void of a material context, is obviously limited. There are, of course, numerous normalizing sites, including the body (which has received particular attention as an inscribed "text"), but my concern here lies with that of the family. As I demonstrate in the following discussion, the family and the home (or household) is a site where normalizing rules of gender and sexual conduct and performance are taught on a daily basis.

More recently there has been a move toward a queer materialist paradigm that asserts that "all meanings have a material base" from which cultural symbols and identities are constructed (Morton 1996; see also Gluck-man and Reed 1997 and Seidman 1996). Furthermore, it is "the examina-tion of the complex social conditions (division of labor, production, distri-bution, consumption, class) through which sexual preference/orientation, hierarchy, domination, and protest develop dialectically at a particular time and place" (Bennett 1996). Thus, in this section I briefly outline a queer materialist paradigm for analyzing the social relations between family, migration, and sexual identity.

The link between "gay" identity and socioeconomic forces[2] has been asserted by gay- and lesbian-studies scholars since at least the late 1960s with the work of Mary McIntosh (1968) and Jeffrey Weeks (1977). In his seminal article "Capitalism and Gay Identity," John D'Emilio (1993) asserts that the modern construction of a gay identity is the result of capitalist development and the migration of homosexuals to urban gay communities in San Francisco, Los Angeles, Chicago, and New York after World War II. In a similar vein, Gayle Rubin argues that gay identity is a result of the rural to urban migration of "homosexually inclined" men and women where communities and economic niches (which Rubin calls a "gay economy") were formed based on a shared identity as an "erotic minority" (1993 [1984]).

Key to these arguments is an understanding of how capitalist develop-ment has shaped and transformed *family* relations and structure. D'Emilio argues, "Only when *individuals* began to make their living through wage labor, instead of parts of an interdependent family unit, was it possible for homosexual desire to coalesce into a personal identity—an identity based on the ability to remain outside the heterosexual family and to construct a per-sonal life based on one's attraction to one's own sex" (1993:470).

D'Emilio's argument thus expanded the historical materialist under-standing of the patriarchal heterosexual-family structure long argued by feminists (cf. Donovan 1992; Hennessy and Ingraham 1997) and even Engels (1993 [1942]) and made more evident the relationship between the political economy of the modern family and sexual identity. This argument asserted that the economic interdependence of family members constrained gay identity formation and that these bonds were loosened by capitalist devel-opment.

Yet, the "capitalism/gay identity" argument is limited in several impor-tant ways. First, it fails to capture the complexity of stratified-power rela-tions beyond a simple class argument even if held to the Western-industrial experience. Racial/ethnic dimensions are notably absent and must also be considered especially when family-economic interdependence plays so central a role in the paradigm. In the case of international migration, family-economic interdependence may continue to play an important role in relations and identity even while reconfigured through migratory processes and when new systems of support are created. Second, while most social constructionists agree that gay identity is linked with capitalist development, this body of literature fails to capture the multiplicity and fluidity of sexual identity and fails to conceptualize capitalist development as a global phenomenon with implications for sexuality and migratory patterns on a global scale. Unfortunately, migration-studies scholars have in turn ignored this literature marked as "gay studies" and have not examined how sexuality may shape migratory processes.

There are a number of theoretical-migration models that postulate the reasons why migration begins or the conditions that perpetuate it.[3] Traditionally, microlevel theories focus either on the rational choice of the individual or on the household;[4] while macrolevel theories examine the structural forces of capitalist societies such as the labor market, trade relations, or economic intervention by nations.[5]

In the 1980s other "social" factors also began to receive analytical attention, but not until Sylvia Pedraza's 1991 article, "Women and Migration: The Social Consequences of Gender," were feminist concerns taken seriously by migration scholars. Part of the reason for the delay (and continued resistance) in recognizing gender as an important dimension of analysis within migration studies has been the limited scope through which migration scholars have viewed the "economic" realm. For many, gender was perceived as a social factor subsumed by the economic or considered to be a variable of analysis, like age or education, that simply needed to be added to migration studies.

Feminist scholars, however, assert that gender is a much more complex dimension. For instance, while migration scholars argue that social networks and modes of incorporation such as ethnic communities and economies are an important aspect of personal transition linking migrants to social, cultural, familial, and economic resources, most studies have conceptualized social networks either in terms of familial relationships or in terms of men's labor networks, without theorizing how gender itself might shape these relations. As Pierrette Hondagneu-Sotelo demonstrates in her book *Gendered Transitions* (1994), gender is more than a variable of migration; rather, it is a dimension of power relations that shapes and organizes migration. Similarly, sexuality is a dimension of power that I contend also shapes and organizes processes of migration and modes of incorporation.

In this chapter I examine the relations between materialist forces, family, migration, and sexual identity. A queer materialist or political economy paradigm is central to my analysis, for such a paradigm allows identity to be understood not only as a social construction but also as being fluid—that is, constructed and reconstructed depending upon social location and political economic context. Furthermore, my analysis is informed by what Anzaldúa (1987) refers to as "mestiza consciousness" (also sometimes referred to as border theory), in which the incongruities of binary systems are made visible as are the intersections of multiple marginal positions and relations of power. My analysis is thus centered on "the borders" in its conscious effort to incorporate structural dimensions of "the borderlands" into an identity that is constructed and draws meaning from marginality.

BORDER CROSSERS: FAMILY, MIGRATION, IDENTITY

THE IMMIGRANT MEN I INTERVIEWED for my research ranged in age from their early twenties to early forties and lived in the greater Los Angeles area. I met these men during my dissertation research fieldwork from 1997 through December 1999 by making initial contacts through organizations, fliers, and friends and then using a snowball sampling technique to meet others. While each of these men's stories was in its own way unique, there were also similarities that became more evident as my research progressed.

Most of the men came from the Pacific states of Mexico, and approximately two-thirds came from the state of Jalisco. About half described their communities of origin as small cities or towns, with only a couple describing their origins as rural; migration to larger cities (such as Guadalajara or border cities such as Tijuana) prior to migrating to the United States was also a common experience.[6] All the men included here were sixteen years old or older when they immigrated. Most came from lower middle-class Mexican backgrounds[7] and had at least a high-school education. Like many of their straight counterparts, many were undocumented. Only two of the men I met were not working at the time of their interview; one man was unable to work due to health reasons related to AIDS/HIV, and the other was looking for work. Several of the men were actually holding down more than one job; one full-time and one part-time. The average annual income of the men was between twenty and twenty-five thousand dollars. Their fluency in English was relative to their time in the United States, but none of the men were completely fluent.[8] Due in part to this, the men interviewed reported daily lives that were for the most part Spanish speaking. In addition, nearly all estimated that more than 75 percent of their social circles were Latino.

In the following paragraphs I introduce seven of the twenty men I interviewed formally.[9] I selected these particular interviews as representative of the range of experiences related to me. However, the interview excerpts I have included should not be considered representative of all Mexican-immigrant men to the United States who have sex with men— the diversity of experiences is far greater than can be captured here. The men I have included identified as either bisexual or homosexual (gay) at the time of the interviews. In addition, I do not include the voice of trans-gendered Mexican immigrants, although some of the men do have experience with cross-dressing.[10] Yet the voices represented here do reveal the complexity of the sexuality of migration and the importance of including sexuality in our analysis. I will first provide a general description of these men and then discuss their experiences as they relate to family, migration, and sexual identity.

Lalo is a thirty-three-year-old immigrant from Guadalajara, Jalisco. The fifth of nine children, Lalo comes from what he describes as a "very poor" class background. He migrated to the United States in 1983 and is a legal resident who currently lives in Fountain Valley.

Armando is a thirty-two-year-old Mexican national born in the state of Jalisco where he spent eight years in a seminary studying to be a priest. He is the oldest of eight children (four boys and four girls). He moved to the United States in 1995 and is an undocumented immigrant. He currently lives in Santa Ana but was living in Los Angeles with his brother when we met.

Gabriel is a twenty-three-year-old undocumented immigrant who has lived in the Orange County area for the past five years. He works as a medical assistant. The fourth of six children, Gabriel moved to the United States from Nayarit, Mexico in 1993 when he was eighteen. Gabriel is now living in Fullerton.

Paco is the youngest of six children, four sisters and a brother. His father died three months after he was born and Paco was raised by his mother and older siblings. Paco is a legal resident of the United States although he immigrated illegally in 1990.

Roberto   is in his early forties and has lived in the United States since migrating from Mexico in 1994. The fourth of five children, he comes from a prestigious and well-to-do family in Nayarit, Mexico. Although never married, Roberto has a teenaged son who lives in Mexico with the son's mother. Roberto now lives in the San Fernando Valley and works as an AIDS educator for a Latino community organization.

Manuel   is thirty years old, identifies as bisexual, and currently is unemployed although he worked as a registered nurse in Guadalajara, Mexico. He is the third of eight children (seven boys and one girl) and grew up in Tlaquepaque, a town famous for its artisans and now considered part of the Guadalajara metro area. A Jehovah's Witness, he considers himself to be very religious. Due to his HIV status, he moved to the United States in 1996 to be with his family and is an undocumented immigrant. He lives with his family in Santa Ana, who know of his condition but are not aware of his sexual identity.

Carlos   migrated from Guadalajara in 1990 and is currently seeking political asylum in the United States based on his sexual orientation. Because Carlos was an active member of the Democratic Revolutionary Party (PRD), an opposition party to Mexico's ruling Institutional Revolutionary Party (PRI), Carlos fears that he may be imprisoned or murdered if he returns to Mexico. He now lives in Los Angeles.

FAMILY LIFE IN MEXICO

SOCIAL SCIENTISTS HAVE HISTORICALLY given great attention to the role of *la familia* in Latino culture. Scholarship often points to Latino "familism"—defined as the value and preservation of the family over individual concerns (Moore and Pachon 1985; Williams 1990)—as the contentious source of both material and emotional support and patriarchal oppression. The stereotype is problematic for a number of reasons, not the least of which is the fact that the same argument could be made of most families regardless of their cultural context.[11] Thus, in this section, while I discuss how the early family lives of Mexican immigrant MSMs influenced migratory processes, my aim is not to reproduce a cultural pathology of *la familia* but, rather, to examine the family as a site where normative constructions of gender and sexuality are reproduced and in which the dynamics of migration are materially embedded.

During my interviews, most of the men remembered their lives as children in Mexico fondly.[12] Yet, even when memories of early family life were positive, the daily lessons of normative masculinity learned by these men often resulted in emotional conflicts. I asked them to share with me their memories of family life and educational experiences in order to understand more fully the processes by which normative gender roles and sexuality are learned. Most early childhood memories were shared with smiles and consisted of generally carefree days: playing typical games and going to school. Most of the men also reported that they were good students who received awards for their scholarship and genuinely seemed to have enjoyed school. However, even men such as Paco, who reported that his childhood was "a great time . . . a very beautiful stage of my life," expressed a sense of inner conflict rooted in normative definitions of masculinity.

These conflicts were even more pronounced for men such as Lalo, whose memories of early life in Mexico were not good ones. Recounting his childhood Lalo told me,

> As I child I was very mischievous. I was sexually abused when I was seven by the neighbor, a man of forty. It was a childhood experience that affected me greatly. This person continued to abuse me, he would give me money, later I would go looking for him myself and I was like his "boyfriend" until I was nine. I knew what he was doing was wrong so I never told anyone.

Paternostro (1998) reports that child sexual abuse by a family member is a common phenomenon in Latin America (whether it is more prevalent than other countries is debatable). In fact Lalo was not the only man I interviewed who was sexually abused as a child, but he was the most forthcoming about the experience.[13] Later in the interview he explained that he had also been abused by two older male cousins and that when he told his father about the abuse, his father's response was to rape him for being a "*maricón.*"

None of the sexually abused men, including Lalo, remember connecting these experiences to homosexuality at the time of their occurrence; in part because they didn't really know what homosexuality was. Lalo explained that although he had never heard the word "homosexual," words such as "*maricón*" and "*joto*" were commonly heard in his home. However, Lalo related these terms to effeminate men or *vestidas* like the man in his neighborhood who dressed like a woman. Many informants related similar experiences. Carlos explained, for example, "Across from us lived the town *mar-*

icón. In every town there is the drunk and the *maricón*, and the *maricón* lived across the street." As children the question of what a *maricón* was remained somewhat of a mystery; although they knew it wasn't anything "good." For instance, it wasn't until later that Lalo started to understand what "homosexual" meant. He explained,

> After about the age of twelve or thirteen there was a lot of sexual play among the boys of the *colonia*. We would masturbate one another. There were about twelve of us in the group and we would form a circle and masturbate one another. Later, couples would form and we would penetrate one another. Now they are all grown up and married but there was a lot of sexual play when we were kids. . . . There were some boys who would refuse to join us, saying, "that's for *maricones*" or "you're going to be a *joto* or a woman." It was then that I started to understand but I never thought that I was going to be like a woman.

Masculine discourse that devalues the feminine and equates homosexuality to the feminine, is of course, not particular to Mexican culture (cf. Fellows 1996 and Murray and Roscoe 1998). However, as Lalo explained, homosexuality and femininity are not popularly understood as synonymous.[14] "Being a *joto* is to not be man. Neither a man nor a woman, it is to be an abomination, a curse." Prieur's (1998) recent work on male-to-female transgendered residents of Mexico City supports Lalo's analysis and suggests that class perspectives are an important dimension of its construction. Thus the relationship of homosexuality to the feminine is more complex than a synonymous equation implies. Homosexuality is not only the opposite of masculinity, it is a corruption of it, an unnatural form that by virtue of its transgression of the binary male/female order poses a threat that must be contained or controlled.

The liminal/marginal location of homosexuality, perhaps best understood as shaped by what Almaguer (1993) refers to as a sex/gender/power axis, is reproduced through messages in everyday life. Discussing his daily chores at home, Paco explained,

> My duties at home in particular, well, they were almost never designated to us. I liked very much to sweep, mop, wash the dishes, and when [my mother and sisters] would make cake I always liked to be there when they were preparing it. But, only when my mom and my sisters were there, because my brother would often be in the United States. I always liked to help my mom and my sisters, but when my brother would get there, I always had to hide or not do it because he would tell me "You are not

a woman to be doing that, that's for the *maricones*." Then, since I was scared of him, I wouldn't do it anymore. But it was what I liked to do, up till now; I like cleaning very much and chores like that. I like to cook very much, I like to have everything clean—I've always liked that.

When I asked Paco to discuss the issue of "women's work" in more detail, he explained,

> In Mexico they say "Oh, a homosexual person or a *maricón* or a *joto* are those persons that are dressed like women." They always have a little of that mentality. For example, there were times that a guy named Luis would pass by and he always left his nails long and his hair long like a woman. He had a bag, and he would put on women's pants or a woman's blouse, and he might have put on make-up but not a lot, but obviously he would go around like a woman. Then all the people, well, they said things, but in my family one time I heard my mother call him, she would call them *frescos* (fresh), there goes this *fresco*, there goes that *fresco*, I would hear my mom say that. Then, I would get angry when I would hear that, because I would say "Well, I am not like that, but I am attracted to young men."

Armando expressed learning the same type of sex/gender message through child's play. Armando explained that he liked to play with paper dolls and more than anything liked to cut out the clothes, yet he hid when he did so. When I asked him why, Armando replied, "It's the only game I remember playing secretly. I knew my parents wouldn't like it. I thought it was perfectly normal, it was only bad because it was something that little girls do."

The struggle that Paco and Armando relate in attempting to negotiate the perceived contradictions of sex, gender, and sexual identities was a common theme of many of my interviews. Participants expressed a certain sense of isolation or "not belonging" and not wanting to disappoint their families. Even learning to emulate normative gender and sexual performances was not, in itself, sufficient to resolve these conflicts. For some men, these tensions were a catalyst for migration itself.

LEAVING HOME

ONE OF THE QUESTIONS that I asked immigrant interviewees was what their top three reasons for immigrating were. After analyzing the answers given, it became clear that sexuality was indeed an influencing reason for migration and that "family" dynamics were often linked to these reasons. However, understanding how sexuality actually influenced these decisions was not always as clear-cut as having people respond, "it was my sexuality"— although that sometimes happened. For example, Lalo told me, "Ninety percent of the reason I migrated was because of my sexuality." Such reasons obviously resonate with D'Emilio's (1993) and Rubin's (1993) models of rural to urban migration by gay men and women seeking greater anonymity and gay life in the cities. Yet, in order to understand more fully how sexuality is linked to other socioeconomic dimensions, one must attempt to connect the micro with the meta and macro dimensions of life. That is to say, one cannot separate individual reasons for migration from the larger processes that shape people's everyday lives and perceived choices. Several themes did arise from the interviews, sometimes from the same source, and these themes are implicated in a queer political economy in different ways.

For example, all of the men I interviewed, in one form or another, gave financial reasons for migrating to the United States. And indeed, immigration scholars have traditionally placed a great deal of emphasis on economic reasons for migration, yet to a great degree their vision of the economic realm is extremely limited. The social inequalities of sexuality, like race and gender, are integrally linked to the economic structures of society. Groups that are marginalized as sexual minorities are constrained by the limits of discrimination and prejudice that may limit their socioeconomic opportunities. Thus, when immigrants, who are a sexual minority, say that they immigrated for financial reasons, part of the analysis must include sexuality. For instance, even the person I interviewed in Mexico who owned his own pesticide and fertilizer business felt the constraints of heterosexism. Business networks, he explained, depend upon having the right image, which means a wife, children, and social events tied to church and school. Clearly, as a gay man he was outside this world. His class privilege and the fact the he is his own boss, however, permit him to remain in Mexico relatively free from some of the pressures that drive others to migrate.[15]

Thus, while men such as Lalo clearly migrate to escape a sense of sexual oppression, for others the decision to migrate to the United States is influenced by a combination of sexual liberation and economic opportunities. For example, Gabriel moved to the United States from Nayarit, Mexico, when he was eighteen but explained that he had begun to prepare himself for immigrating at sixteen. When I asked him why, he explained that he had two major reasons for coming to the United States:

First, I wanted to get a better level of education. And the second reason was sexuality. I wanted to be able to define myself and have more freedom with respect to that. I wanted to come here to live, not to distance myself from my family but to hide what I already knew I had. I knew I was gay but I thought I might be able to change it. I needed to come here and speak to people, to learn more about it, because in Mexico it's still very taboo. There isn't so much liberation.

Gabriel's experience reveals how the tension of sexual desire versus "not wanting to distance" oneself from family may serve as a migratory "push." Yet while he clearly moved to the United States seeking a more liberal sexual environment, it was not just a personal matter, it was also because he felt he had limited economic opportunities as a gay man in Mexico. Staying in Mexico might very well have meant either attempting to create a heteronormative family or dealing with social and economic discrimination as a gay man.

Sometimes homosexual relationships might have subtle influences such as serving to establish or expand social networks or they might have a more direct influence driving migration itself. For instance, Roberto explained to me that he was quite happy with his life in Mexico as a civil servant but that people had begun to gossip about his sexual orientation and he feared for his job security, especially since he had recently learned that he was HIV positive. Roberto had met a man from the United States who was vacationing in Mexico and had maintained a friendly relationship with the man. When the American suggested to Roberto that he move to the United States to live with him, Roberto took advantage of the opportunity and moved to Los Angeles. Although he is no longer in a relationship with the American, they continue to be friends. In such a case, new (transnational) social bonds are created similar to the kinship networks that migration scholars argue facilitate migration, yet these are not blood-based but, rather, based on affiliation–transnational gay networks.

FINDING THEIR WAY HOME

ADAPTING TO LIFE IN the United States is difficult for any migrant, but for immigrants like Lalo, who migrate to the United States expecting a gay utopia, the reality of life in the United States can be quite a blow. Indeed Lalo had returned to Mexico for two years after first migrating to the

United States because of his disillusionment, returning only when he realized that his prospects as a gay man were limited in Mexico. Thus, for Lalo, home was no longer Jalisco. While there are a number of important aspects of an immigrant's experiences adapting to their new home, in this section I focus on how sexuality might be related to a migrant's adaptation and incorporation. Specifically, I am concerned here with both kin networks and the home as mechanisms for adaptation.

In her discussion of gay and lesbian kin relations Weston (1991) demonstrates how gays and lesbians construct "chosen" families based on shared affinities and relationships of both material and emotional support. Kinship (biological) plays a central role in migration as a means through which immigrants receive support and acquire important knowledge for survival and adaptation (cf. Chavez 1992). While the Mexican men I interviewed often utilized kinship networks to these ends, they also depended upon networks that were similar to those described by Weston. About half of the immigrants I spoke with utilized preexisting gay networks to migrate to the United States. They were like Lalo, who migrated with the help of a gay compatriot already living in Los Angeles, and like Roberto, who came with the help of a gay American. But even some of those who utilized kin networks for initial migration also used gay networks for meeting other gay Latino men, finding gay roommates, making job contacts, and acquiring other types of information. The existence and use of these alternative networks depended to a large extent on how the men identified sexually, to what extent they were "out of the closet," and, to some extent, on their ability to speak English (and thus expand their networks into the mainstream gay world).

For instance, although Paco migrated and found his first job using kinship networks, he was soon able to develop a gay network as well.

> My second job was in a company where they made pools. I obtained that job through a [gay] friend, an American, who is the person, the third person that I have to thank about my legal status here in this country. He helped me get the job because it was the company of a friend of his. In the morning I would clean the offices and then I would go to the warehouse and take inventory or I would clean the warehouse or cut fiberglass, or things like that. And they paid me well at that time but I worked only a few hours. So after that, since they said "Oh, you clean so well," and they had some very beautiful houses, over in Laguna Beach. Sometimes I would stay over because I could not finish in the weekend. The

owners of the company were gay. They would go to San Francisco, or wherever there were going, they always traveled on the weekend, they left me the key, "Here is the stereo and here is the television," and everything like that because I had to sleep over. Then I would go home when they returned on Sundays.

Ironically, Paco is one of the people who assured me that sexuality had not influenced his migratory experiences in the least. This excerpt, however, reveals that gay–social networks were an aid in his finding work. In addition, Paco shares a home with a lesbian niece and has allowed other gay immigrants to stay with him temporarily until they are able to move on.

Carlos also made use of gay networks in a similar manner. When he migrated to the United States, he first lived for two months in Watsonville, California, with a brother and then went to live in Milwaukee for two years with his two sisters, who are lesbians. He then moved to Los Angeles after meeting and starting a relationship with a gay man. Like Paco, Carlos revealed that his gay friends had helped him find work and even helped him out financially. "Because of my gay friends, I have never gone without," he said.

Both Paco's and Carlos's experiences also point to the fact that sexuality is an important dimension of immigrant-household arrangements. While recent immigration literature has discussed the importance of household arrangements as "landing pads" for migrant adaptation (cf. Chavez 1992, 1994), the sexual dimensions of these arrangements are missing from the analyses. For an individual who has migrated to the United States seeking a more liberal sexual environment, it makes little sense to live in a home constrained by heteronormative relations. While about half of the Mexican men I interviewed originally lived with family members when they migrated, most had formed alternative living arrangements as soon as they were able to. Lalo's home exemplifies this alternative type of arrangement.

When I first met Lalo he was living in Santa Ana in an apartment he shared with three other immigrant men, all gay. Since our first meeting, Lalo has moved twice and has had a number of different roommates, always gay Latino immigrant men. Sometimes the men, especially if they were recent immigrants, would stay only a short time until they found another place to live. It was clear that Lalo's home was a landing pad, but it was one where Latino men could be openly gay, support one another and share information that was essential for adaptation. Although the men did not explicitly define these relations as "family," they did sometimes refer to each other affectionately as siblings (sometimes as "sisters" and sometimes as "brothers"). Regardless of how these relationships were labeled, it was clear that an alternative support system had been created. It is precisely in this type of living arrangement that many men discover the space that transforms the way they think about themselves and their sexual identities.

MIGRATING IDENTITIES

ONE OF THE CONTRIBUTIONS of postmodern (including queer theory) and postcolonial literature is that identity is no longer understood as something inherently fixed and stable. Rather, identity is understood as mutable and plural—that is, the subject is the intersection of multiple identities (race/ethnicity, gender, sexuality, and so forth) that change and have salience at different moments in time and place. Given the dramatic sociospatial changes that immigrants experience, their sexual identities cannot therefore be assumed stable. As Iain Chambers puts it, "identity is formed on the move" (1994:25). The effects of migration upon the sexual identities of Mexican immigrant MSMs are ultimately linked to their emotional and material relationships to their biological families and the degree to which they have been able to resolve the normative sexuality and gender conflicts that fed their desire to migrate.

I asked the men I interviewed if they felt that they had changed at all since migrating to the United States. Nearly all of the men responded with a resounding yes. The changes they described generally centered around racial, gender, sexual, and class identities. Most of the men inevitably referred to a more liberal sexual environment as a reason for their transformation. Migrating to the United States was for many men one step in a series toward what might be called "a journey to the self."[16] For Gabriel, the desire to live in a place where he could develop his human potential as a gay man was a driving force in his decision to immigrate. He added,

> I have two names, Gabriel Luis, and my family calls me Luis. I've always said that Luis is the person who stayed in Mexico. Once I came here, Gabriel was born. Because, like I've told you, once I was here I defined myself sexually and I've changed a lot emotionally, more than anything emotionally, because I found myself.

This journey of self-discovery is intimately linked to resistance to the normative gender and sex regimes I have described earlier. While earlier scholarship asserted that Mexican male sexual identities were based on the active or passive (*activo/passivo*) role of the participant (where only the passive was deemed homosexual) more recent research, including my own, finds that Mexican sexual identities are more complex.

Most interviewees remembered first being aware of their attraction to boys or men in early childhood. Some remembered being attracted to the same sex as young as age four, but the majority of recollections were a bit later. Carlos remembered, "I was around eight years old. I could recognize the beauty of men. But from then on it was an issue of denial." The pressure to conform, or as Lalo described, "*la lucha de no querer ser gay*" (the struggle of not wanting to be gay) took a toll on most of the men I interviewed but perhaps was most eloquently described by Armando. He explained that he had been tormented by schoolmates after around the fourth grade who would call him *joto* and *maricón*. He stated,

> But I learned how to hide it better, so it wasn't noticeable. I no longer isolated myself, instead I would mix with the troublemakers at school so that their reputation would rub off on me and so no one would tell me anything anymore. A new student arrived who was even more obvious than me and to a certain extent he was my salvation. Everyone focused their attention on him and it was a load off of me. It gave me the opportunity to get closer to the other students and do everything that they did, to act like them, have girlfriends, and not be the "good boy" anymore— to take on the heterosexual role.

Armando would later join a seminary in an attempt to escape his sexual feelings and began to lift weights so that his appearance was more masculine. Eventually, however, he realized he needed to face who he "really" was.

> I feel that I lost a lot of my essence as a homosexual during that time. I see it like that now. At that time I only wanted to be part of a group, to be accepted. It's horrible to feel marginalized, in a corner, abnormal. In my attempts to be like everyone else wanted me to be I lost much of my self.

Two months after migrating to the United States, seeking the freedom to be a gay man, he confessed to a cousin, with whom he was staying, that he was gay. She told him that she accepted and loved him as he was but that he needed to talk to his brothers. Armando told his brothers one by one and they all accepted his homosexuality (although it was by no means easy). He then decided to tell his widowed mother. At the time of our interview it had been five months since he had written his mother a five-page letter explaining his struggle to accept himself. A month later Armando's mother wrote him back asking forgiveness and assuring him that he would have her support and unconditional love. Armando has been able successfully to integrate his calling to service with his desire to be true to himself. He now works as an AIDS educator and program coordinator for an organization that serves gay Latino men.

Like Armando, other men who migrated to the United States also came out to their families and some found acceptance as well. In some of these men's cases it seems that the acceptance is in part tied to a reversal in family roles. Where once they were dependent upon their families for support, now their families are dependent upon them. Thus, while Almaguer (1993) has argued that economic interdependence stifles a gay identity from forming among Latino MSMs, my research reveals that it may actually facilitate familial acceptance. For instance, since migrating to the United States Lalo has also gained acceptance from the family who threw him out of the house. He explained to me that he has sent money to Mexico to have his mother's house repaired and to pay for his brother's tuition and that his family now respects him. Lalo related, "I'm much more secure now. I'm not afraid to say I'm a homosexual. I'm content being gay and I can help others. I'm stronger and have achieved a lot of things."

Thus the transformation in economic roles and physical separation has allowed Lalo the opportunity to be both gay and accepted by his family.

There were, however, a couple of men I interviewed who were openly gay prior to migrating to the United States. In both cases these men had upper-class backgrounds. The difference that class makes in mitigating the effects of homophobia is significant and needs to be studied more closely. For example, when I asked Roberto about his son he laughed out loud and said,

> Oh my son! My son was the product of an agreement. His mother knew that I was gay. My partner of ten years and I lived together [in Tepic, Nayarit] and she lived in front of us. She knew of my relationship with Alejo and the three of us would go out to dance. In a small town, well, it was known that she was the friend of "the boys." We would go out to dance, she would come to our home to watch television, listen to music, or have a drink. Then one day she told me flat out that she wanted to have my baby. Then between the jokes I began to understand and between the jokes we ended up in bed. We had sex for two or three months and one day she called me and told me she was pregnant. I was

twenty-three or twenty-four and was completely out of the closet with my family and I didn't care about anything.

Without a doubt, Roberto's class privilege allowed him to not "care about anything" as an openly gay man. In all probability it also shaped his gay-social networks that allowed him to migrate to the United States.

To be clear, for those men who do not have such privileges in Mexico, migrating to the United States does not necessarily afford them these privileges either. While there may be more space to be gay in the United States, migrating has its costs. For example, as Carlos lamented,

> Being away from Mexico creates a strong nationalistic feeling with a lot of nostalgia. You begin to notice how different the system is here than in Mexico, an economic system that changes your life completely—a system where one forgets about other things that in Mexico were a priority. Here one lives life from the perspective of money. Working and making enough money to pay your bills is more important than having friends and doing what you like. In Mexico it's very different. It's more important to have friends. One lives less a slave to the clock. One forgets these things and becoming aware of that has made me very sad.

Discovering the virulence of racism in the United States seems to counterbalance any feelings of sexual liberation. I asked the men, in an open-ended manner, if they had ever experienced discrimination (without defining the type). Nearly all of the men responded in ways similar to Carlos: "For being Latino, for not speaking English perfectly, for the color of my skin." The irony, of course, is that in their attempts to escape one form of bigotry, most of the Mexican men I interviewed discovered that not only had they not entirely escaped it but they now faced another. As Lalo said, "It wasn't true that homosexuals are free, that they can hold hands or that Americans like Mexicans." Under these circumstances the role of a support system becomes all the more important and for queer Latino-immigrant men this often means that new families must be created.

BUILDING FAMILY

I WAS NAIVELY SURPRISED by the responses I received when I asked immigrant men about their future plans. I suppose that I had allowed myself to become so immersed in the migration literature that I was expecting to hear something more along the lines of "return to Mexico and start my own business." More common, however, were responses such as Paco's:

> I want to be anywhere close to the person I love, to support me. If it's in Mexico, a lot better because I would have my family and that person near me. But, more than anything, right now I worry a lot for my own person and for the partner who I think will be what I wait for in my life. And I see myself in a relationship with a lot of affection, and maybe by then, living with that person, together. And maybe even to get married.

In response to my next question, "So your plans for the future are to have a partner?" Paco answered:

> A stable partner, be happy, and give them all my support, and I would help that person shine, succeed in anything I could help. I will try to do it all the time. If he accomplishes more than I have it will make me very happy because in that aspect I am not egotistical. And still more things that are positive; get more involved in helping people that need me, in every aspect. Be happy, make my partner happy, above all make myself happy, and my family, my friends, all the people that like me, and I like.

This type of response does not exclude dreams of material wealth and entrepreneurship, but it centers and gives priority to affective dimensions— to building new families. The desires for stable relationships reflect not only the difficulty for maintaining such relationships in Mexico but also the isolation that these men feel in the United States. This isolation that gay Mexican immigrant men feel is due in some measure to language difficulties, but racial and class issues also play into it. For instance, Carlos explained to me that although he was in a relationship at the time of our interview he didn't see much of a future in it.

> I don't have many expectations for my relationship because my partner is not Latino. I think that, ideally, for a stable relationship I need to be with a Latino . . . someone who identifies as Latino. Someone intelligent and a little more cultured. Someone who has the capacity to go to an art or photography exhibit and enjoy it. Someone open-minded, open to learning from other cultures and who is financially independent.

The problem, of course, is that the social location of Mexican immigrant MSMs in the United States is a marginal one. Stability is not easily established and financial independence may take years to accomplish, if at all. The problem is exacerbated by the fact that there are few public spaces where Latino gay men can openly meet one another. Thus, creating family or even a sense of community depends in no small part upon the ability of queer Latinos to build a new home with limited resources and external support.

"Who do you turn to for support?" I asked the men I interviewed. The standard response was: "family and friends." Yet it is clear from my discussions with these men, and the data presented here, that these relationships (whether biological or chosen) were sometimes strained, always evolving, and ultimately negotiated. A queer materialist analysis of the experiences of Mexican-immigrant men who have sex with men reveals the ways in which dimensions of family, migration, and sexual identity intersect and are embedded within a political economy. Many of the men interviewed felt marginalized by heteronormative definitions of masculinity reproduced through and embodied in the traditional family. These norms, reproduced in daily activities since childhood, marginalize not only men with "feminine" characteristics but also those able to pass, who were instilled with a fear of discovery. Associations of femininity with homosexuality created a sense of confusion in some men who, although attracted to men, did not identify as feminine. The economic liability that derived from not creating a heteronormative family unit as an adult also influenced the immigration process. These strict gender/sex regimes were powerful enough to drive many men to migrate to the United States in search of a more liberal environment.

A queer political-economy perspective of migration also aids in unveiling how sexuality has shaped processes and strategies for adaptation such as social networks and household arrangements. Alternative relations to biological families, which serve as systems of support, are created based on sexual orientation. The members of these "chosen families" assist one another through the trials and tribulations of being a queer Mexican-immigrant man. Such assistance takes a variety of forms, including helping with migration itself, sharing knowledge and resources such as job information, and even sharing households.

New economic arrangements mean that some men find that they are empowered to come out to their biological families as gay men and maintain a level of acceptance and respect from their loved ones. Shared space is also an important dimension linked to the futures of these gay men. Faced with a sense of isolation and a deep desire to form the stable relationships— which they were prevented from having in Mexico—space becomes the base for adaptation, community, and shared futures. Thus, for many men who have come to identify as gay, new family structures become a means by which dreams may be realized.

Although my focus has been on Mexican-immigrant men, there are larger implications that need to be explored. When we understand sexuality as a dimension of power (that intersects with other dimensions such as race, gender, and class) in which certain groups are privileged over others, then these implications become more visible. For instance, Argüelles and Rivero (1993) argue that some immigrant women have migrated in order to flee violent and/or oppressive sexual relationships or marriage arrangements, which they contest. Little research has been conducted on Latinas in general, far less exists on the intersections of migration and sexuality (regardless of sexual orientation). While it is clear that biological families reproduce normative constructions of gender and sexuality, the ways in which these norms and power relations influence different groups of people in terms of migration and identity is not understood. I hope the research presented here will be a step toward the development of a queer materialist paradigm by which the sexual dimensions of migration can be understood and by which further research may be conducted.

NOTES

1.   This chapter represents part of a larger dissertation research project entitled *Border Crossings: Mexican Men and the Sexuality of Migration*. The author gratefully acknowledges the comments and suggestions of the editors and Nancy Naples, as well as the funding support of the Social Science Research Council's Sexuality Fellowship Program and the Ford Foundation, which made this research possible. In addition, the author wishes to express his gratitude to the men who participated in this project.

2.   While recent debates between social constructionists and what are sometimes belittlingly called essentialists have heated up with genetic research, I assume that sexuality is more complex than the either/or debates allow for. I therefore focus on the social aspects of sexuality, i.e., the social constructionist perspective. The constructionist argument has also been made from a cultural perspective. In his classic study of the Sambia of New Guinea, Anthropolo-

gist Gilbert Herdt (1994 [1981]) examined the cultural meanings of homo-sexuality and masculinity in a nonindustrial society and demonstrated, through his examination of "boy-inseminating rituals," that meanings of homosexuality and norms of gender are not universal but, rather, are cultur-ally constructed.

3.   This section of my discussion is meant to highlight and illustrate only part of the theoretical framework of my research and my ideas for "queering" it.

4.   C. M. Wood (1982) attempts to reconcile these differences by focusing on the household as a unit of analysis that bridges micro- and macroeconomic con-cerns, but the household analysis also has its limitations, including a bias toward the individual actor that obscures some of the macrolevel dimensions of migration such as the role of the state and sociocultural influences. In addition, a focus on the household *exclusively*, tends to conceal dimensions of the transnational or binational household and other adaptive strategies by assuming (in at least some of the literature) a nuclear household configura-tion with one head and fully shared resources-that a household has a choice is a problem of reification as well.

5.   Douglas Massey and his coauthors (Massey, Arango, Hugo, Kouaouci, Pelle-grino, and Taylor 1993; Massey and Espinosa 1995) categorize various theo-ries of international migration into five conceptual frames, which I highlight: neoclassical economics, the new economics of labor migration, segmented labor market theory, social capital theory, and world systems theory.

6.   This urban migration generally occurred during the participants' childhood and was not a common experience of their adult life.

7.   Distinguishing social class was a difficult task in large part because the Mex-ican middle class is quickly disappearing from the country's socioeconomic landscape and also because of the international relativity of social class defi-nitions. My measure of class is, therefore, informant defined and takes into account the men's educational and career backgrounds as well as that of their parents.

8.   Interviews were conducted in Spanish and translated by the author.

9.   The names of research participants are pseudonyms.

10.   I do not mean to suggest that cross-dressing and transgender are the same.

11.   For further elaboration of the ways in which stereotypical cultural arguments pathologize Latino culture see Cantú (2000).

12.   All the men came from households with more than one child.

13.   For ethical reasons, I did not pressure any of my interviewees to discuss trau-matic experiences in more detail than they were comfortable with. I had informed all of them prior to the interview that if there were questions with

which they felt uncomfortable, they could choose not to answer them and/or end the interview at anytime they so wished.

14. While earlier research on Mexican homosexuality found that the homosexual label was applied to only passive (anally receptive) men-*pasivos*—this view seems to be changing (see Carrier 1995).

15. See Cantú (1999) for more on the queer life in Mexico as it relates to migration.

16. I do not mean to imply that there is some essential or "true" sexual nature that awaits "discovery"; rather, I utilize the term as a means to convey informants' expressed understandings of their sexual journeys.

REFERENCES

Almaguer, Tomás. 1993. "Chicano Men: A Cartography of Homosexual Identity and Behavior." In Henry Abelove, Michèle Aina Barale, and David M. Halperin, eds., *The Lesbian and Gay Studies Reader*. New York: Routledge.

Anzaldúa, Gloria. 1987. *Borderlands/La Frontera: The New Mestiza*. San Francisco: Spinsters/Aunt Lute.

Argüelles, Lourdes and Anne M. Rivero. 1993. "Gender/Sexual Orientation Violence and Transnational Migration: Conversations with Some Latinas We Think We Know." *Urban Anthropology* 22 (3/4): 259–76.

Bennett, James R. 1996. Introduction to "Materialist Queer Theory: A Working Bibliography." In Donald Morton, ed., *The Material Queer: A LesBiGay Cultural Studies Reader*. Boulder, Col.: Westview Press.

Cantú, Lionel. 1999. "Border Crossings: Mexican Men and the Sexuality of Migration." Ph.D. diss., University of California, Irvine, 1999.

——. 2000. "Entre Hombres/Between Men: Latino Masculinities and Homosexualities." In Peter Nardi, ed., *Gay Masculinities*, pp. 224–46 . Thousand Oaks, Cal.: Sage.

Carrier, Joseph. 1995. *De Los Otros: Intimacy and Homosexuality Among Mexican Men*. New York: Columbia University Press.

Chambers, Iain. 1994. *Migrancy, Culture, Identity*. London: Routledge.

Chavez, Leo. 1992. *Shadowed Lives: Undocumented Immigrants in American Society*. San Diego, Cal.: Harcourt Brace Jovanovich.

——. 1994. "The Power of the Imagined Community: The Settlement of Undocumented Mexicans and Central Americans in the United States." *American Anthropologist* 96 (1): 52–73.

Cousins, Mark and Athar Hussain. 1984. *Michel Foucault*. New York: MacMillan.

D'Emilio, John. 1993. "Capitalism and Gay Identity." In William B. Rubenstein, ed., *Lesbians, Gay Men, and the Law*. New York: New Press.

Donovan, Josephine. 1992. *Feminist Theory*. New York: Continuum.

Engels, Frederick. 1993 [1942]. *The Origin of the Family, Private Property and the State, in the Light of the Researches of Lewis H. Morgan*. New York: International.

Fellows, Will, ed. 1996. *Farm Boys: Lives of Gay Men from the Rural Midwest*. Madison: University of Wisconsin Press.

Foucault, Michel. 1978. *The History of Sexuality*. Trans. Robert Hurley. New York: Pantheon.

Gluckman, Amy and Betsy Reed, eds. 1997. *HomoEconomics: Capitalism, Community, and Lesbian and Gay Life*. New York: Routledge.

Gutmann, Matthew C. 1996. *The Meanings of Macho: Being a Man in Mexico City*. Berkeley: University of California Press.

Hennessy, Rosemary and Chrys Ingraham, eds. 1997. *Materialist Feminism: A Reader in Class, Difference, and Women's Lives*. New York: Routledge.

Herdt, Gilbert H. 1994 [1981]. *Guardians of the Flutes: Idioms of Masculinity*. New York: McGraw-Hill.

Hondagneu-Sotelo, Pierrette. 1994. *Gendered Transitions: Mexican Experiences of Immigration*. Los Angeles: University of California Press.

Hondagneu-Sotelo, Pierrette and Michael Messner. 1994. "Gender Displays and Men's Power: 'The New Man' and the Mexican Immigrant Man." In Harry Brod and Michael Kaufman, eds., *Theorizing Masculinities*. Thousand Oaks, Cal.: Sage.

Ingram, Gordon Brent, Anne-Marie Bouthillette, and Yolanda Retter. 1997. *Queers in Space: Communities, Public Places, Sites of Resistance*. Seattle, Wash.: Bay Press.

Jagose, Annamarie. 1996. *Queer Theory: An Introduction*. New York: New York University Press.

Martin, Biddy. 1988. "Feminism, Criticism, and Foucault." In Irene Diamond and Lee Quinby, eds., *Feminism and Foucault: Reflections on Resistance*. Boston: Northeastern University Press.

Massey, Douglas S., Joaquin Arango, Graeme Hugo, Ali Kouaouci, Adela Pellegrino, and J. Edward Taylor. 1993. "Theories of International Migration: Review and Appraisal." *Population and Development Review* 19 (3): 431–67.

Massey, Douglas S. and Kristin Espinosa. 1995. "What's Driving Mexico-U.S. Migration? A Theoretical, Empirical, and Policy Analysis." Unpublished paper.

McIntosh, Mary. 1968. "The Homosexual Role." *Social Problems* 16 (69): 182–92.

Moore, Joan and Harry Pachon. 1985. *Hispanics in the United States*. Englewood Cliffs, N.J.: Prentice-Hall.

Morton, Donald, ed. 1996. *The Material Queer*. Boulder, Col.: Westview Press.

Murray, Stephen O. 1995. *Latin American Male Homosexualities*. Albuquerque: University of New Mexico Press.

Murray, Stephen O. and Will Roscoe, ed. 1998. *Boy-Wives and Female Husbands: Studies in African Homosexualities*. New York: St. Martin's Press.

Paternostro, Silvana. 1998. *In the Land of God and Man: Confronting Our Sexual Culture*. New York: Dutton.

Pedraza, Silvia. 1991. "Women and Migration: The Social Consequences of Gender." *Annual Review of Sociology* 17: 303–25.

Prieur, Annick. 1998. *Mema's House, Mexico City: On Transvestites, Queens, and Machos*. Chicago: University of Chicago Press.

Rubin, Gayle. 1993. "Thinking Sex: Notes for a Radical Theory of the Politics of Sexuality." In Henry Abelove, Michèle Aina Barale, and David M. Halperin, eds., *The Lesbian and Gay Studies Reader*, pp. 3–44. New York: Routledge.

Seidman, Steven, ed. 1996. *Queer Theory/Sociology*. Cambridge, Mass.: Blackwell.

Weeks, Jeffrey. 1977. *Coming Out: Homosexual Politics in Britain from the Nineteenth Century to the Present*. London: Quartet.

Weston, Kath. 1991. *Families We Choose: Lesbians, Gays, Kinship*. New York: Columbia University Press.

Williams, Norma. 1990. *The Mexican American Family: Tradition and Change*. Dix Hills, N.Y.: General Hall.

Wood, Charles, H. 1982. "Equilibrium and Historical Structural Perspectives on Migration." *International Migration Review* 16 (2): 298–319.

9 | Constituting Nonmonogamies

R. Jeffrey Ringer

everal years ago I was talking with a student member of my campus's gay and lesbian student association. He was frustrated because he didn't have anyone to whom to turn for advice about his relationship. There were no out gay-male staff members on campus who were available for such advice, and all of his friends who were coupled were straight. His relationship issues, he felt, were different than his straight friends' so he wanted male-couple-role models, but couldn't find any.

Another student addressed the same issue after hearing me give a campus presentation on gay-male relationships. He approached me after my talk and said that he had been in a relationship with someone he loved deeply but discovered after moving in together that, although he expected monogamy, his partner wanted and expected to have sex with other people. He told me he wished that there had been some way to learn about his partner's expectations before moving in together. He had never considered the possibility that a potential partner might want a relationship different from the traditional heterosexual model.

These young men were struggling with their same-sex desires and seeking advice on how to develop relationships. The advice that they might get from a heterosexual parent, friend, or sibling may be useful to construct relationships modeled on normative heterosexual values, but is that right for them? Monogamy is assumed in most heterosexual relationships but was not assumed in at least one of the scenarios above. What should they do differently than their heterosexual family members and friends? Where could they get advice? Clearly, these young men felt a need for advice to help them establish alternative same-sex relationships.

IDEOLOGICAL ASSUMPTIONS AND SAME-SEX RELATIONSHIPS

ADVICE, HOWEVER, IS A TRICKY thing. Any attempt to tell someone how they should do something is based on assumptions about how things should be. Consider the following situation: John and Frank are lovers who have been together for one year. John is considering whether or not to tell his parents about their relationship and seeks advice from friends and colleagues. John's friends tell him that he should tell his parents about his relationship with Frank, convincing him that if he is honest with his parents he will develop a closer relationship with them. This advice is based on the common-sense (at least in the United States) notions that honesty is important and that one should express one's feelings openly. Researchers have recognized, however, that openness and honesty are rooted in ideological conceptions about the nature of intimacy (Parks 1995; Sennett 1977). Such ideological conceptions privilege openness and honesty above such things as privacy, tact, or deception, which all play vital roles in interpersonal relationships. Is it really best for John to tell his family? Or, should he consider other factors such as their likely response, their desired relationship with him, the image they wish to portray to the world, or the material conditions (e.g., financial dependence) of his relationship with them? While there are no easy answers to these questions, it does become obvious that one must carefully examine the assumptions behind advice or recommendations on how to behave.

This is particularly true for advice about gay and lesbian relationships. Much of the knowledge that we have gained about same-sex relationships through research is based on normative heterosexual assumptions and values that view relationships as necessary, consisting of two people, and permanent. Are these assumptions equally appropriate for gay, lesbian, or bisexual relationships? Some individuals may wish to pursue same-sex relationships that model normative heterosexual values. Others, however, may not. Bisexual individuals, or those individuals who discover their homosexuality after already establishing a heterosexual relationship, may desire to create relationships that challenge the normative heterosexual model. For example, someone who is married and then discovers s/he is homosexual may wish to create an alternate form of marriage where the partners can remain married to each other yet pursue erotic connections beyond their marriage partner. The current research on same-sex couples does not examine such issues, however. It generally uses the same models and approaches as the research on heterosexual relationships and, therefore, may unwittingly result in the application of a normative heterosexual value system to gay and lesbian relationships.

Additionally, much of the current research on gay and lesbian couples searches for singular models that attempt to generalize about all or most of our relationships even though variation within the gay and lesbian community is great. For example, McWhirter and Mattison (1984) have proposed a singular model of gay-male relationships that suggests that all gay-male couples' relationships develop through six stages (although each couple may progress through the stages at different rates). Each stage is characterized by several issues that are particular to that stage and that the authors claim were present for most of the couples interviewed.

The value of the McWhirter and Mattison model cannot be understated. It is one of the only models of any type of relationship that describes the development of the relationship over its entire life span. Further, the information included in the model is extremely useful both intuitively and heuristically. But, although the authors state that their goal is not "to create a new typology that becomes the norm against which all such relationships are measured (1984:14), they make totalizing statements in several different essays about the model. They recognize that each relationship is unique but they state that "most relationships, however, do share some characteristics of each stage" (1984:15); that "each relationship passes through a series of predictable developmental stages" (1988:162); and that "considering all the possible variables, there are enough similarities among the couples as their relationships progress to recognize individual stages and to suggest *that most gay relationships pass through them*" (emphasis added) (1988:163), implying that one model will explain the development of most gay-male relationships.

McWhirter and Mattison began their study by interviewing several of their couple friends and then asking those friends to provide the names of other couples to be interviewed. Such a technique, referred to as the snowball technique, is an appropriate sampling method but results in unrepresentative samples. There is no reason to believe that the subjects they interviewed reflect couples other than couples like themselves. Thus, it is a model of "156 couples, mostly white, middle-class, and from the same geographic area" (1984:14). This in and of itself is not problematic, but unless our research considers the ideological differences that may exist among individuals in same-sex relationships these differences may remain invisible and we will be left with a unitary model of same-sex relationships. As Charles Fernandez stated: "Reflected in the ... academy's methodology and theorizing ... is this movement's subject and protagonist: a white and middle-class person" (1991:9).

There are undoubtedly different ideological assumptions about relationships within gay and lesbian communities, and research into their relationships must account for these. The present study is part of a long-term project that considers the question of ideology in gay-male relationships and how these ideologies are constructed in communication. The study began as an ethnographic investigation into the lives of male couples. In *Queer Words Queer Images* (1994), Dorothy Painter noted that people enact their relationships on a day-to-day basis and that much of that occurs in everyday talk. She pointed out that the important question for queer relationships is: "How do we do who we are?" (285). This focus on the day-to-day or the mundane, which became the focus of this project, is important because our beliefs and ideologies about how our relationships should be are reflexively connected to the things that we do. In other words, the things that we do, and the ways that we behave, shape our beliefs and ideologies about our relationships, which, in turn, guide how we behave.

In the remainder of this essay, I will review the communication literature that describes the reflexive nature between communication and ideology. I will then review writings about gay men's relational ideologies. Finally, I will provide a preliminary analysis of ethnographic interviews conducted with gay-male couples that demonstrates how various relational ideologies are reflexively constituted by these couples.

CONSTRUCTING RELATIONAL IDEOLOGIES

SEVERAL LINES OF COMMUNICATION research have begun to focus on the reflexivity inherent in human lives. The first is relational theory. Barbara Montgomery (1992) summarizes four basic assumptions of relational theory. First, "communication and relationships are inextricably intertwined. Neither can exist without the other" (487). Second, the "nature of a relationship emerges from the communication between its members" (478). This assumption revolves around the claim that all messages contain both a content and relationship dimension. The content dimension refers to the subject at hand while the relationship dimension refers to the relationship between the interactants. For example, a message about opening the window involves the content of "opening the window." The relationship dimension of this message would vary depending on how the message was uttered. A request involves a different assumption of relationship than does a command. If one utters a command to an other, one must assume that one has the power to command the other to do something. Additionally, whether or not the other agrees to the request or obeys the command plays a role in how the interactants develop a relationship. Thus, relational theorists argue that "in day-to-day exchanges, interactants are continuously making claims and counterclaims about the nature of their relationship" (478). If one person continually utters commands to another person, and the other person continually obeys these commands, then a particular type of relationship results. If the other challenges the right of the person uttering the commands to utter such messages, or perhaps ignores them altogether, then a different relationship emerges.

The third assumption of relational theory is that these "claims and counterclaims are more often communicated implicitly rather than explicitly" (Montgomery 1992:478). This suggests that interactants frequently do not directly address the relational aspects of messages. Continuing with the same example, the recipient of the command messages can resist the commands in many ways without directly talking about the relationship presumed by a command. The message can be ignored, the subject changed, a return command uttered, ignorance feigned, etc. In this way the relationship assumed by the utterer of the command is not necessarily accepted by the recipient of the message. Instead, the relationship is implicitly negotiated over successive talk turns. The fourth assumption of relational theory is that such a "negotiation process continues throughout the interactive life of the relationship" (Montgomery 1992:478). We continually negotiate and renegotiate our relationships as we interact with each other, and the primary process in which this occurs is communication.

In addition to recognizing the role that communication plays in the development of relationships, Montgomery explains that as couples within a society interact, relational ideologies emerge that guide couple behavior. "A kind of relational ideology emerges in [the social] order that carries with it the power to influence the way couples continue to act, thereby creating a reflexive communication system." (1992:479) As I have noted earlier in this essay, the primary ideologies that govern couple behavior in the United States are based on the heterosexual nuclear family.

Another line of research examines the speech events that characterize various types of relationships. Goldsmith and Baxter (1996) examined routine speech events and how they differed among various types of relationships. They administered surveys to students about their communication with acquaintances, friends, and romantic partners. They found that the use of mundane speech events varied by relationship type. They found that one is more likely to engage in gossip and small talk with friends than with romantic partners. One is more likely to engage in love and involving talk with romantic partners than with friends. And, one is more likely to engage in goal-directed talk with acquaintances and friends than with romantic partners. The authors of this study suggested that routine everyday speech events play an important role in constituting various types of relationships.

Another study by Bruess and Pearson (1997) examined the use of interpersonal rituals in friendships and marriages. Although they found that there are a few interpersonal rituals in which both friendships and marriages engage (such as celebration rituals, enjoyable-activity rituals, and play rituals), there are some rituals that tend to be used primarily in friendships while other rituals tend to be used primarily in marriages. Friends are more likely to engage in getting-together rituals, established-event rituals, and support/event rituals. Marriage partners are more likely to engage in private-code rituals, daily-routine rituals, and intimacy-expression rituals. This study, along with the work of Goldsmith and Baxter (1996), demonstrates that people engage in different routine-speech events with various relational partners.

Seen in the light of relational theory, these studies reveal how communication works reflexively to create and recreate various types of relationships. In other words, people create the relationship "friend" by engaging in particular types of day-to-day speech events (goal-directed talk, gossip, and small talk) and rituals (getting-together rituals, established-event rituals, and support/event rituals). In turn, once one has a friend, one maintains that friend by engaging in the speech events and activities that are appropriate for a friendship. Other types of relationships (such as marriages or acquaintanceships) are similarly constructed.

THE RELATIONAL IDEOLOGIES OF GAY MEN

ARE THERE DIFFERENT TYPES of relationships or relational ideologies among gay men? Early writings in the recent phase of the gay rights movement proposed a variety of types of relationships. In 1972 Carl Wittman (1992) argued that gay men and lesbians should create alternative forms of relationships. He believed that the needs associated with heterosexual marriage could be met through a variety of types of relationships. He wrote that "marriage is a contract which smothers both people, denies needs, and places impossible demands on both people" (1992:333). He proposed that gay men and lesbians should avoid:

> (1) exclusiveness, propertied attitudes toward each other, a mutual pact against the rest of the world; (2) promises about the future, which we have no right to make and which prevent us from, or make us feel guilty about, growing; (3) inflexible roles, roles which do not reflect us at the moment but are inherited through mimicry and inability to define equalitarian relationships. (334)

By arguing that gay men and lesbians should avoid these normative heterosexual values, Wittman was arguing for alternative relational ideologies to guide lesbian and gay relationships.

Rotello (1997) describes two relational ideologies that emerged during this early period. The first might be called the gay-positive ideology. Drawing on ideas similar to those espoused by Wittman, it sought to develop a "nurturing, nonmasculinist and noncompetitive sexual culture" (56). Those who pursued such an ideology began consciousness-raising groups (see A Gay Male Group 1972/1992)and collectives (see Knoebel 1972/1992) or generally "appealed for a transformative gay lifestyle based on love and self-respect" (Rotello 1997:55). The second ideology identified by Rotello views promiscuous behavior as celebratory of gay life. Since gay/lesbian oppression was based on sexuality, freedom from that oppression meant freedom to be sexual. Restraints on sexual behavior were seen as sex-negative; therefore, if one were to be liberated one would remove all sexual restraints. Proponents of this ideology called themselves sex-positive radicals, and they saw promiscuity as an essential aspect of gayness. The existence of these differing ideologies is also discussed by Warner (1993) and Seidman (1993) who trace the development of theorizing about homosexuality and same-sex desires from the liberation theory of the early 1970s through more assimilationist theories in the late 1970s and early 1980s to queer theory in the early 1990s.

AN ETHNOGRAPHIC STUDY OF GAY MEN'S RELATIONAL IDEOLOGIES

GIVEN THAT RELATIONAL THEORY tells us that relationships are created and recreated in communication, that relational ideologies reflexively emerge over time, and that gay men may desire relationships based on alternative relational ideologies, I chose to address the following two research questions. What are the relational ideologies that are reflexively constituted in gay men's relationships? What are the significant speech events or conversations that gay men use to constitute their relationships?

To answer these questions, I conducted ethnographic interviews with thirty male couples. These include twenty-two couples in the Minneapolis/St. Paul area, five couples from New York City, and three couples in northern Denmark (one couple consisted of partners from England and Australia). The interviews were conducted in the couple's homes over a period of three years. Each interview lasted from two to three hours on average, with each couple asked to tell the interviewer the story of their relationship from the day that they met up to the day of the interview. Additionally, the couples were asked to describe their typical week, with follow-up questions probing into specific activities in which they engage, the kinds of conversations and discussions they have, and the ways that they resolve difficulties and conflicts. The couples were interviewed together, and all of the couples agreed to participate in follow-up interviews to be conducted in the future, making this the beginning of a long-term project.

The couples were identified for this project in a variety of ways. The twenty-two couples in Minnesota responded to advertisements placed in a gay Minneapolis newspaper. The couples from New York City were identified by an announcement distributed to a gay democratic party e-mail distribution list. Two of the couples in Denmark were known to me personally, and the third was referred to me by a professional university contact.

Only male couples were interviewed for this study for several reasons. First, it is likely that gay men's relational ideologies will differ from those of lesbian women (Seidman 1993). Second, detailed ethnographic interviewing requires a lot of time (three hours per interview). To interview both male and female couples would reduce the amount of time that could be given to either gender, thus providing less data for understanding the couples. Finally, lesbian colleagues suggested to me that lesbian couples would feel more comfortable being interviewed in their homes by a female rather than a male interviewer.

All of the interviews were tape-recorded, and the transcribing process continues. The following is a preliminary analysis based on these interviews.

RESEARCH QUESTION #1: WHAT ARE THE RELATIONAL IDEOLOGIES THAT ARE REFLEXIVELY CONSTITUTED IN GAY MEN'S RELATIONSHIPS?

SEVERAL OBSERVATIONS CAN BE drawn from the interviews regarding relational ideologies. First, although some of the couples in this study were in monogamous relationships, many of the couples interviewed were not monogamous. This was surprising given that some recent literature has indicated that the threat of AIDS has increased the number of monogamous couples (Huston and Schwartz 1995). Second, they were not monogamous in a variety of ways. For example, one couple agreed that one partner could have sex with someone outside of the relationship, but would have to immediately come home and tell the other partner about it. Then, a discussion would occur in which the partner described the sexual encounter. This discussion might evolve into an erotic episode for the couple. Other couples fully expected their partners to have sexual relationships with other people. Their relationships were governed by the belief that "no two people can completely fulfill each other's needs" and therefore a partner should have another sexual partner. This "other" partner becomes a friend of both partners and, in general, is not just an anonymous sexual encounter but is a person who is fully integrated into the relationship as someone who is important in helping one partner meet his sexual needs.

Other forms of nonmonogamy included couples who allowed their partners to have sex with others, but only when they were out of town on a business or vacation trip. One couple told a story about friends of theirs (not interviewed) who were in a relationship for about a year and had decided that they would eventually be nonmonogamous but would be monogamous for the first three or four years until their relationship was solid. Another couple recognized that it was inevitable that their partner would "cheat" on them because "that's the way men are," but they do not want to know or talk about it when it happens.

At first glance, the multiple ways that these couples do nonmonogamy might appear to be just simple logistical arrangements. Upon further analysis, however, I discovered a variety of different attitudes and beliefs about sex and its role in relationships. On the one hand, there is a set of beliefs that views sex with multiple partners as a natural part of gay men's lives. Even if one is partnered, one should be able to have sex with as many men as one chooses, as often as one chooses, and without the stipulation that a relationship occur beyond the sexual episode itself. The sexual episode can be the extent of the relationship one has with another. On another hand, there is a set of beliefs that sees sex as not something necessarily reserved only for one partner but as an important need, one that should be met through people who play an important role in one's life. These beliefs would not view one-time sexual episodes as a means of fulfilling one's sexual needs. Rather, these needs would be met by men who become significant others in addition to the primary relationship and fulfill one's sexual needs over time, thus enlarging the concept of relationship from two to more people. On yet a third hand, there were a number of gay couples who adopted "traditional" beliefs about sex in relationships, such as the belief that sex is reserved only for one's partner. There are undoubtedly other beliefs about sexuality and relationships that are important to gay men, but the point here is that there seem to be significant differences among gay men's relationships.

These differences reflect the gay-positive and sex-positive ideologies identified earlier. The couples interviewed who believe that no two people can fulfill each other's needs seem to be consistent with the gay-positive ideology. The couples were very nurturing and loving with each other, and they saw their partner's sexual activities with others as fulfilling that partner's needs. In addition, the outside sexual relationship is a long-term one that leads to the sexual other becoming an integral part of the relationship. The other couples I have interviewed, who allow each other to have sex with others but expect their partner to tell them about it and discuss it with them, parallel the sex-positive ideology. Their sexual encounters are mostly anonymous and unlimited, however.

The data collected in this study suggest that there are multiple ideologies that govern the relationships of gay men. These ideologies involve varying attitudes about the role of sex in a relationship, the ways in which gay men relate to one another, and the number of people in a relationship. These ideologies also parallel developments within the gay movement itself. Now that we have identified these ideologies, the next step involves identifying how they are constituted in gay men's lives.

RESEARCH QUESTION #2: WHAT ARE SOME OF THE SIGNIFICANT SPEECH EVENTS OR CONVERSATIONS THAT GAY MEN USE TO CONSTITUTE THEIR RELATIONSHIPS?

TWO DIFFERENT CONVERSATIONS STAND out as important in playing a role in constituting some of these men's relationships. In what follows, I will

describe each conversation and demonstrate how it supports particular ideological beliefs about relationships.

The first speech event is the conversation about an external sexual
episode. This will be called "sexual-episode talk." As I have discussed, several
of the couples I interviewed had a rule that when one partner had sex with
someone outside of the relationship, they must tell their partner about it as
soon as they had an opportunity. The other partner would ask questions such
as "Where did you meet him?," "What did he look like?," and "What did you
do?" This might then lead to a sexual episode between the partners as they
discuss and describe the sexual act engaged in outside the relationship.

I believe this sexual-episode talk plays an important role in constituting and
reconstituting a relationship based upon an ideology that views promiscuous
sex as an important part of gay identity—the sex-positive ideology. It prevents
the announcement of an outside-sexual episode from being perceived as a
threat to the relationship and possibly reinforces the idea that promiscuous sex
is appropriate and exciting behavior in which gay men should engage.

Relational theory tells us that communication and conversations play a
role in the negotiation of our relationships with others. Several theories of
meaning will help us understand how this happens in more detail. Given
that the announcement "I have had sex with someone (else)" is an utterance
that begins the conversation under discussion, it is important to consider
how the meaning of this utterance is managed.

Several theorists see meaning as lying primarily in the utterance itself
(Austin 1965; Searle 1969; Taylor and Cameron 1987). They believe that each
utterance can be considered an act separate from other acts in conversation,
and that one can attribute meaning to the utterance/act itself. Other theorists (such as Wittgenstein 1958 and Xi 1991) believe that utterances only
have meaning within a sequence of utterances. The meaning for the utterance emerges over a sequence of utterances and only in relation to those
utterances. Earlier the utterance "open the window" was described. The first
group of theorists would see this utterance as a command in and of itself.
The second group of theorists would say that whether or not this utterance
is a command depends not only on the way it is uttered but also on the way
it is responded to.

We can examine the utterance "I had sex with someone" in the same
way. One could argue that the meaning of this utterance lies within the
utterance itself. It could be interpreted as a threat to one's relationship—a
violation of a vow of monogamy. But, alternatively, one could also argue
that the meaning for that utterance emerges in the utterances that follow it.

I believe this is what is occurring in sexual-episode talk. Rather than perceiving the meaning to lie within the utterance, the couples I interviewed use the conversation about the sexual episode to construct a meaning that is consistent with their ideologies about the role of sex in a relationship and the appropriateness of multiple sexual partners for gay men. Thus, talking about a sexual encounter that one's partner has had with another allows the couple both to create a meaning that is compatible with their ideology and to resist perceiving the utterance as a threat.

One couple that I interviewed said that shortly after they first met they had to deal with the question of external-sexual episodes because of the way that they had met. They met in a public bathroom and had anonymous sex during a break from work. Since they had met in an anonymous encounter, they both said it was probably likely that they would continue to have such encounters so they had to decide what to do about it. This discussion led to the rule to tell the other about such episodes.

The conversation in which they developed this rule was clearly not a mundane conversation. It was a nonroutine discussion about the nature and future of the relationship. But over time, as such conversations occurred shortly after such a sexual episode, they became mundane and routine. By this I mean that the conversation was not so much about "what might this do to our relationship" but was, rather, a discussion of what occurred and how exciting it was. Once this conversation becomes mundane or routine, then the conversation is one of the ways that the couple (re)produces the ideology for their relationship. In other words, the initial discussion and creation of the rule was an attempt by the couple to create a particular type of ideology and the appropriate behaviors to correspond with it. The continuing mundane and routine conversation about such external-sexual episodes is a way to (re)produce that ideology over time.

This is particularly important given that these couples live in a culture that does not support their relationships. The general population in the United States views nonmonogamy as inappropriate, and even within the gay-male culture, there are those who are critical of promiscuity and are advocating for monogamy (Rotello 1997; Signorile 1997). Even the popular nationally released gay movie *Love! Valor! Compassion!* implicitly promotes monogamy and the goal of a lifetime partner. In the 1997 movie the characters Bobby and Gregory are unable to survive Bobby's infidelity.

Maintaining an alternative ideological configuration of a relationship requires continuous maintenance. Conversation is one practice that allows the couple to reproduce their alternative relationship continuously.

The second example of a speech event that seems to be relevant to relationship ideologies is called "comparison shopping." Comparison shopping is when two people who are in a relationship discuss the attributes of others that they find attractive. For example, one of two coupled–gay men who are standing at a bus stop might say to his partner, "Which of those three guys over there do you find the most attractive?" or, "What do you think of him?" This type of conversation was quite common among the men I have interviewed, but it didn't seem significant to me until one couple said they specifically did not engage in such conversation because it would "hurt" their partner. This statement made me begin to think about the nature of this conversation and what role it might play in relationships, particularly because the couple who did not engage in this conversation is constructing a monogamous relationship in which they believe sexuality is only appropriate within a committed relationship. They also suspect, however, that some day their partner might cheat on them because "that's the way men are." The couples who are nonmonogamous engage in this conversation regularly, and it appears to be a playful and fun conversation for them.

I suggest that "comparison shopping" is a speech event that supports beliefs that sexuality is fun, playful, and not necessarily reserved for the person with whom one is in a committed relationship. Most of the couples who were in nonmonogamous relationships reported engaging in and enjoying such conversation. Thus, comparison shopping may support several different ideologies that do not require monogamy.

This preliminary analysis suggests that ethnographic research on male couples is a rich and valuable endeavor. By listening to male couples talk about their relationships, one can learn about the various relational ideologies that are reflexively produced and reproduced over time in their conversation. The conversations identified here (sexual-episode talk and comparison shopping) appear to play a role in constituting relational ideologies similar to the gay-positive and sex-positive ideologies. Additionally, the lack of these conversations may correlate to the construction of a traditional monogamous ideology. Further analysis of the data will confirm and further elaborate on these processes.

More research needs to be done, however. If we are to provide gay men with relationship advice, we need to fully understand the intricate ways that relational ideologies are constituted in talk. Once this process is more fully understood, our advice will be about showing gay men how to produce the types of relationships they desire rather than telling them which relationships they should produce.

REFERENCES

A Gay Male Group. 1972/1992. "Notes on Gay Male Consciousness-raising." In K. Jay and A. Young, eds., *Out of the Closets: Voices of Gay Liberation*, pp. 293–300. New York: New York University Press.

Austin, John L. 1965. *How to Do Things with Words*. New York: Oxford University Press.

Bruess, C. J. S. and J. C. Pearson. 1997. "Interpersonal Rituals in Marriage and Adult Friendship." *Communication Monographs* 64: 25–46.

Fernandez, C. 1991. "Undocumented Aliens in the Queer Nation: Reflections on Race and Ethnicity in the Lesbian and Gay Movement." *Democratic Left* (May/June): 9.

Goldsmith, D. J. and L. A. Baxter. 1996. "Constituting Relationships in Talk: A Taxonomy of Speech Events in Social and Personal Relationships." *Human Communication Research* 23: 87–114.

Huston, M. and P. Schwartz. 1995. The Relationships of Lesbians and Gay Men. In Julia T. Wood and Steve Duck, eds., *Under-Studied Relationships: Off the Beaten Track*, pp. 89–121. Thousand Oaks, Cal.: Sage.

Knoebel, J. 1972/1992. "Somewhere in the Right Direction: Testimony of My Experience in a Gay Male Living Collective." In Karla Jay and Allen Young, eds., *Out of the Closets: Voices of Gay Liberation*, pp. 301–14. New York: New York University Press.

McWhirter, David P. and Andrew M. Mattison. 1984. *The Male Couple: How Relationships Develop*. Englewood Cliffs, N.J.: Prentice-Hall.

McWhirter, David and Andrew Mattison. 1988. "Stages in the Development of Gay Relationships." In De Cecco, ed., *Gay Relationships*, pp. 161–67. New York: Haworth.

Montgomery, B. 1992. "Communication as the Interface between Couples and Culture." In S. Deetz, ed., *Communication Yearbook* 15, pp 475–507. Newbury Park, Cal.: Sage.

Painter, D. 1994. "Reflections on Interpersonal Communication in Gay and Lesbian Relationships." In R. J. Ringer, ed., *Queer Words Queer Images: Communication and the Construction of Homosexuality*, pp. 278–88. New York: New York University Press.

Parks, M. 1995. "Ideology in Interpersonal Communication: Beyond the Couches, Talk Shows, and Bunkers." In B. Burleson, ed., *Communication Yearbook* 18, pp. 480–97. Newbury Park, Cal.: Sage.

Rotello, Gabriel. 1997. *Sexual Ecology: AIDS and the Destiny of Gay Men*. New York: Dutton.

Searle, J. 1969. *Speech Acts: An Essay in the Philosophy of Mind.* New York: Cambridge University Press.

Seidman, Steven. 1993. "Identity Politics in a 'Postmodern' Gay Culture: Some Historical and Conceptual Notes." In Michael Warner, ed., *Fear of a Queer Planet: Queer Politics and Social Theory*, pp. 105–42. Minneapolis: University of Minnesota Press.

Sennett, Richard. 1977. *The Fall of Public Man.* New York: Vintage.

Signorile, Michelangelo. 1997. *Life Outside: The Signorile Report on Gay Men—Sex, Drugs, Muscles, and the Passages of Life.* New York: HarperCollins.

Taylor, Talbot J. and Deborah Cameron. 1987. *Analyzing Conversation: Rules and Units in the Structure of Talk.* New York: Pergamon.

Warner, Michael. 1993. "Introduction." In Michael Warner, ed., *Fear of a Queer Planet: Queer Politics and Social Theory*, pp. vii–xxxi. Minneapolis: University of Minnesota Press.

Wittgenstein, Ludwig. 1958. *Philosophical Investigations.* Trans. G. E. M. Anscombe. Oxford: Basil Blackwell.

Wittman, C. 1992. A Gay Manifesto. In Karla Jay and Allen Young, eds., *Out of the Closets: Voices of Gay Liberation*, pp. 330–41. New York: New York University Press.

Xi, C. 1991. "Communication in China: A Case Study of Chinese Collectivist and Self-Interest Talk in Social Action from the Coordinated Management of Meaning (CMM) Perspective." Ph.D. diss., University of Massachusetts, Amherst.

10

Communication in "Asian American" Families with Queer Members: A Relational Dialectics Perspective

Gust A. Yep, Karen E. Lovaas, and Philip C. Ho

Being gay is like being born with a compass that is orientated east toward the holy sun of a fiery desire. In the early years, you explore the world with this compass, and it is quite wonderful. You realize soon enough that you walk in a world where most people are going in a different direction. So you try using the maps that family, religion, and culture have given you. But the maps are written with a different compass orientation, and your trip, far from getting better, gets much worse. Because you trust those who gave you the maps, you blame yourself for getting lost. Looking for the safe pasture promised by the maps, you eventually find yourself looking down a cliff edge, wishing you were dead.

—L. L. Lim, 1977

Many of us experience the worlds of Asian America and gay America as separate places—emotionally, physically, intellectually. We sustain the separation of these worlds with our folk knowledge about the family-centeredness and supra-homophobic beliefs of ethnic communities. Moreover, it is not just that these communities know so little of one another, but, we frequently take great care to keep those worlds distant from each other.

—Dana Y. Takagi, 1996

Communication between these separate and "distant" worlds is intricate and complex. Such communication is often filled with personal and relational challenges and difficulties as well as radical possibilities and transformative practices. More simply put, communication in "Asian American"[1] family systems with queer[2] members is characterized by ongoing dialectical tensions of autonomy and connection, secrecy and openness, and certainty and unpredictability. The purpose of this chapter is to examine the relational dialectics in the communicative practices of queer "Asian Americans" with their family systems. To accomplish this, we first discuss the complexity of "Asian American" culture and explore some of the intersections between race, class, gender, and sexuality in our discussions of queer "Asian American" experiences, then introduce the relational dialectics perspective and examine these dialectics in some of the personal narratives of queer "Asian Americans" communicating with their families, and conclude with a discussion of some of the implications of this perspective for the examination of culture.

QUEER IN "ASIAN AMERICA"[3]

ACCORDING TO LISA LOWE (1996), "Asian American" culture is characterized by heterogeneity, hybridity, and multiplicity. By heterogeneity, she refers to differences and differential power relationships under the singular category labeled "Asian American"; for example, "Asian Americans" come from different national origins, generational relation to immigration exclusionary laws, social class backgrounds, gender, and sexual orientation. By hybridity, Lowe refers to the process through which "Asian Americans" survive and invent different cultural alternatives within relationships of unequal power and domination. By multiplicity, Lowe refers to the ways in which "Asian Americans" are simultaneously affected by capitalism, patriarchal power, racial hegemony, and heterosexist ideology.

When asked about whether there is a general "Asian American point of view," Jessica Hagedorn, a renowned Filipina writer and performance artist, noted, "I'm not so sure. Well, perhaps food. Love of food, and a certain sensibility regarding beauty. And I do think our cultures are steeped in traditions of grace and hospitality—we share that with other Asian Americans" (1994:179). In other words, there is no singular "Asian American" perspective.

The diversity of "Asian American" voices and experiences is characterized by interplay and collision between race, class, gender, and sexuality (Aguilar-San Juan 1994; Chin 1997; Eng and Hom 1998; hooks 1990; Jordan and Weedon 1995; Leong 1996; Lowe 1996; Manalansan 1996; Reyes and Yep 1997; Sacks 1999; Stacey 1999; Zack 1998). To illustrate this, let's consider an example. Eng and Hom recall the following situation:

Once, a mutual friend of ours—a Korean American dyke—was washing her hands in a women's restroom when she overheard a conversation behind her. "What's *he* doing here?" one white woman asked another. "Oh, whatever, he probably doesn't read English," her companion replied. (emphasis in the original) (1988:1)

In this scenario, race, gender, and sexuality are clearly intersecting in complex ways. Eng and Hom explain:

> In this compounded misreading of both sexual and racial difference—in this restroom as a public site where dominant images of emasculated Asian American men and hyperheterosexualized Asian American women collide—the Asian American lesbian disappears. In [the previous scenario] it is precisely mainstream stereotypes of an effeminized Asian American male (homo)sexuality that affect the ways in which the Asian American lesbian goes unseen and unrecognized. (1998:1)

In addition, the scenario also illustrates the common perception that "Asian Americans" are "perpetual foreigners" (Nakayama 1997:15) in the U.S., as exemplified by the white woman's automatic assumption that the Korean American does not speak English.

Let's consider another example that one of us encountered while having dinner at a popular restaurant in the San Francisco Castro[4] neighborhood. A young, attractive, well-dressed, and highly limerent[5] gay male couple was seated at an adjacent table. One was "Asian American" and the other Euroamerican. When the "Asian American" finished taking a call on his cellular phone (it sounded as though he was a high-level executive), the two started a conversation. The Euroamerican recounted:

> I talked to my mother on the phone today and I told her about us. She asked me about you . . . and I told her that you are Eurasian and she said, "What? What does that mean?" I explained to her that you were Japanese and Italian but American . . . very American . . . with that strong Italian part of you. I also told her that you have a very good job.

They smiled into each other's eyes seemingly happy with mother's approval. The server came by to explain the "specials of the day," sustaining steady eye contact with the Euroamerican as if he were the only customer at the table. The server returned several times and in each instance he inquired about their meal through the Euroamerican without ever directing his gaze and speech to the "Asian American" partner. In this intricate interplay of race, class, gender, and sexuality, the "Asian American" male becomes invisible. His Japaneseness is erased as he and his partner perpetuate the image that being Japanese is un-American. This is cocreated by his partner's overt Euro-centrism ("very American . . . with that strong Italian part of you") and his own consensual silence. The Euroamerican also included a social-class marker (his partner has a very good job) in the conversation with his mother, almost as an attempt to equalize the status of his partner (given that being Eurasian was perceived as "less than"). Likewise, the interaction with the restaurant server makes the "Asian American" virtually and symbolically invisible (Cissna and Sieburg 1986). One might ask, how is this invisibility and disconfirmation played out through the interlocking axes of race, class, gender, and sexuality? We now turn to some of the features associated with these intersections in the context of identity negotiations.

Identities are political, fluid, nonsummative, and paradoxical (Yep 1998; Yep, Lovaas, and Pagonis in press). As such, race, class, gender, and sexuality are not fixed, coherent, or holistic identity categories. These categories are not additive (hooks 1990; Minh-ha 1989; Yep 1998) as Takagi (1996) reminds us: "marginalization is not as much about the quantities of experiences as it is about *qualities* of experience" (22–23). (emphasis ours) Although these categories are socially constructed (Fuss 1989), they vary in "degrees of vis-ibility"; race is "inscribed in the body,"[6] gender and sexuality are arguably both embodied and performed (Butler 1990; Fuss 1991), and class is enacted (Hunter and Manzón-Santos 1997). In addition, race, class, gender, and sex-uality have different transnational and national (e.g., Brah 1996; Escoffier 1998; Hsu 1981; Katz 1992; Lee 1998; Lowe 1996; Omatsu 1994; Shah 1993; Sinfield 1998; Takaki 1989) as well as local (Chang 1994; Miao 1998; Wat and Shum 1998; Yu 1994) histories that are at times separate and distinct, and in other instances deeply interconnected. For example, queer history focuses on ideologies, politics, and the rhetoric of desire and sexual identity while "Asian American" history emphasizes racist and exclusionary discourses and oppressions (Takagi 1996); on the other hand, however, "class experience in the United States is tied to race and racism in an unhealthy and seemingly inseparable union" (Raffo 1997:5).

Identities and marginalities based on race, class, gender, and sexuality do not necessarily engage in potentially fruitful exchanges; as Takagi (1996) notes, "marginalization is no guarantee for dialogue" (30). For example, Hom (1996), in her interviews with "Asian American" parents and their queer children, reports the reaction of Katherine Tanaka, a Japanese American mother, to learning that her daughter is a lesbian: "I told her we would have to move away from this house. I felt strongly neighbors and friends in the community would not want to associate with us if they knew we had a child who had chosen [sic] to be homosexual" (44). In this example, we can clearly see that marginalization is not necessarily conducive to dialogue: in Tanaka's view, marginalization on the basis of race and possibly class and gender does not lead to dialogue and support for individuals marginalized in terms of sexuality. In other words, the marginalization and oppression that many "Asian Americans" experience based on their race, class, and gender do not always create a space for dialogue with queer "Asian Americans" whose experience might be heightened by intersections between sexuality and the previously mentioned identity markers.

It is our hope in this essay to start engaging these separate yet interconnected spheres in dialogue. To accomplish this, we use personal narratives of queer "Asian Americans" communicating with their family systems. Personal narratives allow us to understand personal experiences and challenges from the perspective of the individual, first, to minimize the discursive dangers of "speaking for" (Alcoff 1995), like those of researchers speaking and writing on behalf of research participants, and second, we hope to diminish the problems of "speaking as" (Fung 1995), like those distant and more general accounts of individuals attempting to represent *the* "queer 'Asian American' experience." In addition, personal narratives of one's experience in a culture honor the individual's history and sociopolitical standpoint and avoid marginalization and objectification so that, as Lee and associates note, "they each sing their songs and tell their stories to make a difference" (1995:285). In order to create a polyphony of voices, we have selected stories of "Asian Americans" from diverse backgrounds and different intersections of race, class, gender, and sexuality. What follows is a collection of voices of recently immigrated as well as U.S.-born "Asian Americans," gay, lesbian, bisexual, and transgender from various Asian cultures (e.g., Chinese, Filipino, Hawaiian, Japanese, Korean, and Vietnamese), social classes, and political ideologies. We now turn to the relational dialectics perspective as a framework where these dialogic exchanges can occur.

THE RELATIONAL DIALECTICS PERSPECTIVE

INFLUENCED BY THE WRITINGS of Russian thinker Mikhail Bakhtin (1981, 1984, 1986), one of the leading intellectuals of the twentieth century,

Baxter and Montgomery (1996) proposed a relational dialectics perspective for the study of communication and human relationships. They describe relational dialectics as

> a way of understanding social interaction that is marked by a healthy dose of irony, a sense that things are both what they seem to be and something else as well. Irony entertains both belief and doubt, both hope and despair, both seriousness and play. . . . Creativity is another hallmark. Relational dialectics demands that we reach beyond our ready-made vocabularies of generalized central tendencies to appreciate the uniqueness of each communicative moment. Inclusiveness is key as well. Our notion of relational dialectics respects different meaning systems, is attuned to their distinct voices, and so, represents a multivocal social reality. Last, we wish to stress the sense of fluidity and unfinalizability that characterizes our relational dialectics approach. All is becoming, but never becomes. (1998:156)

Central to this perspective is Bakhtin's notion of dialogue. It is the cement of social life. Dialogue is both real, such as a face-to-face interpersonal exchange (Baxter and Montgomery 1996, 1998), and metaphorical, such as "culture as dialogue" (Bell 1998:49). Speaking and exchange are fundamental ingredients of dialogue (Holquist 1990), in which fission (separate and distinct voices in an exchange) and fusion (unity through conversation) occur simultaneously. This ongoing interplay between similarity and difference occurs in social life in general and in interpersonal communication in particular.

The relational dialectics perspective has been used to examine communication in a variety of relational types and contexts in recent years. For example, the dialectics approach has been applied to the study of romantic relationships (e.g., Baxter 1990; Brown, Werner, and Altman 1998), friendships (e.g., Rawlins 1992, 1998), family and other social relationships (e.g., Adelman and Frey 1997; Cissna, Cox, and Bochner 1990), and community life (e.g., Adelman and Frey, 1994, 1997). It has also been used to examine a wide array of social and cultural phenomena ranging from stigma disclosure (e.g., Dindia 1998) to cultural artifacts (e.g., Gauvain, Altman, and Fahim 1983).

Communication, according to the relational dialectics perspective, comprises the entire spectrum of human actions, including verbal and nonverbal, intentional and unintentional, genuine and contrived messages that can be potentially and meaningfully interpreted by individuals in social interaction (Montgomery and Baxter 1998). Baxter and Montgomery (1996) further maintain that this view of communication is nonteleological (no ideal goals or ultimate endings) and nonhomeostatic (no final states of balance and equilibrium). They emphatically remind us that "there is only an indeterminate flow, full of unforeseeable potential that is realized in interaction" (Montgomery and Baxter 1998:179). With this in mind, let's now turn to the core concepts of this perspective and examine how they are manifested in interactions within "Asian American" families with queer members.

According to Baxter and Montgomery (1996, 1998), there are four core concepts associated with the relational dialectics perspective. These are totality, change, praxis, and contradiction. Totality acknowledges that all communication between relational partners occurs within social, spatial, and temporal contexts in a web of interdependent, multidirectional relationships. Social dialogues form identities, selves, communities, cultures, and societies and arise from them; that is, both the producers and the products arise dialogically.

Contradiction is commonly viewed as a clash between two opposite phenomena that mutually invalidate each other definitionally, logically, or functionally. This binary, either/or notion makes it fundamentally impossible to reconcile the coexistence of two opposing elements. In the dialogic view, contradiction refers to the complex unity that comprises both centripetal and centrifugal forces. Simply put, dialectical opposites are interdependent and the active interplay between opposites—such as love-anger, love-disappointment, love-shame, and so forth—creates an ongoing, contingent, fluid, and complex relational system that drives change. For example, over time, Jane Nakatani, a Japanese American woman, accepted the fact that she had two gay sons, Glen and Guy, whom she loved, regardless of their sexuality. This realization did not come without struggles. Jane recalls the restless conflicting thoughts within her when she learned about Guy's homosexuality after she had previously discovered that Glen was gay:

> Of course I still loved Guy. But it was as if that feeling was being crowded by so many others—anger, disappointment, confusion, fear, and, worst of all, shame. I couldn't help but think of how others would react. Only a few people in my family knew or suspected the truth about Glen, and even that bothered me. I couldn't imagine telling anyone about Guy. First of all, who would believe it? I'm not sure I believed it, certainly not in those first bitter hours. . . . I watched my husband, desperate to convince our son of our love for him, and I wanted him to be quiet. How

could I, his own mother, claim to love him and not accept him? I remember thinking then that this had to be the worst day of my life.

(Fumia 1997:70)

In this excerpt, we see that the centripetal forces of "love" and "family connection" and the centrifugal forces of "anger" and "shame" exist concurrently, forming a complex unity of contradictions.

In relational dialectics, change, driven by contradictory phenomena, is multidirectional, spiraling, qualitative, and quantitative rather than an unidirectional, linear progress toward shared meanings and balanced homeostatic solutions. Change undertakes "a rightful and significant meaning in the moment" (Montgomery and Baxter 1998:161). It occurs as the dialectical interplay of opposites urges relational partners to modify their actions in response to ongoing, omnipresent dialectical contradictions. Sharmeen Islam, a South Asian American lesbian, discusses how, after she came out to her siblings, this interplay was evident:

> My siblings were initially disappointed . . . but in the last few years they have come a long way. Now they think it would be wonderful if I had a child and raised it with my lover, even though they know I have no desire to have one. . . . [My sister] and my brother seem to have a need to see me in some familiar context. What would be more familiar than a South Asian woman in the role of a mother? (1993:284)

Islam's siblings' first responses did not remain static, as if their relationship with Sharmeen had reached an ultimate, finalized, stable condition. As they moved on to accept Sharmeen's sexuality, "motherhood" became another source of contradiction that would trigger unpredictability and disorder, driving further relational change.

Bakhtin's concept of dialectical praxis, the fourth core concept, considers how all interactions between relationship partners are interwoven with the echoes of distant utterances of the past, responses to what has just been spoken, expected responses to current utterances, as well as a sense of being in dialogue with a generalized other. Within this tapestry, relationship partners make ongoing choices that form new realities; these choices are at once creative and representative of recurring patterns. The creative choices made by relational partners are more likely to have unforeseen results, produce learning, and open new possibilities. Examples of common praxical patterns follow.

When Bryan, a Vietnamese American female-to-male (FTM) transgender, told one of his sisters he "felt this way," her response to him demonstrated a *denial* of the dialectic of openness and closedness: "She said she couldn't see me as a male, because it was against her religion" (Khan, Bryan, and Rhode 1996:239). Her denial, disavowing the possibility of openness, utilized a religious justification for her closedness to accepting him. Alex Chee describes the forbidding consequences of expressing one's gayness in some Korean families, an extreme example of denial: "When you are openly gay in Korea, your family declares you dead and holds a funeral for you. The family book lists you as deceased. Prayers are said for you once a year at the family shrine and incense is burned for your ghost" (1996:317).

Chinese American Susan Chen and her family experienced a long period of *disorientation* in dealing with her lesbianism. Disorientation refers to viewing contradictions as unavoidable, unalterable, and negative. Chen describes her response to learning that she, her mother, and her father were about to have another "meeting":

> I think, "Oh, no, I really, really dread these confrontations. I don't have enough strength to go through with this." This meeting has come as a result of recent months of friction between us over issues such as my going to too many "useless" meetings, receiving what they perceive as too many phone calls (from the wrong people) and, at the center of all the "problems," my homosexuality. (1994:79)

Over time, as Chen found, this disorientation can lead to feelings of pessimism and demoralization.

Conversely, *reaffirmation* accepts contradictions as inevitable but regards them as positive and stimulating rather than negative. Keola, a young Hawaiian man whose mother is a lesbian, talks about how growing up in his family has enhanced his life: "I've met many very nice, supportive people who have helped me grow up to be an understanding, nondiscriminatory person, and have shown me that love comes in many different ways and means" (Drucker 1998:136).

Finally, Kaushala Bannerji and her family provide an example of *integration*, a full responding to opposing dialectic forces:

> I was fortunate that my immediate family was able to come to terms with my lesbianism. . . . Living at home as a South Asian lesbian daughter has

been a complex and sometimes contradictory process for both myself and my parents. Yet it is rewarding and moving to see my parents at a Lesbian and Gay Pride Day. (1993:62)

The act of attending a public gathering affirming Bannerji's sexual orientation symbolizes the family's ability to integrate this aspect of her identity into their relationship.

In applying a relational dialectics perspective to relationships in "Asian American" families with queer members, we address three primary issues of closeness (autonomy/connection), openness (secrecy/openness), and certainty (certainty/unpredictability) (Baxter and Montgomery 1996, 1998). Relational closeness is based on connectedness and separateness, paired concepts only comprehensible in relation to each other. As it is impossible for us to be seen as entirely separate from one another, it is equally impossible for us to commingle in a unitary consciousness. A closely related meaning is interdependence, referring to individuals' dependency not on each other but on their relationship. It is the relational partners' joint construction of connectedness and separateness, a construction that changes in dialogue, over time in a single relationship, and over the life cycle.

In the narratives we have encountered, queer "Asian Americans" construct and deal with this dialectic in their familial relationships in a variety of ways. Bryan, the Vietnamese American FTM, comes from a large family including eight siblings. He describes family members as hoping that he "would grow out of" his feelings (Khan, Bryan, and Rhode 1998:239). In considering the potential need to be at a distance from his family after he "changes over," Bryan stresses the centrifugal force of separateness:

What's important to me is how my family will view me after my change. I told them if that would bother them, I would move. I don't want to be away from my family, but I'm willing to leave my family behind and move to another state for their peace of mind. It wasn't their fault I was born this way, so they shouldn't have to deal with it. (239)

Interestingly, Bryan's motivation for moving also affirms his connection to and affection for his family.

Though her Chinese American family emphasizes its interdependency, Tze-Hei Yong's mother "disowned" her for a time when Tze-Hei came out as a lesbian. Her father's skills as a "peacemaker" provided balance, and as Tze-Hei explains, "for this Asian family, the integrity of the family unit is very important." Thus, "by the next summer, my mom was inviting me to lunches with the family again. In fact, a few years ago my parents (and most of my family) met my second lover, Ann, and my mom even took a liking to her" (1994:10). The family dialogue continued; if Tze-Hei's different sexuality is accepted, preserving their connections, her choice of a lover is still problematic:

> For total acceptance by my family, though, I think Ann would have had to learn Cantonese. Plus, of course, she'd have to somehow metamorphose into a Chinese person. They might accept that she and I are lovers, but that still doesn't stop my mom from making snide comments in Cantonese (when we're all, including Ann, sitting at the dinner table) about "that white one." (10)

For her mother, then, Tze-Hei's sexuality over time became less of a tension in their relationship than the race of Tze-Hei's partner.

In the communication literature, openness is typically presented as superior to its dialectical partner, closedness. This literature also tends to concentrate more on self-disclosure or, degrees of openness and closedness in communicating personal information *with* a relational partner than on openness and closedness *to* receiving information communicated by a partner (Baxter and Montgomery 1996). Attempts to balance a desire to be open with family with a recognition of ways or areas in which they may be closed to receiving information is a frequent theme in the narratives of queer "Asian Americans." Dredge Kang's comments exemplify this negotiation in his Korean American family: "I've thought a great deal about what I am willing to share with others. I want to tell the truth, yet I also want to be respectful of what I perceive to be my parents' wishes. . . . I hope they try to understand my perspective as much as I try to understand theirs" (1996:82).

The dialectics of openness/closedness with and openness/closedness to appear in three multivocal forms: the said and the unsaid, free talk and constrained talk, and inner speech and outer speech (Baxter and Montgomery 1996). The said refers to verbalized words or text, while the unsaid encompasses the contextual meaning of an utterance. Darlena Bird Jimenes, a self-described "multiethnic polyracial" lesbian, offers an example of the latter in reading between the lines of her family interactions:

> In my family, the issue of sexuality was never directly addressed, nor was I ever formally confronted with a "Well, are you or aren't you?" It was

what I termed an unspoken knowledge around the house. . . . But somehow, deep down I knew that there were questions that weren't being asked about marriage, children, etc. (1994:135)

Second is the dialectic of free talk and constrained talk, the interplay of flexible and creative utterances with situationally limited or determined utterances. In noting the growing number of family memoirs of Asian Americans, Justin Chin (1999) suggests that the choice of memoir combines freedom to express one's experience with "a fear of claiming authority":

We are more comfortable writing biographically because then, any challenges made can be dismissed with "Ah! Who should know me and my family better than myself!" But Asians writing about their families is a rather subversive act as well, since we are so often taught to respect the family and never to speak of the family to strangers. (175–76)

The third form is inner speech, an individual's internal dialogue, and outer speech, that which is vocalized. Inner speech includes the remembered and the anticipated, both with a specific other and with a generalized other. Prominent in inner speech are words from previous interactions that deeply registered and appear as influential voices in our internal dialogues as we consider our next words or actions. Chin's previous reference to cultural teachings about how to treat the family are an example of such an enduring voice. The inner speech of each partner in a relationship resonates with the partners' past conversations, differing from each other's as each provides his or her idiosyncratic weighting of earlier messages. What is vocalized, the outer speech, represents the continual dance between the inner and the outer as they "play against one another, perpetually constructing one another's voices" (Baxter and Montgomery 1996:149).

Lastly, the dialectical interplay of certainty and uncertainty marks a *both-and* state; that is, the quality of stability and predictability and the state of fluidity and indetermination concurrently exist in personal relationships (Baxter and Montgomery 1996). The mutual knowledge of one another (certainty or "the given") sets up a seemingly secure, stable, and predictable environment. However, relationships are inherently discontinuous phenomena since relational partners are in and out of each other's presence; the gaps in time and space between one relational encounter and the next ultimately lead to uncertainty characterized by unpredictability, novelty, and/or disorder. Further, certainty and uncertainty are simultaneously experienced by both parties. Neither observes their consistency and predictability from an objective standpoint; rather, they are subjects engaged in dialogue constructing the degree of certainty and uncertainty. In the constant negotiation of their relational space between the centripetal force of mutual knowledge and the centrifugal force of change, they are interdependent and not isolated from each other's influence.

After Maria is caught in bed with a woman, interactions in her South Asian American family illustrate the interplay of certainty and uncertainty:

> Mom and Dad talked to me all night. My mother insisted that I confess to a priest. She and my father alternated in taking me to church, where I confessed my "sin" to an old priest who had no idea what I was talking about. It was a very traumatic time for all of us. (1993:208)

In order to have greater control of Maria's behaviors and whereabouts, Maria's father decided to drop her off at school and pick her up after class, but Maria still managed to skip classes to see other women. Both Maria and her parents jointly participated in the creation of their certainty-uncertainty interaction; her parents took action to negate her sexuality and Maria appeared to comply but continued her lesbian affairs. In response to family tensions, Maria made a decision that led to unforeseen outcomes:

> I joined the army. Not only would it get me out of the house, it would also pay me and teach me something. My parents liked the idea, figuring that the discipline would make me a woman. Little did they know that the army was full of dykes, and there I really came out. (1993:208)

Is there a cultural pattern of stronger centripetal pulls toward closeness, openness, and certainty in "Asian American" families in comparison to other families? Simon Suh refers to such a stereotype in reflecting on his experience as a Korean American:

> This is really generalizing, but everyone says Asian families tend to be very close-knit. Everyone knows what everyone else is doing. . . . So of course everyone watches what they do. I don't know whether I believe that, but I do somehow think that Asian people do have a harder time coming out, both to themselves and to others. (Weston 1991:58)

Consistent with a Bakhtinian perspective, we have neither assumed nor discovered any clear pattern of how relational dialectics play out in "Asian American" families with queer members, beyond noting that the narratives we consulted refer to powerful intersections of sexuality with familial and cultural identities. Three further examples follow. When Leng Leroy Lim was asked to describe his sexual identity, he said that "for Chinese gay men and lesbians, familial and hence ethnic identity may be perceived to be much stronger and more useful than reductionist sexual categorization" (Sadownick 1996:16). When Rafael Chang came out to his parents, he was surprised at the strength of their distress. In a letter from them, Rafael learned that he would not be welcome again in the family unless he was "willing to change [his] mind around being gay" (Andrews 1994).[7] Rafael disowned being Chinese for a while, "because being Chinese meant that I would have a family, or a set of parents to take care of me" (Andrews 1994). Dennis[8] suggests that in a white-dominated society, embracing one's ethnicity and sexuality is analogous, for the queer individual and the family:

> In terms of coming out for gay Asians, I think that one can come out when one can come out as an Asian. And I think that if Asian parents accept themselves as having yellow faces, they can truly accept their children as having different inclinations. (Adair and Adair 1978:190)

IMPLICATIONS FOR THE STUDY OF CULTURE

AS WE HAVE SEEN, communication in "Asian American" family systems with queer members is perplexing and complex. With an emphasis on interactive opposition, multiplicity of viewpoints, dialogism, and multivocality, the relational dialectics perspective provides a framework for understanding "the messier, less logical, and more inconsistent unfolding practices of the moment" (Baxter and Montgomery 1996:46) that are characteristic of family interactions. In this section, we examine some of the implications of this perspective for understanding culture.

Culture is a difficult construct. From a Bakhtinian perspective, Bell (1998) argues that culture can be viewed as dialogue. He further elaborates: "Culture, in this view, is the conversations we have and which we expect to have with various people in various places at various times; it is also the conversations we have which we did not expect with these various people in these various places at these various times (52)."

This definition focuses on the dialogic, creative, and improvisational features of culture. From this perspective, culture is characterized by totality, contradiction, change, and praxis. First, culture operates in both temporal and spatial contexts and individual members interact with each other from their own historical, geographical, and social locations and identifications. Second, culture is full of contradictions. In our previous analysis, we focused on multivocal contradictions—for example, a number of the narratives indicate a simultaneous desire of queer members to be both close to and apart from other individuals in their family systems. Third, culture is emergent and cultural change is more like a spiral than a straight line. Family members go in and out of the closet in more or less predictable patterns. Finally, culture constrains its members while individuals in the culture simultaneously create the conditions for the future of the culture. For example, Dredge Kang recalls the process of coming out to his mother, a Korean woman: "I told her [that] I was gay . . . she asked me how long I had been impotent. I tried to explain that my problem wasn't impotence, but that I wasn't attracted to women. But she assumed, because I told her I was gay, that I was impotent" (1996:87). In this case, cultural views of homosexuality restricted the mother's behavior but at the same time Dredge's open discussion of his sexuality was creating conditions for change as his mother now appears to be more accepting of his affectional orientation.

Through these locations and identifications, we have examined personal narratives of individuals interacting with their family members to understand the relational dialectics at the nexus of the interplay and collision of race, class, gender, and sexuality. Such stories give voice to personal cultural experiences and allow the individual to reflect on the omnipresent dialectical tensions of social existence. Capturing this sentiment, Justin Chin (1999) writes:

> I still think I don't really know what community is, where I fit in, and where I fall out. And in the midst of this queer diaspora, this Asian diaspora, an unapologetically queer Chinese-Malaysian tattooed punkish guy is daily negotiating the spaces between disclosure and safety. (71)

We hope that these stories and narratives of queer "Asian Americans" add to the ongoing, evolving, changing, and unfinalizable dialogue characteristic of their family and community life and help reorient the cultural and family maps so that we can create a compass that honors "Asian American" sexual diversity.

NOTES

1. The term "Asian American" is a label of convenience used by a number of groups including grassroots, community-based, and government organizations. We problematize it by using quotation marks around the label to remind the reader that this is not a singular, natural, fixed, and homogeneous ethnic category. According to the U.S. Census Bureau, there are over forty Asian and Pacific Islander groups from over forty countries and territories, who speak more than one hundred different languages. "Asian Americans" are characterized by tremendous historical, geographical, social, and cultural locations and identifications and personal and collective oppressions; the term "Asian Americans," therefore, may be, according to Lowe, more appropriately viewed as "a socially constructed unity, a situationally specific position, assumed for political reasons" (1996:82).

2. We are using the term in Michael Warner's (1993) sense—"'queer' represents, among other things, an aggressive impulse of generalization; it rejects a minoritizing logic of toleration or simple political interest-representation in favor of a more thorough resistance to regimes of the normal" (xxvi)—and we employ it to refer to individuals with lesbian, gay, bisexual, and/or transgender (LGBT) identifications. Please note that "queer" is not universally embraced by "Asian American" LGBTs.

3. We borrow this title from David L. Eng and Alice Y. Hom's *Q & A: Queer in Asian America* (1998).

4. Although the Castro district in San Francisco has been labeled "a liberated zone" (Castells 1983 as cited in Sinfield 1998:23), it is still a primarily gay, white, male space.

5. McWhirter and Mattison describe limerance as an early stage in gay male romantic relationships characterized by overt physical expressions of affection for each other, both in public and in private (1984).

6. Individuals who can pass as members of another race are exceptions. For a discussion of passing, see Moon (1998).

7. The pages in Andrews's book are not numbered.

8. Dennis refers to himself in the text as Asian.

REFERENCES

Adair, Nancy and Casey Adair. 1978. *Word Is Out: Stories of Some of Our Lives.* San Francisco: New Glide.

Adelman, Mara B. and Lawrence R. Frey. 1994. "The Pilgrim Must Embark: Creating and Sustaining Community in a Residential Facility for People with AIDS." In Lawrence R. Frey, ed., *Group Communication in Context: Studies of Natural Groups*, pp. 3–21. Hillsdale, N.J.: Lawrence Erlbaum.

———. 1997. *The Fragile Community: Living Together with AIDS*. Mahwah, N.J.: Lawrence Erlbaum.

Aguilar-San Juan, Karin. 1994. "Linking the Issues: From Identity to Activism." In Karin Aguilar-San Juan, ed., *The State of Asian America: Activism and Resistance in the 1990s*, pp. 1–15. Boston: South End Press.

Alcoff, L. M. 1995. "The Problem of Speaking for Others." In Judith Roof and Robyn Wiegman, eds., *Who Can Speak? Authority and Critical Identity*, pp. 97–119. Urbana: University of Illinois Press.

Andrews, Nancy. 1994. *Family: A Portrait of Gay and Lesbian America*. San Francisco: Harper.

Bakhtin, Mikhail M. 1981. *The Dialogic Imagination: Four Essays by M. M. Bakhtin*. Ed. M. Holquist, trans. C. Emerson and M. Holquist. Austin: University of Texas Press.

———. 1984. *Problems with Dostoevsky's Poetics*. Ed. and trans. C. Emerson. Minneapolis: University of Minnesota Press.

———. 1986. *Speech Genres and Other Late Essays*. Ed. C. Emerson and M. Holquist, trans. V. McGee. Austin: University of Texas Press.

Bannerji, K. 1993. "No Apologies." In R. Ratti, ed., *A Lotus of Another Color: An Unfolding of the South Asian Gay and Lesbian Experience*, pp. 59–64. Boston: Alyson.

Baxter, Leslie A. 1990. "Dialectical Contradictions in Relationship Development." *Journal of Social and Personal Relationships* 7:69–88.

Baxter, Leslie A. and Barbara M. Montgomery. 1996. *Relating: Dialogues and Dialectics*. New York: Guilford.

———. 1998. "A Guide to Dialectical Approaches to Studying Personal Relationships." In Barbara M. Montgomery and Leslie A. Baxter, eds., *Dialectical Approaches to Studying Personal Relationships*, pp. 1–15. Mahwah, N.J.: Lawrence Erlbaum.

Bell, Michael M. 1998. "Culture as Dialogue." In Michael M. Bell and Michael Gardiner, eds., *Bakhtin and the Human Sciences: No Last Words*, pp. 49–62. London: Sage.

Brah, Avtar. 1996. *Cartographies of Diaspora: Contesting Identities*. London: Routledge.

Brown, B. B., C. M. Werner, and I. Altman. 1998. "Choice Points for Dialecticians: A Dialectical-Transactional Perspective on Close Relationships." In Barbara. M. Montgomery and Leslie A. Baxter, eds., *Dialectical Approaches to Studying Personal Relationships*, pp. 137–54. Mahwah, N.J.: Lawrence Erlbaum.

Butler, Judith. 1990. *Gender Trouble: Feminism and the Subversion of Identity*. New York: Routledge.

Chang, E. T. 1994. "America's First Multiethnic 'Riots.' " In Karin Aguilar-San Juan, ed., *The State of Asian America: Activism and Resistance in the 1990s*, pp. 101–17. Boston: South End Press.

Chee, A. 1996. "These Trees Were Once Women." In Patrick Merla, ed., *Boys Like Us: Gay Writers Tell Their Coming Out Stories*, pp. 312–22. New York: Aron Books.

Chen, S. 1994. "Slowly But Surely, My Search for Family Acceptance and Community Comes." In S. Lim-Hing, ed., *The Very Inside: An Anthology of Writing by Asian and Pacific Islander Lesbian and Bisexual Women*, pp. 79–84. Toronto: Sister Vision Press.

Chin, J. 1997. "Currency." In S. Raffo, ed., *Queerly Classed: Gay Men and Lesbians Write about Class*, pp. 179–89. Boston: South End Press.

———. 1999. *Mongrel: Essays, Diatribes, and Pranks*. New York: St. Martin's Press.

Cissna, K. N., D. E. Cox, and A. P. Bochner. 1990. "The Dialectic of Marital and Parental Relationships within the Stepfamily." *Communication Monographs* 57: 46–61.

Cissna, K. N. and E. Sieburg. 1986. "Patterns of Interactional Confirmation and Disconfirmation." In John Stewart, ed., *Bridges, Not Walls*, 4th ed., pp. 230–39. New York: Random House.

Dindia, K. 1998. " 'Going into and Coming out of the Closet': The Dialectics of Stigma Disclosure." In Barbara M. Montgomery and Leslie A. Baxter, eds., *Dialectical Approaches to Studying Personal Relationships*, pp. 83–108. Mahwah, N.J.: Lawrence Erlbaum.

Drucker, J. 1998. *Families of Value: Gay and Lesbian Parents & Their Children Speak Out*. New York: Insight Books.

Eng, David L. and Alice Y. Hom. 1998. "Q & A: Notes on a Queer Asian America." In David L. Eng and Alice Y. Hom, eds., *Q & A: Queer in Asian America*, pp. 1–21. Philadelphia: Temple University Press.

Escoffier, Jeffrey. 1998. *American Homo: Community and Perversity*. Berkeley: University of California Press.

Fumia, M. 1997. *Honor Thy Children: One Family's Journey to Wholeness*. Berkeley, Cal.: Conari Press.

Fung, R. 1995. "The Trouble with 'Asians.' " In Monica Dorenkamp and Richard Henke, eds., *Negotiating Lesbian and Gay Subjects*, pp. 123–30. New York: Routledge.

Fuss, Diana. 1989. *Essentially Speaking: Feminism, Nature, and Difference*. New York: Routledge.

———. 1991. "Inside/out." In Diana Fuss, ed., *Inside/out: Lesbian Theories, Gay Theories*, pp. 1–10. New York; Routledge.

Gauvain, M., I. Altman, and H. Fahim. 1983. "Home and Social Change: A Cross-cultural Analysis." In N. Reimer and E. S. Geller, eds., *Environmental Psychology: Directions and Perspectives*, pp. 180–218. New York: Praeger.

Hagedorn, J. 1994. "The Exile within/the Question of Identity." In K. Aguilar-San Juan, ed., *The State of Asian America: Activism and Resistance in the 1990s*, pp. 173–82. Boston: South End Press.

Holquist, M. 1990. *Dialogism: Bakhtin and His World*. London: Routledge.

Hom, A.Y. 1996. "Stories from the Homefront: Perspectives of Asian American Parents with Lesbian Daughters and Gay Sons." In R. Leong, ed., *Asian American Sexualities: Dimensions of the Gay and Lesbian Experience*, pp. 37–49. New York: Routledge.

hooks, bell. 1990. *Yearning: Race, Gender, and Cultural Politics*. Boston: South End Press.

Hsu, F. L. K. 1981. *Americans and Chinese: Passage to Differences*, 3d ed. Honolulu: University of Hawaii Press.

Hunter, B. M. and J. A. Manzón-Santos. 1997. "Windows and Water Towers." In S. Raffo, ed., *Queerly Classed: Gay Men and Lesbians Write about Class*, pp. 135–50. Boston: South End Press.

Islam, S. 1993. "Breaking Silence." In R. Ratti, ed., *A Lotus of Another Color: An Unfolding of the South Asian Gay and Lesbian Experience*, pp. 213–18. Boston: Alyson.

Jimenes, D. B. 1994. "Solitary Bravo." In S. Lim-Hing, ed., *The Very Inside: An Anthology of Writing by Asian and Pacific Islander Lesbian and Bisexual Women*, pp. 129–42. Toronto: Sister Vision Press.

Jordan, G. and C. Weedon. 1995. *Cultural Politics: Class, Gender, Race and the Postmodern World*. Oxford: Blackwell.

Kang, D. 1996. "Multiple-Box Person." In E. H. Kim and U. Eui-Young, eds., *East to America: Korean American Life Stories*, pp. 81–89. New York: New Press.

Katz, J. N. 1992. *Gay American History*. New York: Meridian.

Khan, D. K., Bryan, and Rhode. 1996. "Transgender/Transsexual Roundtable." In David L. Eng and Alice Y. Hom, eds., *Q & A: Queer in Asian America*, pp. 227–43. Philadelphia: Temple University Press.

Lee, J. 1998. "Toward a Queer Korean American Diasporic History." In David L. Eng and Alice Y. Hom, eds., *Q & A: Queer in Asian America*, pp. 185–209. Philadelphia: Temple University Press.

Lee, W. S., J. Chung, J. Wang, and E. Hertel. 1995. "A Sociocultural Approach to Intercultural Communication." *Howard Journal of Communications*, 6 (4): 262–91.

Leong, R. 1996. "Introduction: Home Bodies and the Body Politic." In R. Leong, ed., *Asian American Sexualities: Dimensions of the Gay and Lesbian Experience*, pp. 1–18. New York: Routledge.

Lim, L. L. 1997. "Webs of Betrayal, Webs of Blessing." In R. E. Goss and A. A. Squire Strongheart, eds., *Our Families, Our Values: Snapshots of Queer Kinship*, pp. 227–41. New York: Harrington Park Press.

Lowe, L. 1996. *Immigrant Acts: On Asian American Cultural Politics*. Durham, N.C.: Duke University Press.

Manalansan, M. F. 1996. "Searching for Community: Filipino Gay Men in New York City." In R. Leong, ed., *Asian American Sexualities: Dimensions of the Gay and Lesbian Experience*, pp. 51–64. New York: Routledge.

Maria. 1993. "Coming Home." In R. Ratti, ed., *A Lotus of Another Color: An Unfolding of the South Asian Gay and Lesbian Experience*, pp. 204–12. Boston: Alyson.

McWhirter, David P. and Andrew M. Mattison. 1984. *The Male Couple: How Relationships Develop*. Englewood Cliffs, N.J.: Prentice Hall.

Miao, V. 1998. "Coalition Politics: (Re)turning the Century." In David L. Eng and Alice Y. Hom, eds., *Q & A: Queer in Asian America*, pp. 65–78. Philadelphia: Temple University Press.

Minh-ha, Trinh T. 1989. *Woman, Native, Other*. Bloomington: Indiana University Press.

Montgomery, Barbara M. and Leslie A. Baxter. 1998. "Dialogism and Relational Dialectics." In Barbara M. Montgomery and Leslie A. Baxter, eds., *Dialectical Approaches to Studying Personal Relationships*, pp. 155–83. Mahwah, N.J.: Lawrence Erlbaum.

Moon, D. G. 1998. "Performed Identities: 'Passing' as an Inter/cultural Discourse." In Judith N. Martin, Thomas K. Nakayama, and Lisa A. Flores, eds., *Readings in Cultural Contexts*, pp. 322–30. Mountain View, Cal.: Mayfield.

Nakayama, Thomas. 1997. "Dis/orienting Identities: Asian Americans, History, and Intercultural Communication." In Alberto González, Marsha Houston, and Victoria Chen, eds., *Our Voices: Essays in Culture, Ethnicity, and Communication*, 2d ed., pp. 14–20. Los Angeles: Roxbury.

Omatsu, G. 1994. "The 'Four Prisons' and the Movements of Liberation: Asian American Activism from the 1960s to the 1990s." In Karin Aguilar-San Juan, ed., *The State of Asian America: Activism and Resistance in the 1990s*, pp. 19–69. Boston: South End Press.

Raffo, S. 1997. "Introduction." In S. Raffo, ed., *Queerly Classed: Gay Men and Lesbians Write about Class*, pp. 1–8. Boston: South End Press.

Rawlins, William K. 1992. *Friendship Matters: Communication, Dialectics and the Life Course*. New York: de Gruyter.

——. 1998. "Writing about *Friendship Matters*: A Case Study in Dialectical and Dialogical Inquiry." In Barbara M. Montgomery and Lisa A. Baxter, eds., *Dialectical Approaches to Studying Personal Relationships*, pp. 63–81. Mahwah, N.J.: Lawrence Erlbaum.

Reyes, E. E., and Yep, G. A. 1997. "Challenging Complexities: Strategizing with Asian Americans in Southern California Against (Heterosex)isms." In James T. Sears and Walter L. Williams, eds., *Overcoming Heterosexism and Homophobia: Strategies That Work*, pp. 91–103. New York: Columbia University Press.

Sacks, K. B. 1999. "Toward a Unified Theory of Class, Race, and Gender." In

Stephanie Coontz, ed., *American Families: A Multicultural Reader*, pp. 218–29. New York: Routledge.

Sadownick, Douglas, ed. 1996. *Sex Between Men: An Intimate History of the Sex Lives of Gay Men Postwar to Present*. San Francisco: HarperSan Francisco.

Shah, N. 1993. "Sexuality, Identity, and the Uses of History." In R. Ratti, ed., *A Lotus of Another Color: An Unfolding of the South Asian Gay and Lesbian Experience*, pp. 113–32. Boston: Alyson.

Sinfield, A. 1998. *Gay and After*. London: Serpent's Tail.

Stacey, Judith. 1999. "Gay and Lesbian Families Are Here; All Our Families Are Queer; Let's Get Used to It!" In Stephanie Coontz, ed., *American Families: A Multicultural Reader*, pp. 372–405. New York: Routledge.

Takagi, Dana Y. 1996. "Maiden Voyage: Excursion into Sexuality and Identity Politics in Asian America." In Russell Leong, ed., *Asian American Sexualities: Dimensions of the Gay and Lesbian Experience*, pp. 21–35. New York: Routledge.

Takaki, Ronald. 1989. *Strangers from a Different Shore: A History of Asian Americans*. Boston: Little, Brown.

Warner, Michael. 1993. "Introduction." In Michael Warner, ed., *Fear of a Queer Planet: Queer Politics and Social Theory*, pp. vii–xxxi. Minneapolis: University of Minnesota Press.

Wat, E. C. and S. Shum. 1998. "Queer API Men in Los Angeles: A Roundtable on History and Political Organizing." In David L. Eng and Alice Y. Hom, eds., *Q & A: Queer in Asian America*, pp. 166–84. Philadelphia: Temple University Press.

Weston, Kath. 1991. *Families We Choose: Lesbians, Gays, Kinship*. New York: Columbia University Press.

Yep, Gust A. 1998. "My Three Cultures: Navigating the Multicultural Identity Landscape." In Judith N. Martin, Thomas K. Nakayama, and Lisa A. Flores, eds., *Readings in Cultural Contexts*, pp. 79–85. Mountain View, Cal.: Mayfield.

Yep, Gust A., Karen E. Lovaas, and A. V. Pagonis. 2001. "The Case of 'Riding Bareback': Sexual Practices and the Paradoxes of Identity in the Era of AIDS." *Journal of Homosexuality*, forthcoming.

Yong, T. 1994. "New Mexico APL." In S. Lim-Hing, ed., *The Very Inside: An Anthology of Writing by Asian and Pacific Islander Lesbian and Bisexual Women*, pp. 7–11. Toronto: Sister Vision Press.

Yu, Eui-Young, ed. 1994. *Black-Korean Encounter: Toward Understanding and Alliance*. Claremont, Cal.: Regina.

Zack, N. 1998. "Introduction." In N. Zack, L. Shrage, and C. Sartwell, eds., *Race, Class, Gender, and Sexuality: The Big Questions*, pp. 1–8. Malden, Mass.: Blackwell.

PART 2 | *Parenthood*

11 | Affording Our Families: Class Issues in Family Formation

Terry Boggis

I direct Center Kids, the family program of the Lesbian and Gay Community Services Center in New York, the largest regional lesbian, gay, bisexual, and transgender (LGBT) program in the country. Before Center Kids had a paid director, when the program was still run by volunteers, my lover, our son, and I were one of the first families in the program and members of its steering committee since its founding in 1988. As someone involved with the lesbian and gay parenting groundswell on an organizational level for more than ten years, I've had the opportunity to observe a lot.

I receive many telephone calls from lesbian, gay, bisexual, and transgender people needing information on becoming parents and on coping with the tasks of parenthood (plentiful under the simplest circumstances), with the additional challenges of being queer in the mix. These calls have been tremendously instructive, offering a broad view of the range of considerations LGBT people face when planning their families, considerations not usually a part of family planning in heterosexual families, considerations such as: surrogacy or adoption? adoption or alternative insemination? alternative insemination with a known donor, or with an anonymous donor? Will a known donor be a father to the child, an involved parent, or will he be defined and identified as an uncle, a friend, or merely a donor to his biological child? If a couple is adopting, can they be out, or should one partner present as the adoptive "single" parent?

Advances in reproductive technologies and enlightened adoption policies have enabled lesbian and gay people to bring children into their lives without compromising their sexual identities, and these advancements in science and social policy have been hugely celebrated in the LGBT community. The more complex considerations that come with our family planning process are truly stuff of the twenty-first century. Yet this same abundance of choice for nontraditional couples and singles reveals another, less celebratory, aspect of creating families for LGBT people. Not everyone can afford it.

Before we go further, please allow a clarification of terms. My reflections here have to do with the concept of *class*, of fitting in and exclusion. In this culture the perception and assessment of class have so many variables: our parents, our parents' parents, our continents and countries of origin, our first languages, our neighborhoods, our tastes, our hairstyles, the length of our fingernails, what we wear, the things we own, our educations, the possessions and positions to which we aspire, our accents, our pasts, our bloodlines, our accessories. So just to clarify and simplify, when I speak of class issues here, I'm talking about *money*.

Over the past ten years, I've watched and participated as we, the public and self-appointed representatives of LGBT parenting, have presented the out-front, prominent, political face of lesbian and gay parenthood to be white and middle class. But I know through my work that this depiction is deceptive. Queer parents are not *only* educated, comfortable, employed, dual-income "guppy" (gay upwardly mobile professional) couples. We are also people who live in cars with our kids, and people who live in rural areas in economically stressed regions with little to look forward to in the way of work or education. We are lesbian couples who want to have a baby and can't afford to buy sperm, and gay men who are as enthusiastic at the notion of parenting as any could be but who can't possibly afford surrogacy arrangements. We are people with AIDS, sometimes with children who also have the virus. Some of us not only can't afford a copy of *Daddy's Roommate* or *Heather Has Two Mommies* or the other books depicting gay families, but the lives reflected in the pages of these books bear no resemblance whatsoever to the lives we lead. We are families on welfare, living in public housing. We are incarcerated, we are homeless. We are people whose desire to parent is every bit as strong as the middle-class candidate, but we lack health insurance sufficient to cover the most basic care, let alone sperm washing, intrauterine insemination, in-vitro, gamete intra-fallopian transfer (GIFT), and other sophisticated medical technologies, or midwifery, or the funds to cover legal counsel (a basic requirement in a society where our children can still be taken away from us based on our sexual orientation).

In my job I hear from lesbian mothers whose pregnancies have resulted from sex work, drugging or drinking, or from attempts to prove to suspicious peers or family members that they are not gay. I hear from lesbian mothers who have HIV and need to make arrangements for their children while they are working at taking care of themselves. I hear from young single lesbians who became pregnant and don't want to be, who seek to place their babies with lesbian or gay parents. The teenage pressures to conform, to fit in, to go along, to blend, prompt behaviors in lesbian, gay, bisexual, and transgender teens that put them at tremendous risk.

If young lesbians become pregnant, they are more likely to be estranged from families unhappy with their same-sex behavior, more likely to be at odds with sources of support, as well less likely to access healthcare systems they don't trust to understand and support their sexuality. In general, lesbians have historically been less likely to seek medical care due to the heterosexist assumptions and prejudices of the medical care system, and those seeking reproductive health services are perhaps most suspicious of all.

In short, and in fact contrary to the popular truism in the gay parenting community, *not* all of our families are planned, *not* all of our children are wanted, *not* every pregnancy is a carefully planned life transition.

Once, at a Center Kids support group for gay men and lesbians who were considering parenting biologically, I met a lesbian couple of limited means who came to the meeting hoping to meet sperm donors. They had made inquiries at sperm banks and were horrified at the $150 to $200 per shot price quotes, plus assorted adjunct expenses (dry ice storage and shipping, the doctors' fees, etc.). One of them said, "We just want some *sperm!*" Her exasperation at their inability to access a substance generally treated as utterly disposable and valueless was enormous. And the men in the room were even more despairing–the costs for them to reproduce, requiring profound cooperation on the part of a woman (without even getting into the class politics of surrogacy), are even more daunting.

Only men and women of some means are able to gain access to the reproductive technologies that allow lesbians and gay men to have children without compromising their sexual identity or their health. So what is the upshot of this financial challenge for working-class lesbian and gay people? No surprise: the pathways that remain open include heterosexual contact (anathema to many gay-identified people), or insemination at home with fresh sperm from an unchecked donor, involving heath risks that don't come with sperm banks. When women inseminate with sperm from a known donor to circumvent these costs, not only do they risk their health by using untested semen, but they very often have to set aside their sexual identity in order to participate in intercourse with the donor.

Perhaps the most profound risk, though, is the sacrifice of their ability to control the construction and identity of their own families. They risk the donor asserting parental rights, usurping their lesbian partner's role as the child's other parent, court challenges regarding custody and visitation, curtailment of their and their partner's ability to relocate their family, choose a religion and a school, and sometimes even a name, and to decide the people their child will regard as family. I don't mean to suggest that many lesbian mother-known donor arrangements don't work well—in fact, many do. But when they do, they do so without the support of a legal system and without a society that recognizes alternative family structures, and they do so *in spite of* the risks I have listed.

If women are inseminated without the assistance and intervention of a doctor—in other words, if the sperm is administered in their homes with lover or friends as go-between—the donor can always change his mind regarding his interest in the child. Women's power to define their family as they choose, i.e., as their child, their lesbian coparent, and themselves, is sacrificed. A woman who uses sperm from a sperm bank is legally and absolutely protected from paternal assertions of a donor.

And what of "sperm-donor dads"? They too can enter into agreements with lesbians, but their access to their biological children is often extremely curtailed in these arrangements. For some men, this is acceptable, but for others, this limited access is the source of tremendous pain. For gay men seeking to parent biologically, their choices are largely limited to either these severely circumscribed arrangements with lesbians or the employment of surrogate mothers. And although we in the LGBT community may rejoice at the opening of a surrogacy agency in California catering specifically to gay men, we have to recognize that the average cost of a surrogacy arrangement—$35,000 to $50,000—leaves that avenue, which is the avenue that assures full parental rights for the father, closed to all but the most affluent men.

It's interesting to note that throughout the thirty-odd-year-old modern debate on reproductive rights in this country, the argument on which we have unswervingly been focused has to do with a woman's right to choose abortion. The discourse is invariably cast in the negative—the right not to have a baby—and this issue has been interlaced with its own class issues (i.e., women of color and/or working-class women have historically had less access to abortion and family planning services). But reproductive rights also means our rights as LGBT people *to* reproduce, and to have adequate law in support of alternative family structures to make us feel safe enough to take the risk to parent, to love and tend our kids (see Murphy, chapter 12).

So, when alternative insemination, surrogacy, and other biological routes to parenting are so prohibitively expensive, why not adopt? Private (independent) adoption, whether through a private agency or a lawyer, is expensive. International adoption is expensive. Costs for either process can range from $10,000 to $30,000. Public adoption through the foster care system is less expensive, but, ironically, asks that prospective parents with lesser means be willing to take on the additional challenges of special-needs children, children with HIV, infants born drug-addicted or with fetal alcohol syndrome, mixed-race children, children who are older, children who have been abused, children with disabilities—the children most often available through the public system.

LGBT family activists have celebrated the recent, hard-won advent of *second-parent adoption* rights, wherein the other adult in a household, the adult not related to the child by blood or marriage, can legally adopt the child without the legal parent relinquishing custody (see Dalton, chapter 13). This has been a tremendous boon to the integrity of our families, permitting both parents in a gay household to become the legal parents of their child. Yet some of us in the LGBT community question just how jubilant we should be at being granted *the right to adopt our own kids*, a process that is time-consuming, intrusive, and *costly* (several thousand dollars, depending on the attorney and jurisdiction). Ironically and unfortunately, courts in localities where second-parent adoption is permitted are starting to use the fact that parents have not pursued second-parent adoption as grounds for dismissing custody claims when gay couples break up. In other words, if a gay woman or man files for joint custody or visitation with his or her child and they have not (often for financial reasons) legally adopted that child, judges are regarding this absence of second-parent adoption as a lack of intent to parent, contributing to their decisions to deny custody and visitation to nonbiological or "nonlegal" parents.

I've been increasingly distressed at the self-congratulatory nature of the LGBT parenting movement over the years. We position ourselves as saintly liberals with the best children, the light of the next millennium. But who are we talking about when we say "we"? Perhaps more than any other subgroup of this community, the LGBT parenting faction has been the most vigorous in its assertion that "we're just like everyone else," an announcement that sets my teeth on edge every time I hear it. What do we envision when we proudly make this pronouncement? We mean white people with money, education, property, and possessions—the American model, the American myth, not true of all of us, and mostly untrue in the larger culture.

The desperation for acceptance that lies behind the "we're-like-every-one-else" profession makes me cringe. I understand the impulse behind it—as parents, we have a fierce desire for our children to face an unimpeded life, a life without hurt feelings and ostracism for being different. But the fact is, we are different, and so are our families—different from the heterosexual norm, different from one another. Not in every way, and not in specific ways that really count (i.e., we all love our kids, we all want what's best for them, we all do our best for them as parents, we try to see to their nutrition and hygiene and health and education). We all have moments of sublime pride and joy.

But we are different in significant ways—not only in our erotic attractions and attachments but also in how we define community and family. Many of us have lost our families of origin over their unwillingness to accept our sexual orientation and have created families for ourselves, based not so much on blood connections but on intimate friendship, on shared struggle, a family circle that might include ex-lovers, comrades in gay organizing, and so on. And these differences in how we create family do not necessarily make us bad parents *or* good ones. Our differences do require us to remember that we are still considered by many to be bizarre, scary, foreign, dirty, threatening, offensive, and uncomfortable to be around.

The LGBT "community," and our rights struggle, has perhaps been in no way more profoundly moved forward than through the advances in reproductive technologies of recent years, and through increasing enlightenment on the part of the adoption and foster care industries and personnel. Lesbians may now, without having sex with a man, make babies. Gay men may now, without having sex with a woman, make babies. We may now, as openly gay couples, adopt babies. But creating our families costs a lot of money, and many, many of us don't have enough.

Some argue that if prospective parents don't have enough money to afford to obtain a baby, how do they expect to raise a child? Of course others think that only those with money should have access to alternative forms of reproduction. For example, I remember having an argument some time ago with a lesbian who strongly opposed the creation of a "lesbian underclass" through the development of pathways to pregnancy for working-class women.

Children have always been conceived into and raised successfully in loving homes with little money. There is no economic readiness test for straight parents. Despite societal pressure not to, fertile heterosexual couples can conceive children regardless of their economic status. So once again, this time in a profoundly personal, primal, basic human area, it's just not a level playing field. And I know the irony of our situation: that for all time, the one asset, the one abundance that poor people have always had is children. In the queer community, it is our most agonizing area of impoverishment that having children is not always a right we can afford to access safely.

Where to begin? I think we begin with an open and honest discussion of class issues in the queer community. Then, on both personal and political levels, we begin by *forming alliances with other progressive people and movements* that connect to the creation of families and economics–welfare rights, immigration rights, reproductive rights, labor rights. That means we vow to show up on behalf of "other people's" struggles, realizing that "other people" are us. I think we begin by *claiming all members of the LGBT parenting community as our closest kin*, rather than striving to claim alliance with and allegiance to Ward and June Cleaver and the myth of the American family ideal that supports them. We begin *with an expanded, expansive definition of family* that includes many forms of primary connection and households and relationships for which there are not yet vocabulary, only passionate and enduring commitment and love.

12 Should Lesbians Count as Infertile Couples? Antilesbian Discrimination in Assisted Reproduction[1]

Julien S. Murphy

Assisted reproduction not only offers a variety of services for treating infertility but also includes some services useful for fertile women. One method of conception, physician-assisted insemination, can be helpful to fertile women who wish to use insemination as their preferred method of conception. Single women, lesbians, and lesbian couples are among those who rely on this method.[2] A few years ago, my partner and I began using assisted reproduction to conceive our first child, and it occurred to me as I wondered about lesbians' access to reproductive services, insurance coverage, and parenting rights for nonbirthing partners that there was little difference between us and the many infertile heterosexual couples for whom reproductive services were designed. While we lacked a medical reason for an infertility diagnosis, the similarities in the treatment plan and goal suggested that perhaps lesbian couples might be regarded as having a sort of "relational infertility" that could be said to accompany lesbian relationships.[3] Armed with a medical diagnosis, our reproductive concerns would be seen as legitimate. Our access to services would increase, they would be covered by insurance, and we would be granted the crown jewel of benefits afforded married heterosex-

Adapted, with permission from the author and the publisher, from "Making Our Families: Anti-Lesbian Discrimination in Assisted Reproduction Practices," in Anne Donchin and Laura M. Purdy, eds., *Embodying Bioethics: Recent Feminist Advances (New Feminist Perspectives)* (Boston: Rowman and Littlefield, 1999).

ual couples using donor insemination—parental rights for the nonbirthing partner. Despite similarities between our situation and that of those who are routinely diagnosed as infertile, infertility specialists do not regard as infertile lesbian couples who use physician-assisted insemination. But why not? Is it due to antilesbian discrimination in assisted reproduction? I began reading the medical and philosophical literature with this question in mind: Should lesbians pursuing assisted reproduction count as infertile couples? It is a question of strategy with complex theoretical implications.

It may seem foolish to want a diagnosis of infertility, since medical diagnoses are rarely coveted. The fact is that accompanying an infertility diagnosis are some desirable privileges that lesbians currently lack. If lesbians want these privileges, perhaps we should be demanding the same diagnosis and trying to convince the medical establishment that lesbian couples seeking assisted reproduction are as infertile as male-female couples using assisted reproduction. As a result, we might have a good chance of obtaining the same privileges, and we would advance lesbian reproductive rights and increase the legitimacy of lesbian (and gay) families. Many lesbians using assisted reproduction are from the middle class. Their class privilege could be used to garner equity in reproductive services (e.g., from private physicians and insurance providers), with the hope that any hard-won gains could be extended to all women irrespective of economic class.

In this essay I focus on physician-assisted insemination. In order to evaluate the benefits of applying an infertility diagnosis to lesbian couples with no known fertility impairment who are pursuing physician-assisted insemination, I will describe this reproductive method within a lesbian and feminist context. Next, I identify three benefits of an infertility diagnosis accompanying assisted insemination for heterosexual couples, benefits that lesbians lack and that constitute forms of antilesbian discrimination. A review of arguments on physician-assisted insemination in the medical literature reveals common assumptions about lesbians and reproduction that reinforce all three forms of discrimination. Finally, I evaluate parity arguments in favor of applying an infertility diagnosis to lesbian couples. I argue that it is wise to be wary of certain tempting diagnostic strategies when searching for ways to address antilesbian discrimination in assisted reproduction.

LESBIAN INSEMINATION PRACTICES

LESBIANS WHO CHOOSE PREGNANCY without heterosexual intercourse use some form of (alternative) insemination. It has been estimated that as many as ten thousand children have been born to lesbians this way (Cohn 1992:39).[4] Insemination is popular for many reasons. It can be significantly easier, quicker, and less costly than adopting a child (not to mention that many adoption services discriminate against lesbian and gay clients). The most popular insemination is unassisted or self-insemination, whereby a woman is not aided by a healthcare professional. There are no obvious class barriers to alternative insemination. Sperm can be donated by a friend, acquaintance, or relative of the nonbirthing partner, and vaginal insemination requires no technical expertise or expensive equipment. In the late 1970s the feminist self-help movement promoted self-insemination for women wishing to reproduce on their own, and formal and informal sperm banks were established, some specifically for lesbians (Klein 1984). In engaging in self-insemination, usually at home, women directly seized control over conception, enhancing independence from men and a personal sense of freedom from heterosexual relationships and the medical establishment.

While unassisted reproduction represents an advance in reproductive freedom for lesbians and single women and is open to women from all economic classes, the trend in the 1990s is to seek out fertility experts when self-insemination fails to achieve pregnancy. Increasingly, lesbians who can afford to are pursuing assisted-reproductive options (Hornstein 1984). Fertility clinics offer a range of reproductive techniques to increase the chances of pregnancy. They include vaginal as well as intrauterine insemination, hormone injections, ovarian hyperstimulation, egg harvesting for in vitro fertilization and embryo transfer, gamete intrafallopian tube transfer, and other techniques; eventually, human cloning may be possible. I wish to explore antilesbian discrimination in an early intervention, physician–assisted (vaginal or intrauterine) insemination.

ANTILESBIAN DISCRIMINATION

ANTILESBIAN DISCRIMINATION IN ASSISTED reproduction occurs in at least three ways. The first is access. Fertility services are expensive and commonly not covered by insurance plans, excluding women who are insured or cannot afford these services. In addition, some fertility clinics and physicians refuse to extend services to single women and lesbians (Robinson 1997). Restricted access to infertility services is not unique to the United States. It is common for fertility centers throughout Western countries to restrict physician–assisted inseminations to heterosexual couples, although there are exceptions (Arnup 1994; Daniels and Taylor 1993; Knoppers and LeBris 1991). Physicians regulate lesbian access not only to infertility techniques but also to sperm banks (both physician-operated and others requiring physician authorization). Insurance plans that cover fertility services only if there is a diagnosis of infertility also regulate and discriminate against lesbians.[5] Even after one gains access to reproductive services, discrimination can still occur from nurse-clinicians, midwives, and other healthcare providers, who may withhold information and support for lesbian patients or in other ways create a hostile atmosphere for lesbians.

The second form of discrimination already alluded to occurs in the use of infertility diagnosis and perceptions about the value and meaning of lesbians' requests for reproductive services. A lesbian couple in a committed relationship who seek out a physician for insemination services is not regarded as "infertile," unlike a married couple experiencing male infertility problems that require insemination by donor. The diagnosis of infertility legitimizes the heterosexual couple as a "reproductive couple." In the minds of many, the diagnosis declares that the couple's desire to reproduce is not frivolous or optional (as might be thought of a single woman who wishes to reproduce on her own) but, rather, is a necessity for the couple that is central to their very beings. Rare is the physician who regards a lesbian couple's desire to reproduce as similarly "necessary" to their life together. It is commonly assumed that lesbians will not reproduce and are not reproductive couples. This creates a vicious circle.

The diagnosis of infertility not only alters perceptions about couples' reproductive interests, it also provides heterosexuals with certain important benefits. Among them is the important benefit of paternity. In the case of a married heterosexual couple, if the sperm donor terminates paternity claims in advance, the husband of a woman having insemination is permitted to *adopt* any offspring that result from donor insemination. Many states have statutes that grant the husband *automatic* parental rights, provided that the insemination occurred in a doctor's office and that he has acknowledged in writing that he accepts the child as his own. Such statutory rules deem the consenting husband the legal father for all purposes. No adoption procedures, not even stepparent-adoption procedures to examine his suitability to parent, are required (Andrews 1988; Chambers 1996). This is the third form of antilesbian discrimination associated with physician-assisted insemination. The nonbirthing partner in a lesbian couple does not have *any* automatic parental rights and commonly lacks any parental rights whatsoever.[6] Even in places where adoption is permitted, it can be expensive, and social workers and judges can, and occasionally do, insist on longer procedures or additional steps for gay men and lesbians.[7]

Antilesbian discrimination practices in access, perception, and adoption are intimately linked. A review of the scholarly literature on the topic reveals that the main reason for refusing access to lesbians for assisted-reproductive services is a failure to recognize lesbians as reproductive, hence as capable of having treatable fertility problems. It is assumed that lesbians are incapable of having families. Insurance companies, even in states mandating infertility coverage, do not cover sperm bank charges and can refuse to cover lesbians by claiming that fertility procedures are not "medically necessary" (Millsap 1996). Hence conservative judges refuse to legitimize lesbian families by failing to grant adoption requests of nonbirthing partners. The standard assumption is that only heterosexuals *can* reproduce, which comes to mean that only heterosexuals *should* reproduce. If lesbians requested medical assistance in reproductive technology, such requests are deemed special requests. These assumptions and their allegedly "special" status are borne out by the medical literature, albeit scanty and with very little discussion of physician-assisted insemination for lesbians.[8]

Physician–assisted insemination for lesbians was first discussed and sharply condemned in 1979 in letters to a British medical journal in response to an ethics committee report for the British Medical Association (Thomas 1979). Opponents argued that physicians would be unable to foresee possible trauma to the child from being raised in a nontraditional family (Cosgrove 1979), or from not knowing his or her father (Hatfield 1979), or that *the procedure itself was unwarranted lacking a clear medical condition* (Wilson 1979) (emphasis added). How we regard the reproductive interests of lesbians is, at the very least, a philosophical matter. Perceptions about lesbians' reproductive possibilities are often linked with assumptions about lesbian parenting, as well as about lesbians and infertility. Do lesbians "lack a clear medical condition" for infertility? There are striking similarities between lesbians choosing insemination and heterosexuals suffering from some form of male or female infertility that is treatable by donor sperm and insemination. The same treatment yields the same result, a pregnancy. Does that suggest that the "condition" is essentially the same? If so, then lesbians do possess "a clear medical condition."

One issue is whether lesbians are asking physicians to "fix a problem" (i.e., infertility) or to assist in fulfilling a possibility. This is an important philosophical issue, and yet there is very little discussion of lesbians and reproduction or even lesbian parenting in the philosophical literature.[9] If lesbians are asking physicians to assist in fulfilling a possibility, lesbians can be compared to single women desiring the same services and, presumably, *lacking a medical condition*. Conservatives champion this position and use it to restrict access to reproductive services for lesbians and single women. One opponent of physician–assisted lesbian insemination argued that it was more like psychotherapy than infertility medicine. Insemination could not be regarded as medical treatment in lesbian cases, he argued:

> *Treatment for what,* I ask myself. Infertility? No, it can't be that or it would not work. *Treatment for lesbian tendencies?* No, because the women are still lesbians after conception has occurred. *Treatment for the psychological strain of having "married" someone of the same sex and so being unable to conceive naturally?* This seems to me to be the only possible way in which the process can be regarded as "treatment." (Wilson 1979)

As the literature shows in an American case, it is assumed that physicians have a *duty* to treat "medical conditions," but addressing the fulfillment of reproductive possibilities is an optional matter. If lesbians are not perceived as individuals suffering from some treatable form of infertility, services can easily be denied.

Six years after D. H. Wilson's comments appeared, a highly publicized American case of physician–assisted lesbian insemination made its way into the *Archives of Internal Medicine* (Perkoff 1985). The lesbian patient was twenty-eight years old, in a monogamous interracial relationship for over a decade, and the couple wished to use an anonymous donor of the same race as the partner. The physician proceeded with several cycles of insemination after routine genetic screening and social work evaluations. The case came to public attention because of breaches in patient confidentiality that occurred when the patient sought treatment for unexplained abdominal pain and fever that developed during the third cycle of insemination. An anonymous letter to the local newspaper brought journalists to report the story. No doubt, the interracial aspect of their relationship and their choice of donor fueled the controversy, for the story was picked up by national wire services with follow-up stories in local and national newspapers. The breach of confidentiality had disastrous results for the lesbian couple and their physician: the inseminated woman did conceive, but a spontaneous abortion ensued at six weeks' gestation; the couple ceased inseminating; and because of the case and its publicity, their physician's job offer at a Catholic medical school was withdrawn. The lesbian couple was described as "deeply shaken" by the publicity and the repercussions for their physician (Perkoff 1985).

One analysis of this case identifies the breaches of patient confidentiality as unethical but finds no ethical principles violated by physician-assisted donor insemination for lesbian couples. The author did advise caution for physicians considering such requests (ibid.). John Fletcher, a bioethicist commenting on the case, explored whether or not the physician had a professional duty to perform donor insemination for the lesbian couple. He argued that physicians are not obliged to assist lesbian couples with insemination because there is no accepted medical condition requiring treatment, unlike cases of married couples with genetic disorders or male infertility. He concluded that physicians can freely refuse lesbians' requests and have no duty to refer patients to other physicians who might help them. Recognizing that such requests by lesbian couples are "not only 'unusual,' but a real break with traditional practices and the majority religious view on sexuality and parenthood," he urged the leaders of teaching hospitals to provide guidance on the issue (1985).

It is unfortunate that this case introduced American physicians to physician-assisted lesbian insemination, because the severe repercussions for the physician involved cast an ominous light on the issue. Fearful of publicity, no doubt many physicians would thereafter think long and hard about consenting to such a request by a couple who, because of their orientation, might appear "unusual." If there is to be no discrimination based on sexual orientation, then lesbians have as much right to reproduce as anyone else. Fletcher's conservative analysis is equally unfortunate because it refuses to recognize that lesbians have a right to these services and because it was the only response to the case in the medical literature. At the same time, a meeting was convened at the university hospital by the chair of family medicine to discuss the case with the chief of staff, the chair of surgery, the obstetrician responsible for the sperm bank, and the physician who performed the insemination. Opinions about the appropriateness of donor insemination for the lesbian couple were divided.

Lacking good grounds to deny lesbians access to reproductive services, physicians should be compelled to provide reproductive care for lesbian patients or, in cases of religious conflict, refer lesbians to other physicians. Whether or not lesbians are regarded as having a right to assisted reproduction depends in part on whether or not lesbians are seen as assimilated within heterosexual society. Assimilation was an important screening factor in a more extensive discussion that occurred in Europe in response to a

Brussels reproductive center (one of the first) offering donor insemination to lesbians (Brewaeys et al. 1989). Twenty-one of twenty-seven lesbian couples who requested physician–assisted insemination from 1981 to 1988 and who underwent a screening program were accepted in its program. Fourteen pregnancies occurred among the twenty-one couples, with four couples having a second child. Their requests for insemination were termed "special" requests, and careful screening and counseling procedures were adopted. The criteria for psychologically screening lesbian couples required inspection of the personal histories of both women and the relational patterns of the couple, as well as an assessment of their understanding of parenting and desire to parent (ibid.). The reasons cited for refusing insemination services to six of the lesbian couples were: "unresolved problems in the family of origin, doubtful homosexual orientation, lack of acceptance of their homosexual identity, instability in the current relationship, and intolerance of their social milieu towards homosexuality" (ibid.).

It is difficult to evaluate the degree of prejudice, if any, in the screening process without understanding the cultural environment for lesbians in Brussels. For instance, personal history required a positive homosexual self-image; and relational patterns looked for a high degree of social acceptance of the couple in their family of origin, their neighborhoods, and their wider social and professional lives. In the United States good candidates for parenting might not have family acceptance (particularly if either partner comes from a conservative background), may have prejudiced neighbors, and may not be out in their professional lives. The last condition, one could argue, is necessary for good parenting, but the others may fall outside a couple's control. In Y. Englert's opinion piece, the successful applicants were described as highly assimilated into heterosexual society, "surrounded by more heterosexual couples than homosexual ones and certainly could not be considered as a part of a homosexual ghetto" (1994). It is doubtful that the same emphasis on cultural assimilation would be applied to a heterosexual couple from a racial, ethnic, religious, or economic minority. His reference to a "homosexual ghetto" is similarly disturbing. Most likely, the ghetto refers to a lack of heterosexuals, rather than to a lack of economic resources. While any screening mechanism is subjective and can allow prejudice, there was a high acceptance rate for lesbian couples at the Brussels center (twenty-one of twenty-seven couples in one study [Brewaeys et al. 1989] and fourteen of fifteen couples in another study [Englert 1994]). Perhaps this was a function of open-minded psychologists conducting the screening, a high degree of social acceptability for lesbians in Brussels, or a self-selecting applicant pool that sought out the Brussels center with their special requests because they felt they easily matched the criteria.

The link between one's perception of lesbian reproductive interests (whether they are seen as optional or fundamental) and lesbians' access to reproductive services has been demonstrated in this analysis of the medical literature. The same arguments are used to refuse lesbians the more complicated reproductive services.[10] There is little chance, then, that we can improve lesbian access without improving the perceptions about lesbians who wish to reproduce. To battle misperceptions, we must address the claim that lesbian requests for assisted reproduction are "special requests," for this is part of the conservative language that classifies gay civil rights as "special rights." Should we confront conservative perceptions by claiming that lesbians seeking assisted reproduction have medical conditions? Should we argue that lesbians should count as infertile couples? By this, we would mean that lesbians reproducing without intercourse have a treatable form of infertility—temporary or relational infertility—and therefore ought to be granted full access to fertility services. And would this position increase the chances that judges and others would legitimize lesbian and gay families and accept the diagnosis of temporary infertility, so lesbians could be perceived as capable of making families?

A DIAGNOSTIC STRATEGY

IT WOULD NOT BE unreasonable to regard lesbians seeking assisted reproduction as temporarily infertile. The term "infertility" is one of the few relational terms in medicine. Medicine generally assumes that individuals alone have diseases or medical conditions and that the source of a medical problem cannot lie in the relation between the individuals. Infertility is an exception, for the reproductive couple may be the source of the problem. Much of the reproductive literature on this topic refers to diagnosing, treating, and counseling the infertile *couple*. Medical diagnostics allow for the possibility that the source of infertility, in some cases, may lie with the couple and not one of the individuals (Collins 1995; Daley et al. 1996; Seibel 1993). Given the relational aspect of fertility, two people may be fertile apart but infertile together. Infertility can be general or partner specific; it can be temporary or permanent. Approximately 5 to 10 percent of infertility in heterosexual couples is unexplained (Talbert 1992). Lesbians may well be fertile women but could be said to make infertile couples when assistance of insemination is required. By contrast with heterosexuals, lesbians are often not recognized as being in relationships. Medical literature on lesbian couples seeking insemination talks of "insemination in a lesbian" and never a lesbian *couple*. Also, lesbians needing only donor insemination and not other services such as in vitro fertilization are fertile and need only minor medical intervention. The clinical measure of infertility is biased as well. Infertility, as measured in the 2.8 million infertile heterosexual couples who desire to reproduce, is the failure to conceive after one year of unprotected intercourse (Talbert 1992). Attempts to conceive are usually more numerous in noninseminating couples who incur no expense. It might seem reasonable, then, to extend the diagnosis of "temporary infertility," currently applied to some heterosexual patients, to lesbians seeking insemination services.[11]

If we opt to diagnose reproductive lesbians as temporarily infertile, will it change common perceptions of lesbians as nonreproductive, permanently infertile women? Perceptions of sterility are found not only in the medical literature, as mentioned above, but also in legislative arguments favoring state bans on gay marriage. In discussions of gay marriage, conservatives claim that the function of marriage is to raise families, hence gays and lesbians should not be allowed to marry because they cannot biologically reproduce together. The deviant status of lesbianism is associated with an assumed incapacity to bear children in lesbian relationships. Once it is pointed out that there already are gay and lesbian families, conservatives next raise concerns about the welfare of children in these families, even though there is extensive research demonstrating the well-being of children in gay and lesbian families (Golombok and Tasker 1994). Concerns next turn toward fatherhood, considered to be under siege by the practice of lesbian insemination. The belief that manhood is devalued by lesbian insemination, because it makes the role of men inconsequential, is found in discussions about lesbian insemination at the Brussels clinic. The opposition claimed that "the right to equal opportunities cannot entail the right for a woman to procreate without a man any more than the opposite scenario" and that "fatherhood" should not be "reduced to a gamete, or an *anonymous sperm cell*" (Shenfield 1994). These views reflect conservative positions on the family. Lesbian reproduction does eliminate fatherhood in many instances and challenges common sexist assumptions that parents of both genders are necessary for good parenting. Feminists are among the advocates of lesbian motherhood. Advocates for physician-assisted insemination for lesbians argue that "as in other conflicting areas of women's rights it is the law that should adapt to the autonomy of women (where ethically acceptable) and not the other way around" (Englert 1994).

SOME CONSIDERATIONS

THE STRATEGY OF INSISTING on a diagnosis of temporary infertility for lesbians and lesbian couples admittedly targets those who can afford assisted reproduction, with the hope that any gains in access could be extended to all women. Further, the strategy enlists the authority of the medical establishment to legitimize the reproductive interests of lesbians. One can argue that such a strategy is a fair-minded demand for parity in reproductive rights because lesbians are analogous to heterosexuals who also seek donor insemination but who have a diagnosis of infertility. Further, the goal of greater access to reproductive services is an important one. Nonetheless, there are at least five good reasons to question this strategy.

First, in seeking parity with heterosexuals by demanding the same diagnosis, lesbians would be required to fit their reproductive experiences into a heterosexual paradigm. Rather than struggling to confront or resist the dominant paradigms and broaden the models of reproduction, this strategy would encourage greater assimilation by lesbians into heterosexual categories, thereby forgetting important differences among these choices. Some of these differences are identified in a research study on why lesbians request physician-assisted insemination. In a study of fifteen lesbian couples pursuing insemination at the Brussels reproductive clinic from 1988 to 1993, the reasons for physician-assisted insemination were: refusal to sleep with a man and/or break the couple's fidelity (80 percent of the couples cited this reason); desire not to introduce a third party in the couple's project (53 percent); moral reluctance to deceive a male partner by engaging in sex without disclosing one's procreative intent (53 percent); and fear of contracting HIV disease (47 percent) (Englert 1994). There are other differences between lesbian and heterosexual practices of insemination worth considering. One interesting difference is that donor insemination is more likely to be disclosed to children in lesbian-headed than in heterosexual families. In studies of heterosexual couples undergoing donor insemination, most do not plan to tell the child (Klock, Jacob, and Maier 1994).

Second, granting the diagnosis of infertility to otherwise fertile lesbians extends the boundaries of what some call "compulsory motherhood" beyond heterosexuality, a regressive move. Social pressure for women to reproduce is powerful and pervasive. Since lesbians escape this expectation (once their sexual preference is made known), it would be foolish to recreate it. That said, we are in the midst of a lesbian baby boom. The days of lesbians being free of the expectation to reproduce are numbered. A diagnosis of infertility, by increasing access to services, would most likely create social expectations for lesbians to reproduce. This is partly because our society continues to socialize most girls to believe that motherhood should be their primary source of fulfillment in adult life. Also, once new medical technology, especially reproductive technology, becomes available, there is an impetus to use it, and it is widely marketed. While the assumption that lesbians cannot reproduce is oppressive, the assumption that women *must* reproduce is also problematic.

Third, a diagnosis of temporary infertility once again renders an aspect of lesbianism a medical condition. It little matters that initially it would be progressive gynecologists, not conservative psychiatrists, applying the new diagnosis. The inference would remain that there is something medically deficient about the reproductive bodies of lesbians because infertility is generally regarded as an abnormal condition. There is an important difference between lesbian couples and infertile heterosexual couples that we have not mentioned. While some heterosexual couples are regarded as infertile, the majority of heterosexual couples are not. A diagnosis of infertility for lesbian couples would suggest that lesbians are always infertile. In this way, a diagnosis of infertility would be more limiting for lesbians than for heterosexuals.

An important difference between heterosexual and lesbian couples seeking assisted reproduction is that the former can legally marry. Before arguments demanding parity in infertility diagnoses can be fully assessed, we must ask why some privileges accompany donor insemination in heterosexual couples. One important privilege, automatic paternity, applies only to legally married infertile couples. This suggests that paternity rights are grounded in a couple's marital status first and foremost and only secondarily in their infertility diagnosis. The assumption that heterosexuals are normally reproductive and thereby have access to infertility services may also be based on their marital status or at least their right to marry. If legal marriage is the fundamental basis for the benefits currently extended to heterosexual infertile couples, an infertility diagnosis for lesbian couples, barred from legal marriage, may not improve lesbians' access to services or nonbirthing partners' rights to be legal parents of children conceived by donor insemination.

Fourth, medical diagnostics further regulate people. Once lesbians are classified under a particular diagnosis, reproductive concerns shift from the bedroom to the physician's office, we become patients, and the formerly private matter of conception is taken over by the hegemonic practices of institutionalized medicine. Should we relinquish control over reproduction by seeking a diagnosis related to our relationships rather than to our bodies? Already, many who pursue assisted reproduction for infertility problems are subjected to regulatory practices. This regulation includes not only psychological screening, partially ideological in nature, as described above, but the chaotic, short timetables of fertility cycles, implantation procedures, and so forth, that take over normal schedules and priorities, as well as the displacement of the reproductive couple or individual by an extensive team of specialists. Since assisted insemination is a simple procedure, it is unlikely to develop the degree of medical control that may characterize more complex infertility procedures. Nonetheless, extending a diagnosis of infertility to otherwise fertile lesbian couples does further medicalize donor insemination. In addition, sperm banks define and regulate both donors and clients and have become a profitable industry. One researcher claims that since frozen sperm came into common use, "the results have been a major change in the manner that TDI [therapeutic donor insemination] is administered: costs have escalated, commercial sources of semen have expanded their distribution networks and the efficiency of fertilization through insemination has been diminished" (Shapiro 1994:150). The expense of using sperm banks, particularly if many cycles of insemination are required, is another form of regulation, setting up additional economic barriers.

While my strategy of extending an infertility diagnosis to lesbians has not been discussed in the literature, there has been discussion of the trend toward medicalization of donor insemination. Some who argue for self-insemination rather than the medicalization of donor insemination claim that medicalization offers "a measure of confidentiality," but also "involves intrusion and the possibility of some loss of control" (Wikler and Wikler 1991). Lack of access is cited as the most important problem with medicalization. This is interesting, since increased access is a goal of my proposed strategy. If it is likely that increased medicalization leads to decreased access to donor insemination, as the Wiklers have found, then my strategy, accompanied by perhaps new or more scrutinized screening procedures, might prohibit access for more lesbians than it allows. In addition to decreased access, those who argue against the medicalization worry about the increased power it gives to doctors to determine who will and who will not reproduce. The Wiklers argue against doctors' playing such a role in society and prefer that individuals retain full control over their reproductive choices. However, what they do not address is that where lesbians are driven away from fertility clinics and thereby prevented from achieving desired pregnancies, physicians also remain in control.

Those who oppose medicalization of donor insemination argue for the deregulation of donor insemination by encouraging self-insemination and demanding that restrictive practices by sperm banks, such as the requirement of physician authorization, be dismantled. Some such restrictions are especially problematic for lesbians. For instance, in some states, termination of paternity rights of a known donor is more easily accomplished if physician-assisted insemination is used. In light of my discussion, encouraging self-insemination over physician-assisted insemination should include teaching women the techniques for safe intrauterine insemination. Moreover, it does not have the economic barriers associated with physician-assisted insemination. There will be many who will still prefer physician assistance, either because it is easier and more reliable and involves screening for sexually transmitted disease or because medical and legal restrictions never get fully removed. Would an infertility diagnosis be advantageous for addressing discriminatory practices in assisted reproduction?

A final problem with my strategy is that to regard reproductive practices as "treatment for a medical impairment," rather than an elective procedure, is not liberating. A diagnosis of a medical impairment is often stressful. Many couples who currently fit the medical diagnosis of infertility have experienced great angst and frustration because of their inability to reproduce without assistance. They may feel an important function of their bodies has failed them. While lesbians may agonize over fertility matters (such as the inability to produce a child that is the genetic offspring of both women), frustration is largely over social barriers to assisted reproduction and prejudice against lesbian reproduction. By contrast, elective procedures are often liberating, particularly when they involve new medical options and do not presuppose a medical deficiency. Classification as an elective procedure would underscore the deliberate choice of pregnancies resulting from insemination.

If we regard assisted reproduction for lesbians as an elective procedure, we might reject the assumption that lesbian couples are similar to medically infertile heterosexual couples. Were it not for several significant points of similarity, we might find more compelling similarities between lesbian couples and single women pursuing motherhood through assisted insemination. Single women pursuing donor insemination do not seek a diagnosis of infertility. For many, the option to reproduce outside of a relationship is liberating. But lesbian couples are reproducing *within* relationships. This is an important difference. Also, single women may choose assisted reproduction because there is no one with whom they wish to reproduce. Many lesbians long to be able to reproduce with their partners, a difference shared with infertile heterosexual couples.

Lesbian couples seeking physician-assisted insemination are disanalogous in important respects to both infertile heterosexual couples and single women. Yet there are two choices before us: to regard such services as medical treatment for an impairment (hence, a diagnosis of infertility) or as an elective procedure. Currently, lesbian couples are regarded as seeking the latter. In my experiences with assisted-reproductive practices in both a large urban West Coast hospital and a small New England obstetric practice, I was surprised at nurses' responses to us. They were thrilled by the idea of lesbians reproducing in this manner. To them, it was a mark of women's liberation that two women need not marry or be involved with men in order to have children. For these nurses who routinely work with infertile couples, we were not "fixing a problem," we were choosing a new possibility. Would the freedom of this choice be diminished by an infertility diagnosis? Such a diagnosis could not avoid suggesting some impairment or deficiency in need of repair. If there are other ways to improve access to services and diminish discrimination, while still regarding assisted reproduction as an elective procedure, we would retain some measure of the freedom that currently frames the choice of assisted reproduction for lesbians.

Whether or not lesbians should count as infertile couples is a philosophical matter of political importance. Applying an infertility diagnosis to lesbians requesting physician-assisted insemination may normalize these reproductive practices for physicians and even win the support of insurance companies who rely on diagnoses as criteria for medical coverage to reimburse lesbians for insemination services. However, an infertility diagnosis may not greatly increase access to services or persuade adoption judges to approve adoption requests of nonbirthing partners if the process of obtaining the diagnosis fails to diminish antilesbian prejudice. Furthermore, convincing physicians that lesbian couples are "temporarily infertile" would be no easy task. This strategy would most likely be oppressive rather than liberating if any of the five political implications I have listed prove true. Even if it were successful, class prejudice may limit access to assisted reproductive services to those with private insurance. While the strategy of arguing for parity for lesbians at the level of diagnosis may be quite tempting, we must resist it. We are better off seeking these benefits in other ways and steering clear of any infertility diagnosis.

I leave it to my readers who have patiently followed this philosophical thought experiment and are wary of the problems I identify to devise better strategies so desperately needed to improve access to reproductive services, to alter perceptions of lesbian reproductive capacities, and to obtain parental rights for nonbirthing partners.

NOTES

1. This research was inspired by my conversation some years ago with Maggie Magee. I am also grateful to Becky Holmes, Timothy Murphy, Cynthia Sortwell, and Laurel Thom for comments on an earlier draft of this essay and to Barbara Katz Rothman for our conversation at the Women and Genetics in Contemporary Society Workshop on physician-assisted reproductive practices. I appreciate the support for this work provided by the Northwest Center for Research on Women and the Health Science Library at the University of Washington, Seattle, where I was a visiting scholar in 1995 and 1996. I also wish to thank Joan Boggis for typing a final draft of this chapter.

2. Of course, some lesbians and single women do have infertility problems and use assisted reproduction services to address diagnosed infertility conditions.

3. I am grateful to Timothy Murphy for suggesting the phrase "relational infertility."

4. The accuracy of this number is difficult to evaluate since there is no record of the use of self-insemination, and some who use physician-assisted insemination may not identify themselves as lesbian fearing discrimination.

5. State regulation of infertility coverage by insurance companies is not uniform. Three states (Illinois, Massachusetts, and Rhode Island) require insurance companies to cover nonexperimental infertility treatments; seven states (Arkansas, Maryland, Hawaii, New York, Delaware, Ohio, and West Virginia) require infertility coverage in general and limited use of in vitro fertilization. In unregulated states, infertility coverage is quite variable. Low-cost early intervention options are usually covered (Gilbert 1996).

6. According to a review of state adoption laws regarding same-sex second-parent adoption conducted by Lambda Legal Defense and Education Fund (March 3, 1999), the following states had positive decisions in lower courts: Alabama, Alaska, California, Indiana, Iowa, Maryland, Michigan, Minnesota,

Nevada, New Mexico, Oregon, Pennsylvania, Rhode Island, Texas, and Washington. In the District of Columbia and New York State, it was approved in the Court of Appeals. In Illinois and New Jersey, it was approved at the Appellate Level. In Massachusetts and Vermont, it was approved by the State Supreme Court. In Florida, it is prohibited by statute. In Wisconsin and Connecticut, it is prohibited by the State Supreme Court. In Colorado it was disapproved. In Idaho and Ohio, it was disapproved at intermediate court. In the following states, there is no evidence that same sex second parent adoption is permitted: Arizona, Arkansas, Delaware, Georgia, Hawaii, Kansas, Kentucky, Louisiana, Maine, Mississippi, Missouri, Montana, Nebraska, North Carolina, North Dakota, Oklahoma, South Carolina, South Dakota, Tennessee, Utah, Virginia, West Virginia, and Wyoming. See *http://www.lambdalegal.org/cgi-bin/pages/documents/record?record=399*

7. For instance, in some places, a full adoption procedure is required, while in others, stepparent or second-parent adoption, a shorter and less costly procedure, has been extended to gay and lesbian partners (see Dalton, chapter 13).

8. A review of the medical literature on lesbian insemination in *Medline* (1970–96) and other academic databases shows some discussion of HIV risk, access, and prejudice (Shaw 1989:135); and accounts of self-insemination (Hornstein 1984; Klein 1984), of lesbian childbearing (Zeidenstein 1990), and of child rearing (Golombok and Tasker 1994).

9. A review of the philosophical literature from *The Philosophers Index* (1970–96) shows two articles on lesbian parenthood (Hanscombe 1983; Robson 1992) and only one article, a case conference, specifically about physician-assisted insemination in a lesbian couple in London (Forster et al. 1978).

10. See, for example, the discussion concerning a lesbian's request to undergo in vitro fertilization with ova harvested from her partner in Chan et al. 1993.

11. While it may seem more accurate to produce a diagnosis of "relational infertility" to all lesbian couples seeking assisted reproduction through insemination, it is not a term currently used in medicine.

REFERENCES

Andrews, Lori B. 1988. "Alternative Reproduction and the Law of Adoption." In John H. Holinger, ed., *Adoption Law and Practice*, 14.02. New York: Matthew Bender.

Arnup, Katherine. 1994. "Finding Fathers: Artificial Insemination, Lesbians, and the Law." *Canadian Journal of Women and the Law* 7 (1): 97–115.

Brewaeys, A., H. Olbrechts, P. Devroey, and A. C. Van Steirteghen. 1989. "Counseling and Selection of Homosexual Couples in Fertility Treatments." *Human Reproduction* 4 (7): 850–53.

Chambers, David L. 1996. "What If? The Legal Consequences of Marriage and the Legal Needs of Lesbian and Gay Male Couples." *Michigan Law Review* 95 (2): 447–91.

Chan, Connie S., Janis H. Fox, Richard A. McCormick, S. J., and Timothy F. Murphy. 1993. "Lesbian Motherhood and Genetic Choices." *Ethics and Behavior* 3 (2): 211–22.

Cohn, Bob. 1992. "Gays Under Fire." *Newsweek,* September 14: 37–40.

Collins, J. A. 1995. "A Couple with Infertility." *Journal of the American Medical Association* 274 (14): 1159–64.

Cosgrove, I. M. 1979. "AID for Lesbians" (letter). *British Medical Journal* 2: 495.

Daley, Jennifer, Thomas L. Belbanco, and Janet Walzer. 1996. "A Couple with Infertility: One Year Later." *Journal of the American Medical Association* 275 (18): 1446.

Daniels, Ken, and Karen Taylor. 1993. "Formulating Selection Policies for Assisted Reproduction." *Social Science and Medicine* 37 (12): 1473–80.

Englert, Y. 1994. "Artificial Insemination of Single Women and Lesbian Women with Donor Semen. *Human Reproduction* 9 (11): 1969–77.

Fletcher, John C. 1985. "Artificial Insemination in Lesbians: Ethical Considerations." *Archives of Internal Medicine* 145: 419–20.

Forster, Jackie, Carola Haigh, Ian Kennedy, Anthony Parsons, Jennifer Pietroni, Rose Robertson, and Roger Higgs. 1978. "Lesbian Couples: Should Help Extend to AID?" *Journal of Medical Ethics* 4: 91–95.

Gilbert, Bonny. 1996. "Infertility and the ADA: Health Insurance Coverage for Infertility Treatment." *Defense Counsel Journal* 63 (1): 42–57.

Golombok, Susan, and Fiona Tasker. 1994. "Donor Insemination for Single Heterosexual and Lesbian Women: Issues Concerning the Welfare of the Child." *Human Reproduction* 9 (11): 1972–76.

Hanscombe, Gillian. 1983. "The Right to Lesbian Parenthood." *Journal of Medical Ethics* 9: 133–35.

Hatfield, F. E. S. 1979. "AID for Lesbians" (letter). *British Medical Journal* 2: 669.

Hornstein, Francie. 1984. "Children by Donor Insemination: A New Choice for Lesbians." In Rita Arditti, Renate Duelli Klein, and Shelley Minden, eds., *Test-Tube Women: What Future for Motherhood?* pp. 373–81. Boston: Pandora Press.

Klein, Renate Duelli. 1984. "Doing It Ourselves: Self-insemination." In Rita Arditti, Renate Duelli Klein, and Shelley Minden, eds. *Test-Tube Women: What Future for Motherhood?,* pp. 382–90. Boston: Pandora Press.

Klock, Susan C., Mary Casey Jacob, and Donald Maier. 1994. "A Prospective Study of Donor Insemination Recipients: Secrecy, Privacy and Disclosure." *Fertility and Sterility* 62 (3): 477–83.

Knoppers, B. M., and S. LeBris. 1991. "Recent Advances in Medically Assisted Conception: Legal, Ethical, and Social Issues." *American Journal of Law and Medicine* 17: 329–61.

Millsap, D'Andra. 1996. "Sex, Lies, and Health Insurance: Employer-provided Health Insurance Coverage of Abortion and Infertility Services and the ADA." *American Journal of Law and Medicine* 22 (1): 51–84.

Perkoff, Gerald T. 1985. "Artificial Insemination in a Lesbian: A Case Analysis." *Archives of Internal Medicine* 145: 527–31.

Robinson, Bambi E. S. 1997. "Birds Do It. Bees Do It. So Why Not Single Women and Lesbians?" *Bioethics* 3/4: 217–27.

Robson, Ruthann. 1992. "Mother: The Legal Domestication of Lesbian Existence." *Hypatia* 7 (4): 172–85.

Seibel, Machelle M. 1993. "Medical Evaluation and Treatment of the Infertile Couple." In Machelle M. Seibel, Ann A. Kiessling, Judith Bernstein, and Susan R. Levin, eds., *Technology and Infertility: Clinical, Psychosocial, Legal, and Ethical Aspects*, pp. 11–38. New York: Springer-Verlag.

Shapiro, Sander S. 1994. "Therapeutic Donor Insemination." In S. J. Behrman, Grant W. Patton, Jr., and Gary Holtz, eds., *Progress in Infertility*, pp. 149–71. Philadelphia: Lippincott-Ravens.

Shaw, Nancy Stoller. 1989. "New Research in Lesbian Health." *Women's Studies* 17: 125–37.

Shenfield, Françoise. 1994. "Particular Requests in Donor Insemination: Comments on the Medical Duty of Care and the Welfare of the Child." *Human Reproduction* 9 (11): 1976–77.

Talbert, Luther M. 1992. "Overview of the Diagnostic Evaluation." In Mary G. Hammond and Luther M. Talbert, eds., *Infertility: A Practical Guide for the Physician*, 3d ed., p. 2. Cambridge: Blackwell Scientific Publications.

Thomas, Michael J. G. 1979. "AID for Lesbians" (letter). *British Medical Journal* 2: 495.

Wikler, D., and N. Wikler. 1991. "Turkey-Baster Babies: The Demedicalization of Artificial Insemination." *Milbank Quarterly* 69: 5–18.

Wilson, D. H. 1979. "AID for Lesbians" (letter). *British Medical Journal* 2: 669.

Zeidenstein, Laura. 1990. "Gynecological and Childbearing Needs of Lesbians." *Journal of Nurse-Midwifery* 35 (1): 10–18.

13 | Protecting Our Parent–Child Relationships: Understanding the Strengths and Weaknesses of Second-Parent Adoption[1]

Susan E. Dalton

P at and Margaret met in the summer of 1988. For eight months they dated, casually at first, but later exclusively as their relationship became more serious. In April of 1989 they moved in together. That October they began talking about marriage and in November they invited friends and family to a small commitment ceremony where they exchanged rings and vows, promising to treat one another in all respects as a legally married couple.

In the spring of 1990 Pat and Margaret began exploring the idea of raising children together. For nearly a year the couple researched various options including private adoption and artificial insemination. Finally, they decided that they would each have one child, via artificial insemination, and that Pat, because she had better maternity leave, would carry their first. The couple then enlisted the services of a private sperm bank,[2] choosing as their sperm donor a man whose nationality and physical features resembled a genetic blend of both women. In the spring of 1991 they purchased a vial of sperm and used it to inseminate Pat. Several weeks later the couple used a home pregnancy test to confirm their suspicions that Pat was pregnant.

Over the next nine months Pat and Margaret prepared for the arrival of their baby. Both women attended Pat's numerous medical checkups. As the pregnancy progressed they jointly participated in birthing classes and baby showers. And together they slowly accumulated all of the accoutrements that accompany the arrival of infants in Western societies. One winter day in early 1991 Pat went into labor. Margaret rushed her to the hospital where she comforted and coached her until the baby's birth. After cutting the umbilical cord, Margaret kissed the child and gently laid her on Pat's chest to nurse.

To publicly announce the birth of their child, Pat and Margaret designed cards in which both women proclaimed themselves to be the proud mothers of their newborn baby girl. On this card they openly shared their decision to name the child using a hyphenated combination of their two last names.

For the next eighteen months Margaret supported the family so that Pat could remain at home with their daughter. Although Pat officially took on the role of stay-at-home mom, Margaret delighted in sharing in the responsibilities of feeding, bathing, dressing, and nurturing their little girl. To their daughter they became Mama Pat and Mama Maggie, the two most important people in the world.

By the end of 1993, however, Pat and Margaret's relationship had begun to break down, and in the spring of 1994 the two women separated. Following their separation, both women agreed to a joint-custody arrangement and for the next year and a half their daughter lived full time with Pat but stayed overnight with Margaret on the weekends. Throughout this relatively amicable period Pat continually referred to Margaret as her daughter's other mother and supported her attempts to exercise her parental rights and responsibilities.

Toward the end of 1995 this parenting agreement started to unravel, however, and Pat began limiting Margaret's participation in key parenting decisions. As Pat and Margaret's amicable relationship deteriorated, they began increasingly to fight over their daughter's care. In December Pat decided to put an end to the fighting by making a unilateral decision to terminate their joint-parenting agreement, and two months later she proclaimed that Margaret would no longer be allowed to visit with her daughter.

Finding herself painfully cut out of her daughter's life, Margaret hired an attorney and asked the courts to restore her visitation with the child. In court Margaret argued that from the very beginning she and Pat had formed a two-parent family. Evidence supporting this claim was abundant, she argued, and included the fact that she had fully participated in the planning, conception, birth, and rearing of their daughter. With Pat's consent and encouragement she had become an active mother, regularly changing diapers, reading stories, and rocking her daughter to sleep. By all accounts, she had consistently acted as a loving and nurturing parent. As a parent, Margaret argued, she had a right to ongoing contact with her daughter. But more important, she concluded, her daughter had a need for ongoing contact with her.

Pat responded to Margaret's request for court-ordered visitation by arguing that since Margaret had neither given birth to nor adopted her daughter, she was not legally related to the child in any way. Furthermore, Pat argued, even though she and Margaret had attempted to form a two-parent family through marriage, because the state does not recognize lesbian and gay marriage, their attempt had been unsuccessful. Since their marriage was invalid, their two-parent family was legally unrecognizable. Simply put, although Margaret may have acted as a parent, these actions were not enough to make her a legal parent. As a nonparent, Pat concluded, Margaret had no right to ongoing visitation with the child. Even if the court were to determine that ongoing visitation would be in the child's best interest, she insisted, that decision should rest with her, the child's only legal parent.[3]

The court, agreeing with Pat, concluded that despite Pat's initial promise to coparent her daughter with Margaret—her encouragement and consent of Margaret's intimate involvement in the child's conception, birth, and early rearing, and the child's identification of Margaret as her mother—legally Margaret was not a parent. As a nonparent, Margaret had no legal right to visitation with the child. Finally, as the child's only legal parent, Pat retained the right to end any coparenting arrangement she had made with Margaret even if doing so proved detrimental to the child.[4]

DIVORCE IN LESBIAN- AND GAY-HEADED FAMILIES[5]

BECAUSE LESBIAN AND GAY couples cannot legally marry, their relationships remain, for the most part, outside the purview of the courts. Unlike married heterosexual couples who must involve the courts in the dissolution of their marital relationships, lesbian and gay couples can successfully dissolve their families simply by dividing their jointly shared property and moving apart. But what happens to these families when there are children involved?

Lesbian and gay couples who are coparenting children always have the option of developing their own postdivorce coparenting arrangements. These coparenting arrangements may be brokered without the court's assistance, interference, or consent. And, this is in fact what the vast majority of lesbian and gay couples do. A small minority of lesbian and gay couples, however, find themselves unable to broker coparenting arrangements that meet the needs of both parents. For these couples, a court-ordered arrangement may appear to be the only solution.

Child-custody disputes, for the most part, focus the court's attention on two related questions. First, the court asks if each of the adults involved in the dispute has legal standing to bring a case before the court. If the answer to this question is yes, the court then asks the additional question, would ongoing contact with each of these adults be in the best interest of the child?

To answer the first question, the court focuses on the legal relationship each of the adults has with the child. In this equation parental relationships generally outweigh all others, and nonparents are often seen as having no visitation rights at all.[6] In cases such as Pat and Margaret's, where it is determined that the couple was not legally married at the time of the child's birth and only one of the adults is genetically related to the child, if the other adult has not completed a legal adoption, the court generally dismisses the case on the grounds that the nonbiological mother is not a legal parent and thus has no right to sue for visitation. This outcome occurs without any consideration of the child's needs or interests.

CHILDREN OF DIVORCE: WHAT IS IN THEIR BEST INTEREST?

AT THE CENTER OF most child-custody decisions are judicial determinations regarding the best interests of children. These determinations are often based on some combination of factors that are commonly believed to affect the health, safety, and welfare of children.[7] Collectively these factors make up the "best-interest-of-the-child" standard. In addition to their basic physical needs—a physically safe environment, adequate nourishment, mental and physical stimulation—children have a fundamental need for continuity of relationships (Goldstein, Freud, and Solnit 1973). This need emerges for all children who develop strong emotional attachments to those adults they identify as their parents. And, as Patt (1987/88:105) notes, "Maintaining continuity is crucial when the status of the relationship between a child's psychological parents changes."

If a break in the continuity of parent/child relationships is detrimental to children, it is reasonable for judges to consider the continuity of these relationships as a key component of the "best-interest" standard. And, not surprisingly, in most cases of heterosexual divorce the preservation of both of the child's parental relationships is considered extremely important and most judges craft their decisions to facilitate their continuation (Bartlett 1984). In cases of lesbian or gay divorce, however, judges often do not act in ways that facilitate the preservation of the child's relationship with their nonbiological parent.[8] As noted previously, this is because judges often dismiss these cases before the "best-interest" standard is invoked. These decisions force many children in lesbian- and gay-headed families to endure the emotional trauma that comes from losing a parent to whom one is deeply emotionally bonded.

The inability of both of the adults in lesbian- and gay-headed two-parent families to gain legal recognition as coparents has other consequences as well. Many of the financial benefits available to children living in middle- and upper-class families, for example, flow through the parent-child relationship. A parent who is unable to claim a legal relationship to their child may be unable to add that child to their employer-paid health insurance plan; in addition, their property will not automatically transfer to their child, who likewise will remain ineligible for social security benefits should the parent die. For these reasons, many middle- and upper-class lesbian and gay couples have begun searching for alternative ways to legally establish themselves as coparents. Prohibited as they are from entering the legal institution of marriage, some lesbian and gay parents have begun turning to the adoption system for relief.[9]

ADOPTION AS AN ALTERNATIVE MEANS OF CONSTRUCTING TWO-PARENT FAMILIES

OUTSIDE OF MARRIAGE THERE are two legal avenues through which two unrelated adults may form a legally recognizable two-parent family: the joint biological production of a child and adoption. Because same-sex couples are unable biologically to reproduce a child together, their only means of creating legally viable two-parent families is through adoption. The adoption system, however, has a long history of dividing adoption petitioners into two mutually exclusive categories: married couples and single individuals. Within this system married couples create two-parent families by adopting children jointly, while single adults create single-parent families by adopting children individually. What the legislators who created this system did not foresee was that lesbian and gay couples, technically two single adults, would develop a pressing need for access to joint adoptions without the benefit of marriage.

THE TRADITIONAL ADOPTION MODEL

FAMILY LAW IN THE United States has at its core a paradigmatic family structure consisting of married heterosexual adults and their biological children. This structure, it is often claimed, predates the laws of man and reflects the dictates of God himself (Bartholet 1993). Unlike the supposedly preordained structure of the traditional nuclear family, adoptive families, the courts claim, are manmade creations; i.e., they are created through the institution of law. Because adoptive families are creations of the state, it is appropriate, the courts argue, for states to regulate their formation (Hollinger 1996a).

State oversight or regulation of adoption has resulted in the creation, in many states, of a three-tiered adoption hierarchy (see tables 13.1 and 13.2). At the top of the adoption hierarchy sit men who are married to women who give birth to children within the context of their marital relationships.[10] Both presumed-father statutes and many assisted-reproduction statutes make automatic fathers out of husbands whose wives reproduce children, a process known as summary adoptions (Dalton 1999).

At the second tier of the adoption hierarchy are men and women who marry partners who have children from previous relationships. When these adults adopt their spouses' children, they do so using the stepparent adoption. In most states stepparent adoptions are reviewed by the courts to ensure that the child is not being adopted by someone with a violent or criminal history. The investigation of the adopting parent is relatively brief and the resulting information is passed on to a judge who then either grants or denies the adoption petition based on the best interest of the child.

Individuals who adopt children from outside their immediate families[11] occupy the third tier of the adoption hierarchy, the independent adoption. In most states independent adoptions differ from both summary and stepparent adoptions in several important ways. The first difference between summary and stepparent adoptions on the one hand and independent adoptions on the other is the extent to which the state is involved in the adoption procedure. While states generally do not get involved in summary adoptions at all and are involved in stepparent adoption only minimally, they become very involved in independent adoptions. This involvement includes conducting an in-depth investigation into the adopting adults' home and family lives (see table 13.3). As with the stepparent adoption, the information collected during this investigation process is forwarded to a

TABLE 13.1 Adoption Hierarchy

I. SUMMARY ADOPTION (PRESUMED-FATHER AND ASSISTED REPRODUCTION STATUTES)

---

retention of parental rights by birth mother
extension of parental rights to birth mother's husband
no state investigation of the adopting parent
marital requirement
no financial cost

II. STEPPARENT ADOPTION (STEPPARENT ADOPTION STATUTES)

---

retention of parental rights by custodial parent
extension of parental rights to custodial parent's spouse
limited state investigation of the adopting parent
marital requirement
relatively low financial cost

III. INDEPENDENT ADOPTION (INDEPENDENT ADOPTION STATUTES)

---

relinquishment of parental rights by all existing legal parents
acquisition of parental rights by individuals formerly unrelated to the child
detailed state investigation of the adopting family
relatively high financial cost

---

judge, who either grants or denies the adoption based on the best interest of the child.

The second important difference between the first two types of adoption—summary and stepparent—and the independent adoption involves the relationship between the custodial biological parent(s) and their child following the adoption. In both summary and stepparent adoptions the child's custodial parent retains their parental status even as that status is granted to another adult—the custodial parent's spouse—via the adoption process.[12] In both summary and stepparent adoptions, the noncustodial biological parent loses their parental status as a result of the adoption procedure.

In traditional independent adoptions, however, both of a child's biolog-

TABLE 13.2 Action Necessary to Create a Legal Relationship Between a Nonbirth Parent and Child (Across Marital Status)

LEGAL RELATIONSHIP BETWEEN PARENTS	ACTION REQUIRED TO CREATE LEGAL RELATIONSHIP BETWEEN NONBIRTH PARENT AND CHILD				
	NONE	STEPPARENT ADOPTION	INDEPENDENT ADOPTION	SECOND-PARENT ADOPTION	INDEPENDENT AND SECOND-PARENT ADOPTION
biological father married to birth mother at time of birth	x				
nonbiological father married to birth mother at time of birth	x				
nonbiological mother married to biological father at time of birth		x			
nonbiological lesbian mother partnered to birth mother at time of birth				x	
nonbiological parent married to biological parent after birth of child		x			
lesbian or gay parent partnered to biological parent after birth of child				x	
single adult adopting nonbiological child			x		
married couple adopting nonbiological child			x		
lesbian or gay couple adopting nonbiological child					x

TABLE 13.3 Investigation of Adopting Parents (Across Type of Adoption)

ELEMENTS OF STATE RUN INVESTIGATION INTO THE LIVES OF ADOPTING PARENTS	TYPE OF ADOPTION		
	SUMMARY	STEPPARENT	INDEPENDENT AND/OR SECOND PARENT
visual inspection of the home			x
medical history			x
employment and financial history			x
investigation of drug and alcohol use			x
opinions on discipline and punishment			x
child-rearing philosophies			x
relationships with parents and siblings			x
history of prior intimate relationships			x
religious and philosophical beliefs			x
stability of present marital/intimate relationship		x	x
history of past marital/intimate relationships		x	x
criminal records check			x
sexual abuse registry check		x	x
2 two-hour in-home interviews			x
short office interview		x	
approximate financial cost of the adoption	$0	$500–$700	$4,000–$6,000

This table is based on the adoption requirements of the State of California.

ical parents must relinquish their parental rights before those rights may be granted to the adopting adult(s). In independent adoptions, a child is completely transferred from one family to another with their ties to their adoptive family superseding all ties to their biological family. In these adoptions the biological parents end their legal relationship with the child and the adoptive parents become the child's new legal family.

FITTING LESBIAN AND GAY COUPLES INTO THIS ADOPTION MODEL

THE PROBLEM WITH THESE traditional forms of adoption, from the point of view of lesbian and gay couples who wish to use adoption to form two-parent families, is that they do not formally allow unmarried couples to adopt a single child jointly. Both summary and stepparent adoptions, for example, require the adopting adult to be legally married to their partner, the child's legal parent, at the time the adoption takes place. This requirement means that lesbian and gay couples such as Pat and Margaret are unable to use either of these forms of adoption to secure their two-parent families.

At the same time, independent adoptions require that the child's existing legal parents relinquish all parental rights before the adoption may be completed. In families such as Pat and Margaret's, this requirement would mean that Pat would have to give up her parental rights before Margaret could become a legal parent. In other words, Pat would be the child's only legal parent before the adoption and Margaret would be her only legal parent after the adoption. Within this traditional adoption hierarchy there is simply no place for couples such as Pat and Margaret. To solve this dilemma judges in some states have begun adding a fourth tier to the adoption hierarchy. This fourth type of adoption, often known as the second-parent adoption, is created by joining the stepparent adoption with the independent adoption (see table 13.4).

Lesbian and gay couples, like heterosexual couples who complete stepparent adoptions, use the adoption procedure to extend parental rights from one parent to another for the purpose of creating legally recognizable two-parent families. Second-parent adoptions imitate stepparent adoptions in that they allow a parent to extend their parental right to another adult, the child's second parent.[13] At the same time, adults seeking second-parent adoptions are subjected to the same in-depth investigation as adults

TABLE 13.4   Adoption Hierarchy—New Addition

IV. SECOND-PARENT ADOPTION (NO STATUTORY SUPPORT)

retention of parental rights by custodial parent
extension of parental rights to custodial parent's intimate partner
detailed state investigation of the adopting family
no marital requirement
relatively high financial cost

seeking independent adoptions (see table 13.3). What is unique about the second-parent adoption is that unlike other forms of adoption, whose procedures are clearly spelled out in state adoption statutes, second-parent adoptions have received no formal support from state legislatures. This means that lesbian and gay couples wishing to build two-parent families through adoption must convince the judges hearing their cases that the proposed adoption is both in the best interest of their children and permissible under that state's law.

JUDICIAL RESPONSES TO THE SECOND-PARENT ADOPTION

LESBIAN AND GAY PARENTS, faced with the burden of convincing judges that the second-parent adoption procedure is indeed legal, argue that the controlling issue in all adoptions is the best interest of the child (Note 1990). Indeed, in many states judges are required to interpret adoption laws liberally or broadly when doing so will assist them in achieving this primary goal (Hollinger 1996b; Note 1990; Patt 1987/88). When it is clearly in the best interest of the child to be legally related to both of his or her social parents, as is often the case in lesbian- and gay-headed two-parent families, judges have both the ability and the obligation to grant the adoption even if it means creatively interpreting the existing adoption statutes. After all, these parents argue, there is nothing in the adoption statutes specifically prohibiting judges from constructing two-parent families in this way (Note 1990).

Thus far, Supreme Courts in two states—Vermont and Massachusetts[14] —have determined that second-parent adoptions are indeed legal. In these states, all lesbian and gay parents have a right to pursue second-parent adoptions and the only obstacle they must overcome is demonstrating that the proposed adoption is in the best interest of the child.[15] Additionally, Appellate Courts in three states—Illinois, New Jersey, and New York—and the District of Columbia[16] have issued similar rulings. These Appellate Court rulings ensure that all parents living in the corresponding appellate districts have access to the second-parent adoption procedure.[17] Finally, in at least fifteen states—Alabama, Alaska, California, Georgia, Indiana, Iowa, Maryland, Michigan, Minnesota, Nevada, New Mexico, Oregon, Pennsylvania, Rhode Island, and Texas—some second-parent adoptions have been granted. In some of these states, California for instance, although second-parent adoptions are available throughout much of the state, some judges still refuse to grant them, arguing that under current law they are not legal.

At the same time, higher courts in four states—Colorado, Connecticut, Ohio, and Wisconsin,[18]—have ruled against second-parent adoptions. One additional state—Florida—maintains statutes banning all lesbian and gay adults from adopting children under any circumstances. Courts that rule against second-parent adoptions most often reason that while some adoption statutes do formally create the right of custodial parents to share their parental status with their intimate partners, this right is specifically reserved for married couples. Although second-parent adoptions may indeed be in the best interest of children living in two-parent lesbian- and gay-headed families, these courts conclude, the adoption statutes as they are currently written do not give judges the power to grant them.

DRAWBACKS OF THE SECOND-PARENT ADOPTION SYSTEM

WHILE SECOND-PARENT ADOPTIONS do provide important legal rights and protections to those lesbian and gay parents who are able to obtain them, their benefits are remarkably limited, especially when compared to those afforded heterosexual couples through marriage. Additionally, the procedure itself is often problematic.

One drawback for couples who use the second-parent adoption as a legal substitute for marriage is that the resulting legal structure is a family in which the two adults remain legal strangers to one another. Had Pat and Margaret, for example, used a second-parent adoption to secure their family legally, they would have achieved coparent status without ever forming a direct legal relationship with one another. They would have become coparents but not spouses. As the vast majority of legal benefits and protections afforded families in this society are funneled through the spousal relationship (i.e., through legally married couples to their children) Pat, Margaret, and their child would have remained unrecognizable as a family for the purpose of accessing these benefits. Although Pat and Margaret would have both become legal coparents, their family would have remained invisible to the state and federal bureaucracies that dole out family benefits.

Additionally, the fact that only three states currently have Supreme Court decisions favoring second-parent adoptions means that a large number of lesbian and gay parents live in areas of the country in which these adoptions are simply not available. Even those parents living in areas where second-parent adoptions have been granted in the past are not guaranteed their availability in the future. In states lacking Supreme Court decisions affirming the legality of second-parent adoptions, parents' access to the procedure may be lost any time a judge who has granted them in the past is replaced by a new judge. This is because in states lacking precedent, all new judges must decide for themselves whether or not to recognize the procedure as valid. This means that Pat and Margaret's access to a second-parent adoption would depend largely on where in the United States they reside. If they choose to live in a large metropolitan area in the northeastern or western United States, their chances of obtaining a second-parent adoption improve significantly. If they choose to live in a more rural area or in the middle or southern United States, their access decreases remarkably. Of course if Pat and Margaret are financially well off they may be able to simply move to an area of the country that grants second-parent adoptions, returning home after the adoption is completed. If Pat and Margaret are poor, however, temporary relocation would probably not be an affordable solution.

Even if Margaret were successfully to complete a second-parent adoption, however, her parental status could still be challenged. While we generally assume adoptions to be legally robust (i.e., fairly difficult to reverse or dissolve) this is not necessarily the case for most second-parent adoptions. Outside of Vermont, Massachusetts, and New York, no one really knows if any given second-parent adoptions will withstand a court challenge. In Pat and Margaret's case this means that although Margaret may successfully adopt their child using a second-parent adoption, at some later date their state's Supreme Court may decide that second-parent adoptions aren't legally valid after all. If this were to occur, Margaret would automatically lose the legal parental status she had gained through the adoption.

Additionally, because the second parent-adoption procedure funnels lesbian and gay families into the third-tier adoption system, it represents a relatively costly way of forming a two-parent family. Unlike marriage certificates that routinely cost below $50, second-parent adoptions can routinely cost between $4,000 and $6,000. And, unlike marriage certificates that need to be purchased only once,[19] a second-parent adoption must be completed each time a new child joins the family. Let's say that Pat gave birth to three children instead of only one. In this instance Margaret would have to complete three second-parent adoptions, one for each child. Securing their family in this way could easily cost Pat and Margaret $12,000 or more. Parents who have access to few of the financial advantages available to the middle and upper classes may find that the relatively high cost of the second-parent adoption outweighs the limited benefits they are likely to gain as a result of the procedure. At the same time, as second-parent adoptions become more common, judges may begin using them as the sole indicator of a biological mother's intent to share her parental status with her partner.[20] Lesbians who fail to complete these adoptions, for whatever reasons, may find themselves unable to convince the courts to recognize their parental status.

Also, because the second-parent adoption procedure forces lesbian- and gay-headed families into the adoption rubric, it subjects these families to substantial scrutiny by individuals within the adoption system. In an earlier study of the adoption system in California, I found many adoption social workers to be remarkably naïve when it comes to lesbian- and gay-headed families (see Dalton 1999). Indeed, many lesbian and gay parents in that study reported finding themselves in the uncomfortable position of having to educate the social workers who had come into their homes to investigate their families. As one mother recounted regarding her interactions with the state-appointed investigator, "We basically had to do Lesbian 101." Additionally, other mothers reported encountering social workers who used the home study investigation as an opportunity to advocate against those aspects of lesbian and gay parenting about which they felt uncomfortable.[21] Still others reported dealings with social workers who appeared unable to grasp the concept of a female-headed two-parent family and that this was often reflected in the language they used to describe both the family and the adoption procedure.

As a result of these often difficult interactions, many of these lesbian mothers felt angry and frustrated for, as one mother reported, having to "pay all this money and jump through all these hoops to get rights that other people [take] for granted." Another mother who had adopted her partner's two biological children summed up her experience with the overall adoption procedure in this way: "We were very excited that the world was going to let us adopt and be a real family . . . and [so] we really didn't take offense to the fact that we were having to do this process that was so much longer and drawn out than you know any ex-convict murdering stepfather would have to go through. The second time through was a very different experience."

And finally, many of the mothers in this study were acutely aware of their vulnerability during the ten months it commonly takes to complete a second-parent adoption. As one mother angrily proclaimed, "So making us go through all these hoops and ten months worth of . . . a dangerous waiting period . . . , if [my partner] had dropped dead or been hit by a truck, her parents could have broken up our family." Indeed, in most cases, these parents reported that they relied upon considerable resources—financial, educational, and emotional—to negotiate the second-parent system successfully. These relatively high financial and emotional costs work to limit the number of lesbian and gay parents either willing or able to use the second-parent adoption procedure to protect their families.

Finally, in most states the second-parent adoption procedure itself remains extremely vulnerable to political movements aimed at prohibiting all legal recognition of lesbian- and gay-headed two-parent families. In an attempt to avoid political backlash that could effectively eliminate the procedure altogether, many lawyers shy away from publicly broadcasting the availability of the second-parent adoption procedure.

Indeed, in many areas, the primary means of distributing information regarding the second-parent adoption procedure is word of mouth: lawyers and parents who have first-hand knowledge of the procedure pass the information along through personal contact with friends and associates. This particular method of distributing legal information has worked to further limit access to the second-parent adoption to those individuals who are somehow connected to lesbian and gay legal communities. Overall, these multiple shortcomings, imbedded within the procedure itself, work to prevent many of those lesbian and gay parents who exist on the margins of mainstream (white, middle-class, urban) lesbian and gay communities from successfully employing second-parent adoptions to protect their families.

As lesbian and gay communities continue to grow and mature, issues of family formation are increasingly pushed to the forefront of lesbian and gay political and social agendas. The resulting political struggle to open legal institutions such as marriage to lesbian and gay couples is in no small part driven by the fact that an increasing number of these couples are bringing children into their lives, thereby forming socially viable two-parent families (Benkov 1994; Kurdek 1993; McCandish 1987; Patterson 1992, 1994, 1995; Sullivan 1997).

The widespread social discomfort many Americans feel toward lesbian and gay individuals has led some to argue that as a society we should not extend legal recognition or protections and benefits to the families these individuals create.[22] But what of the children living in these families? Our refusal as a society to recognize lesbian- and gay-headed families means that all of the individuals living within these families, including the children, are denied virtually all of the benefits, protections, and privileges we as a society use to support families. One of the most important of these benefits is the right of children to maintain ongoing relationships with parents to whom they become emotionally bonded and upon whom they are emotionally dependent.

When coparenting couples divorce, the children living within their families become extremely vulnerable. Although it would be nice if all divorcing couples were able to jointly construct cocustody arrangements that would satisfy the needs of everyone involved, in some cases this just isn't possible. In these cases we often look to the courts to devise solutions that, although they may not completely satisfy the adults, at least take care of the needs of the children. Unfortunately, however, in the case of lesbian and gay divorce, the courts often decline to take on the role of child-conscious mediator. This unwillingness on the part of the courts to protect the emotional health and well-being of children raised in lesbian- and gay-headed two-parent families derives directly from their inability to recognize these children's families as valid.

Although custody cases are played out in the courtroom, a venue from which the public is largely excluded, the bigger issue of the legal recognition of nontraditional families is being played out in political arenas across the country. Questions concerning whether states should grant lesbian and gay couples the right to marry and thus form legally recognizable two-parent families are being decided by state legislators and increasingly by the voting public.[23] Although these issues are often framed as a battle over lesbian and gay rights, I would suggest that they are more importantly a battle over children's rights. For what is being decided is whether or not we as a society will treat all children living in two-parent families equally.

NOTES

1. This research was assisted by a Sexuality Research Fellowship from the Social Science Research Council, with funds provided by the Ford Foundation.

2. Sperm banks are medical facilities that freeze donations of sperm for later use. An individual wishing to become pregnant may buy frozen sperm from a bank, thaw the sperm to room temperature, and then introduce it into the vagina via a needleless syringe to initiate a pregnancy.

3. This vignette is taken from an actual California Appellate Court case. I have truthfully represented the facts of the case while altering some of the information, such as the names of the litigants, to protect the identities of the family members involved.

4. For legal discussions regarding similar cases throughout the United States see Zuckerman (1986), Delaney (1991), Gavigan (1995), Arnup and Boyd (1995), Berner (1995), and Hollinger (1996b).

5. I am intentionally using the term "divorce," although it does not technically reflect the legal process as it pertains to lesbian and gay couples. As Morton (1998) explains, although lesbian and gay couples may not legally marry and thus do not technically divorce, other terms commonly used to describe the breakdown of lesbian and gay families such as "break up" or "separation" do not capture the profound emotional impact the dissolution of a family has on the members of these families.

6. Some states do give grandparents and/or court-appointed guardians the right to seek ongoing visitation with children.

7. In California the state legislature has instructed judges making best-interest determinations to consider: (a) the health, safety, and welfare of the child; (b) any history of abuse against the child; (c) the nature and amount of contact with both parents (see California Civil Code Section 4608).

8. This is generally true in any family in which one parent is a legal parent and the other is not.

9. For a discussion of lesbians, gays, and the institution of marriage see Chambers (chapter 19). Also see Ettelbrick (1989), Sherman (1992), Eskridge (1996), Sullivan (1997), Cabaj (1997), and Stiers (1998).

10. Here I am specifically referring to married men who are not the biological fathers of their wives' children.

11. Some states allow adults to adopt the children of close family members, such as siblings or first cousins, without undergoing the intense scrutiny of the independent-adoption procedure.

12. In stepparent adoptions, the legal custodial parent may be either a biological parent or an adoptive parent; i.e., someone who adopted the child at an earlier date.

13. Second-parent adoptions have been used to establish other types of coparenting relationships such as between a mother and her adult daughter, both of whom are parenting a close family-member's child (Dalton 1999).

14. See *Adoptions of B.L.V.B. and E.L.V.B.* No. 92–321 Supreme Court of Vermont 160 Vt. 368; 628 A.2d 1271; 1993 Vt; see also *Adoption of Tammy*, M-6219 Supreme Judicial Court of Massachusetts 416 Mass. 205; 619 N.E.2d 315; 1993 Mass.

15. Lawyers sometimes question the importance of distinguishing between states with supreme court, appellate court, and trial court decisions. While this distinction matters less for gays and lesbians who live in urban areas where second-parent adoptions are more readily available, it is significant for gays and lesbians in rural areas where judges often refuse to grant second-parent adoptions until a higher court has addressed the issue directly.

16. See *In re K.M. and In re K.L.*, 1–95–0161 1–95–0238 Appellate Court of Illinois First and Second Divisions 274 Ill. App. 3d 189; 653 N.E.2d 1995; see also *In re H.N.R.*, A-1283–94T5 Superior Court of New Jersey, Appellate Division 285 J.J. Super. 1; 666 a.2D 535; 1995; see also *In the Matter of Jacob*, No. 195 Court of Appeals of New York 86 N.Y.2d 651; 1995; see also *In Re M.M.D. & B.H.M.*, No. 94-FS-620 District of Columbia Court of Appeals 662 A.2d 837l 1995.

17. States are divided into appellate districts. Each district has an appellate court. When a case is appealed to an appellate court, the resulting decision applies to all of the lower courts that operate within the appellate district.

18. See *In re T.K.J.*, No 95CA0531, No. 95CA0532 Court of Appeals of Colorado, Division One 931 P.2d 488; 1996; see also *In re The Adoption of Baby Z.*, (SC 15868), (SC 15869) Supreme Court of Connecticut 247 Conn. 474; 724 A.2d 1035; 1999; see also *In re Adoption of Jane Doe*, Case No. 19017 Court of Appeals of Ohio, Ninth Appellate District Summit 1998; see also *In re Angel Lace M.*, No. 92–1369, 92–1370 Supreme Court of Wisconsin 184 Wis.2d 492; 516 N.W.2d 678; 1994.

19. Of course many people today purchase multiple-marriage certificates throughout the course of their lifetimes. Each couple, however, need only purchase one and that one remains valid until voided through divorce.

20. This is already occurring in California. (See *Nancy S. v. Michelle G.*, 228 Cal. App3d 831, 279 Cal. Rptr. 212 and *West v. Superior Court*, 59 Cal. App. 4th 302, 69 Cal. Rptr. 2d 160).

21. These would include such issues as raising a child without a father in the home and the practice of many lesbian mothers of referring to biological fathers who remain unknown to their children as sperm donors instead of fathers.

22. For examples of these claims see the political discussion surrounding the Defense of Marriage Act, 1996, or the Hawaii marriage case *Baehr v. Miiki*.

23. In 1998 the citizens of both Alaska and Hawaii voted to rewrite their state constitutions for the purpose of preventing their states from issuing marriage licenses to lesbian and gay couples.

REFERENCES

Arnup, Katherine and Susan Boyd. 1995. "Familial Disputes? Sperm Donors, Lesbian Mothers, and Legal Parenthood." In D. Herman and C. Stychin, eds., *Legal Inversions: Lesbians, Gay Men, and the Politics of Law*, pp. 77–101. Philadelphia: Temple University Press.

Bartholet, Elizabeth. 1993. *Family Bonds: Adoption and the Politics of Parenting.* Boston: Houghton Mifflin.

Bartlett, Katharine T. 1984. "Rethinking Parenthood as an Exclusive Status: The Need for Legal Alternatives When the Premise of the Nuclear Family Has Failed." *Virginia Law Review* 70: 879–963.

Benkov, Laura. 1994. *Reinventing the Family: The Emerging Story of Lesbian and Gay Parents.* New York: Crown.

Berner, Nicole. 1995. "Child Custody Disputes Between Lesbians: Legal Strategies and Their Limitations." *Berkeley Women's Law Journal* 10: 31–39.

Cabaj, Robert P. 1997. *On the Road to Same-Sex Marriage: A Supportive Guide to Psychological, Political, and Legal Issues.* San Francisco: Jossey-Bass.

Dalton, Susan. 1999. "We Are Family: Understanding the Structural Barriers to the Legal Formation of Lesbian and Gay Families in California." Ph.D. Diss. University of California, Santa Barbara, Cal.

Delaney, Elizabeth A. 1991. "Statutory Protection of the Other Mother: Legally Recognizing the Relationship Between the Nonbiological Lesbian Parent and Her Child." *Hastings Law Journal* 43: 177–216.

Eskridge Jr., William N. 1996. *The Case for Same-Sex Marriage: From Sexual Liberty to Civilized Commitment.* New York: Free Press.

Ettelbrick, Paula. 1989. "Since When Is Marriage a Path to Liberation?" *OUT/LOOK National Gay and Lesbian Quarterly* 9: 14–16.

Gavigan, Shelley A. M. 1995. "A Parent(ly) Knot: Can Heather Have Two Mommies?" In D. Herman and C. Stychin, eds., *Legal Inversions: Lesbians, Gay Men, and the Politics of Law*, pp. 102–117. Philadelphia: Temple University Press.

Goldstein, Joseph, Anna Freud, and Albert J. Solnit. 1973. *Beyond the Best Interests of the Child*. New York: Free Press

Hollinger, Joan Heifetz. 1996a. *Adoption Law and Practice*. New York: Matthew Bender.

——. 1996b. "The Uniform Adoption Act: Reporter's Ruminations." *Family Law Quarterly* 30: 345–78.

Kurdek, Lawrence A. 1993. "The Allocation of Household Labor in Gay, Lesbian, and Heterosexual Married Couples." *Journal of Social Issues* 49: 127–39.

McCandish, Barbara M. 1987. "Against All Odds: Lesbian Mother Family Dynamics." In F. W. Bozett, ed., *Gay and Lesbian Parents*, pp. 23–38. New York: Praeger.

Morton, Susan B. 1998. "Lesbian Divorce." *American Journal of Orthopsychiatry* 68: 410–19.

Note. 1990. "Joint Adoption: A Queer Option?" *Vermont Law Review* 15: 197–226.

Patt, Emily C. 1987–88. "Second Parent Adoption: When Crossing the Marital Barrier Is a Child's Best Interest." *Berkeley Women's Law Journal* 3: 96–133.

Patterson, Charlotte J. 1992. "Children of Lesbian and Gay Parents." *Child Development* 63 (5): 1025–42.

——. 1994. "Children of the Lesbian Baby Boom: Behavioral Adjustment, Self-concepts, and Sex Role Identity." In B. Greene and G. M. Herek, eds., *Lesbian and Gay Psychology: Theory, Research, and Clinical Applications*, pp. 156–75. Newbury Park, Cal.: Sage.

——. 1995. "Families of the Lesbian Baby Boom: Parents' Division of Labor and Children's Adjustment." *Developmental Psychology* 31: 115–23.

Sherman, Suzanne. 1992. *Lesbian and Gay Marriage: Private Commitments, Public Ceremonies*. Philadelphia: Temple University Press.

Stiers, Gretchen A. 1998. *From This Day Forward: Commitments, Marriage, and Family in Lesbian and Gay Relationships*. New York: St. Martins Press.

Sullivan, Andrew. 1997. *Same-Sex Marriage: Pro and Con*. New York: Vintage.

Zuckerman, Elizabeth. 1986. "Comment, Second Parent Adoption for Lesbian Parented Families: Legal Recognition of the Other Mother." *University of California, Davis, Law Journal* 19: 729–59.

14 | "My Daddy Loves Your Daddy": A Gay Father Encounters A Social Movement

John C. Miller

Like many individuals who grew up in the 1950s, I knew that I was different. I was attracted to my male peers and even to certain television and movie stars—Robert Stack, James Dean, Judy Garland. My Catholic upbringing and even residential junior seminary led me to hide or sublimate all sexuality and to become a somewhat priggish, frightened individual who was afraid of his attraction to boys. To my knowledge I never met a gay person until the mid-1960s when I was in my mid twenties. My uncle, whose life produced my awakening to music and art, so absent in my working-class origin, has never, even at the age of seventy, self-identified with the "g" word. Nevertheless, I read all I could about homosexuals in texts about abnormal and deviant psychology and sociology. I dated and played the social roles but lacked totally any sexual interest in women; they were great friends. The exhibitionism of my fraternity brothers in both their nakedness and their lust toward women fascinated me. I wanted to fulfill my prescribed male role, but to do so I needed to bury my sexual orientation toward men. I lived without any gay role models. The major gay publications were academic—André Gide and Rimbaud in French (of course), and publications within the field of psychology. Not surprisingly, in college I became a French major with a double major in psychology. Outside of academia, the primary gay-related sources available to me were the cheap black and white photo books of young muscular men in posing straps and neoclassical garb that I stole from the magazine company where I worked. Fantasy was possible. In 1961 I went abroad on a Fulbright scholarship, where I permitted myself to be seduced and kept by an older gentleman. I could be homosexual only because the exotic could be made erotic. At the same time I lived in constant fear. Would I lose my U.S. student scholarship if they discovered I was "one of those perverts"? I had grown up during Senator McCarthy's canonization by the nuns in my Catholic schools. Thus it was natural that when I returned to the United States, I assumed once again my prescribed heterosexual role as "best little boy."

During the late 1960s, I began my professional career path. This academic path coincided with a personal journey from a frightened, sexually closeted life to participation in the institution of heterosexual marriage to the emergence of a more authentic self-identity as a openly gay man. During my first academic appointment at Allegheny College, as an instructor in Spanish, working on a Ph.D., I married and became the proud parent of two daughters, Marialisa and Amanda. I tried to fulfill my culturally prescribed heterosexual role as father and husband but my sexual attraction throughout this time was to men.

I became drawn into the emerging men's movement that arose in the shadow of the powerful women's social revolution. Particularly through a consciousness-raising group, I became more open about my sexuality, revealed only in the confidential and sometimes confessional environment of those discussions and dialogues. I first came out to others in 1970 in a consciousness-raising group led by Warren Farrell.

During this time I was torn between the emerging awareness of my sexual orientation and my continuing wish to fulfill my societal role as a father and husband, as modeled by my Roman Catholic, working-class parents. Fatherhood and heterosexuality were the well-defined ideals. Any "deviant" expression of sexuality was a violation of both the social and religious codes that had guided my upbringing.

In an attempt to bridge my conflicts, I fled into the hippie culture of the 1970s, where overt displays of nudity and sexuality, almost always heterosexual but permitting "bisexuality"—for example, by David Bowie, Mick Jagger, Jim Morrison—attracted me. I could be straight but "play around" with bisexuality.

I intellectualized my sexual attractions, reading Gide and Genet, Wilde and Baldwin, yet never entered a gay bar or bath, leaving my decision making to the chance encounters of academic conferences and YMCAs.

My life was fragmented, my sexuality splintered, as I read of the Mattachine Society, *One* magazine, and the far-away protests of Stonewall but concentrated my energy and attention on teaching and completing my dissertation. Only a "chance" encounter on the nude sunbathing deck of the West Side YMCA in New York City in the early 1970s opened my eyes to a romantic, lustful affair with an openly gay man.

Society was also changing. A new group of openly gay biological fathers (gay fathers) appeared. The reasons for the emergence of these groups are complex, reflecting sweeping changes in both mores and political activism, defined best by the emerging openness about sexuality and the Stonewall riots.

The feminist movement stimulated a change in the understanding of the traditional role and perception of males through its critical examination of men's and women's roles and their culturally prescribed responsibilities (Fagan-Fasteau 1974; Farrell 1978; Levinson 1978). The women's movement focused on gender roles, thereby permitting men also to engage in self-exploration and role-change exploration. Men as gendered selves began to examine the ways in which the experience of manhood had structured their everyday activities—both at home and at work.

The feminist movement and the men's consciousness-raising experiences that grew out of the women's movement helped me to explore my emotional side and to better understand both my own expectations of myself as a man and my role as a father. I believed that I was a "good father," but struggled to understand my role as father with the emerging sexual feelings I was experiencing. After my divorce in 1972, I had custody of my two children—supported in serial monogamy by a number of younger women who admired my "single-father" parenting. The most important of these relationships was with Lib, a committed feminist and NOW leader, who became my second wife. There was no clear roadmap for the two of us in understanding ourselves as individuals, our relationship with each other, our sexuality, or our roles as parents and partners. This was uncharted territory for us and for our generation. The result was conflictive. We remained together in the laboratory of our relationship for three years—growing together, growing separately, and sharing in the raising of our children. As our growth pulled us along different paths, we finally chose to go our separate ways.

Soon thereafter I met and fell in love with Paul, a student at Gettysburg College where I was teaching. This new love was both a powerful experience of loving and being loved by a young man and a time of publicly affirming myself as gay. It was a gay adolescence filled with the excitement and passion as well as the doubt and confusion of young love. I was forty at the time and the custodial parent of two children.

As I was exploring my gay self, my older daughter was discovering her own preteen sexuality. I was struggling to understand my own sexuality within a new gay relationship at the very time my daughter was trying to understand hers. In my own adolescent searching, her questions and doubts about becoming a woman went unattended. As she later said, these circumstances left her confused and uncertain and feeling less "valued" as a young woman. She quickly established an intense sibling rivalry with my student lover. My younger daughter, in contrast, loved him and considered him a handsome big-brother figure.

When my older daughter entered high school, my two daughters' lives and my life changed abruptly, not unusual in postdivorce coparenting. My first wife and I had agreed that the girls would move in with her in Columbia, Maryland, for high school. I relocated to New York, lost in the necessarily coded sexual identity of professional life on an urban campus, Jersey City State College. For the first year I was at Jersey City State, my lover and I commuted between Gettysburg College and New York City. Following his graduation, Paul moved in with me in New York. Within eight months, he discovered a gay peer-relationship and we split bitterly. I was left alone in New York without the visible identity of my fatherhood role and without the security of a love relationship to support my identity as a gay man. I was without clear links to the labels that were so important to my definition of self. I was alone in New York and depressed.

Reading the back page of the *Village Voice* early in 1981, I came across a notice of a meeting of the Gay Fathers' Forum—a monthly potluck supper meeting—and a new world opened to me where my needs both as a father and as a gay man were met. I had found an organization that acknowledged my multiplicities—a social movement and my personal identity converged as we fathers discussed children as gay parents.

The phenomenon of gay fathers in society is not new; the openness of their presence and existence at all social levels is. The gay father's role is traditionally expressed through pain and anguish, the confrontation of the traditional heterosexual fatherhood role and the traditional homosexual-male role.

Robert Griswold (1993) describes the overlapping period of 1965 to 1993 as "The Reorganization of Men's Lives" and 1970 to 1993 as "Patriarchy and the Politics of Fatherhood."

Dangerous or nurturing, ever-present or always absent, the patriarch of old or the dad of the new, fatherhood in recent decades has become a Kaleidoscope of images and trend, a sure sign that it has lost cultural coherence. As a result, the identity that men once gained from fatherhood and breadwinning no longer prevails. Buffeted by powerful demographic, economic and political changes, fatherhood in American culture is now fraught with ambiguity and confusion. Not surprisingly, so, too, are fathers themselves. (244)

Barbara Ehrenreich (1984) has discussed how fatherhood in the post–World War II period came to signify maturity, responsibility, and acceptance of appropriate gender and role structures. The bachelor and nonfather was not mature, not responsible, and suspected of deviancy, homosexuality.

The political and social movements of the 1960s and 1970s blurred the lines of sexual conduct; men who had led closeted lives as heterosexuals and fathers began to emerge and accept their double role—gay father. Thus, the gay fathers' movement of the 1970s evolved through the emergence of a heightened awareness of feminism, gay politics, and the newly defined role of fathers in parenting.

The earliest accounts of the gay fathers' movement come from San Francisco, where on a June morning in 1975 a group of gay fathers, mostly hippies, gathered with children, lovers, and friends of both sexes to march in the Gay Freedom Day parade. Nick Lathan, several months before, had published an article in *Gay Sunshine* describing his sense of alienation from the community of traditional self-identified gay men as a gay father (1979). Numerous gay fathers wrote him and when he moved to the San Francisco Bay area, he got in touch with the local correspondents who joined to assemble and march in the annual Gay Pride Parade. History was made as this disparate group of marchers moved through the San Francisco streets. Fatherhood and gayness produced a joyful celebration of identity. That afternoon the folk singer, Blackberri, dedicated songs to them and news reports focused on this new presence in the gay movement. By July the "Fag Dads by the Bay" had met at Lathan's place for a Sunday night potluck supper. This San Francisco group evolved into a very large monthly gathering that broke into smaller workshops after the shared meal. In 1976 a similar gay fathers' group formed in New York, handling growth problems differently. They chose to form smaller organizations evolving into two groups in Manhattan, one in Brooklyn, and one in Westchester—three of which continue today. I was a member of the Gay Fathers One group, located on the Upper West Side in Manhattan. In Toronto, Michael Lynch, Modern Language Association (MLA) gay activist, poet, and a good friend, now dead of

AIDS, wrote an essay on "Forgotten Fathers" in *The Body Politic* (Lynch 1978). Lynch chose to emphasize those biological fathers who continued to function as nurturing, caring parents while forging a gay man's identity. A group of a dozen "organized anarchists" evolved in Canada from this impetus. Also, in the mid-70s, two groups formed in Los Angeles: Gay Fathers and Gay Parents and Children, groups that merged shortly afterward into Gay and Lesbian Parents of Los Angeles. Their agenda included weekly rap sessions, monthly parents and children activities, and bimonthly adult socials. Seattle was not far behind as an active group of forty gay fathers began meeting in March 1979.

The March on Washington, D.C., for Lesbian and Gay Rights on October 14, 1979, produced a meeting in which Dave Berube (Washington, D.C.), Alan Ross (Philadelphia), and Al Luongo (New York) discussed the formation of an international network of gay fathers. The first organizational meeting took place on February 17, 1980, in Philadelphia at the apartment of Alan Ross and Steve Small and was followed by two additional meetings later that year. While the initial meeting was attended by representatives from New York, Washington, San Francisco, and Los Angeles, the subsequent New York gathering on May 10th and 11th included additional representatives from gay father organizations from Brooklyn, Westchester, Rochester, Cleveland, and Toronto. This group officially adopted the name "Gay Fathers Coalition" and elected officers including the chairperson, Al Luongo of New York. A subsequent organizational meeting on November 8 in Washington produced the first statement of purpose and statement of policy. The goals detailed include education of the public as to the existence of gay fathers and their children, support of individuals involved in parenting in their sometimes conflicted role as parent and homosexual, and communicating through the media the reality of gay fathers as nurturing parents.

I knew about my gay male identity. But there were other gay Fathers! The discovery of other gay fathers, mostly biological, a few adopters and partners of gay fathers who were coraising children was wonderful. For some eight years I attended Gay Fathers One and the gay Fathers Forum in New York City. The first Friday of each month, the forum hosted a potluck dinner—the source of great culinary competition—followed by breakout discussion groups. "Coming Out to Your Children," "Coming Out to Yourself," "Fatherhood"—legal and emotional issues—all drew great discussions. The mix was classic—across class, racial, and ethnic lines and gay—from drag queens to Brooks Brothers lawyers, from college professors to cooks, bakers, and waiters.

Few fathers were nonbiological; only three men among the hundreds I met had adopted or had foster children. Most were divorced or separated. A small group of gay married men formed. Typically, the more the man came out, the more likely he was to leave his marriage and to identify as a gay, nonmarried father.

All fathers were concerned about their children; some were involved in long legal custody battles. Many former wives were angry and did not want children to spend time with openly gay fathers. Almost everyone was financially involved with support payments.

These men were responsible, caring, concerned, and *gay*. They wanted to affirm their sexuality *and* their paternity. This dilemma presented conflicts for the society. The gay father as a societal presence had become a visible, if not suspicious, member of the gay rights movement. Was the gay father experimenting with his gay sexuality or was his identity authentic?

After that March, 1981, evening when I attended the Gay Fathers' Forum, my life changed significantly. There I met my life partner/lover of nearly twenty years, Robert Bixler, and shortly thereafter his four-year-old daughter, Rachel, became a part of my life. Rachel quickly made her presence felt as my third child one day when with hands on hips she lectured me, "That's no way to talk to a four year old." I retaliated with hands on my hips, "That's no way to talk to a forty-four year old." Robert watching, simply turned and walked out of the room saying, " It's time for the two of you to get to know each other." Little did we realize how important that would become. Seven years later, Rachel came into our home and life in powerfully new ways after her mother's painful death from cancer.

Robert and I were the poster boys of Gay Fathers' Forum and later Gay Fathers' One—two gay fathers forming a relationship of blended families. For the first time, I belonged to a community—gay men (formerly married with children). This initial identification continued as I further came out in gay academic politics in the MLA caucus leadership.

My daughters welcomed Robert's entry into our lives as hippie carob bunnies and sesame sticks were replaced by Godiva chocolates and colored eggs in their Easter baskets. At age five, Rachel made to Amanda the famous statement that titles this essay—"My Daddy Loves Your Daddy." The occasion for this pronouncement was our first Thanksgiving with the five of us together. While preparing for the dinner, Rachel turned to Amanda and said, "You know, my daddy loves your daddy." So simply put, Rachel's statement was a beautiful expression about gayness, acceptance, and family. Most important to my partner and me it has become a lasting affirmation of the love we share as life partners, gay fathers, and parents of our children.

The 1980s saw growth as new chapters of gay fathers formed in Denver, Houston, and Hamilton. Rival groups even formed in New York, somewhat divided on class and status issues. Gay Fathers' Forum was more diverse while the fathers of Gay Fathers' One represented the professions: doctors, lawyers, and stockbrokers. Annual meetings were held in San Francisco (1981), Toronto (1982), Denver (1983), and New York (1984). The New York conference of 1984 was marked by a debate on expansion to include both lesbian and gay male *Gay Parents* groups. The conference went on record as being supportive of *cosexual* parents' groups and welcomed their participation. In Los Angeles in 1985, at the annual Gay Fathers Coalition International (GFCI), Julie Vallons of the Chicago Parents Groups, reiterated the plea that lesbian mothers be allowed to join GFCI and that a new plan for an *International Parents* association be formed. As an indication of acceptance, she was elected vice president at the GFCI's Seventh Annual Conference (1986). Gay Fathers Coalition International changed its by-laws and the Gay and Lesbian Parents Coalition International (GLPCI) was born. Subsequent annual conferences continue to be held under that name and acronym. Nevertheless, in the GLPCI Directory of Resources, local organizational titles and identities vary. Gay fathers groups still function in Long Beach, Los Angeles, Washington, Atlanta, Baltimore, Boston, Buffalo, Brooklyn, Westchester, Pittsburgh, Houston, New York, Essex Junction, Seattle, Winnipeg, and Toronto. Lesbian mom's groups are present in Los Angeles, Hartford, Santa Cruz, Wichita, and Boston.

Women/biological mothers were always a part of the women's political movement of the 1970s, 1980s, and 1990s. Single women or lesbian couples were accepted somewhat more easily than gay fathers within the societal portrait. The traditional nurturing role of women permitted both maternity and lesbian sexuality in the same individual. In *Families We Choose*, Kath Weston discusses the characterization of lesbians as nonprocreative beings and the invisibility of lesbian sexual identity for biological mothers prior to the 1980s and "the lesbian baby boom." "If motherhood can render lesbian identity invisible, lesbian identity can also obscure parenthood" (Weston 1991). During the 1980s the children of artificial insemination expanded support organizations to include lesbian mothers, a continuation of the groups that had emerged from the feminist political activism of the preceding years. However, the majority of the organizations on both the national and international scene are made up of gay and lesbian parents or families, with affiliates in Canada, South Africa, Finland, France, Norway, and the United Kingdom.

Gay families now create families with children through a variety of means, including alternative insemination, adoption, and surrogacy. Agencies providing adoption and surrogacy services have flourished, creating through legal procedures a new definition of gay fathers. A Lesbian and Gay Family and Parenting Services program is now based in the Fenway Community Health Center in Boston. Nevertheless, full names of leaders are not given in a number of organizations and phone numbers are not available. Homophobia continues to be present among gay and lesbian parents; they still live in fearful times. GLPCI continues to serve other related groups: the Gay and Bisexual Married Men's Group, Center Kids, Colage (Children of Lesbians and Gays Everywhere), and Straight Spouses. The names of groups reflect changing societal attitudes: Free to Be Families, Lambda Family Circle, Love Makes a Family Inc., and Rainbow Families. The gay fathers' movement has become more inclusive and open while simultaneously permitting regional organizational autonomy. Families now regularly attend annual conventions; children's meetings with the participation of infants through college-age children as well as activities for all ages are regularly integrated into the overall programming.

In 1998 the national organization once again changed its name and its mission by establishing "Family Pride, Incorporated," a place for the multiple manifestations of parenthood in today's society. The mission is open to a wide variety of parenting options from artificial insemination to biological parenting, from adoption to surrogate fathers, from the parents to the children. The movement has extended its parameters.

As with lesbian mothers, gay fathers outside the traditional structure of heterosexual marriage have made their presence known in society. Adoption and surrogate parenting have helped redefine the family in the United States.

Recent years have brought many changes to the planned gay parenting option and to gay families in general. Lesbians and gay men have shared leadership in Gay and Lesbian Parents Coalition International (now Family Pride, Inc.). In 1998 the president was a woman, Linda Heller. In 1997 national newspapers focused on the first legal adoption by a gay male couple in New Jersey, Jon and Michael Gallucio. New Jersey became the first state to allow homosexual couples to adopt on an equal basis with married couples (Parker 1997a:1–2). Gay newspapers announce adoptions (Parker 1997b:29). "Focus on the Family" profiles a Sacramento lobbyist, his partner, and their son as well as the daughter of another Sacramento gay educator couple (Moss 1997). Sociologists are reconsidering family values in the '90s, and the first studies of children raised by gay and lesbian parents are being published (Stacey 1996). The *New York Times*, in a magazine dedicated to *status*, stated that for gay men *The Baby* is a symbol that the culture has changed for the millennium (Savage 1998:95). The biological fathers of the 1970s gay fathers movement are still here, but they are being replaced by generations of gay men/couples choosing parenthood.

As for my life partner and me, we have celebrated our middle daughter, Amanda's, wedding to her husband; enjoy visiting with our eldest daughter, Marialisa, who is a lesbian, and her partner; and live ten blocks from our youngest daughter, Rachel. We have moved from gay fathers to gay grandfathers-in-waiting.

REFERENCES

Ehrenreich, Barbara. 1984. *The Hearts of Men: American Dreams and the Flight from Commitment*. New York: Anchor.

Fagan-Fasteau, Marc. 1974. *The Male Machine*. New York: McGraw Hill.

Farrell, Warren. 1978. *The Liberated Man*. New York: Bantam.

Griswold, Robert. 1993. *Fatherhood in America*. New York: Basic Books.

Lathan, Nick. 1979. "Tender Mournings: Progress of a Faggot Father" *Gay Sunshine* (Summer/Fall): 7.

Levinson, D.J. 1978. *The Seasons of a Man's Life*. New York: Knopf.

Lynch, Michael. 1992. "Forgotten Fathers." *The Body Politic* (April): 1.

Moss, J. Jennings. 1997. "Focus on the Family." *Out* (August): 72–74, 104–105.

Parker, Laura. 1997a. "Adoption by NJ Gays Sparks Praise, Criticism." *USA TODAY*, December 19–21, pp. 1, 2.

——. 1997b. "It's Official: Maryland Couple Announces Adoption of Son Keott Gomez-Starnes." *The Washington Blade*, June 20, p. 29.

Savage, Dan. 1998. "For Gay Men, The Baby." *New York Times Magazine*, November 15, Sec. 8, p. 95.

Stacey, Judith. 1996. *In the Name of the Family: Rethinking Family Values in the Postmodern Age*. Boston: Beacon Press.

Weston, Kath. 1991. *Families We Choose: Lesbians, Gays, Kinship*. New York: Columbia University Press.

15 | Alma Mater: Family "Outings" and the Making of the Modern Other Mother (MOM)[1]

Maureen Sullivan

With her famous statement concerning gender identity, that "one is not born a woman, but rather, becomes one," Simone de Beauvoir (1973) highlighted the cultural compulsion with which a human being struggles to become intelligible to the social world. In a gendered social world, an individual who fails to become and appear to others as one of the two prescribed genders is in for some trouble. The same might be said for families who do not conform to the image of mother-father-child. The heterosexual nuclear family is our guiding image of what "real" families look like; it constitutes a kind of truth regime in that its power guarantees that human beings will not only strive to conform to this image but will also recognize as families only those social relationships that do. Those who do not conform, for example lesbian coparent families, are not socially intelligible within this truth regime. Mother-mother-child families are literally inconceivable.

This is especially the case for nonbirthmothers in lesbian coparent families, because unlike their birthmother partners whose identity may be signified through their biological maternity, nonbirthmothers have no recourse to extant familial categories. The identity of the nonbirthmother must somehow be created and articulated within a familial truth regime designed to suppress all nonconformity. What follows is an account of this struggle for intelligibility—the making of the "modern other mother"—as nonbirthmothers in two-mother families confront the heteronormative order with the truth of who they are in relation to their partners and their children. I use the term "alma mater" conceptually to help us think about who non-birthmothers are and what they do.

CONCEPTUALIZING ALMA MATER

NONBIRTHMOTHERS IN LESBIAN COPARENT families have no automatic cultural category by which they can formulate and express their identity as parents. They are not daddies, though sometimes they are primary bread-winners. They are not nannies, though they provide care, supervision, security, and love for their children. They are not aunties or grannies, though often they are presumed to be by strangers. They do everything parents do, though they have no socially intelligible identity. I suggest that they be understood as fostering mothers, or alma mater. "Alma mater" translates from the Latin as "fostering mother," according to *Webster's Ninth*. To foster is to nurture, to promote the growth of and afford parental care, although the persons giving and receiving nurturance are not related by "blood." Through resilient socioaffective cathexes, nonbirthmothers in lesbian coparent families foster their children, with whom they share no blood tie, and their partners, with whom they share no legal tie.

Comothers in two-mom families also act out an educational role in public places, fulfilling the sense of alma mater as school or teacher. Comothers occupy a unique position compared to their partners in that they may choose, but often feel compelled, to explain their relationship with their children to curious others in public places. Unlike a lesbian birthmother who may confidently lay biological claim to a child, or an adoptive hetero-sexual mother whose relationship with her child is legally and thus cultur-ally sanctioned, the lesbian comother who utters the particular truth about her relationship to her child outs herself and her family. The decision to dis-close and the form the disclosure will take, like all phenomena of the closet, weigh mightily on the shoulders of a lesbian co-mom. The spontaneous risk assessment and emotional calculus these mothers face in managing what D. A. Miller (1988) has termed "the open secret" feels more onerous when there are children who factor into these disclosure calculations and whose relationship with comothers is not culturally recognized, much less legiti-mated. This point was summed up nicely by one co-mom I spoke with in a study I conducted in 1994[2]:

> When you're just dealing with yourself and this is your identity, and how you perceive yourself and people perceive you, it has only to do with

you. But in this case, it has to do with a relationship with children, and so it's much more complex. And everything you're taught about a mother's role to the child and involvement is a lot different than just who you are in terms of your personal identity.

Comothers, then, who cannot "pass" precisely because there are few if any intelligible categories for them to "pass as" bear a substantial portion of the collective burden of educating nongay or otherwise uninformed members of society. In short, when they offer an account of their identity, they simultaneously create a new sociofamilial category *and* disproportionately bear the political and social burden of education. A closer analytic framing of how comothers are held to account for their identity is helpful for understanding this conceptualization of alma mater.

NO REST FOR THE WARY

A LESBIAN BIRTHMOTHER OFTEN will experience social respectability or legitimacy for the first time on the basis of her biological maternal status, which is more culturally acceptable than her lesbian status precisely because *she* is presumed *to be* a heterosexual mother. Ellen Lewin (1993, 1994) first noted this dynamic of (biological) motherhood affirming lesbian mothers' personal gender identity and, to a certain degree, their social gender identity, insofar as motherhood provided the single lesbian mothers *she interviewed for* her research with the social cover and legitimation of heteronormative status. Sociologist Arlene Stein (1997) also noted that the equation of motherhood with heterosexuality is so firmly rooted in mainstream culture that some of the lesbians she interviewed, who were also biological mothers, experienced their sexual identities as being effaced by the more acceptable status of motherhood. One of Stein's interviewees reported that she felt acceptable for the first time because she was a (biological) mother, an unambiguous—indeed sacralized—status given the presumption of heterosexuality of which this particular mother often did not disabuse her social interlocutors. While not disabusing one's interlocutors can evoke feelings of shame in the politicized gay person, the point is that this passing and feeling socially legitimate represents something of a choice that will always be an option for a lesbian birthmother.

In the course of her daily rounds, the birthmother can confidently share details of her motherhood with nongay individuals and strangers, persons perhaps predisposed to the heterosexual assumption, knowing that disclosure or nondisclosure of her lesbian identity is fully in her control. She can share stories with interested others about her labor, delivery, breastfeeding, and countless other practices, events, and emotions that will have the socially legitimating effect of persuading her audience that she is *the* mother, as one birthmother in my 1994 study explained:

> When I'm carrying the baby and there's other women with babies and we smile at each other, ask what the baby weighs or whatever, I love that stuff. And I do it all the time. And it doesn't occur to me that I need to tell them I'm a lesbian when I'm doing that.

In contrast, the comother, regardless of whether she would want to, cannot pass as straight (and therefore as Mother) on the basis of the "correct" information about her relationship with the child, which, like the birthmother, she is obliged to manage in face-to-face interaction with others, especially when she is alone with the child in public. Because she has no recourse to existing social categories the comother in lesbian coparent families is acutely burdened with the work of explaining, defending, or concealing—in effect fabricating—her relationship with her child and thus her social identity to others. Stein indicated that nonbirthmothers in her study not only had to "challenge the equation of motherhood and heterosexuality, but they also had to introduce to people the notion of nonbiological or social motherhood" (1997:133).

But nonbiological or social motherhood doesn't quite capture the psychosocial complex of experience that dynamically and relationally constitutes the particular situation of the nonbirth comother. Nor is it likely that, for the co-mom, her sexual identity will be effaced by her maternal identity as with some birthmothers. In fact, it is exactly through nonbirthmothers' sexual identities that their maternal status eventually becomes intelligible: in spontaneous and discrete interactions with individuals, a comother is confronted with inquiries about her particular relationship with a particular child with whom she appears to be close and for whom she appears to be responsible. *The truth is that she is the mother of a child who has two mothers.* A birthmother might use this line or some variation, but she is not compelled to do so as a comother is, if it is full disclosure that the comother wants and pursues. And the comother must provide full disclosure if she is not to be found out later as having lied, if it is likely she will encounter the individual again, or if it is impossible for her to pass as the birthmother (e.g., in the event it is apparent she is too old to have given birth, in which case she may be taken for grandma and must decide either to pass as grandma or disabuse her interlocutor). *The truth is that she is the mother of a child who has two mothers.* But this truth is difficult to comprehend within the regime of mother-father-child family truth.

The comother, as alma mater, must decide when and whom she will educate about her family, among the myriad and initially unpatterned encounters she has with individuals whose attitudes about homosexuality and about gay parents she cannot know in advance. Her face-to-face interactions with grocery store customers, department store clerks, mothers at playgrounds, and countless other strangers with whom she may have the occasion to exchange words or briefly become acquainted become for her a type of recurring game of identity poker. She must be vigilant to the people and situation at hand, assessing every possible sign concerning the risk of exposure she might take in entering what Erving Goffman (1963:13) has called one of the primal scenes of sociology: in this case the encounter of the lesbian comother, who possesses a potentially discrediting attribute, with those whose heteronormative privilege exempts them from having to manage information about their sexual identity. Goffman points out that those who must strategize whether and how to disclose potentially discrediting information in mixed contacts

> will have to be *alive* to aspects of the social situation which others treat as uncalculated and unattended. What are unthinking routines for [hetero]normals can become management problems for the discreditable. These problems cannot always be handled by past experiences, since new contingencies always arise, making former concealing devices inadequate. The person with a secret failing, then, must be alive to the social situation as a scanner of possibilities, and is therefore likely to be *alienated* from the simpler world in which those around him [her] apparently dwell. (emphasis added) (1963:88)

Being "alive" to social situations in ways that others may comfortably approach without calculation and attention is not only (and somewhat paradoxically) alienating, as Goffman suggests, it is also work. We might think of this mental, emotional, educational, and social labor that lesbian comothers do as identity-work or construction work. It is constructive in the sense that comothers are creating new impressions of and expectations for a wider variety of hitherto unrecognized and preemptively delegitimated modes of human affinity. In a sense, comothers are creating more unconcealed space for sexual and familial nonconformists.

A question remains, however, as to why co-moms are compelled to offer accounts of their sociofamilial identity in the first place. If the social circumstances they find themselves in are randomly traversed public spaces, as I illustrate in the next section, why are comothers required to offer identity accounts? What triggers such inquiries from strangers, especially in gay-friendly urban and suburban regions such as the Bay Area of San Francisco from which the families in my 1994 study were drawn and in which gay parenthood is already visible?

Part of the answer is that babies and young children are like social magnets; they draw adult strangers together and provide a common focus and pretext for conversation. A child elicits the amiable interest of strangers, prompting questions from them that the parent is then responsible for answering. In their book *What Is Family?* (1990) Jaber Gubrium and James Holstein refer to these promptings as "challenges," the response to which, and indeed the occasion itself, being what they call "family projects" (58–66). These challenges come in many forms, often with the simple purpose of establishing who is related to whom. When it is a lesbian nonbirth parent with her children, the way in which she is related to the child is not clear *if* it is established that she is not the biological mother—which often occurs with the first question, as we will see. And so one innocuous question is followed by more pointed ones, which then culminate in an interaction in which the gay parent is responsible for the entire (re)presentation of self-and-family. A gay person without children negotiates her identity in public places with only her own well-being, and perhaps that of her group and/or group politics, in mind. When one is with a child to whom one is a parent, however, the entire range of considerations changes. No longer is one negotiating just one's own social (sexual) identity.

It is here where, beyond the immediate attraction of children who draw strangers together, we find another impetus for comothers to provide an identity account: having children means that lesbian mothers are more public in general. They mix socially in straight society, in Goffmanian mixed-contact fashion, more frequently as the needs of their children draw them into spheres that either they rarely entered before, or, when they did, they could choose to be as out with their own identity as they wished. Now, many are mixing more in nongay groups and communities and have their children who elicit interest from strangers. Together these factors provide the conditions that lead to family "challenges" that, for the comother, become complicated information management problems, as co-mom Penny Cipolini[3] reflected:

Normally, if you're just a lesbian at work or something, normally when you go through life, you go to the grocery store, you do anything, and you can just go on and be who you are. You can choose to be out, like maybe wearing a shirt that says something. Or you can go about your life and just assume who you are and it's fine with you and anybody else. But I didn't realize that in order for me to explain how I was becoming a parent, other than that the child showed up from some adoption agency, (and I didn't want to lie, I had already decided that) I didn't realize that in order to go through the whole process, I had to be totally out. And everything, from going through the hospital, the doctors . . . each time we went through a different thing it was another, I had to out myself. And I'm used to it now, but sometimes I wouldn't think about it beforehand and then we'd walk in a room and I'd think, "Oh my God, I've got to out myself again." That was a total surprise to me, it was absolutely, I just didn't expect that I would have to out myself in order to claim myself as a parent.

When I asked Penny's partner, Megan, why it was not the same for her, she responded:

Cause I was a "single mom." I didn't have to explain it to anybody. I was big, I was pregnant. Nobody even asked. I saw a couple of people would look at my hand to see if I had a wedding ring on, that kind of thing. But if Penny says, for example at work, "I'm going to have a baby in two months. I want to go on paternity . . . some kind of leave," there has to be some explanation.

FAMILY "OUTINGS": THREE STRATEGIES

SINCE A CO-MOM MUST OFFER some account, some explanation for who she is in relation to her child, she may decide from a range of non/disclosure options in her information management, given the circumstance she finds herself in with her children. And so, absent a more categorical resolution "not to lie," as Penny had decided, the kinds of discursive strategies available to comothers become all-important in the negotiation of their social identity. The scenes described below highlight in detail three strategies a comother might employ—"full" disclosure, "partial" disclosure through obfuscation or omission, and outright deception or passing—not an exhaustive list but a rendering of the patterns we might begin to think of as movement along a learning curve as co-moms become more experienced inhabiting and performing their identity as lesbian comothers.

The strategies presented begin with "full disclosure" since, in their incipient role and lacking experience interacting with strangers, new comothers struggle to find words and phrases that allow them to control their own utterances about who they are. They enter social situations unprepared with the experience and scripts ("riffs" that later they will have tested) and thus find themselves struggling to convey the truth of the matter, which constitutes "full disclosure," or as I call this strategy, "Telling It Like It Is."

TELLING IT LIKE IT IS

THE SCENE IS A glittering, hypermodern suburban mall in Northern California, where one could easily evaporate into the crushing traffic of anonymous, faceless consumers. Two Japanese-American mothers stroll their infant twins in a lateral two-seater in search of a suitable place for lunch— for the twins. Birthmother Jocelyn will breastfeed both infants. They end up in a department store dressing room, where Jocelyn begins to nurse baby Todd and Amy holds and plays with his twin sister, Hannah, just outside the dressing room area. As Amy told me the story, an encounter with a store salesperson progressed in this way:

> The [Emporium] salesperson comes over, "Oh she's really cute, is this your baby?" I [Amy] sort of stop in my tracks 'cause I know any moment Jocelyn is going to come out and she has a nursing top on and the double, twin stroller, and, I said, " Well, yes, sort of." And she's [salesperson] like, "You're sort of her mother?" And I said, "Yeah, sort of." And here comes Jocelyn, you know, she has a nursing top on, and so I said, "Jocelyn is the birthmother and I'm the co-mom, we're coparenting the children." Jocelyn said later that I didn't have to tell the salesperson that she's the birthmom. But, you know, Jocelyn was wearing a nursing top! We haven't quite gotten things down. It's easier for Jocelyn because people recognize her as being the mom and they address her as being the mom. I haven't quite learned when I should and shouldn't say it, and how to say it. I think it's a matter of practicing, rehearsing it, I'm not real comfortable with that part yet.

What would make that part of Amy's identity-work more comfortable for her?

If I could just tell them simply that I'm their mom, without having to explain it. And that she's the mom and I'm the mom and that that's another kind of family unit. Where right now you can't really say, "Well I'm the mom and Jocelyn is the mom" and everyone says, "Oh, that's really nice." They sort of stop in their tracks. In settings where it's not a personal situation I never receive an affirmative reaction.

The scene at the Emporium described by Amy is important for what it tells us about the disclosure strategies available to her. The clearly visible signifiers of Jocelyn's maternity (e.g., the nursing top) limit Amy's discursive range of motion; they limit her repertoire of symbolic evidence for passing as something recognizable, something familiar. This occurs because the family truth regime of mother-father-child, having first identified and located "mother" in Jocelyn's maternity, now renders Amy's identity incomprehensible. She is produced by this regime as other, as outside the frame of intelligibility. As a result, her identity in relation to her children is not only inconceivable, it is also suspect, for she is a marked woman precisely because she is not marked as something comprehensible. The preclusion of her identity, made palpable by Jocelyn's visible maternity, severely limits the discursive and material evidence Amy might provide for explaining who she is in relation to her children, and thus compels her rhetorically toward "full" disclosure—to a discursive point beyond the threshold of deniability. This struggle to make oneself plausible by means of and in relation to disclosure of gay identity requires not only social intelligence but also extraordinary effort and awareness. This is why co-moms bear a peculiar burden in lesbian coparent families: not only do they support, nurture, care for—in a word, foster—their children and their partners, but they are in the process of creating a familial category and social identity that has not existed in modern Western (nonenslaved) society and for which there is no nomenclature or language that would make it intelligible. Amy's words articulate her experience of this labor-intensive process best:

It's really hard, it takes a lot of energy to have to think about how you're going to deal with these situations and what you're going to say and what you're not going to say. You have to work so hard at it.

Like Penny and Megan, both Jocelyn and Amy agree that social interaction in public places is a little easier for Jocelyn insofar as her biological relationship to the children often automatically imbues her with normative social status. As Jocelyn succinctly put it:

> Well, since people think there is only one mom, they automatically assume I'm the mom. So that puts Amy in the position, 'Well, what am I?"

The full disclosure strategy not only involves new comothers such as Amy testing their wings, earnestly wanting to learn and help others to understand who they are in relation to their children, it also represents a choice available to and made by more seasoned navigators. Melissa Goldstein, for example, seems to have mentally catalogued all the possible situations and individuals with whom she would interact vis-à-vis her children, and deploys her disclosure strategies with laser precision. Here she "tells it like it is":

> We were at preschool one day, just before the end, and we'd taken a day off or something I don't remember why we [parents] were both there. Anyway, Amanda [daughter] was being clingy and she asked me to sit down with her. And so I did. This little girl sitting next to her said, "Who are you?" And I said, "I'm Amanda's mom." And she said, "Oh well who's his mom?" and pointed at Jeremy. And I said, "I'm Jeremy's mom too." And she kind of looked at me and she looked over at Linda and she said, "Well, who's she?" And I said, "Well, she's their mom too." So it was, "Oh, you mean grandma." I said, "No, Jeremy and Amanda have two moms."

After this exchange, apparently the five-year-old asking the questions simply looked at Melissa "like I was crazy." The concept of two moms may be difficult for the young and old alike to wrap their minds around, but it is the most direct and nondefensive way for a co-mom to describe "fully" her relationship with her children. And because the two-moms concept is so difficult, there will always be the occasions where one mother, usually the comother, will be taken for a nanny or for granny or auntie before, during, and sometimes even after the explanation is given (as with the little girl in the encounter described above), regardless of the disclosure strategy used. But telling it like it is still represents the strategy that is the most conducive to the promotion of understanding, however incomprehensible it may be initially, as co-mom Brenda Jacobson explained her selection of the full disclosure strategy:

> I find myself having to come out all the time as a lesbian with Max [son] because they immediately think he's mine and they'll ask, "Oh, did he kick you when he was in utero," you know. And I have a choice to kind of like avoid the question, but what I do is I say, "No my partner had the baby and I'm adopting him." You know, I don't feel totally comfortable with my answers yet but I'm kind of getting it down.

It is important to note that comothers still have no language, no name, for describing precisely *who they are*. The two-mom concept describes the family *form*, and the comother is simultaneously but tacitly inscribed in that configuration. Brenda's account describes what she and her partner have done or are doing in connection with their child. But the comother's specific sociofamilial identity still has no name of its own. And as we've seen, the identity-work, the construction work of comothers—what we might even think of as the meaning-making and being-making work of the comother—takes patience, emotional and mental energy, and a willingness to pursue certain opportunities for fostering understanding. This is why I think of her as alma mater.

Sometimes a comother's desire to tell it like it is may conflict with the abruptness of the turn in conversation or directness of inquiry. She may then find herself uttering partial truths, equal parts fact and fiction, a disclosure strategy I call "Speaking Half-Truths to Power."

SPEAKING HALF-TRUTHS TO POWER

IN A CULTURE THAT has been force-fed an exclusive image of family—mother-father-child—the power of this image lies in the insistence with which its "veracity" is defended, even when empirical evidence to the contrary presents itself. How do "anomalous" cases make themselves intelligible, communicate their existence, and make themselves believed under such a regime? Sometimes it is too strenuous or difficult or one is not in the mood to wage the effort, especially when one has not maintained that level of vigilance to which Goffman refers.

Alana and Eleanor, the proud parents of Brian, a sweet-tempered toddler, recounted a story in which comother Eleanor actually had to exit a social situation because she wasn't prepared with a script and the truth proved too unwieldy to convey.

Ninety percent of the time we tell people the whole story. But one time I got *caught off guard*. I had been staying at home with Brian when he was three months old, and I decided to go out and give blood. Because he was so little they said to me that my iron level was really good after giving birth. And I said, "But I didn't have him." And the only thing I could think of was that I adopted him but then the woman said, "Well did you get him from an agency?" And that threw me off totally to the point where I just got up and left! I didn't know what to say! (emphasis added)

For those comothers finding themselves "caught off guard" and not knowing what to say, this particular scene suggests something more about power that is worth noting. We can see how a comother's "innocent" interlocutor may seem something of an accuser to her (and she the accused) if we understand that ignorance is the flip side of knowledge in assorted power/knowledge nexuses, especially in the organization and management of knowledge around sexuality. Following Michel Foucault (1990/1978), literary and queer theorist Eve Sedgwick (1988, 1990) suggests that ignorance may be just as productive and efficacious as knowledge in its modes of manipulation and coercion, its "opacities," and, most important, its effects. In her attempt to pluralize and specify this discursive terrain of ignorance-as-power, Sedgwick first exposes the duplicitous imputation that ignorance is passive or innocent. Instead, she argues, ignorance is quite generative:

If ignorance is not—as it evidently is not—a single Manichaean, aboriginal maw of darkness from which the heroics of human cognition can occasionally wrestle facts, insights, freedoms, progress, perhaps there exists instead a plethora of *ignorances*, and we may begin to ask questions about the labor, erotics, and economics of their human production and distribution. Insofar as ignorance is ignorance *of* a knowledge—a knowledge that may itself, it goes without saying, be seen as either truth or false under some other regime of truth—these ignorances, far from being pieces of the originary dark, are produced by and correspond to particular knowledges and circulate as part of particular regimes of truth. (emphasis in original) (1990:8)

The capacity of ignorance *to appear* innocent and passive may well be an operation of its power, while the *appearance itself* of innocence and passivity may be one of its effects. The *apparently* innocent question posed to Eleanor by the bloodworker in the scene described earlier constituted *in effect* not an innocuous conversational gesture but, rather, a seizure of Eleanor's freedom and authority to describe her own socioaffective relations and to name her own sexual desire. To put it another way, the bloodworker held most if not all of the rhetorical leverage; she controlled the terms of exchange by virtue of her ignorance and the presumed right to interrogate residing within that ignorance. Further, her privilege-in-ignorance corresponds directly to the truth regime of mother-father-child, for her interrogation would not be possible were it not for the dominant image of family truth against which her comparison could be made. So Eleanor, "caught off guard" and not knowing what to say, saw her epistemological authority usurped in a single thirty-second exchange of words. In this moment of panic, the flight impulse was apparently stronger than the calmer one of fostering understanding, suggesting that the occasions for employing the strategy of speaking half-truths to power may not necessarily be those most favorable for pursuing a pedagogical politics, the opportunity for which, I believe, is always present in these encounters.

In a second mall scene with Amy and Jocelyn, we can glimpse another variation of speaking half-truths to power, in which ignorance-as-power once again works its coercion even though comother Amy seems this time to be on surer footing with her interlocutor.

They are back at the mall, days or weeks after the Emporium encounter, and this time they are at Macy's. Once again, Jocelyn is feeding Todd in a lounge, and Amy carries Hannah into the shopping area to get something to drink. Once again, it was co-mom Amy who narrated the proceedings for me in stream-of-consciousness fashion:

> And so I had Hannah and I sat her down at the counter and I was trying to get my money out and the woman asked me, "So, how old is your baby?" You know, it's really kind of weird, you want to say things like, "this is my baby but I'm not really the birthmom, but this is my baby." *But I'm not saying anything.* And then I said, "Yeah, yeah, she's three-and-a-half months." And she said, "Oh my baby's fifteen months and I remember when she was three-and-a-half months old." And yet I'd be kind of thinking to myself, oh, should I say anything more or should I just walk away? Okay, just walk away. But it's odd because I sort of stop and think [to myself], is this your baby? Yes this is my baby. But I'm not the birthmother! (emphasis added)

Jocelyn's absence in this scene gave Amy more rhetorical room to maneuver than in their first encounter with the salesperson at the Emporium. With the absence of visible cues of biological maternity, Amy's range of strategic options expanded. She might have employed the "full disclosure" strategy, but instead she decided to speak half-truths to power and walk away. Theoretically she could have passed as the birthmother—a third strategy, which I discuss in the next section. In fact, strictly on the level of visual cues and her response to the salesperson, she did pass, but she did not represent herself directly as the birthmother. Rather, she omitted information that would have disabused the woman of her presumption that Amy is the birthmother and, by extension, The Mother, in the mother-father-child model.

Speaking half-truths to power, as Amy did in this second mall scene, is not a particularly comfortable choice. Partial disclosure is a form of dissembling, the product of which, like all things repressed, can return in an oedipal-like fashion to haunt the dissembler. Rather than creating mere conversational awkwardness, Amy's self-censorship gave rise to a fleeting but powerful self-doubt about her relationship to her children. These observations highlight the ways in which an obfuscatory discursive strategy employed in the face-to-face negotiation of a new *social* (parental) identity, without intending to mislead or misinform, can have the unintended boomerang effect of unsettling a newly developing *personal* (parental) identity. Not unlike the loss of control and autonomy Eleanor felt in her encounter with the bloodworker, Amy's partial disclosure strategy resulted in a kind of momentary confusion concerning her personal identity as a parent.

PLAYING IT STRAIGHT

"PLAYING IT STRAIGHT," or passing as the birthmother, is a strategy chosen under duress. Like the closet, which removes lesbian sexual identity completely from view, passing as birthmom represents the most repressive strategy of those available to comothers. Playing it straight actually constitutes a double repression, because it conceals not only homosexual identity but nonbiological parenthood as well. Individually, both categories garner precious little social approbation; combined, they are almost literally unthinkable. A co-mother can therefore avoid much social opprobrium and general tension by passing as the birthmother, especially and perhaps precisely because she is compelled to do so by the particular setting she is in.

Melissa Goldstein, whose encounter with the five-year-old at her twins' preschool I described earlier, has proven an able and loving coparent to Amanda and Jeremy, as everyone in her closest adult circles knows—that is, everyone but her colleagues at work. Melissa is the financial director for a nonprofit housing organization, is "not out at all" to her subordinates, but at the time she took the job knew she would have to inform them that she had kids. "I've known that I would have to take time off, stay home with them, things were going to come up." What's a coparent to do in a conservative work setting where professional relations with her staff depend upon her maintaining her respectability and credibility? Play it straight. Melissa recounted a particularly noteworthy moment in one of her many performances as the twins' birthmother:

> I have their [the kids'] pictures up at work, but they [staff] think I had them myself. One day they were asking me some question about the birth and I'm like, "Ah, yes!" They were asking me where my C-section scar is and I'm trying to remember where Linda's scar is; you don't really see it, it's not like a scar scar. And I'm thinking, now wait a minute, is it over here? I've gotten myself in some pickles.

Playing it straight makes for uncomfortable moments, where comothers must spontaneously assess the likelihood that a false statement will snowball into a tangled thicket of falsehoods so labyrinthine that one could not emerge from it with character intact. To avoid these pickles, as Melissa called them, or "in-deeperism" as Goffman terms it, comothers can mentally sidestep the pressure by making one simple note of the frequency with which they are likely to encounter a particular interlocutor.

Eleanor, the nonbiological parent who left the blood bank in a hurry, chose to pass as birthmother Alana on a later occasion, when she was more experienced and prepared for the seemingly harmless ignorance whose coercive effects she now was able to anticipate with confidence. She also was able to make quick assessments about the probable frequency of contact she would have with her interlocutor.

> One time [at work] I was hiring an instructor. She was new and *I knew I wasn't going to be dealing with her very much.* And I said I'd been off because I was with my son. So she brought a baby present. She said, "Well, where's your son now?" And I said, "He's at home." And he was with Alana at the time. And I said, or something [vague] came out that he was with some-

one [at home]. She looked at me and said, "Oh, is it a full-time nanny?" And I said, "Yeah, it is." (emphasis added)

Passing as the birthmother through direct misrepresentation leaves one feeling uneasy. Facing the ignorance of one's interlocutor occasions shame precisely because the interlocutor's inability or refusal to see the reality before her eyes produces the secret about which she then claims ignorance. Playing it straight—politically regressive, time-honored, and sometimes lifesaving strategy that it is—protects oneself and one's family, but it does so at a psychological and social cost the magnitude of which we as a society are just beginning to understand.[4]

Given these possible strategies (and certainly those I've outlined above do not constitute an exhaustive list of the options but are meant only to be suggestive of a range), we might begin to think about the social settings in which they are employed, the individuals with whom co-moms are likely to employ one strategy over another, and whether there is a certain logic to the use of these strategies.

THE LOGIC OF IDENTITY-WORK: INSTITUTING ALMA MATER

IT IS ONE THING to playfully "perform" a lesbian self so as to signal one's identity to other lesbians and to blur sexual and gender categories for an anonymous public audience. It is a markedly different performance, sometimes playful but more often labor-intensive, for a lesbian parent to enact anew in each social setting a social identity that she must, in a sense, construct "from scratch." The lesbian comother does not perform her own sexual identity per se (Butler 1991) nor does she display lesbian chic through the deployment of a highly cultivated sartorial acumen (Esterberg 1996). Rather, she creates and conveys her sociofamilial *and* sexual identity by way of carefully chosen words. She outfits herself with a lexicon, not with clothing. Her armoire contains her repertoire of scripts—her disclosure strategies outlined above—some of which she has already tested. At the time of the interaction, it is not a sense of bravado she exudes; rather, it is an emotional and mental energy, which she has mustered for following through with her strategy. In short, because it involves both a socially inchoate, unrecognized familial relationship *and* a politically volatile sexual identity, the construction of the Modern Other Mother is something less akin to play and more like the *earlier* phases of the formation of a gay/lesbian identity along with the attendant psychosocial practices of the closet. Similar to the timing and sequence by which some gay people decide to disclose to others their personal sexual identity, lesbian nonbiological mothers in coparent families tell the story of who they are in stages, learning for themselves as they go, and helping to educate others.

None of the strategies discussed earlier is used more frequently than others as co-moms become experienced using them; as we have seen, sometimes passing as the birthmother is easier than explaining the two-mother concept. But it is the fact that co-moms *learn* to choose from the strategies available to them given the circumstances they are in that raises the question of whether there is a "logic in the learning," and thus a logic in the construction of this particular identity. If there is a logic in the learning it is this: as comothers become more experienced interacting with different people in various circumstances and settings, they come to know with precision which discursive strategy, which script from the repertoire, will move them successfully through the interaction, depending on their needs and wants. We saw this with Melissa Goldstein who knew intrinsically that she could (and wanted) to explain to the child interlocutor at the preschool that her children had two moms, while at the same time she maintained with her work colleagues the lie that she had given birth to her children. This suggests that the process of becoming a lesbian comother is quite similar to the process of coming out more generally.

Just as Ken Plummer (1975, 1996) charted "career stages" in his classic interactionist analyses of the process of "becoming a homosexual," we might think of the construction of lesbian comother identities as proceeding in a similarly stagelike fashion. Comothers who are new to the public relations game of managing information about parental status are unaware of the full range of discursive strategies available to them for doing so. With experience, they learn to choose a strategy depending on the likely *duration* of the encounter or relationship with a given individual, its *importance*, or both. Indeed, duration and importance appear to be crucial elements in the learning logic. Co-moms simultaneously formulate and act on responses to the questions: when and with whom is it "worth it" (to use the words of many of the mothers I spoke with) to educate strangers and new acquaintances about one's family; when is it not "worth it"; when is it most important to conceal the information that one's family has two mothers.

Noting that she probably would not be seeing the same person very often if at all, Eleanor knew she could safely pass as birthmother since that was her inclination. She had noted the likely *duration* of the interaction/relationship with her interlocutor. Conversely, precisely because co-mom Clarice felt that she had developed some intimacy over time with the family's regular diaper-service person, whom she called "diaper dude," she decided to have a little fun with the birthmother/comother confusion by speaking half-truths:

> So he thought it would be okay to ask, since, you know, we were going to be on friendly terms. So he says, "I'm confused, which one of you is the mother?" And he's this elderly man. And I said, "What day is it?" And he said, "Well it's Tuesday." "So I'm the mom on Tuesdays." "Okay." He just picked up his diapers and left! He didn't want to play anymore!

By humorously employing half-truths here, Clarice exhibits a certain confidence resulting from her being on "friendly terms" with "diaper dude." The duration, once again, of the family's relationship with him had made him familiar to them, allowing them to have established ground rules for interaction and exchange of information. In a sense, precisely because Clarice and her partner, Kristen, *know* the diaper-service man, they have confidence that the consequences of invoking a particular explanation are well within their control. Mothers' perception of the likely duration of an interaction or relationship is thus a tool enabling them to evaluate—and even disarm with humor—the relational power that might otherwise tip in favor of the interrogator.

So *duration* of the relationship or interaction factors into the selection of a given strategy. Another factor is the *importance* of the relationship or interaction as it is defined by mothers. If the relationship or interaction is with certain people whose knowledge of the family relationships is defined as important to them, mothers will choose the full disclosure strategy. Amy, the Japanese-American comother of infant twins, was relatively inexperienced at this identity-work when she struggled for words and doubted herself in the two mall scenes described earlier. Yet, when I asked her which circumstances were important enough for her to make sure that her relationship was understood—that is, when it was clear that the struggle to explain would have beneficial consequences—both Amy and birthmother Jocelyn responded in rapid succession:

AMY   Well I think they're all important, but then some of it might not be worth it.

JOCELYN   To us personally, I mean it would be an effort to try to *educate* other people. And so some situations it's worth it and other situations it's not.

AMY   So at Gymboree,[5] I thought it was an important enough of a place to let them recognize who I am.

JOCELYN Or if it's a long-term type of . . .

AMY   Or if it's daycare, or school, or if they [the twins] were to become friends with other people then that would be important.

It was less obvious to Amy during the earlier mall scenes that it was "okay" not to explain the whole situation to the department store personnel, mostly because she had not yet experienced a range of situations that would allow her, in a sense, to see her options. Upon reflection and with some experience under her belt, she is able to identify the kinds of situations that are "worth it" to comothers to educate the people involved.

Those situations identified by Amy and Jocelyn as "worth it" were those in which mothers and children will have some type of extended contact with the people involved (duration), but primarily those in which mothers must entrust custodial care of their children for a period of time. And this suggests something about how *importance* is being defined, since the choice of fully explaining the lesbian coparent category as a disclosure strategy appears to be structured to a certain degree by the exigencies of family life itself. For it is their responsibilities as parents that require lesbian mothers to come into contact with family-oriented institutions and organizations such as Gymboree. Beyond the random encounters in public places and the work setting (the latter being an institutional setting in which individual identity management takes place regardless of parental status), there are the institutional settings whose raison d'être is serving families. Because all mothers must necessarily interact with pediatricians, child care providers, family social-service professionals, counselors, teachers, play-school staff, and all such people who serve families in one form or another, the parental status of a lesbian comother must at some minimal level be established with this category of people, if with no other category or group.

Birthmothers and comothers alike come to know this as they increasingly have occasion to come into contact with these societal institutions charged with the socialization, education, and care of their children. When their children are still infants, parents have fewer opportunities to interact with people and social institutions within this category of family service provision, with the exception of hospital obstetric and pediatric personnel.

Newer mothers literally do not have the number and type of interactions with people whose understanding and support of lesbian coparent families is critical for such families to function. As children get older, however, along with the quality of relationships with individuals in this category of organizations and institutions, the sheer quantity of necessary encounters expands substantially for mothers.

For this reason it may be said that lesbian comother identities are both interactional and *institutional* accomplishments, as feminist sociologists Candace West and Sarah Fenstermaker (1993, 1995) have argued about gender and identity construction more generally. The establishment of the comother's identity as a legitimate parent to her children within the context of these family institutions, or what Gubrium and Holstein refer to as "organizational embeddedness" (1990:121) means that the strategy of telling it like it is is somewhat predetermined as a disclosure option, as comother Marlene Fierer confirmed:

> Yeah. Well I knew that, that having a child, we'd have to, you'd be outed at daycare, at school and all that, I knew that that would be part of it.

Comothers thus face a minimal structural constraint or limit on their choice of disclosure strategy—which is to say, they face a constraint on "how out" they will be as lesbians. But as lesbian *parents*, this also suggests that within family-related institutional settings their identity is not only established (accomplished), it is also legitimated. The semi-coercive character of the family-institutional setting, a setting in which the "truth" of familial relationships must be ascertained, virtually guarantees the instantiation of the comother identity and the simultaneous education of all involved. By defining these settings and relationships as "important" and "worth it," lesbian comothers fulfill the twin roles of alma mater as fostering mother and educator.

I have suggested that because lesbian comothers are in the process of constructing a new sociofamilial identity that has hitherto not existed, they are in a unique position to educate members of society about their families. I have tried to preserve a distance from elaborating or fixing the content and form of this identity, believing that as a formative process involving face-to-face interaction and institutional involvement, it is undergoing construction and subject to change. The identity-work done by comothers is qualitatively different from the performative play theorized and described by some queer/feminist theorists. Because it involves highly cathected, socioaffective relationships with children, and because it must operate within a regime of family truth that lends intelligibility exclusively to the mother-father-child family, this work returns lesbian parents to a stage of negotiating the closet all over again, for ultimately it is gay identity—one's status as a lesbian—that renders mother-mother-child intelligible. This time, however, it is not simply one's own sexual identity at stake but also a complex of kin relations that must be *socially recognized as such* if these families are to function in the world.

There is, then, a logic to the construction of the Modern Other Mother, whom I've called "alma mater," to offer a conceptual way of thinking about who she is and what she does. This "logic"—perhaps too strong a word— propels comothers through stages of learning: they not only learn how to represent themselves through identity-work or management of information but they become aware of the discursive strategies available for them to accomplish this work. And—perhaps most important—they learn to assess the potential duration and relative importance of the interactions for which certain strategies are more appropriate than others.

Ultimately, the making of the Modern Other Mother is, I believe, a dialectical process that begins with the unarticulated yet palpable influence of the mother-father-child family truth regime in general, and the heterosexual assumption concerning motherhood in particular. These both become articulated by means of interactional challenge and confrontation between lesbian mothers and their interlocutors—the latter being those whose ignorance has been produced by the heteronormative regime and who are rewarded for their compliance with relative power in these face-to-face contests. Through mothers' deployment of various discursive strategies (for which they develop a facility through repetition and conscious effort), the process moves along until it finally resolves with the recognition and instantiation of the new category of lesbian coparent or comother. This category thus works its way dialogically through and into the public imaginary. I stress public, and have focused here on contacts with nonintimates to highlight the institutional and institutionalizing character of the process and to emphasize that the educational dimension may also be politically transformative in that some institutions will change their definitions of family and their exclusionary practices as a result. This change, I suggest, is currently being initiated and fostered by alma mater.

NOTES

1. I presented different versions of this paper at "Relatively Speaking: A Conference of Gay, Lesbian, Bisexual, and Transgender Families," New York University, May 4, 1997, and the annual meeting of the Pacific Sociological Association, San Francisco, April 18, 1998. I am grateful to the organizers and participants of both sessions for their helpful comments and suggestions, especially E. J. Graff, Lora Lempert, Ellen Lewin, Lonna Malmsheimer and Charlotte Patterson—and of course to the editors of this volume, who organized the New York University conference, Mary Bernstein and Renate Reimann. For their incisive readings of earlier drafts, I extend thanks to Judith Stacey and Linda Morris. Finally, I am indebted to the women who so generously and enthusiastically participated in this study.

2. Empirical data for this paper are based on ethnographic research I conducted over nine months in 1994, wherein I interviewed and observed thirty-four couples with children in the wider San Francisco Bay area. These families are headed by lesbian couples who planned and conceived their children through donor insemination and thus do not include those in which children were born in the context of a heterosexual relationship before their mothers came out as lesbians. A summary of descriptive characteristics of these participants and my research method may be found in my article, "Rozzie and Harriet?: Gender and Family Patterns of Lesbian Coparents," *Gender & Society* 10 (December 6, 1996): 747–67.

3. All names are pseudonyms.

4. The research findings on attempted and successful suicides by gay and lesbian youth as compared to nongay youth are beginning to show more conclusively that homophobic oppression can now count as one of its consequences the self-inflicted loss of life among a generation who might have been expected to be forming their own families in the new millennium. See Remafedi (1994) for a summary of the research on gay and lesbian youth suicide.

5. Gymboree is the free-market answer to the disappearance of public play spaces. For a membership fee and contract similar to those used for adult health clubs, parents can take their toddlers to play classes at a facility where the children romp and expend energy with other toddlers. Of course, parents may also outfit their children in the brand-name clothing marketed by the company.

REFERENCES

Beauvoir, Simone de. 1973. *The Second Sex.* Trans. E. M. Parshley. New York: Vintage.

Butler, Judith. 1991. "Imitation and Gender Insubordination." In Diana Fuss, ed., *Inside/out: Lesbian Theories, Gay Theories*, pp. 13–31. New York: Routledge.

Esterberg, Kristen. 1996. " 'A Certain Swagger When I Walk': Performing Lesbian Identity." In Steven Seidman, ed., *Queer Theory/Sociology*, pp. 259–79. Cambridge, Mass.: Blackwell.

Foucault, Michel. (1978). *History of Sexuality.* Vol. 1. *An Introduction.* Trans. Robert Hurley. Reprint, New York: Vintage, 1990.

Fuss, Diana. 1991. *Inside/out: Lesbian Theories, Gay Theories.* New York: Routledge.

Goffman, Erving. 1963. *Stigma.* New York: Simon & Schuster.

Gubrium, Jaber F. and James A. Holstein. 1990. *What Is Family?* Mountain View, Cal.: Mayfield.

Lewin, Ellen. 1993. *Lesbian Mothers: Accounts of Gender in American Culture.* Ithaca, N.Y.: Cornell University Press.

——. 1994. "Negotiating Lesbian Motherhood: The Dialectic of Resistance and Accommodation." In E. Nakano Glenn, G. Chang, and L. R. Forcey, eds., *Mothering: Ideology, Experience, and Agency*, pp. 333–53. New York: Routledge.

Miller, D. A. 1988. *The Novel and the Police.* Berkeley: University of California Press.

Plummer, Ken. 1975. *Sexual Stigma.* London and Boston: Routledge and Kegan Paul.

——. [1975] 1996. "Symbolic Interactionism and the Forms of Homosexuality." In Steven Seidman, ed., *Queer Theory/Sociology*, pp. 64–82. Cambridge, Mass.: Blackwell.

Remafedi, Gary. 1994. *Death by Denial.* Boston: Alyson Publications.

Sedgwick, Eve Kosofsky. 1988. "Privilege of Unknowing." *Genders* 1 (Spring): 102–24.

——. 1990. *Epistemology of the Closet.* Berkeley: University of California Press.

Stein, Arlene. 1997. *Sex and Sensibility: Stories of a Lesbian Generation.* Berkeley: University of California Press.

Sullivan, Maureen. 1996. "Rozzie and Harriet?: Gender and Family Patterns of Lesbian Coparents." *Gender & Society* 6: 747–767.

West, Candace and Sarah Fenstermaker. 1993. "Power, Inequality, and the Accomplishment of Gender: An Ethnomethodological View." In Paula England, ed., *Theory on Gender/Feminism on Theory*, pp. 151–74. New York: Aldine.

——. 1995. "Doing Difference." *Gender & Society* 9: 8–37.

16 Lesbian Mothers at Work[1]

Renate Reimann

F amily life and work life occupy most of our adult waking hours. Their harmonious coexistence can be a source of great happiness. Work–family conflicts, on the other hand, can produce stress in both areas of life. The relationship between work life and family life becomes further complicated once children demand time and attention within the family sphere.

Children, especially the first child, not only fundamentally alter couples' emotional and relational landscapes but also introduce expanded and different work requirements. While this has been true throughout time and region, families in contemporary American society find themselves confronted with a host of issues unique to modern Western cultures: (a) one or both partners' high time and energy commitments to outside paid labor (Spain and Bianchi 1996); (b) the ideology of intensive parenting, which requires strong commitments to child-centeredness (Hays 1996); and (c) increased expectations of equality between partners (Perkins and DeMeis 1996).

The often contradictory expectations of complete commitment to the job and providing a child-centered and loving family environment leave many parents scrambling for time, energy, and sanity (Coontz 1997; Hays 1996; Hochschild 1997; Spain and Bianchi 1996). Unlike many other Western countries, the United States offers very little public family support. Thus, most families have to rely on individual solutions to social problems.

Two-parent lesbian families experience the same material and emotional constraints as two-parent heterosexual ones. They are even more disadvantaged, however, because they are not eligible for many public programs—both mothers are rarely legal parents (see Dalton, chapter 13) and because such couples do not have access to marriage benefits (see Chambers, chapter 19).

The social and legal invisibility of most lesbian families affects not only their lives at home but also each adult individuals' job advancement, performance, and satisfaction, as well as the interactions between home and work life. The negative consequences of the lack of legal protection and social support for these families range from relatively minor nuisances (such as not being invited to a company picnic as a family) to such matters of importance as health-care coverage and the availability of family leave for comothers.[2] While the general public is increasingly supportive of nondiscrimination policies on the job for lesbian and gay individuals, it mostly continues to find same-sex family issues unintelligible. Thus, workplaces rarely extend family benefits to workers in same-sex parental families because of ignorance if not outright prejudice.

The following discussion illustrates how lesbian mothers in two-parent families address vital work and family issues.

METHODS AND SAMPLE

THIS CHAPTER IS BASED on a study of twenty-five "lesbian nuclear families."[3] All couples had one or more children under the age of six. All children were conceived within the context of the couple's relationship with one partner being the birthmother. I conducted three separate, in-depth interviews per couple: two individual interviews and one couple interview. This technique yielded rich and extensive data allowing each partner to voice her own concerns and interests with respect to paid labor and family life.

The respondents were highly educated (10 percent high school, 10 percent associates, 26 percent bachelors, 26 percent masters, 28 percent professional or doctorate degrees) and 68 percent worked full-time (18 percent part-time, 6 percent on leave, 8 percent unemployed). All mothers who were on leave or unemployed were planning to return to work in the near future. The average annual income per family was $106,000, while the median income was $90,000. Except for one Chinese American, one African American, and three Caribbean American respondents, all participants were European American. (For a more detailed sample description see table 16.1.)

This sample is obviously not representative of the general population,

TABLE 16.1 Sample Profile

Number of participants	25 couples
Number of children	1 child (80 percent); 2 children (20 percent)-a total of 30 children
Age of youngest child	23 months (mean); 14 months (median)
Sex of children	female (n=15); male (n=15)
Years with current partner	9 (mean and median)
Age of participants	38 (mean and median)
Years of education	18 (mean and median)
Place of residence	Brooklyn (18); Manhattan (8); Long Island (8); Other (6); Upstate New York (4); New Jersey (4); Queens (2)
Type of housing	Own house (26); Own apartment (12); Apartment rental (12)

nor is it typical for the lesbian community or even of lesbian mothers (Allen and Demo 1995). However, many studies of lesbian baby-boom families show similar compositions[4] (Patterson 1995a, 1995b; Sullivan 1996). The high levels of education, income, political liberalism, feminist convictions, and racial homogeneity might be due partly to the urban environments that have been studied—mainly New York and San Francisco—and partly to the very deliberate process by which these couples became parents. Twenty-four out of twenty-five couples used donor insemination—a method that requires knowledge and in most cases money and the willingness to involve outside institutions. Also, most mothers were in their thirties by the time they had their first baby. Like heterosexual middle-class women, many postponed childbearing until they were occupationally settled and had reached a point of financial security and personal maturity.

As Boggis discusses (see chapter 11), same-sex parenthood—like few other issues—highlights class differences within the queer community. For example, access to reproductive choices is only available to those in the community who have the financial means, the cultural knowledge, and/or the social privilege to seek out competent and queer-friendly health-care professionals or adoption agents. Furthermore, the violent opposition same-sex parents face from conservatives has led to efforts to control tightly the public image of queer parents from within the lesbian, gay, bisexual, and transgender parent community. I believe, however, that, as the gayby-boom grows in strength and numbers, the diversity among same-sex parent families will become more visible and, it is to be hoped, more accepted.

Despite their relative homogeneity, the families in this study offer important insights into how sexual orientation and motherhood affect work-family interactions. This is not to say that class, race/ethnicity, and location are inconsequential. On the contrary, more research is needed in these areas to understand the influence of family-work choices on the well-being of individuals and families in various cultural and economic circumstances. Thus, I encourage the reader to keep in mind the specific demographic make-up of these families when reading the following text.

FINDINGS

DESPITE THE YOUNG AGE of their children (68 percent of the youngest children at home were under two years old), 86 percent of the mothers in this study were working at the time of the interviews. The high level of labor-market participation indicated a stronger commitment to paid labor compared to the national average of mothers with young children (Spain and Bianchi 1996) and paralleled that of lesbians in general (Dunne 1997). This high commitment to work was motivated by the desire both to work and to be financially independent (Blumstein and Schwartz 1983; Dunne 1997; Morgan and Brown 1991). Although many mothers stated that they would have preferred to stay at home with their children, most thought it desirable only if they were also active in some other ways. Furthermore, many welcomed the return to work after their maternity or parental leaves.

The strong commitment to paid labor on the part of the parents was not always matched with the enthusiasm of employers or even the ability of some mothers to be open about their family arrangements. One of the most pressing issues became whether or not to openly address sexual orientation on the job.

OUT AT WORK

LESBIANS IN THE LABOR force encounter all the basic issues heterosexual women face—e.g., gender-segregated occupations, lower incomes than men for comparable work, and more obstacles to advancement in predominantly male occupations (Reskin and Roos 1990). Lesbians, in general, and lesbians of color in particular, also have to consider to what extent they feel comfortable disclosing their sexual orientation at work (Badgett 1996; Ellis 1996; Ellis and Riggle 1995 and 1996; Friskopp and Silverstein 1995; Levine and Leonard 1984; Rosabal 1996; Schneider 1986).

OUT AS A LESBIAN

ALMOST 50 PERCENT OF the participants in this study were completely out on the job while 12 percent (N=6) had not disclosed their lesbianism to anybody at work.[5] Those who were not entirely out at work tended to work in male-dominated fields (Schneider 1986)—especially in construction and physically demanding occupations. As women they already felt vulnerable and did not want to risk further discrimination on the basis of their sexual orientation. Susan, the mother of a two-year-old and working as a foreman on construction sites, manages her sexual identity on the job as follows:

> [I am not out] to everybody but I am out to my boss. I'm not generally [out] to the regular run-of-the-mill coworker. It's not seen as appropriate. But people know that I have a child and that I raise him with somebody else. I don't make an issue of it. [sighing] But people who want to know, know. If you want to figure it out you're gonna figure it out. But if you don't want to figure it out, you have a back door—you don't have to figure it out.

Many of the women who were not completely out relied on what I call the *open-closet-door policy*. That is, these women stayed in the closet but left the door open for those willing to venture to come in. For example, they would not hide the fact that they were living with another woman but nor would they refer to her as "my lover" or "my partner."

Anne, a mother who worked in another heavily male-dominated industry, described a typical encounter:

> With work, for the most part, people don't know whether I'm gay. In fact, I just had a guy ask me the other day—this is somebody I must have known for fifteen years. He came up to me at this job I'm on, "So, did you get married yet?" [laughing] I'm shocked with these people. Because after a while most people once they get to know me—I don't hide any-

thing about my life. But I don't come up and talk about, "Oh, my lover dadadada." But if you know me for more than a week you know that I have a daughter, that I live with Louise. And if you can't put two and two together then that's too bad. Some people can't put it together, like this guy. When he asked me that I said no. But when I got out of the car I was thinking that I am kind of married—although not legally married.

The open-closet-door policy eases psychological pressure for many who are not comfortable talking explicitly about their "lovers." However, often people they encountered on the job stubbornly ignored the subtle and not so subtle hints the women provided.

When coming out is understood as a relational process rather than a one-sided proclamation, the focus shifts from the person who declares her/himself to the interaction itself, thus including those who receive the message. The attempt of lesbian mothers to invite their colleagues into their lives by opening the closet door is thwarted by the incomprehension of their associates. Coworkers and employers who overlook the open closet door in front of them deny recognition to their queer colleagues' lives. By doing so, they question the legitimacy of queer parents' intimate choices and render their families invisible. Their unwillingness to acknowledge the obvious reflects the power and pervasiveness of heterosexism and homophobia especially with regard to lesbian mothers.

Women of color are at even greater risk of discrimination at work (Badgett 1996; Rosabal 1996). Coming out to their coworkers and superiors increases the potential for bias. Corinne, a lawyer and mother of a one-year-old, explained her reluctance to come out at work as follows:

I'm black. I'm a woman. I get enough negativity based on those things. I am in an environment where being a white male is a premium. I felt like I didn't need to have that other liability.

Being a woman of color did not automatically translate into being closeted. Many other factors influenced the level of disclosure such as work environment and personal relationships on the job.

Another characteristic often negatively correlated with disclosure is the level of income—an important indicator of class position. Schneider (1986) found that women in higher income brackets were less likely to be open about their lesbianism (Ellis and Riggle 1995). Badgett (1996) reports that in another survey, researchers found an inverted V relationship—i.e., those with annual income levels around $50,000 were most likely to be out to coworkers, while disclosure decreased for those making either more or less than that figure.

I did not find a clear income pattern that corresponded with the level of disclosure, although my sample varied considerably in individual income. On the other hand, education, another indicator of class position, had a slight although statistically not significant influence on the willingness to be out at work. Those with professional or doctorate degrees were more likely to be open about their lesbianism than women with less education (77 percent v. 48 percent). Class differences in disclosure thus might be more closely linked to education than to income.

While education and income might have influenced decisions about levels of disclosure on the job, a mother's actual work environment proved more crucial in the coming-out process. Not surprisingly, the most profound deterrent to coming out was anticipated discrimination. The risk seemed too great for some. Loretta voiced the concerns of many others who were not out at work:

> No. I've never been out at any job. . . . They know that I have a child. I guess it's bad. I took a lot of classes in college that told me otherwise—that I shouldn't be this way, not close off so much of myself. But I really feel that if I came out, it would really destroy my career.

The most difficult aspect of anticipated discrimination based on coming out lies in its nonverifiable nature (cf. Wright, chapter 17). The stress of not really knowing what the consequences of being openly lesbian would be took a great toll not only on the workers themselves but also on their families. For example, those women who were the primary providers for their families were much less likely to be out at work than those who shared financial responsibilities with their partners more equally. The possibility of losing most of the household income when coming out posed too great a threat to the family.

Many participants acknowledged that much of their resistance might be a product of internalized homophobia.[6] Yet this internalized homophobia simply reflects the omnipresent privileging of heterosexual intimate choices and the potential for real harm inflicted by bigots and gay-bashers. The frightful stories of sexual or gender nonconformists who have been beaten, raped, and killed instill fear in the most proudly queer person. Thus it is not surprising that Levine and Leonard (1984) found that 25 percent of their sample reported actual discrimination while 60 percent anticipated discrimination if they were to come out. While figures of actual discrimination vary, the fact remains that formal and informal discrimination is a daily reality for many lesbians.

An often overlooked issue in coming-out decisions is the level of commitment to a particular job. Some participants talked about cost-benefit considerations when contemplating disclosure (Badgett 1996). As Danielle told me:

> If I take contract work at [an institution] and I just go there for groups, I'm not gonna tell anybody. There is no point in it. It would be career suicide, I guess. But if it were a job that I would be invested in, then I would. Because I wouldn't want to be going there if I was going there a lot of hours a week.

Danielle, who was looking for part-time employment at the time of the interview, had been very open about her personal life on previous jobs, although it had been difficult. For her the emotional cost of having to hide her affective life clearly outweighed the benefits of passing once she really intended to stay in a full-time job. Danielle's choices once more stress the impact of specific work environments on levels of disclosure. Many women chose to be open about their sexuality in some jobs but not in others. Levels of disclosure not only reflect the self-identity of individuals, they also involve a multitude of considerations that are context-specific. Thus future research would benefit from focusing on the situational and relational circumstances in which sexual (non)disclosure takes place.

OUT AS A MOTHER

LESBIAN MOTHERS, ESPECIALLY THOSE with young children, find themselves in an even more complicated situation. As mothers, they need to be more out because they have to claim benefits and because they require additional support. On the other hand, they become more vulnerable to discrimination because, as mothers and lesbians, they may be seen as less desirable employees.

Motherhood hierarchy[7] and heterosexist assumptions play out differently for birthmothers and comothers. While birthmothers routinely claim their motherhood status, their lesbian identity becomes publicly less visible (Reimann 1997). Mindy related the following episode in which the open-closet-door policy and heterosexist assumptions about motherhood led her colleague to ignore Mindy's lesbian family arrangements.

> I took another appointment recently and I decided at least let me come out to this group and I basically thought I was coming out. . . . But the guy didn't get it. He said, "Well, your personal life is your personal life." And then never asked me about it again. And now when he talks about it, it's clear that he blocked this information out.
>
> I came to tell him that I was pregnant three or four months after he had offered me a position there. I said, "I want you to understand that this is not great timing but I am thirty-nine. It has to happen now. I want you to understand that I am not doing it as a single parent. The woman I have been living with for fourteen, fifteen years will be raising the child with me. Don't look at me as a single parent." Since then he says, "Oh, do you have somebody to take care of the kid?" He just didn't get it.

Seeing one's efforts to come out frustrated to such an extent can be extremely stressful psychologically. But not being able to share important aspects of one's life also takes its toll. Mindy described how it was for her:

> Sometimes it feels bad to not be out. I don't like people assuming that I am a single parent. I don't like misperceptions. But I have done it for so long and I have worked in environments in which it would have been unacceptable to be out—clearly. There was a lot of rampant homophobia. I've just gotten used to it. And I have enough people that I am out to that it doesn't drive me crazy. I can talk with them about it.

Mindy's statement supported Ellis and Riggle's (1995) finding of a strong connection between openness and satisfaction with coworkers. That is, hiding one's sexual orientation in the workplace tends to decrease one's satisfaction with coworkers. Satisfaction with coworkers in turn is an important aspect of overall job satisfaction.

While birthmothers often had to fight for the acknowledgment of their lesbianism, comothers confronted their invisibility as mothers, especially when they were largely closeted. But even when they were very open about their personal lives, motherhood hierarchy assumptions interfered with their perception as mothers. Cordelia, the comother of a one-year-old, vividly described her boss's reaction to her asking for parental leave:

I had been out, very out. And they knew that Delores was trying to get pregnant and they knew within the first three weeks that she was pregnant. When I specifically asked for the leave, my boss seemed a little surprised. I don't know if she was surprised because she was thinking that Delores would do it all or whether she was surprised because she has an ability to ignore things she doesn't really want to cope with.

In the end, it was not difficult for Cordelia to get parental leave and then reduce her hours to part-time. Her office heavily depended on her and was willing to be flexible in order to keep her.

FORMAL AND INFORMAL EMPLOYER SUPPORT FOR LESBIAN FAMILIES

LIKE CORDELIA, MANY OTHERS were able to take advantage of informal as well as formal employer support. While birthmothers' formal benefits were clearly defined, the comothers' situation was often more tenuous. Did they qualify for parental leave as "mothers," as "fathers," or not at all? Cordelia was treated as a "father":

I asked for six weeks. My office has an archaic parental leave provision that mothers are allowed more time than fathers. And I asked for more time than fathers are allowed. The question was did I have it in terms of accrued leave.

Overall, however, her employer was very supportive. As is the case with many other gay or lesbian employees (Friskopp and Silverstein 1995), various personal and situational factors influenced Cordelia's employer's acknowledgment of Cordelia as a mother.

They have been very supportive. They had a [baby] shower for us. Everybody asked about the baby. I think the head of the association is also gay but he is not political. Because everybody assumed or knew that he was gay I don't think that there was ever a question that they would try to not [give it to me]. It's also a very small organization and they do see me as very valuable. For that reason, there also wasn't a question. I think if they didn't like me it might have been different.

This example illustrates not only how a person's position within an organization can help or hinder full acceptance as a lesbian mother but also how important the (perceived) gay-friendliness of a company is to their queer employees. Specifically, those individuals who are out and in positions of power can have a positive influence on the climate of the entire organization. Unfortunately, as I discussed earlier, coming out and being out can derail a career forever (Friskopp and Silverstein 1995).

Not willing to take such a risk, many comothers did not apply for parental leave. Others assumed or were told that they did not qualify for parental leave because they were neither the biological mother nor the father of the child, nor did they adopt. Thus many comothers took vacation time or arranged their schedules to stay with their partners around the birth of their child.

Another rare form of formal support was health-care benefits for partners—or children in the case of comothers. Family insurance is of particular importance if only one partner is employed full-time. Health insurance costs are substantial for self-insured individuals and families. In only two cases was the whole family covered by the comother's health insurance. Vera, the comother of a four-year-old, finally had been able to secure health insurance for her family. Her partner, Bonnie, described the lengthy process:

> City employees got [family insurance for domestic partners]. Where she works is not a city agency and it's not a federal agency. But, on a practical level, it is a city agency. They said that they would abide by the city guidelines. It took them a year to get their act together. They had to bid it out and get guidelines down. When they offered it to Vera I didn't believe it. "I bet they offered it to you without thinking it through. And they will not cover Ellen because she is not your biological child." Lo and behold, she gets the paper and it doesn't cover Ellen. She threatened to sue them. They will cover me also. It's much better insurance than I have too. It saves us a lot of money.

Two other comothers had covered their children for a limited period of time, but because it became more cost efficient they switched the insurance back to the birthmothers.

Another source of support can be union benefits for lesbian and gay families. Anne was trying hard to convince her union to extend domestic-partnership benefits to same-sex couples. The union was stalling the process.

I am going through something with my union right now to get her cov-ered under my insurance. They just don't know what to do at this point. They are stalling right now. Because it's a homophobic union. It's run by men. It's a man's business or world. I don't think they know what to do.

To get other members' support for domestic-partnership benefits, she talked to heterosexual colleagues who where not married to their significant others.

I met a couple of men that do live in that situation who have partners of twenty-odd years who just never married. When I told them that I was looking at domestic partnership they said, "We'll be right there for you. If you need any support we'll be there for you." In fact, there are a lot of people in the union who told me that. It's just dealing with the board and the executives in the union.

The board was afraid that domestic-partnership benefits would be too costly for the union—although domestic-partnership benefit costs tend to be low (Spielman and Winfeld 1996)—and kept tabling the issue indefinitely. This case demonstrates the importance of union support for domestic-partner-ship benefits. Unions can play an important role especially for working-class, same-sex parents and can help create a more positive climate toward queer employees in general.

As important as formal benefits were for these women, informal support often played a crucial role in easing the transition to parenthood and the division of labor in these families. Gloria and Regina worked for the same employer. They had been very open about their decision to parent and the office was extremely supportive emotionally. Gloria told me,

Work, they have been so embracing. I didn't say anything for a long time about Regina. But when I was pregnant, I went door to door to all my colleagues and said, "I need to talk to you. Something is happening. This is how it is going to be. I just want you to know it." And we got flowers and support and hugs.

The employer's practical support was also quite unusual. Both women were able to continue working full-time but compress their hours. As Regina said:

We both work full days Mondays and Thursdays. Tuesdays and Fridays is when we each work half a day. On Wednesday, Gloria's stepmother watches them [while I work in the morning]. Gloria goes to work before I do. I'm responsible for the kids until the babysitters get here. Gloria leaves work before I do, so when she comes home she takes care of them.

And Gloria added:

Childcare, for two days a week Regina's mother and aunt watch the girls. One morning my stepmother [watches them]. Regina and I both work three and a half days.

This way the children only needed childcare half of each week. Informal employer support, however, was rarely available. In most cases, the mothers had to be very inventive about their work arrangements to maximize their time at home.

The above examples of mostly friendly work environments were a result of the mothers' willingness to come out to their superiors and coworkers, as well as to the character of the job. A gay-neutral if not gay-friendly environment seems key. Mothers who had been open about their families prior to becoming mothers had the best chances to receive formal as well as informal employer support.

Birthmothers always had access to formal support. For them, the salient issue often was how colleagues would treat them—as single mothers or as lesbian mothers. Comothers, on the other hand, were never sure of formal support even in cases when they were unabashedly open about their lesbian relationships. Thus, for comothers who had been discreet about their personal lives, coming out did not necessarily secure access to parental benefits, since in most cases they did not qualify as either "mother" or "father" under their companies' policies. Gay-friendly employers offered the greatest potential for, if not formal, at least informal support.

Caught in the dilemma of either forgoing parental benefits or risking their occupational security and advancement, the comothers who were not out at work faced a very difficult decision. Amanda, a comother who was anticipating having their second child, vividly described the stress associated with needing to take care of a child and remaining closeted at work:

It's going to be hard especially when we're going to have another one. There is running around that needs to be done and the school will be calling. I can't pretend that she doesn't exist. People find out anyway. It's been really hard. I try not to get into any conversations where I have to talk about it. It's strange to do that. I hate it. I have to think how I'm going to handle it.

As in Amanda's case, most comothers who feared discrimination at work remained careful about disclosing their family lives. As a result, when both mothers worked full-time, often birthmothers became primarily responsible for the children in crisis situations. Elizabeth, the birthmother of two, described a typical scenario in which birthmothers become primarily responsible for childcare because comothers are reluctant to claim parental responsibilities as a reason for taking time off from work.

> I don't get paid if I don't go to work. That's a little bit of a problem. But if they are sick she wouldn't stay home. But there have been times when I had a job for two hours and she would come home and stay with them. Most of the time I take off when they are sick.

Like most parents, the mothers in this study felt very pressed for time because of the tremendous demands their work and their families exerted. Amanda explains how changing work and child demands can create more stress on family life.

> It was easier [before] because we didn't have to work during our shared leaves. So we managed much better I think than we do now. There were fewer stressors in the relationship, for us individually. She was a lot younger then. She didn't require quite as much time and attention. We took her everywhere and she would just sleep.

Thus, losing one parent in crisis situations added to the overall feeling of stress and strain for families.

Families are profoundly affected by work. Not only are they dependent on the income, but the support or lack of support of employers and coworkers can either intensify or ease the pressure on families. The politics of coming out at work complicate the delicate balance of work–family relations even further. The emotional costs of having to hide one's affective life at work because of fear of discrimination weigh heavy on any person and can result in work and personal dissatisfaction.

Once children are involved, work-related pressures intensify both emotionally and in practical terms. Although parental obligations are not always acknowledged in the workplace, most employers will grant some form of parental benefits to parents. When a comother feels that she cannot risk her job by coming out as a lesbian mother, she has to forgo those benefits and family life becomes more stressful. Comothers face the additional problem of not being viewed as mothers even in cases when they are very open about their lesbian families. Unless they have adopted their children—which in many cases is either legally or financially impossible—comothers are invisible as parents from a policy point of view.

In the absence of access to legal marriage for same-sex couples, domestic-partnership policies that include the acknowledgment of parental obligations could greatly improve work-family experiences for lesbian mothers with children. These policies are not only important because of the practical support they would offer families. They also signal a gay-positive environment in which individuals no longer have to hide their same-sex relationships and families. The open-closet-door policy described earlier would become obsolete. Thus both the practical and emotional benefits of domestic-partnership policies cannot be overestimated. They are desperately needed for the growing number of lesbian families with children.

NOTES

1. This chapter is adapted from the author's dissertation entitled "Shared Parenting in a Changing World of Work: Lesbian Couples' Transition to Parenthood and Their Division of Labor" (1998), which was supported by the Henry Murray Dissertation Award (Radcliffe College) and grants from The Center for Lesbian and Gay Studies (CUNY) and the Birdie Fuchs Memorial Scholarship (CUNY).

2. I chose the term "comother" for the nonbiological mother because it encompasses the social as well as biological implications while stressing the partnership aspect of parenting. Whenever it was necessary to make a distinction between the two partners, I have used the term "comother" for the nonbirthing partner and "birthmother" for the biological mother of a child. In all other cases, I refer to both partners as parents or mothers.

3. The term "lesbian nuclear family" indicates that the family structure of the participants in this study is that of a nuclear family. The couples were together prior to the birth of the child. They planned their families together and rec-

ognized each other as parents. Thus, the household consisted of two adults involved in an intimate relationship and their children.

4.　This impression was also supported by personal discussions with Terry Boggis of Center Kids in New York, as well as other researchers who work with lesbian baby-boom mothers.

5.　This number is slightly higher than reported in most studies. Ellis and Riggle (1995) reported that 38 percent of their respondents were completely open about their homosexuality, while Schneider (1986) only found 16 percent of her sample being entirely open about their lesbianism. The difference between Schneider's and Ellis and Riggle's data is most likely due to their different samples as well as to the changing times. The reason for even higher levels of disclosure in my study are probably a result of the necessities of motherhood and the urban character of the sample.

6.　"Most children internalize society's ideology of sex and gender at an early age. As a result, gay women and men usually experience some degree of negative feeling toward themselves when they first recognize their own homosexuality in adolescence or adulthood. This sense of what is usually called *internalized homophobia* often makes the process of identity formation more difficult" (Herek 1995:335).

7.　Commonly held motherhood ideology only assigns "true motherhood" to one person, generally the birthmother, thus creating a "motherhood hierarchy." Any other claim to motherhood, as in shared motherhood, smacks of substitute parenthood and creates the need to legitimize the relationship to the child (see Sullivan, chapter 15).

REFERENCES

Allen, K. and D. Demo. 1995. "The Families of Lesbians and Gay Men: A New Frontier in Family Research." *Journal of Marriage and the Family* 57: 111–27.

Badgett, L. 1996. "Employment and Sexual Orientation: Disclosure and Discrimination in the Workplace." In A. Ellis and E. Riggle, eds., *Sexual Identity on the Job: Issues and Services*, pp. 29–52. New York: Hayworth Press.

Blumstein, P. and P. Schwartz. 1983. *American Couples: Money, Work, Sex.* New York: William Morrow.

Coontz, S. 1997. *The Way We Really Are: Coming to Terms with America's Changing Families.* New York: Basic Books.

Dunne, G. 1997. *Lesbian Lifestyles: Women's Work and the Politics of Sexuality.* Toronto: University of Toronto Press.

Ellis, A. 1996. "Sexual Identity in the Workplace: Past and Present." In A. Ellis and E. Riggle, eds., *Sexual Identity on the Job: Issues and Services*, pp. 1–16. New York: Hayworth Press.

Ellis, A. and E. Riggle. 1995. "The Relation of Job Satisfaction and Degree of Openness about One's Sexual Orientation for Lesbians and Gay Men." *Journal of Homosexuality* 30 (2): 75–85.

Friskopp, A. and S. Silverstein. 1995. *Straight Jobs-Gay Lives: Gay and Lesbian Professionals, The Harvard Business School, and the American Workplace*. New York: Scribner.

Hays, S. 1996. *The Cultural Contradictions of Motherhood*. New Haven: Yale University Press.

Herek, G. 1995. "Psychological Heterosexism in the United States." In Anthony R. D'Augelli and Charlotte J. Patterson, eds., *Lesbian, Gay, and Bisexual Identities over the Lifespan: Psychological Perspectives*, pp. 321–46. New York: Oxford University Press.

Hochschild, A. 1997. *The Time Bind: When Work Becomes Home and Home Becomes Work*. New York: Metropolitan Books.

Levine, M. and R. Leonard. 1984. "Discrimination Against Lesbians in the Work Force." *Signs* 9 (4): 700–710.

Morgan, K. S. and L. S. Brown. 1991. "Lesbian Career Development, Work Behavior, and Vocational Counseling." *The Counseling Psychologist* 19 (2): 273–91.

Patterson, C. 1995a. "Families of the Lesbian Baby Boom: Parents' Division of Labor and Children's Adjustment." *Developmental Psychology* 31 (1): 115–23.

——. 1995b. "Lesbian Mothers, Gay Fathers, and Their Children." In Anthony R. D'Augelli and Charlotte J. Patterson, eds., *Lesbian, Gay, and Bisexual Identities Over the Lifespan*, pp. 262–90. New York: Oxford University Press.

Perkins, H. W. and D. K. DeMeis. 1996. "Gender and Family Effects on the 'Second-Shift' Domestic Activity of College-Educated Young Adults." *Gender & Society* 10 (1): 78–93.

Reimann, R. 1997. "Does Biology Matter? Lesbian Couples' Transition to Parenthood and Their Division of Labor." *Qualitative Sociology* 20 (2): 153–85.

Reskin, B. and P. Roos. 1990. *Job Queues, Gender Queues: Explaining Women's Inroads into Male Occupations*. Philadelphia: Temple University Press.

Rosabal, G. 1996. "Multicultural Existence in the Workplace: Including How I Thrive as a Latina Lesbian Feminist." In A. Ellis and E. Riggle, eds., *Sexual Identity on the Job: Issues and Services*, pp. 17–28. New York: Hayworth Press.

Schneider, B. 1986. "Coming Out at Work: Bridging the Private/Public Gap." *Work and Occupations* 13 (4): 463–87.

Spain, D. and S. Bianchi. 1996. *Balancing Act: Motherhood, Marriage, and Employment Among American Women*. New York: Russell Sage Foundation.

Spielman, S. and L. Winfeld. 1996. "Domestic Partnership Benefits: A Bottom Line Discussion." In A. Ellis and E. Riggle, eds., *Sexual Identity on the Job: Issues and Services*, pp. 53–78. New York: Hayworth Press.

Sullivan, M. 1996. "Gender and Family Patterns in Lesbian Coparents." *Gender & Society* 10 (6): 747–67.

17 "Aside from One Little, Tiny Detail, We Are So Incredibly Normal": Perspectives of Children in Lesbian Step Families

Janet M. Wright

Years ago I was trying to explain homophobia to one of my sons, who was five years old at the time. He looked at me with confusion, "Mom, I don't understand. How can it be wrong to love someone?" Recently, when I was doing research on lesbian step families,[1] the children in the families echoed this same sense of surprise and confusion—how was it that something so good and secure as their families was considered so disgusting and awful by so many people? Alcoholism in families has been described as being like an elephant in the living room. Everyone can see it and they politely step around it, but no one talks about it. This leads to a sense of inauthenticity in the children of such families. In lesbian and gay families, however, children have a very different experience. There is no elephant in the living room at home, but many outsiders insist that there is. This creates a sense of mistrust and fear of the world outside the family.

Saffron (1996) interviewed twenty British people who have lesbian mothers or gay fathers or both. She writes, "Many believed that their experiences were unexceptional and couldn't understand how such ordinary lives might provoke such interest" (5). She quotes one of her participants, Mary, who was twenty at the time of the interview: "At the time I was

---

Parts of this chapter are reprinted, with permission from the Haworth Press and from Janet Wright, *Lesbian Step Families: An Ethnography of Love* (1998).

growing up, the fact that my Dad was gay was a normal part of my life. I never thought about it as a phenomenon."

There have been many studies about the children of gay and lesbian people directed at examining what harm, if any, might come from growing up in such an atmosphere (see Patterson 1996; Pollack 1987). Pollack identifies three erroneous assumptions commonly addressed by the courts in custody cases: that lesbians/gays are sexually maladjusted and therefore liable to sexually harm their children, that children of gay parents will grow up to be gay or to have confused sex-role identification, and that the children could be seriously harmed by the social stigma of having lesbian/gay parents. However, as Patterson (1992) summarizes, "despite psychological, judicial, and popular prejudices, a substantial body of research now attests to normal adjustment among mothers and normal development among children in these families" (420). There have been fewer studies examining gay and/or lesbian families from the children's perspective. Lewis (1980) interviewed twenty-one children from the Boston, Massachusetts, area, ranging in age from nine to twenty-six years. Much of her information, however, concerns the children's reactions to their biological parents' divorces. Rafkin (1990) presents stories from thirty-seven sons and daughters of lesbians, ages five to forty. But it is difficult to draw conclusions for children growing up today since the social climate for lesbians, especially the increased awareness/ acceptability of lesbianism, has changed so drastically in the last ten to twenty years. Tasker and Golombok (1997) interviewed thirty-nine British children raised by lesbian mothers in 1976 when the children were around ten years old and then interviewed them again in 1991, when they were about twenty-five years old. This comprehensive and fascinating study focused in 1976 on "the quality of the mother-child relationship, the mother's psychological adjustment, the child's gender role behavior, and the child's peer relationships" (39). In 1991 the interviews with the young adults covered four main areas of interest: "family relationships, peer relationships, intimate relationships, and psychological adjustment" (44). While the data and results are rich and informative, the inquiry and findings still focus on affirming that children raised in lesbian families are not harmed by the experience. They conclude:

> What is clear from the present study is that it is not necessarily the case that children who are raised in a lesbian mother family will experience difficulties in adulthood. Indeed, the findings from the present study show that young people brought up by a lesbian mother do well in adulthood and have good relationships with their family, friends, and partners. (155)

My own study attempts to shift this focus on normal adjustment (i.e., just like children with heterosexual parents) to an examination of the unique benefits as well as challenges that children in lesbian families experience. This inquiry concentrates on how children raised in lesbian families may have different, but not necessarily less healthy, family experiences. It also suggests that some of those experiences may even be quite beneficial for the children of lesbians.

This chapter describes a small piece of a larger, comprehensive ethnography of five lesbian step families (Wright 1998).

Ethnography is the study of groups and people in their natural setting as they go about their everyday lives. It involves not only seeing how others react to various events in their lives but also examining one's own reactions. The ethnographer uses him or herself as a research tool to deepen his or her understanding of the participants and their lives.

I studied five lesbian step families and used intensive interviewing of each family member, a limited number of observations of each family, and an analysis of structured journals that were kept by family members. With each family I began with a short meeting with the entire family, explaining the process and the research topic, as well as issues of confidentiality and potential problems. At that point, if the family elected to continue with the project, we arranged as many of the interview and observation times as we could. I always interviewed the couple first. After that, the schedules for interviews and observations was based on the family's needs, although I generally tried to do most of the interviewing before I did the observations.

There were a total of seventeen participants in this study. The ten mothers and step mothers ranged in age from thirty-one to forty-seven. The "children" ranged in age from seven to twenty, with two clusters at either end of the range. The children include two boys and five girls/young women.

This is a middle-class sample, with annual family incomes of $45,000 to $140,000. Individual adult incomes ranged from $15,000 to $90,000. Four of the five families owned their own homes. The education level of the adults included four high school graduates, one college graduate with additional training, four master's degrees, and one Ph.D.

Three of the participants identify themselves as mixed race. One is Asian/African-American/Caucasian. One is African American/Caucasian. And one is one-quarter American Indian and Caucasian. One person identifies herself as one-eighth Jewish. Three children are partially Hispanic, including two who are one-half Hispanic and one child who is one-quarter Hispanic. Other ethnicities identified by participants as part of their heritages are German, Danish, Norwegian, Swedish, English, Welsh, Spanish, Scottish, Hungarian, and Polish (see table 17.1).

The adult partners have been in their present relationships for an average of 7.4 years. The relationships range from four plus to more than fifteen years in duration. The children in the study were between ages one and seven when their moms got involved in the present relationships. One family had a child who was thirteen when the parents became involved, but she was not interviewed because she was not living at home at the time of the study. Four of the biological mothers were married to men before the present relationships and their children are products of those marriages. The length of those marriages were three, four, fourteen, and fourteen years. Only one step mother was previously married—for a year and a half. One biological mother had had her children by alternative insemination by donor in the context of a nine-year lesbian relationship.

The qualitative data was analyzed through thorough readings of the transcribed interviews, notes on observations, and journals. Broad themes were identified and searches for confirming and disconfirming evidence were conducted. I took a feminist stance in collecting and analyzing the data. This included attempting to balance the integrity of the data with respect for and appropriate protection of the participants. Children, in particular, do not have the same ability as adults to screen material from the researcher. They may say something about a parent, for example, that could be potentially damaging to the family. I felt it was crucial for me to take responsibility to report the truth but to do so in a manner that would not harm the participants. I made an effort to collaborate with the participants by sending my chapters to them for feedback before the final draft. But I also attempted to be clear that the interpretations were mine—the research was ultimately my responsibility. For a more thorough discussion of the data analysis see Wright (1998).

"NORMAL" FAMILIES

IN THE DICTIONARY, THE definition of "normal" includes two aspects. On one hand it means usual, not abnormal, regular, natural. On the other hand, it means sane, free from any disorder or disease. The contradiction raised by the dual definitions is whether or not only the usual and regular

TABLE 17.1

| FAMILIES | | | SEX(ES) AND AGE(ES) OF CHILD(REN) | COMBINED ANNUAL INCOME | EDUCATION | | ETHNICITY/RACE | | |
BIOLOGICAL MOM	STEP MOM	CHILDREN			BIOLOGICAL PARENT	STEP PARENT	BIOLOGICAL PARENT	STEP PARENT	CHILDREN
Tanya Norden	Terry Westby	Kevin Engleking	Kevin: male, 8	$48,000	Master's degree	Some college	White	Multiracial: White/Black/Asian	Biracial: Black/White
Delia Iliff	Kathy Dubrovsky	Diana Iliff, Natalia Iliff-Hernandez	Diana: female, 20; Natalia: female, 17	$60,000	Bachelor's degree & paralegal	Master's degree	White	White	White/Hispanic
Nisi Uphoff	Florence Dillard	Dale Uphoff, Frannie Uphoff	Dale: male, 8; Frannie: female, 8	$58,000	Master's degree	High school	White	White/ 1/4 Native American	White
Cady Peterson	Lori Timms	Molly Taylor	Molly: female, 15	$140,000	Master's degree	Ph.D.	White	White	White
Dory Stark	Becky Stark	Pauli Stark	Pauli: female, 7	$48,000	High school	High school	White	White	White/Hispanic

can also be considered sane and free from disorder. The children in this study clearly testify to the fact that their families, while not usual in one or more aspects, are still healthy. As Talia, a sixteen-year-old girl, said:

> I mean, look at our house, it is extremely normal. That's what I told my . . . , just the other day in school, the teacher told us to write something different about our family. I'm sorry, my family is just too normal. He just looked at me and said, well, they're really not. Come on I said, aside from one little, tiny detail, we are so incredibly normal.

Indeed, the challenges faced by their families that the children addressed, outside of homophobia, were all typical challenges faced by heterosexual families and step families. For example, in step family situations, the children sometimes resented the intrusion of the step parent into disciplining. Molly, age fifteen, complained about her step mother:

> I can hear her saying things to my mom like, 'Well you had better punish her for that or what do you plan on doing about this?'

However, Molly later also conceded:

> Sometimes, though, Lori can, like, see things my mom doesn't. Like with certain situations. It's weird.

Teenaged children also complained about the discipline that the mother and step mother developed together. Talia talked about her parents sitting together at a table, waiting to talk with her when she got home:

> Oh yes, it drives me nuts, because you come home and they will be sitting at the table and you're like—"Oh God! Oh shit! What did I do this time? They called school and they know I've been skipping." So, they don't let us get away with much at all.

Certainly, struggles over discipline issues are common in families of all types. Lesbian families appear to be no exception.

In heterosexual step families, the other parent (the divorced parent) is often a challenge to the stability of the step family (Sager et al. 1983). In lesbian step families, this issue is particularly troublesome when the other parent is critical of the lesbian family or the new partner. Twenty-year-old

Diana discussed how her biological father constantly criticized her mother's partner, Kathy:

> He used to put down Kathy all the time and I didn't understand why, you know, because I didn't see her as an evil person. But he always said, "She's so bitter. Don't be bitter like Kathy. Don't get a hard heart like Kathy. Be like your mom—she's so creative." And I'm like—excuse me, you don't know this woman. OK. You probably didn't know [mom] when you were married to her and you don't know Kathy at all. And I would just—for a really long time that really bothered me because then I'd come back and . . . I'd be thinking, Dad said Kathy was nasty. And Kathy wouldn't do anything nasty to us, you know. Yes, she'd punish us when we did stupid stuff, but that's because she was our mom and she had a right to do that. That really [confused] and hurt me.

Other problems that confronted these families, and are also common in straight families, included diseases and disorders (such as attention deficit disorder (ADD) and juvenile arthritis), problems with families of origin, and job stress (including working different shifts, long hours, or unhappiness with a job). However, when I asked the children if there was anything they wished that they could change about their families, they identified problems that were unrelated to family structure, such as illness. Frannie, eight years old, answered, "Well no . . . maybe not Florence (step mother) having a broken leg." And Pauli, seven years old, said:

> That my grandma would be alive and Becky [step mother] and me never had arthritis and we never had the [car] accident and that my grandmas were alive, and that I never had ADD and my mom didn't either. And my mom and I never had any of the other things—either of my moms.

Clearly these families confront problems that are similar to all kinds of families—"the challenges of creating cohesion while nourishing individuality, of monitoring and constantly adjusting parental guidance to fit the changing needs of children, of providing safety and security and love for all family members, and of nurturing the couple relationship as well as all family relationships" (Wright 1998:95–96).

The children in this study felt that the challenges their families faced, as well as the nurturance and love they held, were "normal" or not very unusual.

The lesbian family challenges the societal prescription of male domination, refuting the splitting of human traits along gender lines. These children, whether they had contact with their biological fathers or not, did not express concerns or fears about their gender development. Diana stated:

> I don't need a father, and I get really resentful when people tell me I do, and [that] I'm not going to be as good as someone who has one. I need two loving parents who will love me and respect me as a person. And that's what I have.

Silverstein and Rashbaum (1994) suggest that the terms "mothering" and "fathering" be degendered and retired in favor of "parenting."

> "Parenting" is something that any caring person of either gender and any sexual persuasion can do. If there are two people—or more—doing it, whether it's a man and a woman, two women, two men, or any conceivable combination of loving, competent adults who are passionately committed to the well-being of the child, so much the better for the child as well as for those who are taking care of him or her. (239)

The dissonance, confusion, and fear that the children experienced, then, came from the homophobic reaction and/or complete erasure of their kind of family by society outside the homes they experienced as healthy and normal.

THE EXPERIENCES OF CHILDREN IN A HETEROSEXUAL SUPREMACIST ENVIRONMENT

HOOKS (1987) DESCRIBES WHITE SUPREMACY as an all pervasive ideology and behavior in the United States' society—a value/belief system that is still embodied by whites, even when they do not embrace racism. The term "heterosexual supremacy" is used here in a similar sense. In a heterosexual-supremacist society the male/female bond is idealized as superior—spiritually, morally, physically, emotionally, and intellectually. As Pharr (1988) has explained, the system of heterosexual supremacy enforces a rigidly gendered and patriarchal society. Children are forced into stereotypical gendered roles in part by the fear of being identified as a "faggot" or "dyke." It is difficult to even imagine a world without homophobia. Rich (1980) illuminated many years ago how compulsory heterosexuality warps the freedom of both boys and girls to grow into themselves. It should be no surprise, then, that children who grow up in lesbian families may be more secure in their own identities (Patterson 1992). How then do children growing up in lesbian homes (which they perceive as healthy and normal) experience, cope with, and at times triumph over heterosexual supremacy?

The children in this study were sometimes teased about having lesbian mothers. Pauli reported that she had been teased about having two moms. She said that "a lot" of kids teased her about having two moms when she was in the first grade—calling her "mental" and "retarded."When I asked her why she thought that they teased her, she replied,"They think it is funny that I have two moms."

Some of the older children have been accused of being gay themselves. ("The apple doesn't fall far from the tree," a girl in eighth grade once told my daughter.) Talia talked about her boyfriend's confusion. Once when she made a comment about another girl looking quite beautiful when she was dancing, her boyfriend wondered if she might be lesbian like her mothers.

Children also hear a lot of negative misinformation about gay and lesbian people. Talia "freaked out" when she was in the fifth grade and read a pamphlet on AIDS that was distributed at her school. She thought that it implied that if you were gay, you were likely to die from AIDS. She was so upset that she ran home and asked her mom if she had AIDS. Certainly, children often hear derogatory statements about gay and lesbian people. "Faggot" is a commonly heard put-down. And these negative characterizations are almost never refuted by adults (the same adults who might refute racial slurs). In addition, children are sometimes misinformed or even rejected by their extended family. Diana was told as a child by her maternal grandmother that her mother was "abnormal."

However, these children have experienced very little overt trauma from being teased by friends and classmates about their different family structure. Eight-year-old Dale reports that no one really teases him about it. Frannie says that none of her best friends tease her at all, and writes in her journal: "Yosily nobody hurts my feelings about having lesbian moms."[2] Therefore, it was somewhat surprising for me to repeatedly hear these children talk about their fear. The children seemed to carry around with them a certain uneasiness and anxiety, even when they had not experienced any overt homophobia. When I asked Dale if he was sometimes afraid that people would find out about his mom's lesbianism, he replied:

DALE   Well, not bad—but it's just if they tease me.

JANET   But you said . . . has anybody ever teased you, yet?

DALE   No, not really.

Pauli, who has experienced very little homophobia up to this point, tells me that she will definitely be straight when she grows up—because she doesn't want her children to be teased.

PAULI   I think that I don't want. I don't want to go through the hassle of my kids being teased by some other kids. So I'm going to get married. I'm going to get married with a man, because I don't want my kids to be teased. And I'm going to have four of them, so I don't want the four of them being teased. And I don't want to hear everything coming home saying that they got teased. I don't want to hear that. I want to hear a good report, like they didn't get teased today.

JANET   Do you think kids get teased about a lot of things though?

PAULI   YEAH, I DO.

JANET   I mean, you said that you get teased about your name.

PAULI   Lots of kids get beat up in that school. Lots of kids get pushed. Lots of kids get their teeth ripped out—well, not the teeth. But, you know, it's an angry world out there, you know.

JANET   So, even if you get married, your kids may get teased about something else, huh?

PAULI   You know, like maybe because they, boys go to ballet, you know. But I hope that my kids don't do it, because it's awful hard to grow up being teased. And I don't like being teased so I certainly know that if I do grow up having four kids, I don't want to hear them being teased because it's awful for me. Because, you know, if it's hard, it certainly will be hard for them. So I don't want that happening, though. But, I do want, you know, I will do, would like to pass on what my mom did— you know, get married with a gay . . . but I think that my kids would get teased a lot. I don't want that to happen. But I would like to pass it on, you know. I would like to pass it on if kids would be more nicer.

Pauli, at age seven, is so afraid of teasing that she has already determined that she will not be lesbian and will not put her own children in this position.

The key point here is the extent to which all of these children had fears about being in lesbian families—regardless of whether or not they had any personal experience with homophobia. Nisi, a biological mother, describes it as a "free-floating anxiety" and tells this chilling story:

NISI   I think it was a year and a half ago, we went to a winter solstice—you were there. As part of the ceremony, the celebration was letting go, you know, what do you want to let go of as a family. What do you want to leave behind as a family. And we went like into a blanket amongst this group of trees and then talked about it ourselves. And what Frannie said at that time was what she wanted was she was afraid that somebody would kill us because we were a lesbian family.

JANET   Wow, that gives me the chills.

NISI   And that was what she wanted to let go of was that feeling. And so it really is a big issue for them. So I think life would just be less anxious [if there were no homophobia]. They'd feel like they wouldn't have to be on guard, they'd feel safer, they'd feel like it was easier to be themselves with their friends and let everybody know who they were and what their core identity was. Introductions would be easier—I mean, everything would be easier.

For the most part, in these families, it is the fears that stress the children more than the actual occurrences of homophobia. Patterson (1996) found that "children of lesbian mothers reported greater reactions to stress than did the children of heterosexual mothers, and they also reported a greater overall sense of well-being than did children of heterosexual mothers" (427). What causes such strong fears in the children of lesbians? I believe it may have more to do with the covert messages of heterosexual supremacy than with the overt teasing that children experience.

The scarcity of positive images and feedback, in conjunction with the abundance of negative stereotypes, combine to create a sense of fear and secrecy. Society sends the clear message that children of lesbians should not be proud of their mothers or their families—they should be ashamed.

Children, like their parents, use various strategies to cope. Some children, such as fifteen-year-old Molly, simply don't tell anyone. Younger children, who don't yet understand situational ethics, may feel particularly torn by this strategy's similarity to lying. When I asked Dale if there were times when he had been afraid to tell people about his mothers, he answered yes. When asked what he did then, he responded, "I don't tell—I don't lie—because they don't ask me." Frannie suggests a compromise strategy. She says she will often wait until kids get to know her before she tells them about her moms.

> But then, after the kids start to get to know me, and I tell them that I have three moms,[3] you know, they don't really mind because after they start to know that I'm not different or I'm not mean or I'm not different just because I have lesbian moms, they start to realize that it's OK to have a friend.

Other children, particularly very young or older children (middle-school years seem to foster the most fear and hiding) simply use the strategy of coming out. Diana's mother tells this story about Diana and her friend, Tilly, who had a gay father:

> Well, when Diana and Tilly got to high school, I think in order to jump the gun on the other kids, realizing that everybody by now knew their situations . . . and so they would kind of skip down the hall and say things like, "Oh, so how's your gay dad doing?" and "Oh, fine, and how's your lezzie mom?"

Both Diana and Talia found that joking about it was a way to disarm their potential attackers. Talia says, "Now I just basically come out and say it, kind of like in a joking manner—like, just warning you, my mom is gay."

The strategy of coming out works as a way to separate our friends from our enemies, or a way of identifying peoples' levels of acceptance and/or comfort. It is easier to come out when one can accept the idea that everyone doesn't have to be a friend or to like oneself. As Delia and Kathy comment, Talia was able to stop lying about her moms when she matured enough to realize that "if they are so stupid [to react negatively], I don't need to have them as friends and I don't care." This attitude change occurred as Talia went from middle school to high school. It may also be easier to come out when we are in touch with our righteous anger. Anger can be an empowering emotion when it names oppression. As Dale wrote in his journal, "It makes me mad when I think about Lesbian parants not giting as much rights." And Frannie said in her interview, when asked why she thinks some people don't like lesbians:

> Well, they might think that someone is different and they don't like that. They might think that we are mean, just because we have a partner. But I don't think its any different—they just love a woman instead of a man. I mean, there's no law about not liking a man or something, liking a woman instead. And . . . I mean, it wasn't very, I don't think it's very, not really good thinking that someone is different makes them mean.

Children, then, are empowered as they understand that lesbianism is not the problem—homophobia is. In fact, children may find strength in being a member of a lesbian family. As Dale wrote in his journal, "Being in a Lesbian family [makes] me more unekie." How do children get to a place of feeling acceptance of and even pride in being a member of a lesbian family? These children talked about two crucial factors that made a difference in their lives: positive books and other media about lesbians, and contact with other children of lesbians and/or gay men. Several children talked about the influence of positive media on their ability to accept their situations. When I asked Pauli why she thought that some people didn't like that she has two moms, she gave a response that illustrates the power and importance of books. Children need to see their families reflected in books.

> They think it is weird, you know. Like in the book, it says that some grown-ups don't like other grown-ups that are gay. And one of the signs that this person is holding [says], Please go away. So you know some kids don't like people that, kids that have gay [parents].

Media may have an even more powerful impact on Pauli because she is one of the more isolated children. She does not know other children with lesbian or gay parents. Books and movies and TV shows that depict lesbians and gay men in a positive light are very powerful for children because they address that aspect of invisibility in their lives. They also convey the message that there are lots of people out there somewhere, powerful people, who accept lesbians and gay men. They are not alone. Diana talked of watching movies about lesbians as a way of increasing her understanding of the issues. It also may help children to name their anger at homophobia and to label that anger as righteous and justified.

The second factor these children mentioned as an important influence in their lives is knowing other children of gay and lesbian parents. One of the crucial aspects of knowing other children from similar family structures is that children are reassured that they are not alone. As Talia put it, "So I always knew that there were other kids like me. I always knew that I was not alone." And Dale wrote in his journal,

> I was talking with Nicky. He is in a Lesbian family to. I said to him I have three moms! Nicky has two moms and a dad.

Although Dale mentions here that he talked about his family structure with his friend, the children mostly do not talk about it. Talking about and processing their lesbian families seem less important to them than simply hanging out and playing. Further on in his journal, Dale reports, "I went over to Nickys and I like plaing with pepel that [have] Lesbian prants." And when I asked Diana if she and her sister ever talked with their friends who had lesbian parents about their family structure, she replied:

> Really, I don't think that when we were with Kelly and Tara or any other kids when we were really young, we never—we took it for granted that they [our families] were, we knew that they were different. And we knew that they were different in a way that other people would find unacceptable and we knew why. But we never, it wasn't a strange thing for us. It wasn't like, it wasn't until recently that even like now that I'll sit down and go, wow, you know, my mom is a lesbian, and I'll think about what that is and then I'll think about the images we see in the media, and stuff, and I'll go—that's not my mom, you know. She's just mom and Kathy and they've been there all my life. But I'll sit down with Sara and I'll go—Sara, our moms are lesbians. And she goes, I know. And like, wow. But no, I never personally saw it as anything weird [when I was little].

The need to talk about having a lesbian mom with friends may come later in life, then, but it seems most important for younger children to simply have play connections with children from lesbian families.

Both media about and connections with other lesbian families seem to be extremely effective ways to combat the pervasive sense of invisibility that can haunt the children of lesbians. While I did specifically ask children about whether or not they knew other children who had lesbian moms, the issue of the importance of the media came up entirely spontaneously as a children's concern. While their parents have other strategies they use to help their children combat heterosexual supremacy, these were the factors that the children themselves were aware of and mentioned.

When I asked the children if they had any advice to give to other lesbian step family members, they addressed several of the issues that were important to them. Molly suggested that it is just something that you have to accept—"you can't control other people, you know." And that, if you are lucky, you will get someone decent who joins your family. "But even if it is a struggle at times, it can still be OK." Dale said, "It's not different. It's OK. It's not bad at all. . . . Well, it is different—it's not something worse, though." And his sister Frannie echoed his advice of acceptance:

> If they were scared that people would tease them, I could say to them, like, nobody will tease you if they get to know you. It's really not that big of a deal, you know.

Kevin agreed with Dale and Frannie, saying that "it's fun having two moms."

Diana and Talia's advice was to moms and kids—don't hide. Talia explained that it was harder when she tried to hide her family situation— "If anything was hard it was me making it hard, like me trying to hide it, you know."

And Diana told this story to illustrate how important it is for parents to be proudly out:

> I think it helped that my parents were out. Because then it was me who was doing the hiding and it wasn't them. If they were telling me that this is right and this is OK, our relationship, but then they weren't out in the public, then that would have given me a real clear signal, and I probably would have had a lot more hard time.

STRENGTHS

ONE OF THE GREAT strengths mentioned elsewhere in research on lesbian families (Patterson 1996; Pollack and Vaughn 1987; Saffron 1996) and certainly corroborated by this study is the ability of the children to accept and enjoy human differences. Rafkin (1990) concludes from her interviews with children of lesbians that, compared with heterosexual parents, lesbians "are bringing up kids who are more socially responsible, less prejudiced, more open to difference" (17). Tasker and Golombok (1997) found that young people from lesbian families had significantly more positive attitudes toward lesbians and gay men than did young adults from heterosexual families. This positive attitude toward lesbian and gay people has a protective function for the children of lesbians because they come to understand that all differences, including their own, have value and something to offer the world. As Pauli's mother said:

> If I'm going to teach Pauli anything it's that, you know, that everybody is entitled to live their life the best and the fullest that they can, whatever it is. And that God loves you just the way you are.

And Pauli's step mother proudly told this story:

> I remember watching the Thanksgiving parade yesterday and Pauli thought that those outfits, you know, the real high cut legs, were gross. And she's on and on about this. And I said, "Well, you know, men really like that kind of stuff. They think that's real great. I personally don't think that they need to be stereotyping women like that." And she goes, "Well, the band looks beautiful without them." And I was so happy.

Molly told me that she thought racism was "stupid" and based on "ignorance." Diana refused to buy a camera case with the insignia "Stars and Stripes" because "that was the name of that awful boat that beat the women's boat in the America Cup race." Talia spoke with distaste of a kind of minority quota system in her school—since the school wants to show that 25 percent of its student body are minority students, the administration wants Talia to identify herself as Hispanic.

In fact, the children in this study also taught their parents about acceptance of diversity. Talia's mom told this hilarious story:

> The funniest time was when Talia brought over this boy, and, Jan, he had tattoos. He had a Mohawk that was, I think, that fluorescent kind of blue. He had more pierces than, at that time, this was a few years back, that I'd ever, this was when piercing just started and I didn't, I'd heard about it but I hadn't really seen anybody with these things in their noses, a guy with a safety pin in his eyebrows, and oh, I don't know how you can do this. And I'm sitting here, trying not to stare, but this is amazing. A very nice young man. You know, you go through the whole thing, he's a very

nice young man; some of my best friends are pierced, you know. But, just that, again, that acceptance (that the kids have)!

Because the children of lesbians have personal experience with prejudice and see how it affects their mothers intimately, they may integrate it more easily and have a deeper understanding than children who have not had this personal experience.

IMPLICATIONS

CHILDREN IN LESBIAN FAMILIES encounter an ongoing tension between their experience within their families, which feels "normal" and safe and nurturing, and their experience outside their families, in which they often feel invisible or vilified. These children must uphold the value of difference and uniqueness in the face of a society that enforces conformity. The invisibility of their kind of families and of lesbian people in general in the institutions outside the family creates a sense of unreality—as if one is seeing something that others cannot see. And when the information that children do find outside the home about lesbian and gay people is negative, this plants the seed of fear in the child's heart. As one of my sons put it, "*I* know it isn't bad, but other people don't."

One set of strategies that seemed to be particularly helpful for children was that which worked to reduce the invisibility—to stop the erasure of lesbian people and their families. These strategies include seeking out and inundating the child with positive images of lesbians and gay men—from books, TV, movies, newspaper articles, herstories, pictures, and identified lesbians and gay men who are famous. It also means finding and spending time with other lesbian and gay families, lesbian and gay people in general, and heterosexual people who are accepting and affirming of the child's family. The importance of affirming heterosexual allies in our lives was strongly supported in this data. Our children are bombarded with invisibility and unacceptance. We strengthen them by presenting a broad and diverse community that stands with them.

Perhaps most important, since our children spend so much of their time in the institution of school, we should work toward increasing the inclusion of gay and lesbian people and families in the school curriculum and atmosphere. It is crucial that our children see themselves and their parents reflected positively in a school setting. This inclusiveness will ease the fears born of erasure.

Second, we need to consider how to "normalize" (in terms of accepting as healthy) our families to society. Either same-sex marriage or a legal equivalent would help legitimize our relationships and our families. While some of us may reject all marriage as the creation of a patriarchal paradigm, as long as we exist within that paradigm we must demand legitimate status from it. Even if this step is seen as a transitional goal along the way to some new system of family formation, it is one worth pursuing because of the crucial impact on our children's security. When asked what he liked best about his lesbian family, Dale replied:

> Oh boy, everything. Let's see. They are not mean at all. They, when something gets broken, they always fix it for us—they are real good about that. They have enough time for me usually. They are not a yelling family. We play games like Chinese checkers. Two nights ago we played cribbage. We watch TV shows. We go camping. We hug a lot.

Our children, as they grow up, are becoming, for the most part, allies to the gay and lesbian communities. They are also supporters of human diversities. As we make the world safer and more nourishing for them, we create an environment that will support creativity and positive self-determination for all.

NOTES

1. I use the word "step" as an adjective to describe a type of relationship. I reject the use of the words "stepfamily" or "stepmother," which imply something qualitatively different from "family" or "mother."
2. In quoting from the participant's journals, I have used the spelling as it was originally written.
3. Frannie's biological mom was in a relationship with a woman before this present relationship. Frannie acknowledges all three women as her mothers.

REFERENCES

hooks, bell. 1987. *Talking Back*. Boston: South End Press.

Lewis, Karen Gail. 1980. "Children of Lesbians: Their Point of View." *Social Work* 25 (3): 198–203.

Patterson, Charlotte. 1996. "Lesbian Mothers and Their Children: Findings from the Bay Area Families Study." In Joan Laird and Robert-Jay Green, eds., *Lesbians and Gays in Couples and Families*, pp. 420–37. San Francisco: Jossey-Bass.

——. 1992. "Children of Lesbian and Gay Parents." *Child Development* 63 (5): 1025–1042.

Pharr, Suzanne. 1988. *Homophobia: A Weapon of Sexism*. Little Rock: Chardon Press.

Pollack, Sandra. 1987. "Lesbian Mothers: A Lesbian-Feminist Perspective on Research." In Sandra Pollack and Jeanne Vaughn, eds., *Politics of the Heart: A Lesbian Parenting Anthology*, pp. 316–24. Ithaca, N.Y.: Firebrand Books.

Pollack, Sandra and Jeanne Vaughn, eds. 1987. *Politics of the Heart: A Lesbian Parenting Anthology*. Ithaca, N.Y.: Firebrand Books.

Rafkin, Louise, ed. 1990. *Different Mothers*. Pittsburgh: Cleis Press.

Rich, Adrienne. 1980. "Compulsory Heterosexuality and Lesbian Existence." *Signs* 5: 631–60.

Saffron, Lisa. 1996. *What About the Children? Sons and Daughters of Lesbian and Gay Parents Talk About Their Lives*. London: Cassell.

Sager, Clifford J., Hollis Steer Brown, Helen Crohn, Tamara Engel, Evelyn Rodstein, and Libby Walker. 1983. *Treating the Remarried Family*. New York: Brunner/Mazel.

Silverstein, Olga and Beth Rashbaum. 1994. *The Courage to Raise Good Men*. New York: Penguin Books.

Tasker, Fiona and Susan Golombok. 1997. *Growing Up in a Lesbian Family: Effects on Child Development*. New York: The Guilford Press.

Wright, Janet M. 1998. *Lesbian Step Families: An Ethnography of Love*. Binghamton, N.Y.: Harrington Park Pres an imprint of The Haworth Press.

PART 3 | *Political Activism*

18 | Building Common Ground: Strategies for Grassroots Organizing on Same-Sex Marriage

Irene Javors with Renate Reimann

For several years, I have been involved in organizing, educating, and advocating for same-sex marriage. This chapter will take a critical look at strategies currently being used for grassroots organizing on this historic issue. My information is based on my experiences as president of United for The Freedom to Marry, Inc. a grassroots group based in New York City.

Conservative groups who are intent on curtailing the rights of lesbian, gay, bisexual, and transgender people have chosen same-sex marriage as one of their main battlegrounds. The religious right has lobbied for numerous state and local laws and policies that are designed to exclude queers from the rights and privileges heterosexual families so freely enjoy, and was instrumental in passing the 1996 Defense of Marriage Act (see Haider-Markel, chapter 21).

Since these groups only represent a small percentage of the larger heterosexual society, it is vital to counter their efforts by educating straight people who are not prejudiced but are often uninformed. Many, in fact, are unaware that same-sex couples are excluded from the right to legal marriage. They are ignorant of the sometimes dire consequences of this exclusion be they financial, with respect to children, or in cases of sickness and disability (see Chambers, chapter 19 and Dalton, chapter 13).

Organizing within the various queer communities, on the other hand, has been an education unto itself. In these postmodern times of fluid identities, limitless boundaries, and deconstructed institutions, the subject of marriage has taken on problematic dimensions for many queer radicals. Marriage is viewed as singularly reactionary if not outright *retarditaire*.

Central to the marriage critique is the position that patriarchy privileges the institution of marriage as the sole form of relational intimacy that is recognized and rewarded by the state. Queer critics of marriage argue that the individual and not the state has the right to define significant relationships and that all such constructions should be equal to each other in the entitlement field (see Walters, chapter 20). Although I basically agree with the feminist critique of marriage, marriage bestows privileges on couples that cannot be claimed through other means (see Chambers, chapter 19).

As advocates of marriage for same-sex couples, members of my group have had to launch a major educational campaign within the lesbian, gay, bisexual, and transgendered communities in order to counterbalance those who oppose marriage on the grounds that it is not a "queer" thing to do. By framing the issue of marriage as one of choice, we tried to create common ground for people from diverse political and cultural camps within the larger community. However, we have been categorized as "retro-conservatives" and exiled from the "greater activist body."

On a personal note, my partner and I registered as domestic partners at City Hall in New York City. We basically did it for financial reasons since the partnership registration gave us access to joint benefits. Similarly, given the financial, legal, and social privileges it bestows on couples, I might consider marriage. On purely philosophical grounds, however, I would not get married because of my opposition to the state interfering with my private life. The spiritual aspect of marriage is also a personal matter. It disturbs me enormously that the state has conflated the material aspects of marriage with religion.

Thus my personal attitude was not the primary motivation for my getting involved in the struggle for same-sex marriage. My interest in the issue stems more from my work as a therapist and my experiences with friends who died of AIDS. As a therapist, I have counseled many people who desperately wanted marriage because of the social validation it offers for their lives and their relationships. For mental health reasons alone, marriage needs to be available to same-sex partners. The constant refrain is, "Why am I a second-class citizen? Why can't I have what everybody else in my family has?" Many feel very angry about their exclusion from this pervasive and powerful social institution. Also, when working with the families of lesbians and gays I encountered real sadness: "My child won't have access to things that others have. And we can't celebrate in the same way." Lesbians and gays are the only people in this country who cannot get married.

The other impetus to organize came from watching some of my gay male friends who were dying from AIDS and whose families would come in and disregard their relationships without hesitation. The horror stories that I witnessed and tried to prevent still sadden me. For example, I had friends, a gay couple, who both had AIDS and who became terminally sick at the same time. Their individual families put them into separate hospitals against their previously stated will, and there was nothing anybody could do about it. Thus both my personal and my professional experiences motivated me to enter into the fight for same-sex marriage.

Once we had started organizing, the problems we encountered surpassed my worst nightmares. Because of my experiences in the feminist movement in the 1970s and 1980s, I thought that people would be eager to join the good fight. To my surprise, the marriage issue turned out to be extremely volatile and created many dysfunctional dynamics within the queer movement. In addition, those who are most invested in gaining access to marriage are often the most closeted individuals and couples.

GRASSROOTS ORGANIZING WHEN THE CLOSET LOOMS LARGE

A MAJOR TASK OF organizing is to identify your constituent base of support. We have focused our outreach on persons and groups not usually targeted for political organizing within more activist, queer communities i.e., those living in the boroughs, suburbs, and rural areas, couples, singles seeking spouses, immigrants involved with American citizens, those belonging to a broad spectrum of racial, ethnic, religious, economic, and political identities, loyalties, and categories, union groups, and those who have little or no experience with politics, especially activist politics.

To reach these diverse groups, we employ various outreach methods well-known to seasoned organizers (see the next section). In the best of all possible worlds, your efforts prove so successful that your group is inundated with volunteers ready to sign up for the duration. In the worst of all possible scenarios, you do everything there is to do and no one comes forward and you feel like a character right out of the *X Files* who is left wondering, "Is the truth really out there?" You blame yourself and feel that you must do more only to discover that still there is no overwhelming response, just a drop-by-drop drizzle of volunteers who show up for one meeting and then disappear into the ozone. Or, if you manage to get them to reappear, you find that they give you an address and phone number that is unreachable or they leave only a first name on a mailing list.

This "don't ask, don't tell," mode makes it very difficult to build a consistent volunteer base. These "invisible visibles" who come to meetings, sign mailing lists, pay dues only in cash, and refuse to commit themselves openly, even though they claim to support the issue, are all inhabitants of the closet. Many supporters of same-sex marriage are charter members of the closet. They pose as singles when in reality they are coupled. They hide their relationships. They are terrified of being found out, yet they want the right to marry and long for the day when their relationship will receive public blessing and recognition.

Those most in need of access to marriage are the most closeted and thus unable to join the struggle for same-sex marriage. The very fact that they deeply crave public recognition of their relationships and lives within the heterosexual world immobilizes their ability to openly demand acceptance of their intimate choices. Not surprisingly, this kind of supporter of gay marriage is indeed more conservative and "traditional" than more openly queer individuals.

As organizers, we are challenged by the task of working with supporters in different stages of the coming out process. To accommodate this reality, we have structured our outreach activities to be as flexible as possible in order to meet the needs of members. We communicate by fax, E-mail, snail mail, newsletter, phone call, web site, post office box, plain brown envelope, and just about anything that will facilitate an exchange of information. We have learned to adapt ourselves to the demands of the closet culture.

Many of our volunteers have never before been involved in political work. They see themselves as "family oriented," or the "marrying kind," or as singles looking for life partners. They span the social, ethnic, religious, and economic spectrum. They have three things in common: they want the right to marry, they are activist novices, and they hate politics. This dislike for politics was often reinforced by the lack of response from politicians and the media we contacted and by the internal political turf battles among queer organizations.

We respond to this dislike of politics and politicians by focusing attention on the issue itself. We maintain a nonpartisan stance and steer clear of involvement with party politics. Instead of embroiling ourselves with caucuses and cabals, we encourage our volunteers to develop leadership skills as advocates and educators on the issue of same-sex marriage.

Disillusionment with politics and politicians is pervasive at the grassroots level. Similarly, there is an equal amount of distrust toward paid professional organizations and activists within the gay, lesbian, bisexual, and transgender communities. Many view these groups and their spokespersons as not really representing the needs of grassroots queers. There is perceived to be a great divide between those involved in grassroots work and those working for national gay and lesbian organizations.

Much of the disillusionment is a result of disregarding the hard work of grassroots volunteers. For example when the initial positive decision was handed down in the groundbreaking Hawaiian same-sex marriage case, *Baehr v. Lewin* (1993) (see Chambers, chapter 19), a well-known professional organization with whom we had worked closely for an extended period of time never called to invite us to join them in "their" victory celebration. There was no communication conduit and no appreciation for any of the hard work that we had voluntarily done for them. Politically, this inattentiveness served to alienate many of our committed volunteers from further involvement with our organization as well as managing to cause tremendous ill-will toward the national organization.

In addition many volunteers who are working for same-sex marriage feel betrayed by those professional gay/lesbian organizations that have not actively supported marriage. These groups have been criticized by grassroots workers for "playing politics" with the straights and neglecting the very population that they allegedly claim to represent. In my experience, many of the grassroots activists feel that such national organizations do not take seriously the needs of the "common queer." Their agendas are driven by political expediency rather than by an understanding of what the majority of lesbians and gays find politically most relevant to their lives.

All of this bickering and infighting does not serve us well. These internecine struggles work only to weaken and separate us. Far too much time is spent attacking each other rather than fighting our real enemies: prejudice, hate, inequality, and ignorance. Both grassroots and professional activists must learn to work with each other more effectively or we risk losing even more ground to homophobes and the cynical politicians who represent them.

Let us continue our journey through the byzantine world of grassroots activism with a discussion of how a small, volunteer, unfunded group educates and organizes.

EDUCATING THE MASSES

EDUCATING OTHERS ABOUT THE importance of the freedom to marry for same-sex couples is one of our main purposes. For this reason, we have put together a broad range of educational efforts.

- *Speakers Bureau*   As a grassroots group with a minuscule budget, we have found that sending out speakers to different groups is a very economic and successful means of educating people. There is a great deal of ignorance and misinformation about the issue. Audiences really appreciate the question-and-answer sessions.
- *Public Events*   We have cosponsored as well as initiated many public activities from a town hall meeting at the Lesbian and Gay Center to a Wed-In at Bryant Park, to marching in the Heritage of Pride Parade, to demonstrating against the Defense of Marriage Act (DOMA) in front of the Clinton/Gore campaign headquarters. These activities have increased our visibility as well as provided a venue for distributing flyers and other educational materials.
- *Web Site and Newsletter*   We have established a web site wherein we encourage information sharing and dialogue. At the site, couples can participate in our "Wedding Album" by sending a photo and information about themselves. We provide ongoing news updates and list announcements about upcoming events happening in the metropolitan area. We also publish a quarterly newsletter that contains news related to the freedom to marry. The newsletter is sent to our membership and is available on our web site (see editor's note).
- *Educational Packet and Marriage Archive*   We have developed an educational packet on the right to marry. This resource is designed to answer many of the questions that have been raised in regard to same-sex marriage. We plan to update the package regularly. Another organizing tool has been to establish an archive documenting the struggle for the freedom to marry. This project includes oral histories, videos, cultural materials, stories, etc. (see editor's note).
- *Media*   Sadly, New York City does not have a large and/or varied gay/lesbian press presence. We have had great difficulty getting the gay/lesbian media to take note of our existence. We continue to fax information in the hope that the existing newspapers, as well as cable and radio shows, will eventually realize that we are for real.

- We are also having difficulty involving the mainstream press on this issue in an ongoing manner. For the most part media attention is only paid when some sort of sensational event is happening to a well-known celebrity such as Melissa Etheridge or when the visual image has entertainment value. In fact, media visibility and political efficacy has become highly dependent on celebrity involvement. Issues such as same-sex marriage remained obscure until recently, when celebrities such as Ellen Degeneres started to support the cause.
- A group member managed to get a letter to the editor published in the *New York Times* after the passage of DOMA. The newspaper printed the letter with her name but without her group affiliation. When asked to account for this omission, the *Times* employee said that she had never heard of the group. This explanation was supposed to suffice as reason enough not to credit the organization. We queried back, "How do you get to be known if not through such venues?" This question was answered by a momentary silence, an irritated, "that's our policy," and then the ever-equalizing dial tone of oblivion.

We persist in our efforts to cultivate the media. We are developing a roster of "poster couples" who are willing to be interviewed by reporters about their desire to be legally married. We search for the winning media "spin" on this issue.

BUILDING COALITIONS

ANOTHER CENTRAL INTEREST OF our organization is to build coalitions with other groups who are involved in similar issues or who are open to becoming allies for the cause. Our efforts within the heterosexual world have been a mixed bag of hits and misses. In pursuing some of the time-honored avenues for organizing, we have found that these have met with a modicum of success. We have been confronted by the double headed dragon: homophobia and homoprejudice. We have learned that we stand a better chance of advancing our issue by working with individuals within groups rather than by trying to influence and take on the larger organization as a whole.

Working with Clergy   Those who are already lesbian/gay positive are open to our efforts; however, since they must work within the confines of the larger church body, the efficacy of their support is conditioned by the current status of gay/lesbian concerns within the context of institutional policy. Unfortunately, there has been a conservative backlash within many denominations, which has resulted in homophobic decision making in regard to lesbian and gay status, i.e., the ordination controversies and prohibitions against same-sex commitment ceremonies within the Episcopal, Presbyterian, and Methodist churches.

Historically, support from clergy has helped to advance the goals of human liberation movements. During the 1960s many churches worked for civil rights and challenged congregants to confront their prejudices. Today, the religious right uses their church(es) as locations for rallying support against the rights of lesbians and gays. Within queer communities, there exist no equivalent institutional churches capable of organizing their members as effectively as does the Christian Coalition.

We are compiling a list of organizations that are also engaged in fighting against the extremist views of the religious right and the Christian Coalition. We plan to distribute our educational materials to groups such as reproductive choice advocates, anticensorship groups, and immigrant-rights groups. Since the religious right is working very hard to abridge everyone's rights, this threat should help us to develop alliances with others who oppose the right's hate-filled agenda. Over time, we hope to build a broad-based coalition of groups concerned with extending and upholding equal rights for all Americans.

As advocates of same-sex marriage, we must pursue our goals within such a homoprejudiced environment. In dealing with clergy, even those within more liberal and moderate congregations, we have come to realize that for every step forward, the specter of conservative and orthodox reaction threatens to overturn all our hard-won victories.

Identifying and Working with (Gay/Lesbian Positive) Straight Organizations
We have had success in gaining support from organizations such as the National Organization for Women (NOW), the ACLU, Workmen's Circle, the Ethical Culture Society, and so on. They have provided important venues for outreach to their membership. As one member of United For The Freedom To Marry has said, "They are great but isn't this speaking to the already converted?" Indeed! How-

ever, when there is such a negative climate around an issue, the endorsements of these groups encourage us to "hang in" and value our efforts.

We view the "right to marry" as a nonpartisan issue. Therefore, we have attempted to meet with groups from all points on the political spectrum. This has not been successful as a vehicle for changing minds. We pursue this merely as an educational outreach strategy.

Reaching Elected Officials   We have been involved in distributing educational material on national and local levels. During the struggle against the passage of the 1996 Defense of Marriage Act, we engaged in a direct-action letter-writing campaign, "Parent to Parent," encouraging parents of gay, lesbian, bisexual, transgendered children to write to the president and other elected officials and ask them how they might feel if they were the parent of a gay or lesbian or transgendered child who was prohibited from legally marrying?

We have distributed our material to all the candidates running for the year 1998 New York City mayoral race. To our amazement, all four democratic candidates have publicly endorsed the right of same-sex couples to marry. However, to date there is no politician in New York City willing to present a promarriage bill or actively fight for such legislation.

Developing alliances with other organizations who are struggling to achieve civil rights and human liberation is the key to successful grassroots organizing. At this point we are finding it very difficult to identify straight groups willing to publicly stand with us on the issue of same-sex marriage. From elected officials to clergy to professional activists, there has been a reluctance to come out and openly fight for the right to marry.

Our efforts to organize and educate in queer and straight communities have revealed to us several outstanding issues in regard to the marriage question. At the present time our focus must be to develop and cultivate a cultural climate that is receptive to an open discussion on same-sex marriage. In order to do this, work needs to be done on raising awareness about the deleterious effects of homophobia and homoprejudice on all facets of our society as well as on our psyches. As grassroots organizers, we are at the front lines of the battle against fear, prejudice, and discrimination.

FRAMING THE ISSUE

GROWING UP IN A FAMILY of labor activists, I learned about organizing by listening to my grandmother tell stories about sitting on stoops in Brooklyn listening to disgruntled workers complain about conditions in the shop. She'd ask them some questions, but mostly she let them run off at the mouth about "their lousy boss," or the "foreman who had roving hands." After they said their say and this could go on for quite a while she'd tell them about the union and what the union could do for them. She'd then proceed to have a Q & A session right there on those stone steps while kids played hopscotch and a baby was having her diaper changed. After several hours, maybe days, she managed to get a few of the workers to come to a meeting at the union hall.

My grandmother was a very successful organizer who understood the importance of listening to people's stories in order to understand their needs. By getting someone to tell you what they want, you can figure out a way to present what you want in terms that are mutually beneficial. A win-win situation. Organizing on the issue of same-sex marriage requires the same strategy used by my grandmother: listen, clarify, understand, build common ground; pursue tangible outcomes.

When speaking about the marriage question to individuals and groups, we structure our presentation to fit the concerns of the listener. In our presentations to local chapters of Parents, Families, and Friends of Lesbians and Gays (PFLAG), we have stressed that marriage is a civil right of all Americans and that as members of PFLAG it is in their interest to support the right to marry. In our interactions with Pride-At-Work, a lesbian and gay group working for the equal rights of lesbians and gays in the workplace, we have discussed the benefits lesbian and gay workers would gain if they had marriage rights. We have emphasized that the many economic and health care privileges fought for by unions for married heterosexuals should be available to gay and lesbian couples.

In speaking to groups such as the Butch/Femme Society and Just Couples, we have focused our talks on the difficulties of living as an out couple in a heterosexual world. We stressed that gay and lesbian couples and families exist in a limbo-land of second class citizenship while their heterosexual counterparts have special rights to marriage.

We have given speeches at Unitarian and Ethical Culture groups to raise awareness about the struggle for same-sex marriage. In these presentations, we have related stories about gay and lesbian couples who have been discriminated against because of their sexual identity. We have described terrible situations wherein one member of a couple is hospitalized and his partner of ten or more years is *not* allowed to visit because he isn't a blood relative. We have stressed that the importance of securing the right to marry rests not only in marriage's entitlements and benefits but also in conferring society's blessing on the fortunate couple.

THE FUTURE OF GRASSROOTS ORGANIZING

SINCE THE INITIAL WRITING of this article, United for The Freedom to Marry, Inc. has been disbanded. The many frustrations and obstacles discussed above culminated in profound disillusionment among the members of the organization. The well-organized opposition of the religious right to same-sex marriage, plus the lack of substantial support for it in the larger lesbian, gay, bisexual, and transgender community, combined with frustrating experiences with professional queer organizations made it impossible for the group to continue.

Single-issue organizing at this time can only be successful on a short-term basis. Strong pushes for or against specific legislation or giving visibility to a concrete positive or negative cause can be supported by this type of organizing. For example, professional organizations can spontaneously use the grass roots to advance a specific cause within a given time, and the grass roots can dissolve when that particular issue is taken care of.

Long-term organizing will have to adopt broader political themes. For example, rallying around family issues versus same-sex marriage has some long-term promise. Parental rights provided by second-parent adoptions are central to the lives of many queer families. The ability to register as domestic partners is another critical concern.

With respect to the marriage issue itself, working with younger generations might prove more fruitful than did our experience. Younger people are not as hostile to the issue! They have had a different coming-out experience and more diverse family experiences than an older generation who came out at a time when being gay or lesbian was still considered a crime and a "homosexual" would have had no concept of entitlements. The entire notion of marriage and family as an acceptable choice would rarely have entered the minds of this generation of gays and lesbians.

Gender differences also play an important role in organizing around marriage. I often wondered whether we would have been more successful if the organization had been led by two men rather than two women. I wonder how seriously we were taken as women by many of the gay men. The sexism and the misogyny we faced were enormous. There was a continuous challenge to our authority by males both inside and outside the organization who were constantly seeking to undercut our power and position. Often at meetings with other gay organizations we experienced being ignored and not heard by male leadership. Our efforts to be recognized proved futile. We did not have a style that was aggressive and competitive enough to strong-arm our way into the discussions. As a result we came to feel that the old boy network is very much alive and well in our rainbow community. Within the gay male world, men network extensively and can gain access to money and power. As lesbians (let us not forget that we self-identified as women), we weren't even on the proverbial screen for consideration.

Moreover, many men have a very romanticized notion of marriage. We offended them when we critiqued marriage from a feminist point of view. It was equally disturbing that when we supported the freedom to marry, we offended people who were critical of marriage. In my view, if we gained access to marriage the whole institution would be turned upside down. For that perverse reason alone, I wholeheartedly support our right to marry.

With respect to organizing methods, they have to adjust to the new political and technological climate. I would now use the internet and other advanced communication techniques for mobilization if I were to get involved in another grassroots organizing effort. We can also learn much from analyzing the methods the religious right has been successfully employing to generate large-scale support for their conservative agenda.

Professional organizing and lobbying has become absolutely indispensable in this day and age. In fact, when we finally decided to break up the organization, I felt that I could do the job if I were paid full-time. There was so much going on in terms of political machinations that only a full-time person could have dealt with it. The current political conditions require increasing professionalization of social movements in order to be effective in Washington, the state capitol, or city hall, as well as to gain media access. Yet the grass roots are still playing a vital role.

The face of grassroots organizing is rapidly changing in its scope, methods, and political efficacy, however. Instead of being the creative engine behind issue development, the grass roots are increasingly becoming simple foot soldiers for queer professional organizations who have the ability to lobby politicians and reach the media. To maximize the impact of grassroots involvement, however, these professional organizations need to honor the contributions of the volunteers committed to the shared cause. Mutually respectful cooperation is vital to achieving our goals of eradicating homophobia and creating a world in which our families can thrive and be free from discrimination.

Editor's Note: Since this chapter was originally written, United For The Freedom to Marry, Inc. was unable to survive for many of the reasons described herein. Although their Web site no longer exists, you can request a copy of their educational packet from Raffles20@hotmail.com. The story of United's demise warrants its own chapter.

Mary Bernstein, August 2000

19 What If? The Legal Consequences of Marriage and the Legal Needs of Lesbian and Gay Male Couples

David L. Chambers

Laws that treat married persons in a different manner than they treat single persons permeate nearly every field of social regulation in this country—taxation, torts, evidence, social welfare, inheritance, adoption, and on and on. In this chapter I identify the patterns these laws form and the central benefits and obligations that marriage entails, a task few scholars have undertaken in recent years. I began this inquiry after a decision of the Supreme Court of Hawaii in 1993 came close to holding that, under the Hawaii constitution, same-sex couples must be allowed to marry on the same terms as opposite sex couples[1] and prompted a virulent national debate on the subject. I wanted to know the benefits and burdens that legal marriage carries with it and to determine whether or not these legal consequences would fit the circumstances of lesbian and gay male couples. In other words, would this institution molded over time for persons of different sexes, apply to those with different differences. The inquiry has taken on more immediate relevance because, shortly before this book went to press, Vermont's legislature extended all of marriage's legal consequences to gay and lesbian couples who join in a "civil union."[2]

My findings form the core of this chapter: that the laws assigning consequences to marriage today have much more coherence than has been com-

---

Adapted with permission from the *Michigan Law Review* 95 (1996): 447–91, and the author.

monly recognized, largely falling within three sorts of regulation; that each of these three sorts of regulation would, as a whole, fit the needs of long-term gay male and lesbian couples; that while the law has changed in recent years to recognize nonmarital relationships in a variety of contexts, the number of significant distinctions resting on marital status remains large and durable; that in some significant respects the remaining distinctive laws of marriage are better suited to the life situations of same-sex couples than they are to those of opposite-sex couples for whom they were devised; and, most broadly, that the package of rules relating to marriage, while problematic in some details and unduly exclusive in some regards, is a just response by the state to the circumstances of persons who live together in enduring, emotionally based attachments.

Just at the point that I finished the article on which this chapter is based, Congress acted to limit the effects that legal marriage would have, if Hawaii or Vermont, or any other state permitted same-sex couples to marry. The 1996 Defense of Marriage Act declares that all federal statutes and regulations that refer to married persons or to spouses shall be read as applying to opposite-sex couples only.[3] This chapter persists in reviewing both federal and state laws that bear on married persons, for the purpose of my exercise of imagination—the "what if?"—is to ask how opposite-sex married persons are treated under the law today and hold these laws up to the situations of lesbian and gay male couples.

POSTURES TOWARD MARRIAGE

A LARGE PROPORTION OF American adults who identify themselves as lesbian or gay live with another person of the same sex and regard that person as their life partner. Exactly how many gay or lesbian adults there are in the United States and what proportion live with another in a long-term relationship are not possible to calculate on the basis of existing information. Still, every survey of adult Americans willing to identify themselves as lesbian or gay finds that a majority or a near majority are living currently with a partner (Hatfield 1989a, 1989b:A-19; Lever 1994:23, 1995:29). Increasing numbers of these couples are celebrating their relationships in ceremonies of commitment (Butler 1997; Lever 1995:29; Sherman 1992:1, 5–7). Those who participate commonly refer to the ceremonies as weddings and to themselves as married (see Lewin, chapter 3; Sherman 1992:13), even though they have known that the ceremonies were not legally recognized. If states extend the legal right to marry, it is highly probable that large numbers of gay and lesbian couples would choose to participate. In a recent survey of nearly 2,600 lesbians, for example, 70 percent said they would marry another woman if same-sex marriage were legally recognized (Lever 1995:27).[4]

Exactly what lesbians and gay men hope to obtain from legal marriage is uncertain. Since public ceremonies of commitment are already so common, one might expect that when debating state-sanctioned marriage, they would focus on what law itself can accord that other institutions cannot: a range of legally protected benefits and legally imposed obligations. In fact, they do not. In the vigorous public discussion, few advocates address at any length the legal consequences of marriage. William Eskridge, for example, devotes only 6 of the 261 pages in his fine book, *The Case for Same-Sex Marriage*, to the legal consequences (1996:66–71), and his, with one exception, is the longest discussion I can find.[5] Whatever the context of the debate, most speakers are transfixed by the *symbolism* of legal recognition. It is as if the social significance of the marriage ceremonies gay people already conduct today count for nothing—as if, without the sanction of the state, those who marry have merely been playing dress-up.

That the social meanings of state recognition draw so much attention is nonetheless understandable. In our country, as in most societies throughout the world, marriage is the single most significant communal ceremony of belonging. In a law-drenched country such as ours, permission for same-sex couples to marry under the law would signify the acceptance of lesbians and gay men as equal citizens more profoundly than any other nondiscrimination law that might be adopted.

Skeptics about marriage within the lesbian and gay communities also largely ignore the legal consequences of marriage. They focus instead on the negative meanings they attach to the institution itself. To many, marriage signifies hierarchy and dominance, subjugation, and the loss of individual identity (Ettelbrick 1989; Homer 1994; Polikoff 1993). To them it marks a tombstone over the graves of countless generations of married couples; one stone reads "Herbert Smith," the other simply reads "Wife." And even if the legal institution of marriage has changed in the recent past, they resist the assimilation of queer couples into an oppressive heterosexual orthodoxy of ascribed roles and domesticity (Robson 1993).

THE LEGAL CONSEQUENCES OF MARRIAGE

EACH OF THE FIFTY states defines the incidents of marriage for its residents. Federal laws add hundreds of other legal consequences. Some scholars have characterized the multitude of legal attributes of marriage today as largely incoherent,[6] and in their details they surely are. Yet it is possible to identify three central categories of regulation, within each of which a certain coherence obtains: some laws recognize affective or emotional bonds that most people entering marriage express for each other; some build upon assumptions about marriage as creating an environment that is especially promising or appropriate for the raising of children; and some build on assumptions (or prescriptive views) about the economic arrangements that are likely to exist (or that ought to exist) between partners.

As you read, you will encounter occasional ghosts from an authoritarian and formally gendered past. The laws dealing with married persons have undergone a massive transformation during the last century.[7] Well into the nineteenth century, all assets of a married couple, including those that the wife brought into a marriage, were controlled by the husband. In fact, the wife's personal property became the husband's property. The husband also, as a matter of law, controlled all decisions that related to a married couple's children. This male-controlled relationship was also difficult or impossible to leave. At the beginning of the nineteenth century, marriage was indissoluble under the laws of nearly all states. Later in the century, it was dissoluble, but only on proof by one sinless spouse of a serious marital sin committed by the other.

Today, legislatures or judicial decisions have removed virtually all rules that explicitly provide different status or authority for husbands. They also permit marriage to end without proof of marital fault. The compulsory sex-linked aspects of the law of marriage have, during the latter half of this century, been withering away (Glendon 1976, 1989; Regan 1993; Schneider 1985), sometimes at the price of providing insufficient protection to women economically ill-positioned to protect themselves. As we will see, for example, the rules of divorce commonly treat marriage as a partnership with an equal division of property, but, because of their lower earnings, women are generally left significantly worse off financially than men are. Most gay and lesbian couples can, however, appropriately regard the legal aspects of marriage today as serving primarily, though not entirely, a facilitating function—offering couples opportunities to shape satisfying lives as formal equals and as they, rather than the state, see fit (Schneider 1992).

REGULATIONS THAT RECOGNIZE EMOTIONAL ATTACHMENTS

SOME LAWS AND REGULATIONS dealing expressly with married persons can best be viewed today as promoting the emotional attachments that most spouses feel toward each other. Here are a few examples. Statutes or common law doctrine in all states grant decision-making powers to relatives when a person becomes incompetent to make decisions for herself. Two broadly different sorts of laws exist. The more narrow sort authorizes a family member to make an emergency medical decision when the person has become incompetent and has failed to execute a formal document authorizing some other person to make decisions on her behalf. When such incapacity arises for an unmarried person, state laws designate a parent or an offspring or some other blood relation as decision-maker, but, for persons who are married, they typically turn first to the person's spouse.[8] The second sort of law, broader in scope, provides for the formal appointment, of a "guardian" or "conservator," who typically makes not only medical decisions but also other decisions about residence, care, and financial matters. These statutes also differ widely, but commonly provide first for the appointment of a blood relative for a single person and a spouse for a married person. The *Uniform Probate Code*, for example, has been adopted in fourteen states, and establishes an order or preference for the appointment of relatives as the guardian for an incapacitated person, with the spouse first in line, followed by an adult child or a parent.[9] Upon death, other laws or court decisions provide that the spouse has first right as "next of kin" to claim a person's remains[10] and to make anatomical gifts of parts of the deceased person's body when the deceased person has made no directive of their own.[11]

In a similar manner, state laws designate the spouse as the person to receive part or all a married person's assets when they die without a will.[12] These "intestacy" laws vary widely among the states.[13] In some states, if there are surviving children, a spouse receives as little as a third; in many others, a fixed-dollar amount and a share of the remainder; in still others, the entire estate.[14] In most states, if there are no surviving children and no surviving parents, the spouse receives everything.[15]

The laws relating to incompetency and death serve fairly obvious functions but ones worth explicit recognition. Some relate to the control of property, a subject taken up later. But most fundamentally, for couples who see themselves in an enduring relationship, the spouse is the appropriate person for the state to designate as decision-maker during a period of incompetency and as primary beneficiary after death on the basis of a reasonable guess that that is the person whom the now-incompetent or deceased person would have chosen if they had addressed the question in advance. That is, the rule fulfills their probable wishes.

Do gay men and lesbians with partners need the protection of such laws to ensure that their partners make decisions for them or inherit their estates? A very few states designate a long-term unmarried partner as the preferred decision-maker for the incompetent person, but most states ignore the unmarried partner altogether.[16] Similarly, only a very few states provide that an unmarried partner shall receive any portion of the estate of a person who dies without a will and, to date, no state provides anything for a same-sex partner. Despite this, one could argue that gay couples do not need such protections because they can protect themselves fully by simply executing a will or a medical power of attorney. But gay men and lesbians who are in relationships need these protections for the same reason that heterosexual persons need them. Like most heterosexuals,[17] most gay men and lesbians are reluctant to think about their mortality and procrastinate about remote contingencies. They fail to execute wills and powers of attorney, even though they are often aware of the unfortunate consequences of failing to act.[18]

Even if all persons with a same-sex partner remembered to execute the proper documents and had access to the needed legal services, other forms of government regulation that recognize special emotional and spiritual ties could not be adequately handled by a scheme of private designations. Consider four examples. Federal law places severe restrictions on the opportunities for foreign-born nationals to immigrate legally to the United States. One significant exception to this rule of exclusion is that a foreign-born national who enters into a nonfraudulent marriage with an American citizen has a presumptive right to enter the United States immediately as a long-term resident.[19] No such special provisions are made for a friend or lover. Even brothers or parents of a U.S. citizen are not automatically entitled to preferential treatment, but typically face long waiting periods before entry.

Another federal law, the *Family and Medical Leave Act of 1993*, requires all employers with fifty or more employees to extend unpaid leave of up to twelve work weeks during each year to an eligible employee to care for a spouse with a "serious health condition."[20] The statute also provides for leaves to care for children and for parents, but makes no provision of any kind for friends, lovers, or unmarried partners.

The federal government and many states also extend an advantage to married people when called to testify in a criminal proceeding that bars the state from forcing a married person to testify against their spouse (Regan 1995:2045, 2052–2054; Strong 1992:66). Nearly all states offer a related protection, typically in both civil and criminal proceedings, for confidential communications made between spouses during the marriage (Strong 1992:78–86 at 112–19).

Finally, under the law of many states, if a third person injures a married person negligently and by so doing deprives the spouse of care and companionship, the spouse can typically sue the injuring party for what is called loss of "consortium," compensation not for financial loss but for the loss of companionship (Clark 1987:12.5 at 672–83).

The immigration preference for spouses, the family-leave provisions, the evidentiary rules, and the consortium rules have a common current justification: that it is fitting for the state to recognize the significance in people's lives of one especially important person to whom they are not biologically related. Lesbians and gay men in long-term relationships attribute a similar level of importance to their partners (even if they have other gay and lesbian friends they also consider significant) (Sherman 1992; Weston 1991:117–29). They need these rules as much as heterosexual people do.

Gay men and women would experience as a burden, not as a benefit, a few regulations that attach to marriage and that also build, in substantial part, on assumptions about the emotional salience of the marital relationship. Public and private employers, for example, adopt antinepotism regulations that prohibit employees from participating in decisions to hire, promote, or discharge their spouse or from supervising their spouse in the workplace.[21] Resting on views about both emotional and economic ties, these regulations are as justifiably imposed on lesbians and gay men in enduring relationships as they are on heterosexuals: no one can be expected to be sufficiently objective when decisions about one's own long-term partner must be made.

REGULATIONS DEALING WITH PARENTING

GAY MALE AND LESBIAN couples raise children in this country in three common contexts. In the first, numerically the most common, one of the partners has already become the biological parent of a child (usually in the course of a prior relationship with a person of the opposite sex) and has later formed a relationship with a same-sex partner. This new partner is functionally in the position of a "stepparent." In the second context, a same-sex couple, *after* beginning a relationship, agree to raise a child together. They plan that one of them will be the biological parent and that, after birth, they will serve as coparents. In the third context, a same-sex couple seeks to adopt or to become the foster parents of a child who is biologically related to neither of them.

Opposite-sex couples also raise children in each of these sorts of contexts and, in each, laws and practices in all states treat such couples, when married, in specially favored ways. By contrast, in each of the three situations, a gay or lesbian partner who is not the biological parent of the child typically faces formidable, often insuperable, difficulties in becoming recognized as a legal parent at all. The laws that advantage married couples are needed by *some* heterosexual married couples who wish to raise children, but these same laws would be helpful to almost *all* lesbian and gay male couples who wish to raise a child as legal equals because, for them, it is always the case that neither partner or only one is the biological parent of the child.

In each context, most of the rules would be defended today as intending to serve the best interests of children. I will focus on the value of these rules both for children and for lesbian and gay male adults who wish to raise children. As to the interests of children, a great deal has been written on the adequacy of gay men and lesbians as parents in the past two decades. I do not intend to review this literature. It is well reported elsewhere.[22] In overwhelming measure, it concludes that a person's sexual orientation has no significant bearing on their parenting capacities or skills and that children raised by lesbian and gay male parents fare as well day-by-day and over time as children raised by other parents.[23]

As we will see, some of the difficulties currently experienced by gay men and lesbians who wish to raise children are not formally imposed by law. Some arise under rules that courts and agencies already have the discretion to extend to gay people or to same-sex couples, but rarely do. Thus, in some contexts, the benefits of legal marriage for same-sex couples may lie less in the rules that would become applicable to them than in a changed attitude toward homosexual persons that a change in marriage laws might help bring about on the part of legal actors exercising authorities that already exist. Here the symbolic and the legal intertwine.

The Stepparent Relationship

When a lesbian or gay male parent with custody of a child begins to live with another person of the same sex, the new person assumes a parenting role functionally comparable to a stepparent. The state of the law in the United States about such parenting relationships outside of marriage is clear: no matter how long the gay "stepparent" lives with the child, no matter how deeply they become involved in the care of the child, they and the child will rarely be recognized as having a legally significant relationship with one another. The state of the law is essentially the same for stepparent figures in opposite-sex unmarried couples. They are just the "boyfriend" or "girlfriend" or "live in" of the custodial parent and have no legal significance.

Perhaps surprisingly, until the recent past, the legal position of the opposite-sex partner who *marries* a custodial parent has been little different. In all but a few states, the stepparent married to a biological parent has not been legally obliged to contribute to the support of the child during the marriage.[24] In no state has the stepparent been required to contribute to the child's support upon divorce, no matter how long he or she lived with the child or the extent of his or her voluntary contributions. The stepparent has also had no legal entitlement upon divorce to be considered for court-ordered visitation or for sole or joint custody of the child (Mahoney 1994:124–48). It has been the absent biological parent who remained financially liable for support, who remained the one parent eligible for visitation (even if never having lived with the child), and who remained second in line for custody.

Recently, however, stepparents married to a custodial parent are coming to be recognized as parent figures for at least some purposes, and it is to the benefits of these laws and court decisions that gay and lesbian "stepparents" need access. A few states have begun, for example, to protect the relationship between a child and a stepparent whose marriage to the biological parent comes to an end. No state has imposed on the stepparent a general obligation of support upon divorce, but some courts and a few legislatures have given courts the authority to grant visitation and, in unusual circumstances, custody, even over the objection of the biological parent (Mahoney 1994:124–48).

States have also expanded the opportunities for stepparents during their marriage to a biological parent to become the full legal parent of a stepchild through adoption. If the absent biological parent consents, most states permit the married stepparent to adopt without any of the home visits and family studies usually required as a part of the adoption process (see Dalton, chapter 13; Hollinger 1990a). Consensual stepparent adoptions now account for over half of all adoptions that occur in the United States (Hollinger

1990b).Within the last few decades, most states have recognized certain circumstances in which stepparents living with and married to a biological parent are permitted to adopt even over the objection of the absent biological parent (Chambers 1990:102, 118–21; Hollinger 1990b).

A further change regarding stepparents is found in laws relating to employment in the labor force. State worker's compensation programs (Clark 1987:21.12 at 688–89) and the federal Social Security survivor benefit program (Mahoney 1987:496–514; Mason and Simpson 1995:457–60) permit a minor stepchild living with and dependent upon a stepparent to receive benefits after the stepparent's death. These programs replace much of the income lost to a child upon the death of the supporting stepparent. Similarly, the *Federal Family and Medical Leave Act of 1993* requires employers to permit a worker to take up to twelve weeks of unpaid leave to care for their seriously ill child, including a stepchild.[25]

Despite these reforms that apply to stepparents married to a biological parent, unmarried stepparent figures, of the same or opposite sex as the custodial parent, remain almost totally ignored by the law, wholly ineligible, for example, for the special treatment for stepparent adoption, wholly unable to secure for a child the benefits of worker's compensation or Social Security survivor benefits, and ineligible for the protections of the *Federal Family and Medical Leave Act*. They also remain free of the legal obligations that would come with adoption—most notably the obligation to provide financial support for the child they adopt. Extending these benefits and obligations to lesbians and gay men by permitting them to marry would serve well their needs and the needs of their children for the same reasons that they serve the needs of married opposite-sex couples and their children: children who live with a stepparent figure who is in a committed relationship with their biological parent often become attached to and financially dependent upon the stepparent and these attachments warrant recognition.

Artificial Insemination, Sperm Donors, and Surrogacy

The second parenting context for gay men and lesbians includes the same-sex couples, already formed, who agree that one of them will become the biological parent of a child whom they will raise together. Here the issues are rather different for women than for men.

When a lesbian couple plan that one of them will become pregnant—and large numbers of lesbian couples seek to have babies today in this manner (Martin 1993; Pies 1988)—they first must find a source of sperm. Some face problems that are not formal barriers of law but that are probably aggravated by the outlaw status of their relationship. Sperm banks in all states provide insemination services to women, most commonly in circumstances in which the woman is married and her husband is sterile. While no state expressly prohibits sperm banks from providing services to unmarried women or to lesbians (Lacey 1987), some doctors and sperm banks apparently decline to do so (see Murphy, chapter 12).[26]

Clearly legal problems arise after birth, at the point that the lesbian partner seeks to become recognized as a legal parent. She will be able to achieve such recognition only if she successfully completes a formal process of adoption. In most states, her petition to adopt will be rejected, either because her partner and she are of the same sex,[27] or because they are not married to one another,[28] or both. In a growing number of states, the lesbian partner can be considered for adoption, but even in these states, the best the couple can hope for is that, after completing elaborate forms and enduring an intrusive home study and an individualized inquiry into the child's "best interests," a court eventually, many months after the child's birth, will approve the application of the nonbiological parent to adopt (see Dalton, chapter 13). The whole process is likely to cost thousands of dollars.

Lesbian couples need a simpler and more welcoming process. They need, at a minimum, the procedures available in most states to legally married couples in comparable circumstances. For such couples, most states' laws provide a straightforward procedure governing artificial insemination through clinics or sperm banks.[29] The sterile husband simply acknowledges in writing his concurrence in his wife's insemination and his acceptance of the child as his own. He is then treated for purposes of the law in exactly the manner that he would be if he had been the biological father. No home study is required. No court hearing is held. The child's birth certificate simply records him as the father of the child. Lesbian couples need access to the same automatic registering of parenthood for the nonbiological female partner.

Similarly problematic are the situations for gay male partners when they wish one of them to serve as the biological father for a child they plan to raise together (Hollandsworth 1995:197 n. 53). This situation is troublesome for it necessarily involves a much more substantial involvement by the other biological parent—the surrogate mother—than in the case of artificial insemination through a surrogate father, involvement under circumstances in which there are well-founded concerns for the interests of the mother and of women in general (Field 1990; Gostin 1990; Kandel 1994; Rae 1994).

Reflecting differing resolutions of these concerns, state laws vary widely today regarding the legality and enforceability of surrogacy arrangements. Some prohibit surrogacy agreements altogether; some refuse to enforce them but do not prohibit the arrangements if voluntarily carried out; and some permit enforcement if the parties comply with various state-imposed requirements and if the mother does not change her mind within a statutorily prescribed period. Among the requirements in many states is that only married couples may enter into surrogacy arrangements with a donor mother (Hollandsworth 1995:205). Thus, under these varying schemes, few gay men could legally enter into an enforceable surrogacy agreement, and when they are able to do so, they would still have to overcome the adoption problems that lesbian couples face when both partners seek to be recognized as the legal parents of the child born to one of them. The issues surrounding surrogacy are complex, but, whatever their resolution, gay male couples need access to whatever scheme is made available to opposite-sex married couples.

When Neither Partner Is the Biological Parent: Adoption and Foster Care

Today, a few states prohibit lesbians and gay men from adopting under any circumstances and a few others prohibit them from serving as foster parents (Evall 1991:352–54; Sullivan 1989:1643). Most other states make adoption or foster care difficult in practice for persons who are openly gay or lesbian (Ricketts and Achtenberg 1987:89–111). Single heterosexual individuals are also disfavored in practice in most places (Bartholet 1993:70–72). When single persons, gay or heterosexual, are permitted to adopt, they are often offered only the most hard-to-place children, children who are older and have had multiple foster placements, or children with multiple handicaps (Bartholet 1993:70–72; Hollandsworth 1995:197 n. 54).

By contrast, while procedures for adoption and foster care vary widely across the country, it is the case everywhere that, whatever the procedure, the married heterosexual couple stands highest in the hierarchy of preferred units for placement of a child (Bartholet 1993:70). The status that is accorded to married opposite-sex couples today would provide fully adequate legal protection for the interests of gay male and lesbian couples and for the children they would raise.

LAWS REGULATING THE ECONOMIC RELATIONSHIP OF COUPLES OR BETWEEN THE COUPLE AND THE STATE

A CONSIDERABLE MAJORITY OF the laws that provide for differing treatment for married persons deal with the married couple as an economic unit. They build on beliefs or guesses about the economic relationships that married persons actually have and on prescriptive views about what those relationships ought to be. They assume that married persons differ from most single persons, including most single persons who share a residence with another person, in one or more of the following ways: the married partners will live more cheaply together than they would if they lived apart (that is, that there are routine economies of scale); the two will pool most or all of their current financial resources; the two will make decisions about the expenditure of these resources in a manner not solely determined by which party's labors produced the resource; the two will often engage in divisions of labor for their mutual benefit; and one partner, typically the woman, will often become economically dependent on the other.

To the extent that these laws have an empirical foundation, it is unclear whether the images of opposite-sex relationships that lie behind them will fit the circumstances of the sorts of gay male and lesbian couples who would marry under a change in the law. What evidence there is suggests that most lesbian and gay couples in long-term relationships believe in pooling resources and practice it today,[30] and that pooling is particularly common among those who engage in ceremonies of commitment (Sherman 1992:115, 127, 145, 153, 163, 208, recorded interviews).

The review that follows divides the many financial regulations that treat married persons differently than single persons into two rough sorts—those that fix the relationship between married persons and the state and those that fix the economic relationship between the two married persons themselves—because these sorts of regulations typically serve quite different ends.

THE REGULATION OF THE FINANCIAL RELATIONSHIP BETWEEN MARRIED PERSONS AND THE STATE

TAX LAWS AND LAWS pertaining to government benefits commonly treat married persons in a distinctive manner by regarding them for most purposes as a single economic unit. Consider some examples. Federal and state income tax laws create a system of joint returns for married couples that treats the couples as a single economic entity.[31] Under these provisions, when only one spouse earns any income, the total tax liability for the couple will be less than it would be if the income-earning spouse filed as a single person, a result that may be thought justified because two people are living off the single earner's income. On the other hand, when both spouses work and each earns even a fairly moderate income, their total tax liability will often be higher than it would have been if each had filed as a single person, a result that may again be thought justified because, by pooling incomes, they can live together more inexpensively than two single persons living separately. In many situations, these two sets of rules produce wholly justifiable outcomes, but their paradoxical impact in practice is that many working men and women maximize their incomes by living together but not marrying, each filing a separate return, even though they might otherwise prefer to marry. The same rules also discourage some married women from seeking employment outside the home, because they conclude that the marginal tax rate on any earnings they produced would be so high as to make the economic contribution of their earnings trivial (McCaffery 1993a, 1993b).

Similar rough justifications and undesired effects characterize the rules that apply when low-income married persons who are aged, blind, or disabled apply for federal welfare benefits under the program of Supplemental Security Income (SSI). If a married couple apply together, their grant will be lower than it would be if they were treated as two individuals applying separately.[32] Similarly, if only one member of the couple applies, the income of the applicant's spouse will be assumed to be available to the applicant and will be taken into account in determining both the applicant's eligibility for the benefit and the size of the grant.[33] Much the same rules of income attribution apply when a married person seeks a government-backed educational loan.[34] For couples who in fact pool their income and resources, these government benefit rules make sense, but they can impose hardships when the rules attribute more income as available than the spouse can comfortably contribute (Drizner 1987:1036–1047) and can sometimes deter couples from marrying who otherwise would.

Government taxing and benefit regulations of other sorts also build on the expectation that married couples will share resources and recognize that one spouse is often economically dependent on the other. Some of these programs, fortunately, avoid the undesired behavioral incentives we have just discussed. When a long-employed worker retires with a spouse who has been a homemaker and has not worked in the labor force long enough to be entitled to full Social Security benefits in his or her own right, the non-working spouse, if over sixty-two, is entitled to benefits through the worker.[35] Similarly, when a long-employed worker dies, Social Security benefits will typically be available for a surviving spouse over sixty who is not entitled to full benefits through their own contributions as an employee.[36]

Gift and estate taxes also reflect a view of the married couple as a single economic unit in which dependencies arise. When a well-heeled spouse transfers property to the other spouse during the marriage, the transfer is not subject to the federal gift tax that would apply to gifts to others, including the donor's children.[37] When appreciated assets held in the name of one spouse are transferred at divorce to the other spouse, no capital gains tax or gift tax is due at the time of the transfer.[38] And, when a spouse dies, bequests to the other spouse are not taxed under federal estate tax laws.[39] Public and private employers further recognize the economic interdependency of spouses by making health care benefits available to their employees' spouses, and, just as federal and state income tax laws exempt from taxation the value of a worker's own employer-provided health care benefits, so too these same laws exempt from taxation the value of the benefits for the worker's spouse.[40]

Gay and lesbian couples are subject to none of these rules, neither the benefits nor the burdens (Cain 1991:123–29). No joint return. No attributed income. Even when employers provide health benefits to both married employees and to employees with a same-sex domestic partner, only the married employees obtain the benefit of the tax exemption for the value of their partners' health coverage; the employee with the same-sex partner must report the value of the benefit to his or her partner as income and pay taxes on it.

Would gay and lesbian couples be advantaged by being treated like heterosexual married couples across this range of state and federal legal consequences? They would be subject to the same unfortunate behavioral incentives that these rules create today for opposite-sex couples. A gay man with HIV on Medicaid, for example, might choose not to marry on learning that, if he did, he would cease to be eligible for benefits even though his partner and he did not actually earn enough to pay the couple's medical bills. Indeed, it is possible that an even higher proportion of gay male and lesbian couples would be economically disadvantaged by the application of the current tax laws than are married opposite-sex couples. The only couples who consistently benefit from the current laws are those in which one partner works in the labor force, and taxes aside, both partners prefer this arrangement. Given enduring sex-ascribed roles, the employment of only one partner is likely to be the situation more often in opposite-sex than in same-sex couples. Moreover, the premise of the current rules is that married couples actually share in the control of resources and expenditures (Kornhauser 1993:73–80). When that premise fails, it is doubtful whether the burdens of the joint return should be imposed. Some observers have raised doubts about the actual degree of sharing of control in most heterosexual married couples (Kornhauser 1993:73–80), and it is quite possible that an even higher proportion of gay men and lesbians who would marry, would be persons who in their day-to-day lives would share only some of their income.

On the other hand, remember that not all tax and welfare rules work to the harm of gay couples who would marry. In some couples, only one partner works in the labor force, and for them the benefits of health coverage and the joint tax return might be substantial. In others, both partners work, but only one has a job with medical benefits. For them, the value of tax-exempt benefits through the partner with coverage could be considerable. And for those at the highest end of the income scale, the benefits of the estate- and gift-tax exemptions might more than offset the disadvantages of a joint return.

Moreover, in actual practice, even for the couple in which both partners work and both earn significant incomes, the income tax and other rules may in actual practice less frequently cause behaviors experienced as painful by the parties. When neither partner in a couple considers themselves the "secondary" worker—when both partners, that is, have strong ties to the labor force—then, while the perversities of the tax laws may affect some decisions to marry, they are less likely to lead either partner to drop out of the labor force or feel economically useless in a manner that they resent or later come to regret. And, viewed from another perspective, the opportunity for legal marriage, at the very least, provides a choice to opposite-sex couples whether to marry or not, a choice from which lesbian and gay couples could benefit for the same sorts of reasons.

THE REGULATION OF THE FINANCIAL RELATIONSHIP BETWEEN MARRIED PARTNERS

IN THE UNITED STATES today, states employ either of two broad schemes of regulation to define the economic relationship between married partners.

Nine states (mostly in the West and Southwest) employ "community-property" regimes (Elrod and Walker 1994:695, table),[41] under which, to oversimplify, the spouses own separately whatever they bring into the marriage or receive by gift or bequest during the marriage and own jointly any other assets either of them acquires during the marriage, including all assets acquired from their labors (Cunningham, Stoebuck, and Whitman 1982:5.14 at 232–33; McClanahan 1982:1:6, 1:8). The earnings of each partner are owned jointly by the pair. In the remaining states, called "common-law states," again to oversimplify, the spouses own separately whatever they acquire in their separate names and jointly whatever they buy in both names or whatever one by deliberate act puts into joint control.[42] Their earnings are their own. These differences in law sound significant and may affect many married persons' perception of the nature of their relationship,[43] but it is probable that social conventions linked to gender have greater impact than formal legal rules on the way that assets are controlled by married persons who live together.[44]

The rules of property do, however, become crucial at the point of divorce, for all states impose rules of distribution that have significant impact on the separate spouses' financial well-being. State divorce laws differ widely in their structures and in their details, but commonly produce similar outcomes.

In community-property states, each divorcing spouse is entitled to one-half of the property acquired during the marriage. In some states judges may deviate from this division in extraordinary circumstances (Elrod and Walker 1994:723–25). The remaining states have adopted more flexible schemes of property division generally called "equitable distribution." In these states, courts are permitted to divide all property acquired during the marriage in an equitable manner (Elrod and Walker 1994). In practice in many equitable-distribution states, lawyers for divorcing persons begin negotiations with an assumption of a division closely similar to the division imposed in community-property states: in the absence of special circumstances, the couple will divide equally all assets acquired by either during the marriage (Blumberg 1986:1251; Cheadle 1981:1269). And in practice in many community-property and equitable-distribution states, the actual division of property negotiated by parties often deviates from a fifty-fifty distribution in ways that have little to do with formal legal rules (Garrison 1991:621).

What is critical for our purposes is that at the point of divorce, under either regime, married persons encounter formal systems of forced allocation of assets that treat married persons as economic partners while they were together. Thus, as a single important example, for many long-married couples today, the largest single asset owned by either is a pension account accumulated in the name of one of them. In both community-property and common-law states, that part of the pension assets attributable to the period of the marriage will be subject to division between the partners (Ellman, Kurtz, and Bartlett 1991:253–57).

State law also responds at divorce to imbalances in earning capacity between spouses, imbalances that have often been magnified during the "partnership." It does so in common-law states by allowing judges to consider the disparate financial positions of the parties in the distribution of property.[45] Many states have also devised doctrines that permit courts to compensate a spouse in some manner for helping to increase the human capital of the other partner, most commonly by bearing the costs of putting the partner through professional school (Elrod and Spector 1996:774, table 5). In addition, both community-property states and common-law states permit courts to award periodic payments, called alimony or maintenance, for the support of a spouse unable adequately to provide for himself or herself after separation (Clark 1987:220–334; Elrod and Spector 1996:770, table 1).

Death is another occasion when the law imposes financial obligations because of marriage. Under the laws of nearly all states, a married person with personal assets cannot unilaterally prevent his or her spouse from inheriting part of them. Thus, when a married person dies with a will and the will fails to provide for the surviving spouse, the laws of nearly all common-law states permit the surviving spouse to claim a "forced" or "elective" share of the estate, commonly one-third or one-half (Brashier 1994:99–104; Waggoner 1992:720).[46] Much the same result is reached in long-term marriages in community-property states because, no matter what one spouse considers to be their separate property and attempts to bequeath by will to others, one-half of the assets acquired by the couple during the marriage will be considered the property of the other spouse at death (Brashier 1994:97).

Thus at both divorce and death, states impose on married couples a prescriptive view of the appropriate financial relationship between them. Most states now permit couples, at the point of marriage or during the marriage, to contract for a different arrangement on death or divorce than the law would otherwise impose, though also placing some limits to ensure that the decision to contract was "voluntary" and "informed" (Ellman, Kurtz, and Bartlett 1991:662–87; Schultz 1982:280–88).

How, by comparison, does the law treat the income and assets of single persons with a long-term partner? Very differently indeed. In both community-property and common-law states, the earnings of an unmarried person and the resources bought with those earnings are entirely the property of the earner. Moreover, in no state today does the state impose on the estate of an unmarried person a forced share for a surviving partner (Waggoner 1994:62–63). Unmarried persons can leave their money to whomever they please, no matter how long a relationship they may have had with a partner.

The rules relating to the breakup of unmarried couples vary widely among the states. Until the last thirty years or so, courts in nearly all states refused to intervene at all, even when the parties had agreed to share assets, on the ground that the cohabiting relationship itself was immoral.[47] A few states still retain this approach.[48] In most states, however, the law has changed, responding to the huge growth in the numbers of unmarried opposite-sex couples living together and to the changed social perception of the acceptability of such cohabitation.[49] Courts will enforce express agreements between unmarried persons to support each other or to divide property titled in the other's name.[50] Some of the cases have involved same-sex couples.[51]

A few states have gone further than the enforcement of agreements, coming closer to imposing a marital regime. Some will enforce "implied contracts," the contents of which courts infer not from words of agreement between the partners but from the partners' conduct—and which may in fact not reflect any actual agreement between the parties. In a few more states, judges will, at the request of a separating long-term unmarried partner, simply impose a property division that seems "just," even in the absence of any express or implied agreement between the parties.[52] In most states, however, unmarried partners still have no state-prescribed obligations to each other that apply in the absence of agreement. Each can walk away taking whatever is titled in their name.

At first blush, the rules currently applied in most states to the unmarried may seem to most gay men and lesbians preferable to the rules of forced sharing imposed on married people. Most states, as just described, impose on unmarried couples only what the couple itself has agreed to. Such a regime may well appeal to couples who are suspicious of the state and couples in which neither partner is economically dependent on the other. And, even if they saw themselves as having some continuing responsibilities, many would reject the notion of the state, through its judges, having the power to apportion fault or responsibility between them under the discretionary guidelines found in common-law states.

Yet I think that the rules regarding the financial aspects of divorce now in place for married couples would serve lesbian and gay male couples reasonably well. In the first place, the property rules of divorce are given life as part of a larger set of procedures governing divorce proceedings, procedures that encourage, or force, couples to wind up their financial relationship prior to moving on to another relationship. In the second place, the rules regarding the division of property for married people are, to an increasing extent, subject to alteration by the agreement of the parties. Before or during marriage, the parties may contract for different outcomes between them that will be honored by courts if voluntarily entered (Blumberg 1985:354). So seen, the rules of marriage operate as a default regime for couples who marry and do not choose a different scheme for themselves.

Of course, just as only a small proportion of opposite-sex married couples enter agreements today to vary from the rules otherwise imposed at divorce, so it is probable that few gay male and lesbian couples would do so in the future. My own belief, however, is that a default rule of imposed sharing is preferable for gay male and lesbian couples to the default rule of separate property and no continuing obligations that now exists for unmarried couples.

The moral claims for independence and separate ownership have their own weaknesses. Some may look at the world of forced sharing and alimony, remember a time when married women could own nothing in their own name, and wish to reject any reminders of the dependence of women on their husbands (Kaye 1987:1). But the world of independence has its own poisoned roots. Independence in law means that the person with legal title wins, and title, standing alone, bears little necessary relation to the efforts that lie behind the generation of the asset or to the moral implications of a long-shared life.

Taken together, these considerations even support the claim that the default property rules for marriage will not merely serve most gay and lesbian couples reasonably well but will, in general, serve gay and lesbian couples who choose to marry better than they serve opposite-sex married couples today. Gay men and lesbians compelled on separation to share assets will be hurt less frequently when the law's promise of sharing fails to produce economic parity between the partners. Because the members of such couples are always of the same sex, they more often earn similar incomes and are less likely to have gender-assigned expectations of divided responsibilities for income production during the relationship.

OBSERVATIONS

AMERICAN STATES AND THE federal government, as we have seen, treat married individuals differently than single individuals in three broad respects—privileging their relationship to their spouse in certain contexts because of their affective ties, providing them and their partners opportunities for legally recognized parenting that are not provided to others, and extending benefits and imposing obligations based on a view of the partners as economically intertwined. Taken together, the rules bearing on marriage offer significant advantages to those to whom they apply. The case I have tried to make for gay and lesbian couples is that they need these opportunities and choices to much the same degree that heterosexual couples do.

Heterosexual conservatives object to same-sex marriage either on the ground that sex between persons of the same sex is immoral or pathological or on the ground that permitting same-sex couples to marry will somehow contribute to the crumbling of the "traditional" family. Feminists among gay and lesbian scholars are also often critical of marriage for same-sex couples, fearing different undesirable consequences for lesbian and queer communities (Ettelbrick 1989; Homer 1994:505; Polikoff 1993:1535; Robson 1993:124–27). Neither objecting group focuses on the fit of specific legal rules with the lives of same-sex couples and, for this reason, this chapter has not addressed their claims. Two other sorts of doubts that *do* address the legal consequences of marriage might nonetheless be raised about legal same-sex marriage, even by some gay men and lesbians who might be expected to be sympathetic.

One objection is that there is a better vehicle than something called "marriage" for extending the appropriate protections and opportunities to same-sex couples. Especially for those for whom marriage is indelibly associated with male-female relationships, the alternative of permitting same-sex (and opposite-sex couples who want it) to register with the state as "domestic partners" and extending to such partners some or all of the consequences attached to marriage may seem attractive.

Formal registration of domestic partners has been instituted in several Scandinavian countries, where registered partners are treated very similarly to "married" couples. Within the United States, Hawaii now permits same-sex partners (and others) to register as "reciprocal beneficiaries" and obtain a few of the benefits that opposite-sex couples can obtain through marriage.[52] And one American state, Vermont, has quite recently adopted legislation that treats same-sex partners who enter "civil unions" precisely like married couples with respect to all the benefits and responsibilities of state law.[53]

The Vermont "civil union" legislation signifies an enormous change in American law. For those who disdain the term "marriage," "civil union" offers the legal consequences that Vermont extends to married persons without the historical baggage of the word "marriage." For others who believe that the rose by any other name will not smell as sweet, "civil union" provides significant legal benefits, as well as the hope that eventually Vermont and other states will take the final step and accept the sacred name.

A second doubt about pursuing changes in the laws of who may marry is that the benefits of marriage are likely to be unevenly distributed among same-sex couples. Nitya Duclos, a Canadian scholar, has argued, for example, that the rules of marriage would primarily benefit lesbians and gay men who are members of the middle class—"those who are already fairly high up in the hierarchy of privilege" (1991:31, 55, 58). She does not argue that this lopsided allocation of benefits is a reason not to permit same-sex marriage, for surely it is not, but rather is a reason to be less exultant about what will be achieved by it (Duclos 1991:59).

Duclos may possibly be right. Those high in the hierarchy of privilege usually come out ahead. Still, at least in this country, many lower-income same-sex couples will find great benefits in marriage. Duclos claims that "[t]hose who rely for most of their income on state benefits are more likely [than middle-class persons] to be economically penalized for marrying" (1991:55) and it is true that a significant cost of marriage for some lower-income persons who marry a working person is the loss of government benefits, such as Medicaid or Supplemental Security Income. It is also true that some other rules, such as those exempting bequests to a spouse from the estate and gift taxes, are of value only to those who have large sums to give away. Still, there may be compensating gains for low-income persons. Social Security retirement benefits for a nonworking spouse and Social Security survivor benefits are of most importance to those without long ties to the formal economy. Medical benefits tied to employment—including employment of some low-earning government employees—are of immense significance to spouses with jobs that carry no health coverage at all. And other benefits, such as the immigration rules or rules that relate to intestate succession, are likely to be at least as frequently invoked by people of modest incomes as they are by the well-heeled. It is impossible for all sorts of reasons to make a confident prediction of what class-groups among gay men and lesbians would benefit most from being permitted to marry, but there is ample reason to believe that the rules relating to marriage will be appealing to many people of all economic classes.

A final criticism of the laws bearing on married persons is more fundamental: even if legal marriage would offer benefits to a broad range of same-sex couples, some might claim that all these advantages are illegitimate—illegitimate for both same-sex and opposite-sex couples—because they favor persons in two-person units over single persons and over persons living in groups of three or more, and because they favor persons linked to one other person in a sexual-romantic relationship over persons linked to another by friendship or other allegiances (Homer 1994:530; Jaff 1988:238–42; Weston 1991:209–10). Those of us who are gay or lesbian must be especially sensitive to these claims. If the deeply entrenched paradigm we are challenging is the romantically linked man-woman couple, we should respect the similar claims made against the hegemony of the two-person unit and against the romantic foundations of marriage.

Still, nearly all reform to correct disparate treatment in our society is incremental. It comes at points at which the state finally recognizes the legitimacy of the claims of some long-disfavored group. Thus, within this century, governments have gradually changed their posture toward the legal position of the child born outside of marriage and toward unmarried opposite-sex couples in their relationships with one another.

A next appropriate step is the step discussed in this chapter—the recognition of same-sex couples who wish to marry. And although it is conceivable, as some have feared, that permitting gay people to marry will simply reinforce the enshrined position of married two-person units in our society, it seems at least as likely that the effect of permitting same-sex marriage will be to make society more receptive to the further evolution of the law (Hunter 1991:9, 12). By ceasing to conceive of marriage as a partnership composed of one person of each sex, the state may become more receptive to units of three or more (all of which, of course, include at least two persons of the same sex) and to units composed of two people of the same sex but who are bound by friendship alone.

NOTES

1. *Baehr v. Lewin*, 852 P2d 44 (1993). Five years later, in 1998, Hawaii's voters amended their constitution to give the legislature unreviewable authority to limit marriage to opposite-sex couples.
2. 2000 Vermont Laws 91.
3. See Defense of Marriage Act, Pub. L. No. 104–199, 3(a), 110 Stat. 2419, 2419 (1996).

4. In a comparable survey of gay men, 59 percent said that they would marry if they could, and another 26 percent said maybe. Seventy-one percent of men said they preferred long-term monogamous relationships (Lever 1994:23–24). In the national telephone survey undertaken for the *San Francisco Examiner*, 92 percent of lesbians and gay men indicated approval when asked, "How do you feel about two people of the same sex living together as a married couple?" (Hatfield 1989b:A-21).

5. See Eskridge (1996); see also *Hawaii Commission on Sexual Orientation and the Law Report*, pp. 1–23 (1995) discussing the legal consequences of marriage at great length.

6. "[C]ontemporary marriage cannot be legally defined any more precisely than as some sort of relationship between two individuals, of indeterminate duration, involving some kind of sexual conduct, entailing vague mutual property and support obligations, a relationship which may be formed by consent of both parties and dissolved at the will of either" (Clark 2.1 at 81 [1987]).

7. For a history of the early law, see Salmon (1986). For accounts of the changes, see Glendon (1981, 1989); Rheinstein (1972); and Schneider (1985).

8. See e.g., *Ky. Rev. Stat.* 311.631 (Michie Supp. 1994), which lists, in order, the spouse, an adult child, a parent.

9. See *Uniform Probate Code* 5–305(c) (guardian of the person), 5–409(a) (guardian of property), 8 U.L.A. 466, 487–88 (1983); see also Brown (1990:1029, 1045–1047).

10. See, for example, *New Mexico Disposition of Dead Bodies Act, N.M. Stat. Ann.* 24–12–1 to 4 (Michie 1994).

11. See *Uniform Anatomical Gift Act* 3(a), adopted in some form in every state; see also *N.Y. Pub. Health Law* 4301(2) (McKinney 1996).

12. See Henner (1985). The rules about intestate succession also reflect legislative views about the financial obligations of spouses to each other. See infra section III.C.

13. As a starting point, intestacy laws "build upon the rules that allocate original ownership" during the marriage (Waggoner 1994). As will be discussed later (under the heading "The Regulation of the Financial Relationship Between Married Partners"), two quite different regimes of marital-property ownership exist within the United States.

14. See Fellows et al. (1978:357–58 nn. 128–29); and Waggoner (1994:37–38).

15. In Europe and the United States, intestate succession laws have progressively moved toward reducing or excluding shares for blood relatives when the person who died has a surviving spouse (Glendon 1989:238–40).

16. Section Five of the *Uniform Health-Care Decisions Act* (1993) gives priority over everyone except a spouse to "an individual in a long-term relationship ... with the patient in which the individual has demonstrated an actual commitment to the patient similar to the commitment of a spouse and in which the individual and the patient consider themselves to be responsible for each other's well-being." As of 1996, the act had been adopted in a few states. See, for example, *N.M. Stat. Ann.* 24–7A-5B(2) (Michie Supp. 1996). Arizona has recently adopted a statute that provides that a patient's "domestic partner" can be designated by a court as the surrogate decision-maker for an incompetent person, but such a person is given lower priority than an adult child or a parent. See *Ariz. Rev. Stat. Ann.* 36–3231 (1995).

17. Fellows et al. (1978:337–39) report that in a survey of 750 adults, 55 percent of those interviewed said that they did not have a will, and laziness was the most commonly cited reason.

18. Thompson and Andrzejewski (1988) relate the story of Sharon Kowalski, a young woman who had failed to execute a power of attorney before a severely debilitating car accident, and whose lover was excluded by Sharon's parents from playing any role in her care. One of the gay men interviewed by Suzanne Sherman (1992) who had united with a partner in a ceremony of commitment said, "We haven't put together a will yet, but we're planning to do it," and his partner conceded, "we won't get motivated until something forces us to" (208). They had been married for five years.

19. Gordon, Mailman, and Yale-Loehr (1996) report there is a narrow context in which marriage hurts. Under current rules, an American citizen can secure a preference for entry as a resident for his foreign-born child if, but only if, the child is not married (36.02[2]).

20. See 29 U.S.C. 2611–54, 2612(a)(1)(C) (1994).

21. See, for example, 5 U.S.C. 3110 (1994), which prohibits federal officials from employing, promoting, or advancing any of a list of family members in or to a position in an agency in which they serve or over which they exercise control; *Tenn. Code Ann.* 8–31–103 (1993), which prohibits state employees from being placed in the direct line of supervision of a relative.

22. For a brief review, accessible to lawyers, of the research on gay men and lesbians as parents and for abundant references to the social science literature, see Herek (1991) and Patterson (1992). On lesbians as parents, see Polikoff (1990). On gay men as parents, see Bozett (1989).

23. See Patterson (1992).

24. See Mahoney (1994:13–51). Utah, for example, is a partial exception, imposing a duty of support during the course of the stepparent's marriage to the

biological parent, but not at the point of divorce. See *Utah Code Ann.* 78–45–4.1 (1992); see also Chambers (1990:108–09).

25. See 29 U.S.C. 2611(12) & 2612(a)-(d) (1994). The act includes "stepchild" but does not define the term. I assume from its use in other legal contexts that, for purposes of the act, a stepchild is a child of a person to whom the employee is actually married and does not include the child of a person with whom the employee is cohabiting outside of marriage.

26. See Curie-Cohen et al. (1979:585), which reports on a survey of physicians, 90 percent of whom said that they would not perform artificial insemination on an unmarried woman; and Sparks and Hamilton (1991:311–12) report that lesbians often face special difficulties obtaining services form clinics.

27. Florida and New Hampshire prohibit adoptions by gay men and lesbians. See *Fla. Stat.* ch. 63.042(3) (1995); *N.H. Rev. Stat. Ann.* 170-B:4 (1994). In a few other states, appellate courts have declared homosexuals unsuitable to be adoptive parents. See Hollandsworth (1995:197 n. 53).

28. See, for example, *In re* Adoption of T.K.J. and K.A.K., Nos. 95CA0531, 95CA0532, 1996 WL 316800 (Colo. Ct. App. June 13, 1996) holding that only a person married to the biological partner is eligible for the rules regarding stepparent adoption.

29. See Andrews (1991:14.02), which notes that thirty states have adopted statutory rules that a properly consenting husband becomes the legal father for all purposes, and that courts in most other states have reached the same result by relying on the common law presumption of legitimacy for children born within marriage and on the agreement of the parties prior to conception.

30. The best available information about the economic behavior of gay and lesbian couples comes from Blumstein and Schwartz's pioneer study from the early 1980s of the handling of money by American couples. See Blumstein and Schwartz (1983:94–111).

31. See I.R.C. 1(a) (1994).

32. See 42 U.S.C. 1382(b) (1994).

33. 42 U.S.C. 1382c(f)(1) (1994).

34. See 20 U.S.C. 1087pp, 1087nn(b)(1)(A) (1994).

35. 42 U.S.C. 402(b)-(c). See *U.S. Social Security Administration, Social Security Handbook*, 305 (12th ed. 1995). In much the same manner, a divorced spouse not fully covered through their own employment will be covered through the former spouse on reaching the required age. See *id.*

36. See *id.* 401.

37. See I.R.C. 1041, 2523 (1996); also Cain (1991:123–29).

38. See I.R.C. 1041(a)-(c) (1996).

39. See I.R.C. 2056 (1996).

40. See I.R.C. 105, 213 (1996).

41. The states are Arizona, California, Idaho, Louisiana, Nevada, New Mexico, Texas, Washington, and Wisconsin.

42. See Cunningham, Stoebuck, and Whitman (1993:5.15) and McClanahan (1982:1:07), which compare common-law and community-property states.

43. Lawrence Waggoner believes that the two sets of rules serve to "reinforce the profoundly different symbolical and psychological feelings within the ongoing marriage" (1994:27).

44. See generally Blumstein and Schwartz (1983), which describes the personal and social characteristics motivating heterosexual relationships and compares them to those motivating homosexual and lesbian relationships.

45. See *Uniform Marriage and Divorce Act* 307(a), 9A U.L.A. 239 (1987), adopted in many states.

46. See also *Uniform Probate Code* 2–102, 8 U.L.A. 59 (1982), which divides the marital assets on a 50/50 basis.

47. See, for example, *Wallace v. Rappleye*, 103 Ill. 229, 249 (1882).

48. See, for example, *Hewitt v. Hewitt*, 394 N.E.2d 1204 (Ill. 1979).

49. On the demographic changes, see Thornton (1988:497; Waggoner 1994:63).

50. See *Marvin v. Marvin*, 557 P.2d 106 (Cal. 1976), which held that courts should enforce contracts between unmarried partners; *Morone v. Morone*, 413 N.E.2d 1154 (N.Y. 1980); see also Kandoian (1987:1829).

51. Only a few states have appellate decisions on the question whether such contracts will be honored for same-sex couples. See, for example, *Jones v. Daly*, 176 Cal. Rptr. 130 (1981).

52. 1997 Hawaii Act 383.

53. 2000 Vermont Laws 91. Vermont's marriage law limits marriage to the union of a man and a woman. The "civil union" legislation was prompted by a decision of the Vermont Supreme Court holding the marriage statute unconstitutional under a term of the Vermont Constitution, and leaving to the legislature the choice between altering the marriage statute to permit same-sex couples to marry or creating a new institution that carried the rights and responsibilities of marriage under some other name. The legislature chose the latter course.

REFERENCES

Andrews, Lori B. 1991. "Alternative Reproduction and the Law of Adoption." In Joan H. Hollinger, ed., *Adoption Law and Practice*, 14.02. New York: M. Bender.

Bartholet, Elizabeth. 1993. *Family Bonds: Adoption and the Politics of Parenting.* Boston: Houghton Mifflin.

Blumberg, Grace G. 1985. "New Models of Marriage and Divorce." In Kingsley Davis, ed., *Contemporary Marriage: Comparative Perspectives on a Changing Institution*, pp. 349–72. New York: Russell Sage Foundation.

——. 1986. "Marital Property Treatment of Pensions, Disability Pay, Workers' Compensation, and Other Wage Substitutes: An Insurance of Replacement Analysis." *UCLA Law Review* 33 (June): 1250–1308.

Blumstein, Philip and Pepper Schwartz. 1983. *American Couples: Money, Work, Sex.* New York: William Morrow.

Bozett, Frederick W. 1989. "Gay Fathers: A Review of the Literature." *Journal of Homosexuality* 18 (1/2): 137–62.

Brashier, Ralph C. 1994. "Disinheritance and the Modern Family." *Case Western Reserve Law Review* 45 (1): 83–184.

Brown, Amy L. 1990. "Broadening Anachronistic Notions of 'Family' in Proxy Decisionmaking for Unmarried Adults." *Hastings Law Journal* 41 (4): 1029–1076.

Butler, Becky, ed. 1997. *Ceremonies of the Heart: Celebrating Lesbian Unions.* Seattle: Seal Press.

Cain, Patricia A. 1991. "Same-Sex Couples and the Federal Tax Laws." *Law & Sexuality* 1 (Summer): 97–132.

Chambers, David L. 1990. "Stepparents, Biologic Parents, and the Law's Perception of 'Family' After Divorce." In Stephen D. Sugarman and Herma Hill Kay, eds., *Divorce Reform at the Crossroads*, pp. 102–29. New Haven: Yale University Press.

Cheadle, Elizabeth A. 1981. "The Development of Sharing Principles in Common Law Marital Property States." *UCLA Law Review* 28 (August): 1269–1313.

Clark, Homer H., Jr. 1987. *The Law of Domestic Relations in the United States.* 2d ed. St. Paul, Minn.: West.

Cunningham, Roger A., William B. Stoebuck, and Dale A. Whitman. 1993. *The Law of Property.* 2d ed. St. Paul, Minn.: West.

Curie-Cohen, Martin et al. 1979. "Current Practice of Artificial Insemination by Donor in the United States." *New England Journal of Medicine* 300 (11): 585–90.

Drizner, Paul. 1987. "Medicaid's Unhealthy Side Effect: The Financial Burdens on At-Home Spouses of Institutionalized Recipients." *Loyola University of Chicago Law Journal* 18 (Spring): 1031–1052.

Duclos, Nitya. 1991. "Some Complicating Thoughts on Same-Sex Marriage." *Law & Sexuality* 1 (Summer): 31–62.

Ellman, Ira M., Paul M. Kurtz, and Katharine T. Bartlett. 1991. *Family Law: Cases, Text, Problems.* Charlottesville, Va.: Michie.

Elrod, Linda D. and Robert G. Spector. 1996. "A Review of the Year in Family Law: Children's Issues Take Spotlight." *Family Law Quarterly* 29, no. 4 (Winter): 741–74.

Elrod, Linda D. and Timothy B. Walker. 1994. "Family Law in the Fifty States." *Family Law Quarterly* 27, no. 4 (Winter): 515–746.

Eskridge Jr., William N. 1996. *The Case for Same-Sex Marriage: From Sexual Liberty to Civilized Commitment.* New York: Free Press.

Ettelbrick, Paula. 1989. "Since When Is Marriage a Path to Liberation?" *OUT/LOOK National Gay and Lesbian Quarterly* 9: 14–16.

Evall, Joseph. 1991. "Sexual Orientation and Adoptive Matching." *Family Law Quarterly* 25, no. 3 (Fall): 347–80.

Fellows, Mary Louise et al. 1978. "Public Attitudes About Property Distribution at Death and Intestate Succession Laws in the United States." *American Bar Foundation Research Journal* 3 (2): 319–91.

Field, Martha A. 1990. *Surrogate Motherhood: The Legal and Human Issues.* 2d ed. Cambridge: Harvard University Press.

Garrison, Marsha. 1991. "Good Intentions Gone Awry: The Impact of New York's Equitable Distribution Law on Divorce Outcomes." *Brooklyn Law Review* 57, no. 3 (Fall): 621–754.

Gill, Thomas P. 1995. *Report of the Commission on on Sexual Orientation and the Law.* Honolulu: The Commission.

Glendon, Mary Ann. 1976. "Marriage & the State: The Withering Away of Marriage. *Virginia Law Review* 62 (4): 662–720.

——. 1981. *The New Family and the New Property.* Toronto: Butterworths.

——. 1989. *The Transformation of Family Law: State, Law, and Family in the United States and Western Europe.* Chicago: University of Chicago Press.

Gordon, Charles, Stanley Mailman, and Stephen Yale-Loehr. 1996. *Immigration Law and Procedure.* New York: Bender.

Gostin, Larry, ed. 1990. *Surrogate Motherhood: Politics and Privacy.* Bloomington: Indiana University Press.

Hatfield, Larry D. 1989a. "Methods of Polling." *San Francisco Examiner,* June 5, p. A-20.

——. 1989b. "New Poll: How U.S. Views Gays." *San Francisco Examiner,* June 6, pp. A-19, A-21.

Henner, M. 1985. *A Compendium of State Statutes and International Treaties in Trust and Estate Law: A Reference and Referral Guide for Practicing Attorneys.* Westport, Conn.: Quorum Books.

Herek, Gregory M. 1991. "Myths About Sexual Orientation: A Lawyer's Guide to Social Science Research." *Law & Sexuality* 1 (Summer): 133–72.

Hollandsworth, Maria J. 1995. "Gay Men Creating Families Through Surro-Gay Arrangements: A Paradigm for Reproductive Freedom." *The American University Journal of Gender and the Law* 3, no. 2 (Spring): 183–246.

Hollinger, Joan Heifetz. 1990a. "Introduction to Adoption Law and Practice." In Joan Heifetz Hollinger, ed., *Adoption Law and Practice*, pp. 1.05[2] 1–53 through 1–61. New York: M. Bender.

———. 1990b. "Consent to Adoption." In Joan H. Hollinger, ed., *Adoption Law and Practice*, pp. 2.10[3] 2–93 through 2–112. New York: M. Bender.

Homer, Steven K. 1994. "Against Marriage." *Harvard Civil Rights-Civil Liberties Law Review* 29, no. 2 (Summer): 505–30.

Hunter, Nan D. 1991. "Marriage, Law, and Gender: A Feminist Inquiry." *Law & Sexuality* 1 (Summer): 9–30.

Jaff, Jennifer. 1988. "Wedding Bell Blues: The Position of Unmarried People in American Law." *Arizona Law Review* 30: 207–42.

Kandel, Randy Frances. 1994. "Which Came First: The Mother or the Egg? A Kinship Solution to Gestational Surrogacy." *Rutgers Law Review* 47, no. 1 (Fall): 165–246.

Kandoian, Ellen. 1987. "Cohabitation, Common Law Marriage, and the Possibility of a Shared Moral Life." *Georgetown Law Journal* 75 (August): 1829–1873.

Kaye, Herma Hill. 1987. "Equality and Difference: A Perspective on No-Fault Divorce and Its Aftermath." *University of Cincinnati Law Review* 56 (1): 1–90.

Kornhauser, Marjorie. 1993. "Love, Money, and the IRS: Family, Income Sharing, and the Joint Income Tax Return." *Hastings Law Journal* 45, no. 1 (November): 63–112.

Lacey, Linda J. 1987. "The Law of Artificial Insemination and Surrogate Parenthood in Oklahoma: Roadblocks to the Right to Procreate." *Tulsa Law Journal* 22 (Spring): 281–324.

Lever, Janet. 1994. "The 1994 Advocate Survey of Sexuality and Relationships: The Men." *Advocate* August 23, pp. 23–24.

———. 1995. "Lesbian Sex Survey." *Advocate*, August 23, pp. 27–29.

Mahoney, Margaret M. 1987. "Stepfamilies in the Federal Law." *University of Pittsburgh Law Review* 48 (Winter): 491–537.

———. 1994. *Stepfamilies and the Law.* Ann Arbor: University of Michigan Press.

Martin, April. 1993. *The Lesbian and Gay Parenting Handbook: Creating and Raising Our Families.* New York: HarperCollins.

Mason, Mary Ann and David W. Simpson. 1995. "The Ambiguous Stepparent: Federal Legislation in Search of a Model." *Family Law Quarterly* 29, no. 3 (Fall): 445–82.

McCaffery, Edward J. 1993a. "Taxation and the Family: A Fresh Look at Behavioral Gender Biases in the Code." *UCLA Law Review* 40, no. 4 (April): 983–1060.

——. 1993b. "Slouching Towards Equality: Gender Discrimination, Market Efficiency, and Social Change." *Yale Law Journal* 103, no. 3 (December): 596–676.

McClanahan, W. S. 1982. *Community Property Law in the United States.* Rochester, N.Y.: Lawyers Co-operative.

Patterson, Charlotte J. 1992. "Children of Lesbian and Gay Parents." *Child Development* 63 (5): 1025–1042.

Pies, Cheri. 1988. *Considering Parenthood: A Handbook for Lesbians.* Duluth, Minn.: Spinsters Ink.

Polikoff, Nancy D. 1990. "This Child Does Have Two Mothers: Redefining Parenthood to Meet the needs of Children in Lesbian-Mother and Other Nontraditional families." *Georgetown Law Journal* 78, no. 3 (February): 459–576.

——. 1993. "Commentaries: We Will Get What We Ask For: Why Legalizing Gay and Lesbian Marriage Will Not 'Dismantle the Legal Structure of Gender in Every Marriage.'" *Virginia Law Review* 79, no. 7 (October): 1535–1550.

Rae, Scott B. 1994. *The Ethics of Commercial Surrogate Motherhood: Brave New Families.* Westport, Conn.: Praeger.

Regan, Milton C., Jr. 1993. *Family Law and the Pursuit of Intimacy.* New York: New York University Press.

——. 1995. "Spousal Privilege and the Meanings of Marriage." *Virginia Law Review* 81, no. 8 (November): 2045–2157.

Rheinstein, Max. 1972. *Marriage, Stability, Divorce, and the Law.* Chicago: University of Chicago Press.

Ricketts, Wendell and Roberta Achtenberg. 1987. "The Adoptive and Foster Gay and Lesbian Parent." In Frederick Bozett, ed., *Gay and Lesbian Parents,* pp. 89–111. New York: Praeger.

Robson, Ruthann. 1993. "Lesbian (Out)law: Survival Under the Rule Law." *Harvard Women's Law Journal* 16 (Spring): 279–85.

Salmon, Marylynn. 1986. *Women and the Law of Property.* Chapel Hill: University of North Carolina Press.

Schneider, Carl E. 1985. "Moral Discourse and the Transformation of American Family Law." *Michigan Law Review* 83 (August): 1803–1879.

——. 1992. "The Channelling Function in Family Law. *Hofstra Law Review* 20 (3): 495–532.

Sherman, Suzanne, ed. 1992. "Introduction." In S. Sherman, ed., *Lesbian and Gay Marriage: Private Commitments, Public Ceremonies,* pp. 1–10. Philadelphia: Temple University Press.

Shultz, Marjorie M. 1982. "Contractual Ordering of Marriage: A New Model for State Policy." *California Law Review* 70 (March): 204–334.

Singer, Jana B. 1992. "The Privatization of Family Law." *Wisconsin Law Review* (5): 1443–1568.

Sparks, Caroline H. and Jean A. Hamilton. 1991. "Psychological Issues Related to Alternative Insemination." *Professional Psychology, Research and Practice* 22, no. 4 (August): 308–14.

Strong, John William. 1992. *McCormick on Evidence*. 4th ed. St. Paul, Minn.: West.

Sullivan, Kathleen M. 1989. "Unconstitutional Conditions: Developments in the Law-Sexual Orientation and the Law." *Harvard Law Review* 102 (May 7): 1413–1506.

Thompson, Karen and Julie Andrzejewski. 1988. *Why Can't Sharon Kowalski Come Home?* San Francisco: Spinsters/Aunt Lute.

Thornton, Arland. 1988. "Cohabitation and Marriage in the 1980s." *Demography* 25, no. 4 (November): 497–508.

Waggoner, Lawrence W. 1992. "Spousal Right in Our Multiple-Marriage Society: The Revised Uniform Probate Code." *Real Property, Probate and Trust Journal* 24, no. 4 (Winter): 683–774.

——. 1994. "Marital Property Rights in Transition." *Missouri Law Review* 59 (1): 21–104.

Weitzman, Lenore J. 1985. *The Divorce Revolution: The Unexpected Social and Economic Consequences for Women and Children in America*. New York: Free Press.

Weston, Kath. 1991. *Families We Choose: Lesbians, Gays, Kinship*. New York: Columbia University Press.

20 | Take My Domestic Partner, Please: Gays and
Marriage in the Era of the Visible

Suzanna Danuta Walters

I n this supposedly hip "gay '90s" Americans seem unusually
vexed when it comes to gays and families. In poll after poll,
even when respondents are in favor of nondiscrimination,
the numbers shift radically when it comes to family issues. In a 1993 *US
News and World Report* poll ("Straight Talk" 42), 60 percent opposed recognizing legal partnerships for homosexuals, 73 percent opposed same-sex
marriages, and 70 percent opposed allowing gays to adopt. In a 1994
Newsweek poll (Ingrassia 47), 65 percent of those polled opposed gay adoptions, 62 percent believed gays should not be allowed legally to marry. This
is all in the context of polls that show that people overwhelmingly oppose
discrimination in housing, employment, health care, and so on. Indeed, in
the same *Newsweek* poll, 74 percent favored protecting gays from job discrimination and 81 percent favored equal housing laws. An earlier poll by
Time magazine, in 1989 (Isaacson et al. 101), showed something quite similar: 69 percent opposed legal recognition of gay couples, 75 percent opposed
gays adopting, while 65 percent believed gays should be allowed to inherit
each other's property. More recent polls paint a similar picture of increasing
support for antidiscrimination legislation while at the same time steady
resistance to adoptions by gays, foster parenting by gays, and, of course, gay
marriage: an October 1998 Time/CNN poll (Lacayo 32–36) showed that 64
percent opposed gay marriage and 57 percent opposed adoptions by gays.

Yet as much as the right wants to go back to the (fictional, of course) days
of June and Ward, Ozzie and Harriet, times do seem to be a-changin'.

Domestic partnership laws, gay marriages, donor insemination, adoption—while unthinkable a few years ago—are now part of the larger cultural landscape. Hundreds of universities, cities, towns, and private businesses (including major corporations such as Apple Computers and Disney) have instituted domestic partnership policies, allowing unmarried couples (both homosexual and heterosexual) to share health benefits, housing rights, and other amenities typically accorded only to married heterosexuals. Gays are having children in record numbers, prompting the term "gayby boom" to enter the public lexicon.

Into this changing social field emerges the specter of gay marriages. This is not to say that the subject of gay marriage has never been broached before. Rather, it is to say that "the gay marriage debate" as a public spectacle emerges in the context of a heightened visibility of lesbians and gays. This new visibility affects gays and straights alike, altering gay sensibilities and political strategies and inhabiting straight consciousness as never before. In other words, to understand the gay marriage debate we must have some sense of the strange and confusing moment in which this debate emerges onto the public stage. Gay understandings about marriage, gay desires, gay identities are forged not just through some internal logic but also through the complex negotiations with (heterosexist, hegemonic) popular culture. The huge academic, legal, and journalistic discourse around gay marriage (a discourse I will examine in this chapter) is produced in and around a new public visibility of lesbians and gays. Thus I am interested here in locating this debate within this changing social and cultural field. For surely it must be different to broach gay marriage now than in the context, say, of the 1960s when gay liberationism, the women's movement, and hippie culture explicitly challenged traditional familial models, disavowing marriage and its detritus of commercialized legitimacy. The *historical* question "Why now?" must be merged with the *cultural* examination of how and why marriage gets produced as a "gay desire" and a straight fear.

Gay life and identity, defined so much by the problems of invisibility, subliminal coding, double entendres, and double lives, has now taken on the dubious distinction of public spectacle. But beyond the odes to openness, diversity, and "tolerance," few (except on the right of course!) have questioned the value of this almost obsessive fascination with gay life. At first glance, these stunning changes seem all for the good. But if gays seem like the paragons of trendiness, then they are being simultaneously depicted as the very anti-Christ, the sign of a culture in decay, a society in ruins, the perverse eclipse of rational modernity. As religious fundamentalism grows, becomes mainstream and legitimate, so too does hard-edged homophobia. Hate crimes are on the rise—not just in pure numbers but in the severity and brutality of the acts.[1]

It is assumed that visibility is an unmitigated "good thing," inherently promoting awareness and producing sensitivities. Most people believe that the more lesbians and gays are assimilated into the everyday life of American society, the more readily straight people will "understand" and "accept" them. To some extent, I believe this to be true. As an openly gay person I have ample evidence that seeing gays and lesbians in all walks of life helps to shatter old stereotypes and challenge misinformed judgments. I have seen numerous students and colleagues reevaluate their prejudices when faced with a lesbian professor. Indeed, several years ago, when I announced my pregnancy, a colleague's first words were, "But I never thought *you* wanted to have a *family!*"—the assumption being, of course, that lesbians and gay men were beyond the realm of family life. While my colleague is not quite on the barricades for gay rights, my everyday presence and that of my daughter has surely made her more aware of the multiple ways of forming family.

Yet, unfortunately, the processes of assimilation and cultural visibility are not solely beneficent. History has shown us—with horrifying detail—the ways in which forms of bigotry sustain themselves and even grow in the face of assimilation. Never have we had so many openly gay elected officials, or so many antigay initiatives. Gay weddings abound on TV as they are being denounced in Congress. Gays are at once the new "Willie Hortons" and the chic flavor of the month. The age of visibility produces both realities: the hopeful moments of rights and inclusion and the fearful moments of victimization and reaction.

As with any minority group, the moment of public visibility marks the beginning of a complex process. The emergence into public view can aid in the process of liberation; surely liberation cannot be won from the space of the crowded closet. Yet the glare of commercial culture can often produce a new kind of invisibility, itself supported by a relentless march toward assimilation. The debates about assimilation are as old as the movement itself. Indeed, every social movement has at some point been faced with similar questions, questions about the benefits of assimilation into the dominant order versus the elaboration of visionary alternatives to that order. But what *is* new today is that these debates are now taking place in full public view, around the watercoolers of corporate America, the hallways of university campuses, the barbecue grills of genteel suburbia, and the streets and malls of both urban and rural areas. No longer restricted to closed-door meetings and internecine battles, these internal debates have been irrevocably externalized. If the enemy was once perceived as invisibility itself, then how is an enemy defined in an era of increased visibility? Is the penetrating gaze of the popular a sign of public acceptance or, rather, the construction of the homosexual as commodity fetish, as sideshow freak?

What profound (and new) alienation must be felt when a gay person looks at a gay wedding cheerfully depicted on TV and then has her/his partner studiously ignored at a family gathering? What does it feel like to be depicted as the cutting edge of chic postmodern style as you are getting fired from your job, rejected by your family, and targeted by right-wing activists? These are new problems, surely, for those coming of age in this new era of visibility. The gap between new expectations and old realities can produce a postmodern funnyhouse of the soul, as gays live out the paradoxes of our times.

NOT ALL IN THE FAMILY: HETEROSEXUAL UNEASE IN THE ERA OF VISIBILITY

INTO THIS STRANGE REGISTER of the visible enters the soundbite-ish gay marriage debate, a debate played out in the pages of gay journals but also played out on our TV sets, in glossy mainstream magazines, in prime-time news specials, in our legislative bodies, in legal argumentation, in everyday talk. Gay marriage has wreaked havoc on the public imagination. Indeed, the peculiarly public display that is the marriage ritual emphasizes the centrality of the visible to marriage, in a way that domestic partnerships or even commitment ceremonies can never quite manifest. Weddings are highly commercialized public signs;[2] it is no accident that this imagery has captivated public imagination, pushing aside the more mundane and everyday images of lesbian and gay life by making visible that which we cannot have.

Nowhere is this new gay visibility more pronounced—and more problematic—than on television. Gay weddings have appeared on numerous series, including *Friends* (with Candace Gingrich playing the lesbian minister), the since canceled *Northern Exposure*, and *Roseanne*. For all the obvious newness of this—and its pathbreaking quality—most have forgone the taboo gay kiss and presented gay marriage ceremonies as cuddly, desexualized mirrors of the more familiar heterosexual ritual. Notably absent are the odes to same-sex love and the revisions of traditional vows that most assuredly accompany many gay commitment ceremonies. The *Friends* wed-ding—while carefully sensitive—went out of its way to portray the gay wedding as an exact replica of its heterosexual counterpart, only with two bridal gowns. The episode focused much more on the heterosexual response to the gay environment than on the gay participants themselves. Indeed, the gay wedding was framed by a secondary plot line concerning the impend-ing divorce of a characters' traditional mom, implicitly linking heterosexu-ality and homosexuality in a liberal scenario of sameness.

It is interesting to note that in three of the major gay weddings handled on TV, it is a heterosexual character who brings the nervous and fighting homosexual couple together when the nuptials are threatened. In *Friends*, *Northern Exposure*, and even the typically more innovative *Roseanne* one of the series regulars has a heart-to-heart with one member of the bickering gay couple and helps convince the wavering one to go through with the planned wedding. Often, it is the character who is initially most resistant to the wedding (ex-husband Ross in *Friends* and rich town leader Maurice in *Northern Exposure*). This strange pattern is not, I'm afraid, merely coinciden-tal. Rather, the confidential tête-à-tête between gay outsider and heterosex-ual insider renders not only homosexuality but *homophobia* benign and palat-able. The appalled Maurice, who complains about these "tutti fruttis" ruin-ing the very concept of marriage by engaging in a same-sex version of it, becomes not a bigoted homophobe but, rather, a befuddled and ultimately good-hearted traditionalist. The straight character is reformed and redeemed through his/her expertise in prewedding cold feet, thereby avoiding reck-oning with the actual homophobia that surrounds such events. And the gay characters are "redeemed" by participation in a very familiar ritual—the said cold feet.

In this scenario, straight people know more about family life and rela-tionships and are needed to pass that knowledge on to their floundering gay brethren. The implication here is that gays are simply not knowledgeable about the real-life issues of forming families, making commitments, raising kids.[3] Not only does this infantilize the gay characters, it also reintroduces an old canard about homosexuals as childlike, immature, unformed versions of heterosexuals. This backlash scenario argues for the "acceptance" of homosexuals but not as full-fledged people who can handle their own lives.

In addition, there is a certain amount of hubris at the specter of the straight homophobe playing Dear Abby to the jittery gay person. Do these gay people on TV never have *any* gay friends to consult in their various tra-vails? Isolation and assimilation are often the price of tokenism. But at least the *Cosby* family had each other. Gay people on TV appear to have sprung full-blown from the Zeus's head of heterosexuality—the social, political, and cultural context that "births" gay people gives way to the fiction of the fully formed fag, parented by bravely reconstructed heterosexuals. Homophobia is rarely portrayed as just that; rather, it is usually reduced to ignorance, bewilderment, and discomfort. In the television land of gay life, the perpetrators of homophobia (aside from the obvious gaybashers) are not *offenders* but are basically good-hearted souls whose liberal inclinations will win out in the end.

Contrast this delusional neoliberalism with the realities of antigay politics. The same year that witnessed ratings-successful gay weddings on TV also saw the U.S. Congress overwhelmingly support an antigay marriage bill— and a putatively progay president sign it. Television abounds with gay weddings while our elected officials rail against marriage (and state after state votes to restrict marriage to heterosexuals)—and polls suggest most Americans agree with the officials and not with the television shows they watch so assiduously. For the religious right, gay marriage is most assuredly the proverbial line in the sand, keeping heterosexuals safe from the invading hordes of gay barbarians eager to say their "I dos" in the Chapel of Love. A full-page ad by the Family Research Council in *The Washington Post* quite explicitly locates marriage as the glue that holds society together—and that keeps out the undesirables. Above a picture of a crumbling wedding cake, the ad encapsulates the "family values" rhetoric and reveals its political heritage: "The institution of marriage was built to last. . . . It was made in heaven . . . Recognized by the state . . . Sanctioned by faith and honored by the community. It has gone hand-in-hand with the rise of civilization. Marriage has survived Marxism. Outlasted Free Love. Outlived Woodstock. Toughed-out the Playboy philosophy. Even endured radical feminism." Opponents of gay marriage are explicitly linking the supposed evils of same-sex love to all the other supposed evils of a secular-humanist society—the ogre of sixties-style sex, drugs, and rock-n-roll meets up with the shibboleth of radical feminism, which encounters the Godzilla of gay marriage. Because the right has used this as a wedge issue in recent elections, gays must, unfortunately, fight the battle on the limited turf that has been set out for us. So mainstream and conservative gays assert the centrality of marriage and pledge their commitment to maintaining its traditions. They respond to right-wing hysteria (e.g., William Bennett's assertion that same-sex marriage "would be the most radical step ever taken in the deconstruction of society's most important institution") by assurances of shared family values and reverence for traditional marriage. It is difficult to hear the more radical gay voices, those that would say to Bennett and his ilk: "Would that it were so! Forward deconstruction! Onward challenge! Hi ho revision!" In this truncated battle, then, the complicated and difficult politics of marriage gets evaporated in a sea of assimilationist paeans to heavenly coupledom.

A PLACE AT THE ALTAR: THE EQUALITY ARGUMENT

IF THE LIBERAL POPULAR culture depicts gay weddings as cheerfully hetero we-are-the-world assimilation, and straight homophobes depict them as the satanic rituals of secular humanism run amok, then what are gays themselves saying about this contested institution? There are really two debates surrounding the whole issue of gays and marriage. The first is the one we are most familiar with—that between gays arguing for rights to marriage and heterosexuals attempting to limit legally recognized marriage to heterosexual couples. This debate as it stands is fairly simple and one can take a position without much ado. The public gay argument is basically one of equality: how can one justify denying one group of people access to a practice, simply on the basis of their sexual preference? At the most basic level, gays argue that they are being both socially disenfranchised (because marriage brings with it such large and meaningful social approval) and economically discriminated against (marriage confers all sorts of financial rewards, including inheritance, tax filings, health and pension benefits, etc.) by being denied access to such a fundamental social institution. For gays—at least publicly—this is another in a long line of civil rights issues, analogous here to interracial marriages and other forms of systematic exclusion. Prohibiting gays from marriage is one more insult, perpetuating the belief that gays are second-class citizens, unable or unworthy to take up the mantle of full civic membership.

The civil rights/equality arguments for marriage are by now quite familiar and need not be reiterated here. Indeed, I will focus more in this piece on the ideological agendas that underlie—in both explicit and implicit ways—the more impassioned advocates of gay marriage who are *not* relying solely on an equality argument. That marriage rights would confer benefits—both social and economic—to many lesbians and gays is undeniable. Given the structure of our social and legal system (including our tax structure, inheritance laws, health benefits and responsibilities, childcare and custody and parenting issues—to name just a few), it is certainly understandable that many gay couples would desire access to the same rights and responsibilities, benefits and assumptions that married heterosexuals receive as a matter of course. Numerous writers, including David Chambers (chapter 19 and 1996), have explicitly spelled out the financial and legal ramifications and strongly argue that gay access to marriage is not only just and fair but would also positively confer tangible benefits that far outweigh additional responsibilities or burdens.

However controversial the phenomenon may be within the gay community, gay wedding ceremonies have become a part of the political landscape. Mass weddings now regularly mark gay pride days and gay rights demonstrations; over five hundred couples participated in such a rite during the 1993 March on Washington and the recent Millennium March began with a similar mass betrothal. In the few polls that have been done, there does seem to be general support within the gay community for legalizing gay marriage. Certainly even those who think the energy misplaced and the institution suspect agree that full civil rights for gays must include the right to marry. In a thoughtful editorial for the *St. Louis Post-Dispatch*, Amy Adams Squire Strongheart writes with humor and fairness about both sides of the debate within the gay community and concedes the point that the institution of marriage has, at best, a misogynist history. Yet she takes up the mantle of gay marriage, in part because "we lesbians and gays have been told by religion, government and business that we don't matter and that our relationships don't count. But they do count" (1994). She goes on, however, to argue that we must "create a new covenant that is more applicable to the unique nature of our love relationships." Yet for her, I fear, the "unique nature" of our relationships has a decidedly biological bent. Citing the Bible, she argues for a "born with it" thesis, implying that our "differences" are natural and innate (genetic?). So it seems that the difference is not so much about ideology, or history, or vision, but rather that since we are "born different," God surely means for us to have different ceremonies.[4]

However, there is a more complex issue that often gets ignored in the media light of this highly polarized and acrimonious debate, and that is the differences amongst gays *themselves* over marriage. Before I delve into that more complex subject, I must of course note that the basic equality/equal access argument is persuasive and important. Obviously, no thoughtful gay activist should or would take a position that argues for the continual exclusion of lesbians and gays from any institution or practice they choose to join—be it marriage or the military. That said, and my nod to fundamental principles of equality duly noted, the rest of this essay will engage in a much more critical analysis of gay *desire* to join such dubious institutions, and the kinds of ideological positions and cultural assumptions that surround such desire. For desire is, of course, constructed. No one—gay or straight—is born with some inherent desire to throw themselves on the altar, pledging fidelity to one true love and filing joint income taxes. No gene for that. So gay desire to marry must be interrogated, its seeming transparency compromised in order to reveal the complex of cultural and political imaginings that have produced a moment such as this.

There is, of course, a more pragmatic and strategic dimension to this discussion. Like the gays in the military debate, many lesbians and gay men are reluctant to focus so exclusively on this particular issue, believing that the impossibility of victory here will foreclose action on more winnable initiatives. Indeed, the overwhelming support of the Defense of Marriage Act, even among those considered allies and who had previously voted for antidiscrimination legislation, was a sign to many activists that foregrounding marriage was a strategic error of Olympian proportions. In many ways—like the military debate—this issue was forced on gays. While it was never the highest priority among gay organizations and activists, the developments in Hawaii and, later, Vermont, helped push the issue of gay marriages to center stage. It is strangely disconcerting that the two most public issues identified with lesbian and gay rights have been inclusion in marriage and the military, two institutions notorious as sites for the reproduction of some of the most troublesome values and practices around masculinity and violence. But in a dominant culture in which masculinity and violence are such recurrent and persistent tropes, should this be any surprise?

TIES THAT BIND: THE FEMINIST CRITIQUE

FOR MANY GAY ACTIVISTS and theorists, access to marriage seems as straightforward as access to any social institution. Yet, for many others—lesbians in particular—access to marriage is like asking to have a piece of a very, well, *tasteless* pie. For lesbians—many of whom have been influenced and shaped by feminism—the institution of marriage is irrevocably mired in inequality and male dominance. Feminists from both the second and first waves (I think here particularly of Charlotte Perkins Gilman's eerie documentation of marriage as imprisonment in the feminist classic *The Yellow Wallpaper*) have analyzed marriage as one of the central mechanisms for the subordination of women. In more recent years, of course, feminists have skillfully revealed the violence at the heart of the marital bond. Wife battery and sexual abuse are now understood not to be simply an unfortunate outcome of idiosyncratically violent men but, rather, deeply embedded in the unequal structure of marriage and its sexist ideological underpinnings. Indeed, women are more likely to be violated by spouses than by anyone else. I am always surprised, in fact, when writers supportive of gay marriage blithely speed past this bleak fact, as if to imply that these overwhelming statistics speak nothing of *marriage itself.*

Lesbian feminists (and many feminist gay men) argue that the institution of marriage has a long and rather ugly history that should mitigate against participation by gay people of conscience. Marriage has historically been built on the suppression of women and the ownership of women and children by the male "head of household." While ownership no longer *literally* occurs, heterosexual marriage continues to operate to limit women's options and curtail women's independence. It is only recently that rape in marriage was even conceptualized as a crime, and wife battering continues to be one of the most underreported and underprosecuted offenses. Many gays and feminists argue that marriage is not some neutral institution—or an empty vessel—that can be blissfully transformed by the addition of same-sex participants. Indeed, marriage was built and organized as a means to institutionalize and enforce very particular and unequal divisions of gender, property, and childcare—divisions that both assumed and attempted to enforce female responsibility for childcare, food production, home maintenance, and male responsibility for mediating the outside world through wage labor and property ownership.

If, as many have argued, gay rights and women's rights are absolutely intertwined, then any gay argument for marriage that ignores or downplays the relationship of the marriage institution to institutionalized male dominance is problematic at best. Indeed, in recent years we have seen a restigmatizing of single women and single mothers—portrayed as either pathetically lonely career gals gone sour (*Ally McBeal*) or as the cancer in the body of domesticity, creating social havoc through reckless child rearing and neglectful daycare. While feminists pushed legislation to make it easier to leave marriages, the push now is to make it more difficult, through challenges to no-fault divorce and a rise in fundamentalist "covenant marriages." If feminists are right—that marriage is one of the cornerstones of the patriarchal family and a central site for the reproduction of gendered ideologies and behaviors—then gay inclusion must be seen in that light and therefore examined through that feminist lens. In other words, gay access to marriage

must be understood in terms of both sexual exclusion *and* gender domination. Paula Ettelbrick, in particular, has written eloquently of the unavoidable history of marriage as an institution of ownership, property rights, violence, and control that cannot be simply overturned with gay inclusion. In
her much-cited debate with Tom Stoddard in the now-defunct gay journal
Out/Look, Ettelbrick makes a convincing antimarriage argument that hinges
on a sophisticated gender-based critique joined with an antiassimilationist
gay rights analysis.[5]

Marriage advocates such as William Eskridge, writing in *The Case for
Same-Sex Marriage*, grant that marriage has historically been a form of subordination for women but do not believe that it *must* be the case. That seems
analogous to the fiction that there can be a "kinder, gentler" capitalism or, in
the words of George W. Bush, a "compassionate conservatism."[6] In addition,
it ignores the current status of marriage as an institution perpetuating gendered identities and gendered inequalities. Marriage has not only a check-
ered past; its present is equally troublesome.

TO TAME THE WILD BEAST: GAY MARRIAGE AS ANTIDOTE

IF MARRIAGE ITSELF REINFORCES structural inequalities within families,
it also privileges state-regulated, long-term pairing over other forms of intimacy and connectedness. Many in the gay movement—like their counterparts in the women's movement—have been critical of marriage not only
for its gender inequity and history of violence but also for the ways in which
it contributes to a *devaluing* of other ways of being sexual, loving, and nurturing. Many gays believe that families of choice are at least as valid as traditional marriage structures—and certainly as lasting. Anthropologist Kath
Weston (1991) and others have written convincingly of the ways in which
lesbians and gay men—so often disenfranchised from their families of origin—have created families of choice that serve many of the personal, emotional, and social functions of more traditional familial formations. In creating vast and intricate networks of friends and lovers, gay people have forged
intimacies and connections that often seem more lasting and durable than
the often tenuous family of origin. Weston argues that these families of
choice are not merely replicas of heterosexual families but actually create
new forms of mutual responsibility that are outside the more typical—and
typically gendered—roles inhabited by women and men in heterosexual
families.

This is not just a banal argument for diversity of familial forms; rather, it is about advocating models of love, support, and intimacy that actively dethrone the sexual/familial couple and present instead ever-expanding webs of relationships—ex-lovers, their partners or lovers, old friends, blood kin, and so on. Indeed, one can see this as a gay gift to the bankrupt models of middle-class white heterosexuality that "tend to isolate couples from their larger families and sometimes from friends—especially if they are ex-lovers" (Browning 1997:133).

Yet if gays succeed in sanctifying the couple as the primary social unit (the one that gets financial and legal benefits), does that help to set up a hierarchy of intimacy that replicates the heterosexual one rather than challenging or altering it? Gay marriage might grant visibility and acceptance to gay marrieds, but it will not necessarily challenge homophobia (or the nuclear family) itself; indeed, it might simply demonize nonmarried gays as the "bad gays" (uncivilized, promiscuous, irresponsible) while it reluctantly embraces the "good gays" who settle down and get married. Many gays therefore argue that to participate in this institution is not only to assimilate into the dominant heterosexist way of relating but also to give further credence to an institution that has been built on the backs of both sexism and heterosexism.

While certainly there is no direct correlation between desire to marry and desire to assimilate, testimonies and anecdotal evidence suggest that many gays who desire marriage ceremonies are precisely those gays who are most interested in exhibiting their sameness to straight America. In particular, they are often more religiously identified and more anxious to assert the absolute validity of long-term commitments over other forms of loving. There is no doubt that many gay people—in constructing ceremonies of commitment—try very hard to find ways to render them differently. Because of their very nature, gay ceremonies have a variety and diversity not often witnessed in heterosexual ceremonies. In Ellen Lewin's thoughtful and fascinating tour of lesbian and gay commitment ceremonies (see chapter 3, this volume), she rightly stresses the often uneasy mixture of the traditional with the "queer" in the formation of these ceremonies, the mixing of genres and ideologies implying a sort of postmodern pastiche of gender-bending imagery.

Nevertheless, the desire to mimic heterosexual pairings is strong (and understandable, given the relative invisibility of alternative forms of loving). Indeed, Lewin betrays just such an assumption when she refers to our "failure to marry." But is it simply a failure, an exclusion, an omission, or can we imagine it as a rejection, a challenge, a bold act of refusal? Lewin identifies gay unease at heterosexual weddings as "excruciating" because of our inability to be "recognized as worthy of such celebration" rather than resulting from our rejection of an institution we find deeply flawed (see chapter 3, this volume). Is the dream of a seamless inclusion really so foolproof?

Many gays, such as conservative writer and former editor of the *New Republic*, Andrew Sullivan, strongly believe that the right to marry is crucial to the "maturity" of the gay movement. Writing early on in 1989, Sullivan argues against domestic partnerships and for legalizing gay marriage. He is wary of the legal ramifications of domestic partnerships (who qualifies?) but is even more concerned that the concept of domestic partnerships undermines the centrality and hegemony of the institution of marriage, arguing that "Society has good reason to extend legal advantages to heterosexuals who choose the formal sanction of marriage over simply living together" (1989:20). His argument, like those of many other conservative gays, is actually a familiar and vaguely Victorian one: marriage tames and civilizes the wild beast that is Man; without it we would be awash in a sea of sexual depravity, flitting madly about from partner to partner, never tending to the business of the day. Like his family values counterparts on the Christian right, Sullivan sees marriage as the "anchor . . . in the chaos of sex and relationships to which we are all prone" (1989:20). Now, many would disagree, arguing instead that the metaphor might not be an anchor but rather an albatross, particularly heavy around the necks of women. Not coincidentally, Sullivan's arguments for marriage are framed within an understanding of the gay movement that interprets the Stonewall generation as washed-out radicals, too blinded by their own perverse desire for liberation to be able to grow up and assimilate. But brave young souls like himself have reckoned with this immaturity and now agree that "a need to rebel has quietly ceded to a desire to belong" (1989:20). More recently, Sullivan has testified before the House Judiciary subcommittee hearings on the Defense of Marriage Act, arguing that endorsing same-sex marriage means being in favor of stability, monogamy, and responsibility (U.S. House Hearing 1996); in short, being "profamily" in the worst sort of antifeminist way. His is, as he himself admits, a conservative argument for gay marriage, a claim that same-sex marriage will have two beneficent outcomes: forcing homosexuals into more committed and monogamous relationships and reinforcing the centrality and dominance of marriage as the primary social unit.

Georgetown University law professor William Eskridge recently published a more sophisticated and scholarly version of the Sullivan argument.

For Eskridge, there are many reasons to pursue marriage, including the one I find most compelling—the civil equality issue, and Eskridge makes a strong case here. But beyond the obvious (gays should not be excluded from any realm of society), Eskridge echoes Sullivan's argument about the "civilizing" influence of marriage on gay men in particular, men whose wanton promiscuity needs to be tamed by the imposition of marriage. Not only does Eskridge invoke the same ideology of naturally wild men,[7] he also joins Sullivan in framing the argument around a very particular and truncated historical narrative. Eerily like mainstream heterosexual stories of gay life (see particularly Maria Shriver's voice-over in her TV special on the "gay '90s"), Eskridge creates a history of radical gay activists and sexual liberationists giving way to commitment-bound, home-owning, AIDS-fearing "guppies" for whom marriage is the bright light at the end of the tunnel. Not only does this paint a false picture of the demise of gay radicalism (it is still alive and well, thank god) but it also completely ignores the reality of nonwhite, poor, working-class gays—the majority of course. So marriage will civilize nasty promiscuous gay men (and what of lesbians?) and, in so doing, will make them more acceptable (his language) to straights. Like Sullivan, Eskridge too argues for marriage over domestic partnership, because "most lesbians and gay men want something more than domestic partnership; they want to be in a committed relationship at some point in their lifetime" (Eskridge 1996:78). Thus, for these gay men, marriage is the *real* sign of a committed relationship (thank you Dan Quayle!)—everything else is just silly kid's play. In making his argument for gay marriage as profamily, Eskridge joins in the chorus of single-mother bashing that has characterized the family values debate since Dan Quayle let fly at Murphy Brown by claiming that "some studies have found that children of lesbian couples are better adjusted than children of single heterosexual mothers, presumably because there are two parents in the household. If this finding can be generalized, it yields the ironic point that state prohibitions against same-sex marriages may be antifamily and antichildren" (Eskridge 1996:13). So, in arguing that gay marriage promotes a sound environment for raising children, Eskridge (perhaps unintentionally) falls into the worst sort of conservative assumptions of two-parent stability over just about anything else.[8] In explicitly linking marriage with parenting, Eskridge (and many others, for this has been a consistent point among gay marriage advocates) forgoes a more radical and nuanced critique of the family (and thus ignores the substantive work of feminist scholars) and further conflates partnering (a presumably sexual relationship between consenting adults) and parenting (a relationship of profound structural dependency). This conflation and merger (memorialized in the nursery rhyme "first comes love, then comes marriage, then comes baby in the baby carriage") is the fulcrum of the heterosexist nuclear family, confusing sexual intimacy with family, the desire to parent with sexual desire, interdependency with dependency.[9]

In this conservative argument for gay marriage—and for its civilizing influence on gays in need of civilizing—there is an implicit and often explicit denigration of radical attempts to challenge both marriage and the family. During the early days of both the women's movement and the gay movement, a critique of the family and of marriage was integral to a critique of patriarchy and heterosexism generally. The Gay Liberation Front made a statement in 1969—right after Stonewall—that was crystal clear in its denunciation of marriage: "We expose the institution of marriage as one of the most insidious and basic sustainers of the system."[10] For writers such as Eskridge, Sullivan, and Bruce Bawer (and, one might add, most heterosexuals), this kind of statement is one they would like to forget. For them it is a remnant of an extremist and liberationist past that must be transcended if gays are to fully enter into mainstream society and take their rightful place alongside Mr. and Mrs. Cleaver. But for many of us these are glorious statements of which we are proud. They indicate a thoughtful and thoroughgoing critique of social institutions that have played a serious role in the subjugation of women and the enforcement of heterosexuality. To be liberated from these institutions—and then perhaps to create ones that build not on those shaky foundations but on new and sturdier ones—is seen as a worthy and ethical goal.

Like many others, Eskridge seems to want to have it both ways. He argues that gays have no desire to "shake up" the institution of marriage and familial structures, they only want to be allowed access to them. But these same marriage advocates simultaneously argue that legalizing same-sex marriages will radically alter marriage as we know it and bring substantial change to an historically fraught institution. Typically, the second argument is made by more progressive gay activists and scholars who are painfully aware of the problems in the institution of marriage and are trying to support gay civil rights without promoting a thoughtless assimilationism. But it is not at all clear that adding lesbians and gays to the marriage stew will necessarily alter its flavor, just as it is not at all clear that allowing open gays to serve in the military would alter the structure of the military. Embedded, powerful institutions are funny things. True, no institution is impenetrable or completely inelastic to change. Nevertheless, powerful and hierarchical ones such as the military or marriage are not going to be easily transformed.

BEYOND MARRIAGE: RETHINKING INTIMACY, SEX, COMMUNITY

YET I DO HAVE some sympathy for the internal transformation argument. Indeed, the extraordinary Vermont decision sent unexpected shivers up my spine even as I winced at much of the language used to support it. In that sense, the Christian right is right: the creation of gay and lesbian families *does* pose a fundamental challenge to traditional family values. For if "traditional family values" is just another way of stating the claim that heterosexual, nuclear families (with Dad bringing home the bacon and Mom cooking it up for him and the kids) is the single "correct" form of family, then our families most certainly do stir things up. As much as straights and many gays might want to argue that there is no difference between the way gays create families and the way heterosexuals do, it seems hard to believe that the structure of exclusion and discrimination that surrounds gay life cannot in some way impact gay family life. Because gays parent and partner in a world brimming with hatred, where they have little legal recourse to fight either overt or covert discrimination, gay families can never be simple replicas of heterosexual families.

Yet it is not at all clear that, say, same-sex marriages will present a *fundamental* challenge to the institution of marriage or that gay parents will construct truly new ways of raising children. Is it possible that the creation of gay families through marriage (or commitment ceremonies) and the raising of children is the *least* challenging aspect of gay and lesbian life? Is the formation of gay families the nail in the assimilationist coffin, linking gays irrevocably with mainstream heterosexuality? Or do these moves shake up heterosexual dominance like nothing else, permanently altering the very definitions of family? These are, as we social scientists like to say, empirical questions. But the argument that gay marriage, for example, will *necessarily* alter (sexist, heterosexist) marriage as we know it seems far-fetched. Have the Log Cabinites altered the GOP? If gays marry from within the dominant heterosexual frameworks—invoking dangerous ideologies of familialism, faith, and fidelity—the prospect of internal combustion fizzles out.

In addition, the very place of family is often a fraught one for lesbians and gay men. While the larger social world offers few sites of freedom for gays, the family is all too often the site of the most outrageous rejection and brutality. For so many lesbians and gays, the family is not only the first place where they experienced homophobia but also the place where they felt most betrayed, most alone, most violated. Like battered women beaten by those who pledge their love, the rejection of gay people by their families is one of our ugliest social secrets. Some of the saddest stories gay people tell are the stories of family—remaining in the closet for fear of rejection, being kicked out of the home, being told you are no longer a son/daughter, being kept away from the other kids, being beaten, being told you are sick, telling your mother it is not "her fault," being disinherited, being shunned. It should be no surprise then, that "family" remains a highly charged arena for lesbians and gay men. It is ironic that one of the coded ways gays have of acknowledging other gays is to ask if they "are family." And in this referencing, we hint at a utopian construction of "families of choice" that is not bound by definitions of blood, of law, of sex, of gender.

My objection to marriage, therefore, rests on any number of arguments. The feminist critique of marriages's past and present is, in itself, enough for me. And the gay liberationist argument against assimilation into the dominant heterosexual gestalt—and the way that this assimilation can denude us of our specificity and cultural uniqueness as it claims our allegiance—is a powerful statement against easy adoption of heterosexual mores. But my objection is not simply to marriage as it exists (e.g., with the implication being that if it were less sexist, had a different history, less homophobic, I would embrace it) but, rather, to the valorization of coupledom and familialism that marriage implies.

If granted inclusion in the marriage club, will gays and lesbians be similarly pressured to marry as are their heterosexual counterparts? As many have argued,[11] marriage is hardly a choice. Like its partner in crime, heterosexuality, marriage is largely *compulsory*: if the economic benefits don't get you, the social ones surely will do the trick. As feminists consistently argue, the institution of marriage is inextricably tied to the heterosexual nuclear family, as well as to the merger of parenting and partnering, intimacy and financial interdependency that is so central to our truncated vision of family. Marriage is not simply an isolated institution, nor some innate desire. On the contrary, marriage signifies a whole chain of equivalences and relationships that are therefore naturalized and valorized as the single true model for intimate life: the linking of long-term sexuality with financial interdependence, the merger of partnering with parenting, the assumption of sexual desire chained to emotional intimacy. Lesbians and gays should do all they can to dismantle those conflations and to continue to envision and enact ways of caring and loving that reinvent family, intimacy, parenting. Working to end *all* marriage as a legal institution (and to instead provide meaningful social and financial supports for relations of dependency and need) would do much more to challenge the noxious politics of family values than getting married ourselves. I'd much rather see a utopian future of unmarried love and lust—for our heterosexual brothers and sisters too—than a dystopian future where marriage and familialism continue to trump values of community and care.

NOTES

1. According to statistics from the Human Rights Campaign (garnered from the FBI), hate crimes against lesbians and gays (or those perceived as lesbian or gay) increased to 14 percent of the total of all reported hate crimes in 1997, up from 11.6 percent in 1996. In addition, attacks against lesbians and gays are becoming more violent, indicated most dramatically by the brutal murder of Wyoming gay student Matthew Shepard in October 1998.

2. The commercialization of marriage is obviously disturbing as well. What does this say about the supposedly "natural" drive to marry, given its relentless marketing? Gays have gotten in on the act as well. Just the other day I received a catalogue in the mail for "Family Celebrations," billing itself as "America's First Wedding & Special Occasions Catalog for the Gay and Lesbian Community." Yet the emphasis is clearly on weddings or other such ceremonies and firmly embedded in a traditional family motif (even the kid's stuff references two mommies or two daddies). Where is the paraphernalia to celebrate single motherhood? Deep and abiding friendships? Political alliances?

3. The construction of gays as congenitally unable to negotiate the vicissitudes of adulthood (read marriage and kids) is a common theme not only in TV neoliberal discourse but also in gay conservative discourse. (See particularly Bawer 1996; Sullivan 1997).

4. Sullivan has used the biological argument to different effect in his testimony before the subcommittee on the 1996 Defense of Marriage Act.

5. Paula Ettelbrick (1989) in the much cited debate with Tom Stoddard.

6. This is not to suggest that marriage is identical to capitalism but, rather, to argue *rhetorically* that institutions forged in the fires of structural inequality cannot simply be remade.

7. This ideology is not only Victorian but clearly neoconservative as well: neocon guru George Gilder was making the same argument for the Moral Majority in the '80s.

8. In this chapter I am focusing rather narrowly on gay marriage. For a more extended discussion of gay family life, including issues around child rearing, see my forthcoming book *All the Rage: The Story of Gay Visibility in America*.

9. Feminist legal theorist Martha Fineman has made a controversial and compelling argument that has important implications for rethinking this debate. In her book *The Neutered Mother, the Sexual Family, and Other Twentieth-Century Tragedies* (New York: Routledge, 1995), Fineman argues that in order to create a less gendered social order (and a less unequal one as well) we need to separate parenting and partnering and socially and economically valorize relations of dependency instead of supposed peer relations. The conflation of parenting and partnering (and the assumption that one leads to the other) sets the stage for the conflation of relations of dependency and relations of mutuality. As Fineman argues, most of our social supports go to preserving the marital union, and our supports for dependent children are bound up with our valorization of a two-spousal unit (1995). Indeed, as Chambers reports (see chapter 19), spouses cannot be summarily written out of a will, whereas children can. Yet, presumably, the relation of parent to child (or any other relationship of dependency) is not comparable to that of adult sexual partners. Dependencies are in all relationships, to be sure, but to economically and socially support a relationship in which fundamental dependency is not the presumption seems to help create a context for the confusion of intimacy with dependency, social legitimacy with state support. Perhaps gays would do better to support legislation that removes marriage as a legal and economic category, while at the same time creating frameworks to socially, legally, and economically support relations of real dependency: parent to child, caretaker to caretakee, able-bodied to the disabled they care for, etc.

10. "Gay Revolution Comes Out," *The Rat*, August 12–26, 1969, p. 7, cited in Eskridge 1996, p. 53.

11. See especially Polikoff 1996.

REFERENCES

Bawer, Bruce, ed. 1996. *Beyond Queer: Challenging Gay Left Orthodoxy*. New York: Free Press.

Browning, Frank. 1997. "Why Marry?" In Andrew Sullivan, ed., *Same-Sex Marriage: Pro and Con*, p. 133. New York: Vintage (originally in the *New York Times*, April 17, 1996).

Chambers, David. 1996. "What If? The Legal Consequences of Marriage and the Legal Needs of Lesbian and Gay Male Couples." *Michigan Law Review* 95 (2): 447–91.

Eskridge, William N. 1996. *The Case for Same-Sex Marriage: From Sexual Liberty to Civilized Commitment.* New York: Free Press.

Ettelbrick, Paula. 1989. "Since When Is Marriage a Path to Liberation?" *OUT/LOOK National Gay and Lesbian Quarterly* 9: 14–16.

Fineman, Martha Albertson. 1995. *The Neutered Mother, the Sexual Family, and Other Twentieth-century Tragedies.* New York: Routledge.

Ingrassia, Michele. 1994. "The Limits of Tolerance?" *Newsweek*, February 14, p. 47.

Isaacson, Walter et al. 1989. "Should Gays Have Marriage Rights?" *Time*, November 20, p. 101.

Lacayo, Richard. 1998. "The New Gay Struggle" *Time*, October 26, pp. 32–36.

Polikoff, Nancy. 1996. "Marriage as Choice? Since When?" *Gay Community News* 24, no. 3/4 (Winter/Spring): 26–27.

"Straight Talk About Gays." 1993. *U.S. News & World Report*, July 5, p. 42.

Strongheart, Amy Adams Squire. 1994. "A Foundation for Same-Sex Marriage," *St. Louis Post-Dispatch*, February 10, p. 7B.

Sullivan, Andrew. 1989. "Here Comes the Groom" *The New Republic*, August 28, p. 20.

Sullivan, Andrew, ed. 1997. *Same-Sex Marriage: Pro and Con.* New York: Vintage.

U.S. House Hearing. 1996. *Subcommittee on the Constitution of the Committee on The Judiciary, on H.R. 3396,* Defense of Marriage Act. 104th Cong., 2d sess., May 15.

Weston, Kath. 1991. *Families We Choose: Lesbians, Gays, Kinship.* New York: Columbia University Press.

21

Defense, Morality, Civil Rights, and Family: The Evolution of Lesbian and Gay Issues in the U.S. Congress

Donald P. Haider-Markel

CONGRESS AND EVOLVING ISSUE AREAS

DRIVEN BY CONCERNS OVER same-gender marriage litigation in Hawaii and scoring political points during an election year, the 104th Congress passed the so-called Defense of Marriage Act (DOMA) during the summer and fall of 1996. The law defines marriage as the union between a man and a women, prevents same-sex married couples from receiving federal benefits, and allows states to refuse to recognize same-sex marriages from other states. While the necessity and constitutionality of DOMA has been questioned, the bill may be the most important piece of national legislation to date affecting the lives of lesbians, gays, and their families. DOMA, however, was not the first time Congress dealt with homosexuality or homosexual family issues. In fact, since 1964 Congress has voted on over 270 amendments, motions, and bills that, in one form or another, have addressed issues concerning lesbians, gays, and their families.

As students of the policy process we might ask several questions related to gay politics in Congress, including (1) how have issues involving homosexuality evolved in Congress; (2) how do legislators make decisions when voting on a relatively new and evolving issue area, such as homosexuality; and (3) how have gay issues fared in Congress? I address these questions in the three sections of this chapter. In the first section I explore the historical evolution of lesbian and gay issues in Congress. Section two explains the findings from legislative voting behavior research on gay issues in Congress.

In the third section I examine the legislative outcomes in the conflict over homosexuality and how these outcomes have changed over time.

FRAMING THE ISSUES AND ISSUE EVOLUTION: GAY ISSUES IN CONGRESS

LEGISLATORS MUST SOMETIMES DEVELOP policy to deal with new issues, but issues do not appear on a blank slate—politicians, interest groups, and citizens all play a role in defining (or framing) issues. How an issue is framed will determine whether or not it reaches the political agenda, what venues are suitable for its discussion, what actors will be mobilized and/or allowed to participate in the policy process, the focus of policy proposals, and who wins and who loses within political institutions (Baumgartner and Jones 1993:16–30). I argue below that homosexuality reached the political agenda of Congress because of concerns raised by the defense community over national security, by Evangelical Christians over traditional values and the family, by lesbian and gay activists over civil rights, and by medical practitioners and civil libertarians, among others, over AIDS.

Each of these groups defined homosexual issues differently, but most important, each tried to tie homosexual issues to strong and positive symbols (or frames) in American politics. For example, during the 1950s members of the defense community linked homosexuality with the threat posed by communism (D'Emilio 1992:68). Evangelicals framed their opposition to homosexuality in terms of declining moral standards, the rise of secular humanism, and the troubled American family in the 1960s (Vaid 1995:320–21). Meanwhile, throughout the 1960s and 1970s lesbian and gay activists argued that homosexuals were an oppressed group facing discrimination (Vaid 1995:106). In the 1980s the AIDS epidemic was linked to homosexuality, thereby expanding the scope of homosexual issues. AIDS also brought new political actors into the debate over homosexuality, and these actors each brought their own values, judgments, and issue frames to the debate.

SETTING THE AGENDA ON HOMOSEXUALITY: HISTORICAL OVERVIEW

EARLY CONGRESSIONAL ACTION ON homosexuality focused on homosexuals as a national security threat. Framing homosexuality in terms of national defense not only gave Congress jurisdiction to address the issue of homosexuality, it also limited what actors could participate and what specific issues could be addressed. Congress first addressed homosexuality during a 1920 Senate investigation into " 'immoral conditions' of a homosexual nature at the naval training station in Newport, Rhode Island" (D'Emilio 1992:64).

In the 1950s members of Congress expanded the debate over homosexuality by linking homosexuality to communism, thereby placing homosexuals on the wrong side of Cold War politics. The Senate released a report on the security threat homosexuals posed to the federal government in December 1950, and the issue was also raised during the 1953 McCarthy hearings when witnesses suggested that homosexual government employees could be blackmailed by communist spies (Adam 1995:60–65; D'Emilio 1992:59–60). Members of Congress also attacked homosexual activist groups; in 1954 Senator Wiley (R-WI) convinced the U.S. postmaster to block a gay magazine (*ONE*) from using the U.S. mail because of its devotion to the "advancement of sexual perversion" (Streitmatter 1995:32, 343).

Framing homosexuality as a security threat and as immoral created an alliance between cold warriors and Evangelical Christians in the early 1960s and also limited the ability of homosexual activists to participate in the debate. The alliance reflected broader trends in American society and the Republican Party. At the time, Evangelical Christians were increasing their political involvement because of the threat to traditional values posed by a Supreme Court ruling on school prayer and the increasing demands of the black Civil Rights movement (see Diamond 1995:104–6; Horne 1996).

This political debate set the stage for the first known congressional vote on a gay-related issue. The early lobbying efforts of a homosexual group, the Mattachine Society, so enraged Representative John Dowdy that in May 1963 he initiated hearings on the issue and introduced a bill to revoke Mattachine's permit to raise funds. During congressional hearings, Mattachine representatives tried to frame homosexuality as a civil rights issue, but committee members used the venue to speak against the immorality of homosexuality and to question witnesses on deviant sexual behavior. The bill, H.R. 5990, overwhelmingly passed the House on August 11, 1964 (D'Emilio 1983:156–57). While gays and lesbians had gained limited political access during the consideration of H.R. 5990, cold warriors and Evangelicals were still firmly in control of how the issue was framed.

In the early 1970s gay activists increasingly attempted to frame homosexuality in positive terms, stressing that discrimination should be the issue under consideration. Gay activists achieved limited success in their efforts to redefine the issue when a bill was introduced by two New York Democrats in May 1974 to extend civil rights protections to gays and lesbians (Thompson 1994). The bill would have prevented discrimination against lesbians and gays in employment, housing, credit, and public accommodations. It failed in committee but was reintroduced in 1975 (Vaid 1995:62). Both bills would have changed civil rights policy by revising the 1964 *Civil Rights Act* to include sexual orientation, a clear effort by a few Democrats (lesbian and gay civil rights were not endorsed by the Democratic Party until the late 1970s) to define the issue as civil rights and to frame the policy change as incremental. Framing the issue as one of civil rights allowed gays to expand the definition of homosexual issues and thereby mobilize nonparticipants, such as ethnic minorities and other traditional Democrats.

The effort to mobilize nonparticipants continued as bills to protect gays from discrimination were introduced in Congress every year following 1974. House committee hearings were first held on the issue in October 1980; six witnesses provided testimony in support of the law and two witnesses opposed the measure (Congressional Information Service 1981:H341–25). A Senate version of the bill was first introduced in 1979. After two decades without a floor vote, legislation concerning antigay discrimination was narrowed to cover discrimination in employment in 1994 (Vaid 1995:7). Even this limited legislation, however, did not reach the floor of either chamber until the Senate voted against it (50–49) in September 1996.

As shown in figure 21.1, gay-related issues increasingly reached the congressional agenda as the 1970s progressed.[1] The Congressional Information Service (CIS) lists the participation of gay activists at several congressional hearings dealing with diverse issues, including cutting Washington D.C. funding of homosexual venereal disease clinics (1976:H181–77.29, S181–55.4), television portrayal of homosexuals (1977:H501–16.4), and alcoholism treatment for lesbians (1977:S541–9).

Gay family issues also began to emerge, including the issue of adding questions in the census to identify homosexuals and gay couples (1979:H621–37.2) and the repeal of federal welfare benefits to homosexuals and their partners under H.R. 4122, the *Family Protection Act* (1979:H782–45). Congressional attention to such diverse issues suggests that gay groups, and their opponents, were able to expand the scope of conflict over homosexuality. Furthermore, gay groups were able to change the institutional venues where homosexuality was addressed. Homosexuality was increasingly discussed in nondefense-related congressional committees.

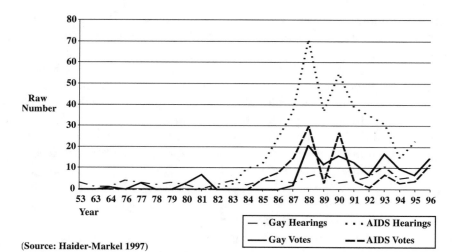

FIGURE 21.1 Congressional Committee Hearings and Floor Votes on Lesbian and Gay Issues 1953–1996

The greatest expansion of homosexual issues, however, occurred during the 1980s with the advent of AIDS—as AIDS reached the congressional agenda, gay-related legislation was increasingly discussed in committee hearings and voted on in each chamber (see figure 21.1). The expansion of homosexual issues by AIDS constituted an expansion of the scope of conflict over framing homosexual issues; as gay issues were expanded to include AIDS, new actors were brought into the debate, including civil liberties groups, medical professionals, and members of Congress who had previously been uninterested in gay-related issues.

While the attachment of AIDS to homosexuality delayed government response to the disease, it eventually allowed gay activists and interest groups to find more support in Congress (an issue I return to later). The AIDS epidemic brought renewed visibility to gay issues, with each chamber increasingly considering floor votes on AIDS and homosexuality. In fact, with the first congressional hearing on AIDS in 1982, AIDS became the focal point of most 1980s congressional activity regarding homosexuals (see figure 21.1). Gay lobbyists were successful in convincing Congress to spend money on AIDS by 1985, but nearly all legislation increasing AIDS funding in later years contained amendments prohibiting any of the funds from being used to promote homo-sexuality (Vaid 1995:139–40). For example, in 1989 the Senate adopted, by voice vote, an amendment to AIDS-funding legislation that prevented the distribution or production of materials for schoolchildren that would "promote or encourage homosexuality, or use words stating that homosexuality is 'normal,' or 'natural,' or healthy'" (Congressional Quarterly 1989:712). Also, not all AIDS legislation was directed at research and education. For example, S 1352 (1987), would have required mandatory HIV/AIDS testing.

Evangelicals expanded the conflict again in the late 1980s by prodding conservative members of Congress to repeal funding for the National Endowment for the Arts (NEA) after controversy erupted over the homo-erotic photography of Robert Mapplethorpe (Bull and Gallagher 1996:164; Streitmatter 1995, 289). While Congress did cut $45,000 from the NEA's budget in 1989, the expansion of conflict also helped to rally liberal members of Congress who hoped to save the NEA from extinction (Bull and Gallagher 1996:164). And in 1990 Democrats were able to remove language from the NEA reauthorization that characterized homoerotic art as obscene (Tuller 1990). As had occurred in the past, each time homosexual issues were expanded, new actors became involved and existing actors became more divided along ideological and partisan lines.

During the early 1990s gay lobbyists achieved some of their greatest gains in Congress—the *Ryan White CARE Act* was passed to provide funding for AIDS, sexual orientation was included in the *Hate Crimes Statistics Act*, and the *Americans with Disabilities Act* prevented discrimination against persons with HIV/AIDS. In 1992 gays saw their political stature increase as they were credited with assisting in the election of Bill Clinton, gay members of Congress retained their seats, and gay PACs contributed more than $760,000 to congressional candidates (see Bull and Gallagher 1996:95).

As the 1990s progressed, however, gay lobbyists faced a number of devastating losses. In 1993 an increasingly conservative Congress defeated the attempt to lift the ban on gays in the military, replacing existing administrative rules with the now infamous "don't-ask, don't-tell" policy. In part, the battle over gays in the military was along the old issue-cleavage created by cold warriors. Other setbacks included increasing levels of opposition to funding for AIDS programs (such as project Aries), the ongoing efforts by Congress to prevent Washington, D.C., from using federal funds in providing domestic partners benefits, and the passage of the so-called Defense of Marriage Act.

DOMA (H.R. 3396) sought to deny federal benefits to same-sex married couples and to allow states to deny the recognition of such marriages. The bill was introduced by Representative Robert Barr (R-GA) as part of a Republican package of "family-values" legislation.[2] Barr argued that proponents of same-sex marriage wanted "to throw open the doors of the U.S. Treasury . . . to be raided by the homosexual movement" (Dupuis 1998). Representative Barney Frank (D-MA) failed 103–311 in his attempt to amend the bill to limit its scope. With the support of openly gay Representative Steve Gunderson (R-WI), a California Democrat tried to amend the bill with language that would have required the General Accounting Office to study the differences and benefits, rights, and privileges available to persons in a marriage and persons in a domestic partnership. This amendment failed as well, and the bill finally passed 342–67, with some Democrats (65), one independent (Bernard Sanders, VT), and one Republican (Steve Gunderson, WI) opposing the measure (Haider-Markel 1997:328–29).

House hearings on DOMA contained arguments on morality, civil rights, and gay families. For example, Representative James Sensenbrenner (R-WI) argued that "one of the problems our society faces today is the erosion of the family and the erosion of the marriage because the marriage is the bond that keeps the family together, and that's why I strongly support this legislation" (U.S. House Hearing 1996:33). Meanwhile, gay activist Andrew Sullivan argued against DOMA, countering that allowing same-sex marriages would "promote stability, responsibility, the disciplines of family life among people" (U.S. House Hearing 1996:119).

DOMA hearings in the Senate also revolved around the notion of a "normal" family and the decision as to whether that definition could be expanded. The hearings included testimony from religious conservatives and gay activists, including the president of Parents, Families, and Friends of Lesbians and Gays (PFLAG). While Senate Democrats questioned the constitutionality and political timing of DOMA, Senator Orin Hatch (R-UT) argued that of those values deserving protection, "family values . . . rank at the highest level . . . [this] . . . isn't a political issue. It is a very important moral and family issue" (U.S. Senate Hearing 1996:16). Gary Bauer, president of the Family Research Council, testified that there "is mounting evidence that the mother-and-father family is the foundation of civilization. . . . [DOMA] . . . is a powerful antidote to the destructive trend that has gripped this country. . . . It is not hatred to prefer normalcy. It is not bigotry to resist radical redefinition of marriage. It is not intolerance to believe in traditional morality" (U.S. Senate Hearing 1996:22–3). The president of PFLAG countered these arguments by saying that "you cannot defend marriage by attacking our gay sons and lesbian daughters" (U.S. Senate Hearing 1996:49).

House and Senate floor debate on DOMA largely mirrored the committee testimony. In referring to DOMA, Representative Steve Largent (R-OK) argued that there "is absolutely nothing that we can do that is more important than protecting our families and protecting the institution of marriage" (U.S. House Debate 1996:7276). House Democrats who opposed the bill chose not to argue their point in terms of the legitimacy of gay families but instead to argue that DOMA was unconstitutional and a political maneuver during a presidential election year. However, Representative Steve Gunderson (R-WI) did argue that Congress should consider adopting a national domestic-partnership law for gay couples (U.S. House Debate 1996:7493). Finally, perhaps the most dramatic element in the Senate debate was Senator Robert Byrd (D-WV) holding up his family Bible to support the legislation and his definition of the American family.

With the 104th Congress and DOMA, Congress has generally grown more conservative in the 1990s, even though the 105th Congress (1997–98) did provide some victories for lesbians and gays, especially on gay-family issues. For example, efforts to overturn President Clinton's 1998 ban on sexual-orientation discrimination for federal employees were defeated and AIDS funding reached record levels—exceeding $4 billion.

Gay groups gained a large victory for gay families by eventually blocking Republican efforts to pass legislation prohibiting unmarried couples from jointly adopting children in the District of Columbia. Republicans had introduced similar legislation in the Appropriations Committee for three years, but each time the measure was defeated. In 1998 the measure, introduced as an amendment to the D.C. budget bill, was again defeated in committee. The defeat came after openly gay Representative Jim Kolbe (R-AZ) gave an impassioned speech against the amendment, pointing out how two gay men he knows have provided a "loving home to an orphan child from Russia" (Chibbaro 1998). However, Republican leaders chose to ignore the committee action and allowed Representative Steve Largent (R-OK) to introduce the amendment on the House floor. Ironically, Largent argued that "these are real kids. . . . It is simply wrong to turn them into trophies from the culture war" (Holland 1998). The amendment passed along party lines 227–192 but was later removed in conference committee.

Gay activists also killed legislation that would have denied certain federal funds to localities with domestic-partnership laws. Representative Frank Riggs (R–CA) had introduced a measure that would have prevented San Francisco from using federal housing money to enforce its requirement that city contractors provide same-sex partner benefits (Holland 1998). This measure was also removed in conference committee.

Recent failures for gay lobbyists include efforts to pass a stronger hate-crime bill that would include sexual orientation; progress toward having James Hormel, a gay activist and philanthropist, confirmed as U.S. ambassador to Luxembourg; efforts to block an amendment cutting funding for an AIDS housing program; and yet another amendment that prevented federal money from being used in needle-exchange programs to reduce the spread of AIDS (Chibbaro 1998; Holland 1998). In each case arguments framing the issues as moral concerns won over those who argued in terms of civil rights.

To summarize, the main actors in the congressional debate over homosexuality have each tried to frame the debate in their own terms. Prior to the 1960s the dominant actors in the congressional venue were able to define homosexuality in terms of national security and along the ideological divisions of cold war politics. Cold warriors and Evangelicals within the Republican Party formed an alliance around the notion of homosexuality as immoral. These groups were able to frame the debate in their terms until the 1970s when gay activists gained limited access to Congress and the congressional agenda. As gay activists gained access, they began a process of expanding the debate over homosexuality to include the notion of gay civil rights. The advent of AIDS in the 1980s allowed gay activists *and* Evangelicals to expand the debate over homosexuality— gays gained increasing access to the congressional agenda and were able to enlist the support of medical professionals. Evangelicals, meanwhile, tried to create a negative connection between AIDS and homosexuality by arguing that AIDS was God's retribution on homosexuals for immoral behavior.

If recent trends are a good indicator, lesbian and gay issues will remain on the congressional agenda and a multitude of actors will have input as to what this agenda includes. No single group or coalition has been able to dominate the framing of gay issues since the mid-1980s, making it unlikely that gays will always lose or win in Congress. Understanding the historical evolution of gay and lesbian issues in Congress, however, does provide a framework for understanding how legislators might vote on these issues.

UNDERSTANDING LEGISLATIVE VOTING BEHAVIOR ON
LESBIAN AND GAY ISSUES

WHILE MANY ACTORS IN the congressional arena clearly have strong opinions on homosexuality and the issues involved, it is not immediately clear how the average member of Congress makes decisions on these or other relatively new issues. Because of the multitude of ways gay issues have been defined, the average member of Congress is likely to be confused when these issues reach a floor vote—is the issue about morality and threats to traditional values, as argued by Senator Jessie Helms (R–NC) and others, or is it about civil rights and the American notion of private life, as argued by Representative Barney Frank (D–MA), among others? Which values an individual member attaches to gay issues will likely influence his or her voting decisions. Theoretically, a number of forces come to bear on how legislators vote, including partisan affiliation, personal ideology, religious affiliation, constituency preferences, and interest groups (Smith 1995).

The party affiliation of legislators is most often the single best predictor of voting behavior (Fiorina 1974; Kingdon 1989). On its surface, the debate over gay issues has involved a rather high degree of partisanship, with the Republican party's view of homosexual issues being dominated by a morality interpretation and the Democratic party's view dominated by the civil rights interpretation (see Bull and Gallagher 1996). When making voting decisions, however, legislators do not simply rely on how their party defines an issue; they are also likely to be influenced by their political ideology (Tatalovich and Schier 1993). Conservatives from either party are likely to be less sympathetic to gay issues, whereas liberals should be more likely to support a progay position (Yang 1998:7).

On issues that may be perceived as involving morality, such as abortion or homosexuality, the religious affiliation of legislators can play a role in legislative decision-making (see Benson and Williams 1982; Day 1994). Legislators affiliated with more conservative religions should be more likely to interpret gay issues in terms of morality, making them more likely to oppose any legislation positive toward gays.

Political scientists have also assumed that constituencies influence legislative voting behavior. The idea is that more liberal districts will tend to elect more liberal candidates (probably Democrats) and those that are more conservative will tend to elect more conservative candidates (probably Republicans). Once elected, however, legislators continue to track and respond to the preferences of their constituents (Buchanan and Ohsfeldt 1993; Fiorina 1974).

Finally, some research suggests that interest groups can influence legislative voting behavior through lobbying and campaign contributions. However, interest-group influence is often limited by the predispositions of legislators and the characteristics of the issues (Smith 1995). Gay groups may be particularly disadvantaged in Congress simply because they often face opposing interest groups, their issues tend to receive public and media attention, and gay issues often lead legislators to divide along partisan and ideological lines—all factors that tend to decrease interest-group influence (see Smith 1995). Although gay groups are not likely to have a large influence on legislative voting, two national gay groups have formed for this purpose—The National Gay and Lesbian Task Force (NGLTF) and the Human Rights Campaign (HRC). Both of these groups lobby Congress and track important votes on gay issues. HRC also funds political campaigns. In 1996 HRC contributed more than $1 million to candidates to national offices.

SUMMARY OF PREVIOUS RESEARCH

RECENT QUANTITATIVE RESEARCH DOES indeed suggest that legislators' voting behavior on lesbian and gay issues is similar to voting behavior on many other issues but is most similar to voting on other morality issues (see Haider-Markel 1997, 1999).[3] Legislators tend to vote along party and ideological lines, with Democrats being more supportive than Republicans and liberals being more supportive than conservatives. However, the influence of partisanship on voting varies across chambers and over time, with the greatest influence during the initial votes on AIDS in the 99th House (1985–86), when some of the first AIDS votes were taken (see figure 21.1). The influence of partisanship decreased in the House over the 100th and 101st Congresses (1987–90) and increased over the 102d to 103d Congresses (1991–94) before dropping back to its earlier level in the 104th Congress (1995–96). The influence of partisanship in the Senate is similarly erratic, with the lowest levels of partisanship occurring in the 99th Senate (1985–86). The results from both chambers then, suggest that while partisanship consistently influences legislative voting behavior, its influence is likely to vary widely, especially on votes concerning AIDS. Also, while AIDS was initially a partisan issue in the House, it was not in the Senate— perhaps not too surprising considering that gay issues are generally more partisan in the House.

Legislators who identify as Protestant fundamentalists are also less supportive on gay issues, but this tends to be more true for House members than for senators. In the House the influence of religion has dropped considerably over time but became more of a factor in the 104th Congress (1995–96). Religious affiliation in the Senate exhibits a similar pattern, suggesting either that more religious conservatives are being elected to Congress or that members with conservative religious affiliations are increasingly voting in line with their religious beliefs on homosexuality.

Perhaps not surprisingly, legislators are also quite responsive to constituency opinion on gay issues—when their constituents do not support gay civil rights, legislators often take an antigay position (see Haider-Markel 1999). In both the House and the Senate responsiveness to constituency opinion on gay issues has generally increased over time. However, constituency opinion had less influence in both chambers during the 104th Congress (1995–96). This finding may indicate that as more conservative legislators have been elected since 1994, their voting behavior on gay issues has become more inconsistent with the more moderate opinions of their constituents.

Also, AIDS appears to have decreased the influence of religion and constituency opinion on legislative voting behavior, at least temporarily. The influence of religion and constituency opposition decreased significantly during the 99th Congress (1985–86), when only AIDS votes were taken, but the negative influence of each variable steadily increased back to its previous position in the following Congresses.

Interestingly, gay interest groups, through PAC contributions and membership mobilization, have a significant positive influence on progay support in most congressional sessions. Although interest group mobilization appears to have more influence in the Senate than in the House, the influence of gay financial contributions has increased over time in the House but declined in the Senate. This could be because the Senate has become more polarized on gay issues, leaving little room for campaign contributions to make a difference. The only firm conclusion we can make is that gay groups have increasingly obtained more "bang for their buck" in the House and that financial contributions had less of an influence during the 104th Congress (1995–96).

The influence of grassroots mobilization by gay interest groups does not show a simple pattern in either the House or the Senate, which may suggest that gay groups have been inconsistent in their ability to mobilize their constituents for legislative campaigns. Interestingly, the influence of gay mobilization has increased slightly in the House over the 103d and 104th Congresses (1993–96) and declined slightly in the Senate. There are too few data points, however, to draw firm conclusions about possible patterns.

A brief example of Haider-Markel's (1999) analysis of legislative voting behavior is displayed in table 21.1. The votes analyzed here are the four votes taken on DOMA in the House. Column one shows the results for the full House, column two for House Democrats, and column three for House Republicans. The pattern matches the overall pattern of voting on gay issues, suggesting that gay family issues evoke the same legislative response as other gay-related issues. Interestingly, constituency opinion has a greater

TABLE 21.1 Multiple Regression Analysis Predicting Four House Roll-Call Votes on DOMA

INDEPENDENT VARIABLES	FULL HOUSE	HOUSE DEMOCRATS	HOUSE REPUBLICANS
Member Ideology	-.51**(.06)	-.19(.12)	-.053(.057)
Democrat	22.16** (2.66)	—	—
Fundamentalist Religion	-4.81* (2.11)	-4.61 (3.22)	-1.09 (1.86)
Simulated Constituency			
Opposition to Gay Rights	-6.56** (1.30)	-4.73* (1.94)	-1.00 (1.26)
HRC Contributions	.0047* * (.0006)	.0030* * (.0007)	.013** (.0018)
Gay Mobilization	10.19** (2.34)	11.02** (3.67)	3.68# (1.99)
Previous Congress			
Pro-Gay Support	.32** (.05)	.81** (.11)	.048 (.034)
Intercept	64.05** (13.23)	39.09# (22.02)	12.60 (12.44)
R squared	.73	.73	.28
Adjusted R squared	.73	.72	.26
Standard Error	400.01	471.92	146.59
F Ratio	154.90	84.92	13.41
F Significance	.0000	.0000	.0000
Number of Cases	406	192	214
Mean of Dependent			
Variable	27.59	53.11	4.66

NOTES: Coefficients are unstandardized regression coefficients. Standard errors are in parenthesis. One-tailed significance test = ** Sig. < .01; * Sig. < .05; # Sig. < .10. For a complete description of variable measurement and analysis of roll call votes see Haider-Markel (1999).

influence on Democrats than Republicans. This suggests that Republicans are less responsive to shifts in public opinion concerning gays–they will still generally oppose gays, even when the public supports gays.

In summary, the results summarized from Haider-Markel (1999) provide fairly strong evidence that voting behavior on gay issues is highly partisan, ideological, and is often grounded in religious teachings. Legislators who are more moderate and less partisan, however, are also influenced by constituency opinion, campaign contributions, and grassroots mobilization. It seems clear that the lesbian and gay movement has made a significant impact on the voting behavior of at least some legislators. Through the use of both financial contributions and the mobilization of constituents, gay interest groups have become a factor in congressional decision-making. This has occurred despite relatively high-issue salience, the opposition of antigay interest groups, and negative public attitudes toward homosexuals. As gay and religious interest groups become more institutionalized in congressional policy-making, the voting patterns uncovered by my analysis are likely to continue.

PATTERNS OF CONGRESSIONAL SUPPORT ON GAY AND LESBIAN ISSUES

WITH AN UNDERSTANDING OF how legislators make voting decisions on gay and lesbian issues, we can now examine the aggregate outcomes of these decisions. This section examines changing levels of progay support in Congress and explains the factors leading to changes in levels of support. Before examining the data, what might we expect to find? First, the findings in sections one and two suggest that partisanship plays a large role in legislative voting behavior on gay issues; thus we might expect that as the partisan composition of Congress changes, so too will progay support. Second, because AIDS expanded the scope of homosexual issues and the number of actors concerned with homosexual issues, we might expect progay support to increase or decrease.

Figures 21.2 and 21.3 display the progay support of the average member in each chamber as well as the Democratic composition of each chamber. While levels of support in each chamber do follow the chamber's Democratic composition, the evidence is not convincing. For example, average progay support in the 102d House (1991–92) dropped even though Democratic composition increased (see figure 21.2). Furthermore, while Democratic

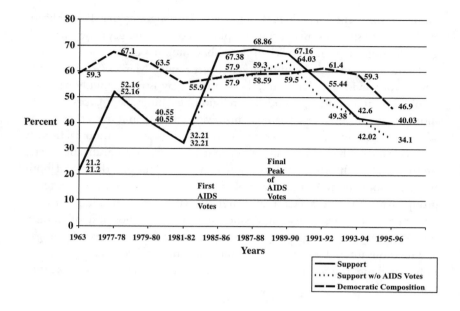

FIGURE 21.2   Average Progay Support in House, 88th to 104th Congress

composition in the House decreased by only 2 percent between the 102d and 103d Congress (1991–94), progay support dropped by more than 13 percent.

The introduction of AIDS as a homosexual issue may provide the best explanation for changing levels of progay support. Recall that neither chamber voted on AIDS issues until 1985, in the 99th Congress. The number of AIDS votes increased through 1988 (the 100th Congress), dropped in 1989 (the first session of the 101st Congress), peaked again in 1990 (during the second session of the 101st Congress), and dropped again until a slight increase in 1996 (the 104th Congress). As the figures show, progay support has been highest precisely at the points when AIDS issues represented a significant portion of the congressional agenda on gay issues—the 99th to 101st Congress (1985–90).

If we examine the difference in progay voting support for the average Democrat and the average Republican, the connection between progay support and AIDS becomes even more apparent. In figure 21.4 the average House Republican increased his or her progay support by almost 10

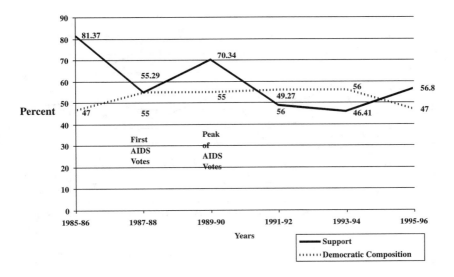

FIGURE 21.3   Average Progay Support in the Senate, 99th to 104th Congress

percent from the 99th to 101st Congress (1985–90) and by 5 percent between the 103d and 104th Congress (1993–96), precisely at the points when the greatest number of AIDS votes were taken. Figure 21.5 shows a similar pattern for Senate Republicans, but there are some differences. Republican progay support was highest during the 99th Congress (1985–86); of the six votes taken in the 99th Senate (1985–86), all six votes concerned AIDS funding and none specifically mentioned homosexuals. With only a 14 percent difference in progay support between Democrats and Republicans in the 99th Senate (1985–86), it seems likely that Senate Republicans did not immediately tie AIDS to negative attitudes toward homosexuality.

During the 100th Congress (1987–88), however, this pattern changed when Senator Helms (R–NC) proposed amendments to all AIDS legislation that would prevent any AIDS funds from being used to "promote homosexuality or the homosexual lifestyle." Progay Republican support took a sharp drop—nearly 40 percent. Senate Democrats also reduced their progay support during the 100th Congress (1987–88), but to a lesser degree. Finally, although the 104th Congress (1995–96) has been widely considered the most conservative modern Congress, progay support increased during the

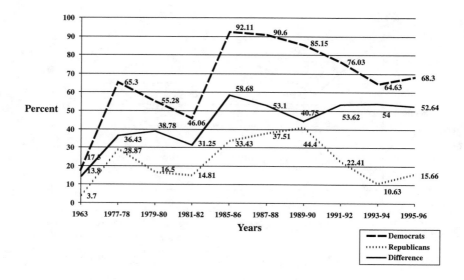

FIGURE 21.4 Difference in Averge Progay Support in House by Party

104th (1995–96) in both the House and the Senate (see figures 21.4 and 21.5). This increase might be attributed to a slight increase in the number of AIDS votes during the 104th Congress (1995–96), the increased support among moderate Republicans for gay rights (see Yang 1998), or the fact that Republican attacks on gay families became difficult for moderates to support during both the 104th and 105th Congress (1995–98).

Overall the evidence suggests a number of points. First, while Democrats have clearly provided more progay support in Congress, progay support among members of both parties increased when gay issues were expanded to include AIDS during the 1980s. Second, increased progay support proved fickle—both parties became less supportive when legislation directly connected AIDS to homosexuality. Furthermore, as AIDS moved off the congressional agenda, average progay support returned to levels near those that existed before AIDS reached the agenda. Third, the degree of partisanship on gay issues has remained fairly high, especially in the House. Partisanship on gay issues, however, has also remained fairly stable since the mid-1980s, with some conservative Democrats and moderate Republicans easing their opposition to gay activists.

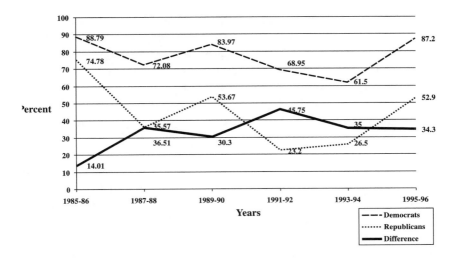

FIGURE 21.5 Difference in Average Progay Support in Senate by Party

This chapter has examined the evolution of lesbian and gay issues in Congress, legislative voting behavior on gay issues, and how progay support has changed over time. My analysis of these issues raises several important conclusions. First, to gain a political edge, the main actors in the congressional debate over homosexuality have each tried to frame the debate in their own terms. Prior to the 1960s the dominant actors in Congress were able to define homosexuality in terms of national security and along the ideological divisions of cold war politics—a frame that was mirrored in the 1993 debate on gays in the military. Cold warriors and Evangelicals within the Republican Party formed an alliance around this and other family and social issues, framing the debate in their terms until the 1970s when gay activists gained limited access to Congress. As gay activists gained access, the issues addressed by Congress began to change and include gay civil rights and family issues. The appearance of AIDS created political opportunities and liabilities for both sides. By the 1990s a temporary stalemate was reached, with both sides claiming victories and losses.

Second, my summary of research on legislative voting behavior suggests that legislators base their voting decisions on their party, religious affiliation, ideology, and the preferences of their constituents. Gay interest groups have also been able to influence legislative voting behavior and their influence may be increasing in the House but declining in the Senate. It also appears that religion may play an increasing role in legislative voting behavior as the influence of partisanship, constituency opinion, and ideology declines. Although greater interest-group resources will likely translate into greater political power, this power will be limited by the ability of groups to mobilize their constituents for legislative campaigns. To influence policy, interest groups must coordinate both financial contributions and mobilization.

Third, my examination of the aggregate outcomes of individual voting behavior in Congress suggests that while gays have received greater support from Democrats, increasing the number of Democrats in Congress does not immediately translate into more progay support. More important was the expansion of homosexual issues to include AIDS, which significantly increased progay support in Congress, even though this support was weak and dropped in the 1990s. Furthermore, the overall level of progay support in Congress has declined over the past ten years. While this may be because Congress has become more conservative and more Republican, the decline is most likely a result of the rise and influence of opposition groups, such as the Christian Coalition.

Finally, gay issues in Congress have evolved from a focus on national defense and federal-employment issues to a focus not only on the "threat" posed by gays to traditional families but also on redefining the traditional family to include lesbian and gay conceptions of the family. Religious conservatives in Congress will likely continue to attack gay families with legislation such as the Defense of Marriage Act, legislation denying domestic-partner benefits, and legislation preventing gays from adopting—but these extremist attacks may also be offending the broader public, which increasingly views such measures as unfair (see Yang 1998). Regardless of who is winning or losing these issues in Congress, gay family issues are likely to increase their prominence on the congressional agenda.

NOTES

1. All figures used in this chapter are based on data from Haider-Markel (1997, 1999).
2. H.R. 3396 had 105 Republican and 12 Democrat cosponsors. The Senate companion bill was S 1740.

3. Haider-Markel's (1999) examination of legislative voting behavior on gay issues from the 95th to 104th Congress using multiple regression analysis is summarized in this section.

REFERENCES

Adam, Barry D. 1995. *The Rise of a Gay and Lesbian Movement.* Rev. ed. New York: Twayne.

Baumgartner, Frank R. and Bryan D. Jones. 1993. *Agendas and Instability in American Politics.* Chicago: University of Chicago Press.

Benson, Peter L. and Dorothy L. Williams. 1982. *Religion on Capitol Hill: Myths and Realities.* San Francisco: Harper and Row.

Buchanan, Robert J. and Robert L. Ohsfeldt. 1993. "The Attitudes of State Legislators and State Medicaid Policies Related to AIDS." *Policy Studies Journal* 21: 651–71.

Bull, Chris and John Gallagher. 1996. *Perfect Enemies: The Religious Right, the Gay Movement, and the Politics of the 1990s.* New York: Crown.

Chibbaro, Lou Jr. 1998. "D.C. Bill Faces Adoption, Needle Exchange Votes GOP Leaders Seek to Reverse Committee." *The Washington Blade,* August 7.

Congressional Information Service. Various years. *Congressional Information Service Annual.* Washington, D.C.: Congressional Information Service.

Congressional Quarterly. Various years. *Congressional Quarterly Almanac.* Washington, D.C.: Congressional Quarterly, Inc.

Day, Christine L. 1994. "State Legislative Voting Patterns on Abortion Restrictions in Louisiana." *Women & Politics* 14 (2): 45–63.

D'Emilio, John. 1983. *Sexual Politics Sexual Communities.* Chicago: University of Chicago Press.

——. 1992. *Making Trouble: Essays on Gay History, Politics, and the University.* New York: Routledge.

Diamond, Sara. 1995. *Roads to Dominion: Right-Wing Movements and Political Power in the United States.* New York: Guilford Press.

Dupuis, Martin. 1998. "State Legislative Response to Hawaii's Same-Sex Marriage Case." Paper presented at the annual meeting of the Midwest Political Science Association, Chicago.

Fiorina, Morris P. 1974. *Representatives, Roll Calls, and Constituents.* Lexington, Mass.: Lexington Books.

Haider-Markel, Donald P. 1997. "From Bullhorns to PACs: Lesbian and Gay Politics, Interest Groups, and Policy." Ph.D. diss. University of Wisconsin-Milwaukee.

——. 1999. "Redistributing Values in Congress: Interest Group Influence Under Sub-Optimal Conditions." *Political Research Quarterly* 52 (1): 113–44.

Holland, Judy. 1998. "House Would Ban Gays From Adopting Children." *New York Times*, August 7.

Horne, Gerald. "Marshall-FBI News Reminder of Movement's Compromises." *Detroit News*, December 15, sec. C.

Kingdon, John. 1989. *Congressmen's Voting Decisions* 3d ed. New York: Harper and Row.

Smith, Richard A. 1995. "Interest Group Influence in the U.S. Congress." *Legislative Studies Quarterly* 20: 89–139.

Streitmatter, Roger. 1995. *Unspeakable: The Rise of the Gay and Lesbian Press in America*. Boston: Faber and Faber.

Tatalovich, Raymond, and David Schier. 1993. "The Persistence of Ideological Cleavage in Voting on Abortion Legislation in the House of Representatives, 1973–1988." *American Politics Quarterly* 21 (1): 125–39.

Thompson, Mark, ed. 1994. *The Long Road to Freedom*. New York: St. Martin's Press.

Tuller, David. 1990. "Gays Note Success in Congress." *San Francisco Chronicle*, December 24, p. A8.

U.S. House Debate. 1996. *Proceedings and Debates of the 104th Congress, Second Session*, Defense of Marriage Act. House of Representatives, July 11.

U.S. House Hearing. 1996. *Subcommittee on the Constitution of the Committee on The Judiciary, on H.R. 3396*, Defense of Marriage Act. 104th Cong., 2d sess., May 15.

U.S. Senate Hearing. 1996. *Committee on the Judiciary, United States Senate, on S. 1740, A Bill to Define and Protect the Institution of Marriage.* 104th Cong., 2d sess., July 11.

Vaid, Urvashi. 1995. *Virtual Equality: The Mainstreaming of Gay and Lesbian Liberation*. New York: Anchor Books.

Yang, Alan S. 1998. *From Wrongs to Rights: Public Opinion on Gay and Lesbian Americans Moves Toward Equality.* Washington, D.C.: NGLTF.

22

GENDER TRANSGRESSIONS AND QUEER
FAMILY LAW

Political Organizing and the Limits of Civil Rights:
Gay Marriage and Queer Families

Randall Halle

Transformations in kinship structures to forms that deviate from the nuclear family have been decried as marking the decline of "Western values" and as undermining the state.[1] Conservative, far right, and Christian organizations, recognizing such transformations, search for the motor behind the changes and continually draw connections between a homosexual agenda and an aggressive attack on family, morality, and the "American way of life." A discussion broadcast on "Straight Talk from the Family Research Council" makes clear how connections are typically drawn to a "gay agenda" in the expression of anxieties about the family.[2]

Kristi Hamrick, the moderator, asserted that

> legally destroying the exclusive territory of marriage to achieve a political end will not provide the real benefits of marriage to homosexuals, but it may be the blow that the shattered American family does not survive.

Robert Knight, Director of Cultural Studies at the Family Research Council, explained that

> support for these kinds of special set-asides would erode if the institution [of bourgeois heterosexual marriage] itself suddenly ceases to be that special man-woman unique relationship that is the heart of civilization. We can't do without it, and that's the bottom line. The state knows

that. . . . There is no society on Earth that has functioned without marriage, and there are many that have gone into the dust bin of history as
soon as they cheapened marriage: Rome, Greece, some of the middle
Chinese dynasties. When marriage became cheapened, the social fabric
began to unravel.

And we're seeing that in this country.

From these quotes we recognize a number of typical rhetorical maneu-
vers: (1) there is an elision of the difference between marriage, sexuality,
and kinship; (2) the historical specificity of state, legal, and cultural forms
is ignored—glossing over, for example, the way various forms of non-
heterosexuality have historically been socially supported and legally sanctioned; (3) a direct connection is drawn between family and state, and this
connection is presented as an alarming vision of the decline of the state
in which the transformation of kinship acts as the chief signifier; (4)
although heterogeneous forms of desire and social arrangements have
always already existed, a moral line needs to be drawn. Such a line in effect
does not mean other forms cease to exist, however it does rob them of
legal legitimacy and leaves them subject to repression and inviting perse-
cution.[3] Finally, these quotes show that lesbians and gays have a very real
vested interest in examining and understanding the relationship of family
form and the state.

It would be a mistake to view positions such as those expressed by the
Family Research Council to have emerged in bad faith. They are not made
out of an organization's desire to use the spread of anxiety to gain financial
support and political clout—although certainly that is one of the effects of
such statements. It is important to recognize that an intimate connection
between the family and the nation-state does exist. It is also important to
accept that the preachers and broadcasters relying on such rhetoric have an
effect because an attentive audience exists. The iterations of such anxiety
address the fact that indeed much of our world is changing in ways they
rightly identify.

We can accept the proposition of "good faith" here, because a myriad of
transformations, active and passive revolutions alike, have brought about the
transformations they describe. We could compile a long list, the examples of
which would run from an increase in single-parent and extended-family
households to a broad redistribution of wealth and poverty, from changes in
school curriculum, services, and funding to mass political change regarding
insurance and social security, from the prolongation of childhood and ado-

lescence to shifts in the representation of adolescent sexuality, etc., etc. Yet, rather than approach these changes with fear and anxiety, we can experience a sense of anticipation, standing on the threshold of the new, a new era, a new modernity that has indeed fundamentally transformed the family and state.

The simple structure of mother, father, child only ever existed in middle-class urban pockets. Its claim to be the ideal family form lasted less than one hundred years, and now it wanes. In approximately the same time span the nation-state rose and declined.[4] While various conservative groups struggle to maintain the hegemony of outdated familial and political forms, transnational geopolitical configurations sublate the nation-state. Furthermore economic and demographic transformations mark the kinship structure of the bourgeois nuclear family as superseded.[5] It is hardly a homosexual world conspiracy that acts as motor of change. At the same time gays and lesbians can indeed be understood as subjects of these changes, positive agents in historical change.

A BRIEF HISTORICAL REVIEW OF THE FAMILY, CIVIL SOCIETY, AND THE STATE

WHILE THOSE OPPOSED TO the "gay agenda" might be able to gloss over historical specificity, a (brief) reflection here on the historical interconnection between family and state may prove significant for organizers, activists, and academics interested in crafting a response. In the eighteenth and nineteenth centuries, at the dawn of the modern era, liberal political theorists relied on the recognition and promotion of a significant and intimate interconnection between the family and the state. Those political theorists who drew this interconnection of family and state once claimed revolutionary ascendance in the face of feudal social structures. They derived from the family a form of human universalism, autonomy, and equality that countered absolutist hierarchies and privilege.[6]

Hegel was the original family-values man. Writing in the first quarter of the nineteenth century, Hegel's social philosophy occupied a position at the emergence of the bourgeois nuclear family as well as the nation-state. At the dawn of modernity Hegel set the Owl of Minerva out on a flight to gather observations of new forms. From such actual observations he sought to distill the rationale of the real or the truth of society. As the original family-values man, family values in their liberal phase, Hegel's philosophy provides texts filled with insights significant for our own contemporary understanding of the politics of the family and its intersection with queer organizing.

In the *Philosophy of Right* (1821), Hegel identified the family as the origin in each individual of the awareness of the common good at the heart of society, the source of ethical values.

> The Family thereby makes him [the individual] a member of a community which prevails over and holds under control the forces of particular material elements and the lower forms of life, which sought to unloose themselves against him and to destroy him. (452)[7]

In the designation of the family as such, neither God's grace nor ordained hierarchies nor knowledge of tradition—all limited to a guiding few—but a new universal "birthright" to ethical sovereignty and citizenship emerged. The family acted as a filiative group that provided the first experiences of society and its mores. Filiation stood in stark contrast to the Enlightenment conception of ethics. The *Lumières* right up to Kant had understood ethics, based as they were in education and inherent human rationality, as a project of affiliation.[8] The promotion of the family in this manner was new.

The theoretical deployment of family at this point in time did not promote just any kinship structure. Distinct from other contemporaneous terms such as "house" or "lineage," family marked the substantial emergence of the modern middle-class man/woman, mother/father, parents/children family structure.[9] This new kinship structure, subsequently designated as the bourgeois nuclear family, provided the ethical base for the liberal nation-state: "The expansion of the family, as its transition to another principle . . . becomes a people or *nation*" (PR, 181).

Until this time marriage had been an institution reserved primarily for the aristocracy, i.e., the propertied class. Now marriage more generally formed the family as the primary ethical union. The legal institution of marriage became the intermediary between the state and the family, making the state into an arbiter of family form. Hegel in particular recognized how marriage could act as an apparatus of state ideology, not only to determine outward state and family form but also to construct ideologically inner consciousness.

> Marriage, as the immediate type of ethical relationship, contains first, the moment of physical life; and since marriage is a *substantial* tie, the life involved in it is life in its totality, i.e., as the actuality of the race and its

life-process. But, secondly, in self-consciousness the *natural sexual union* . . . is changed into a union on the level of mind, into self-conscious love." (*PR*, 161) (emphasis added)

In this paragraph, typical of nineteenth-century legal and social thought, Hegel ideologically links marriage, family, and a specific sexual practice, i.e., the heterocoital form of sexual expression, by invoking the concept of a "natural sexual union."[10] This assertion of the naturalness of this "sexual union" opposed forms equally real, equally present, and equally "natural." This conflux of sexuality, legal form, and (middle-) class interest central to the (liberal) state was based, however, in a tautology. "Natural" heterosexuality became the basis of the modern legal rationale, and this became proof of its "naturalness." Later Hegel went beyond drawing a connection between heterosexuality and state form, to include monogamy, love-marriage, and women's "place in the home," as rational and natural.[11] As a result of this tautology, homosexuality along with so many other varieties of sexual expression was not sanctioned by the state. Heterosexuality, marriage, and kinship, on the other hand, became tied directly to the state.

Yet this (liberal) vision of the state also afforded a social space that gays and lesbians would come to inhabit fully. Hegel's social structure was not one in which a simple expansion of kinship provided the direct foundation of the state, i.e., the state was the sum of clans, which were the sum of families. Such a vision of society would have been more in line with the form of the feudal state. Rather precisely, Hegel presented the possibility for a social realm distinct from filiation, an arena of (possible queer) affiliations. In his description of how ethics as substance expanded from the values of the family to the values of the state, Hegel positioned a stage before the state and after the family: civil society.[12] Civil society, like family and state, is part of ethical life, but in civil society the individual becomes the central subjective moment.

> In civil society, each individual is his own end, and all else means nothing to him. But he cannot accomplish the full extent of his ends without reference to others; these others are therefore means to the end of the particular [person]. (*PR*, 182)

Clearly related to the family, given that all individuals must come from a kinship structure of some sort, civil society is, nevertheless, distinct from the family as the dynamic active economic sphere of public negotiations.

Clearly related to the state, given that public negotiations take place within the institutions and the legal purview of the state, civil society is, nevertheless, distinct from these institutions as the real lived experience of individuals. This discussion of civil society, new here with Hegel, proves significant for us. It was here that a social space was theorized that allowed for a radical ethics of individual liberty and the free development of the personality.

In the subsequent century and a half, feudal society and aristocratic privilege have all but disappeared. The bourgeois nuclear form of the family has risen to ascendance and civil society and the nation-state have likewise become the defining terms of modern political science. Our notion of "proper" family form has changed little. But separate from the politics of filiation, civil society, as the realm of affiliation, has to this point been and continues to be a dynamic and experimental sphere, the main social arena for the expansion of individual freedoms and rights. It is in the area of civil society that gays and lesbians have been most active and have made the greatest contributions to individual freedom, autonomy, and universal human emancipation. It is in civil society that gays and lesbians have furthered the conceptualization of a realm of human interaction distinct from state and family.

NOW FOR SOME REFLECTIONS ON THE RELATIONSHIP OF QUEER ORGANIZING TO FAMILY, CIVIL SOCIETY, AND THE STATE

IT IS APPROPRIATE NOW, at the dawn of a new modernity, to set the Owl of Minerva to flight once again to survey the current social and political terrain. "Family values" continue to occupy a central position in the definition of the modern state. Of course those who now draw connections, as the early modern liberals once did, between family and state can hardly themselves be considered liberals. Whereas Hegel was cognizant of his ideological promotion of the bourgeois nuclear family over older forms, the Family Research Council et al. promote this form as if there had ever been a time when it was the only form of filiation. If this form, supported by state legal structures, has become ideologically ascendant, that does not mean that historical processes have come to a grinding halt. In order for legislative bodies such as the U.S. Congress to hinder further expansion of civil autonomy and equality, they must fetter society through the codification and ossification not only of family form and the institution of marriage but also of state form and institutions.[13] The 1996 Defense of Marriage Act, for instance, seeks to force an end to history through legislation—an odd proposition at best.

Those of us involved in analyzing and promoting queer politics benefit from a reflection on the terms of our political activity. For instance, we can recognize how demands for gay marriage and the presence of queer families in civil society present varying degrees of challenge to exclusionary and repressive social forms. But as is the case with every political challenge the queer community presents, there are a number of variables organizers confront when framing the challenge.

First and foremost, organizations may promote issues on an inclusionary or a transformative level. I mean by these terms quite simply whether the direct intention of the political organizing is to seek admittance to existing institutions and forms without attempting to alter their structure. That is to say more familiarly, are we looking for our place setting at a dinner table without even asking what is being served? Or, do the organizers frame their challenge in such a way that it can be resolved only by the transformation of existing institutions and forms or even the creation of new forms? That is to say, are we proposing that Thanksgiving take place at our house for a change, and "don't worry we'll do the cooking!"

Furthermore, with every political challenge there exists a question of address. Is the challenge directed at the state or at civil society. We can note a certain elasticity that allows state and civil society to meet certain challenges easily. This elasticity is in part due to the dynamic developments of civil society and the state during the modern period. Hence some of the challenges presented to the state or to civil society are radical attacks; others are more easily contained.

For instance, an inclusionary demand on the state for gay marriage reduces (but does not entirely negate) the ability of the state to treat marriage as a site of reproduction. It does, however, negate the valorization of heterocoital practice in the state, requiring a slight but not insignificant transformation of state institutions. At the same time the challenge to civil society of "queer families," as a definite public presence, does not inherently undo a system of reproduction for the nation. However, such families do inherently result in a transformation of civil society, introducing new life possibilities, diversifying social forms, and providing greater individual choice.

At this point, in order to continue this examination, I would like to shift my discussion from the heady heights of social philosophy to the gritty streets and backrooms of contemporary urban political practice. In fact, I would like to talk about Cambridge, Massachusetts—hardly the grittiest urban setting, but one of the few progressive communities that dot the otherwise bleakly conservative political landscape of the United States. Even Cambridge, however, is in a state of transition, with conservatives successfully undoing progressive gains. My observations will be drawn from the fact that during my four years as a resident there, from 1992 to 1996, I was very active in the politics of the city, especially in the area of queer politics. I quickly became chair of the Cambridge Lavender Alliance (CLA), the center of lesbigay politics in the city.

At the time, the CLA was undergoing transformations that are part of general trends in lesbigay politics in the United States and beyond. We can note a general shift in the structure and political interest among gays and lesbians. From the '60s onward a politics of affiliation and activity in civil society had dominated the agenda of gay and lesbian liberation. For many, the nuclear family as central filiative moment was experienced as a site of repression. Individuals moving out of their family setting took on a new role in civil society as lesbians and gays. The gay and lesbian community presented them with an affiliative community, a queer family of choice, or a family of affection. The move out of the nuclear family was thus experienced as a moment of liberation. Attempts by the state to coerce, control, or regulate these affiliations met with resistance, even active rebellion.

While in general it continues to be the case that gay and lesbian politics center on questions of affiliation, we can also recognize a shift to a politics of filiation. It should be emphasized that there is no need to see these concerns as intrinsically replacing a politics of affiliation. However the increasing presence of new kinship structures has transformed and expanded our definition of family, making visible the presence of "queer families."[14] To be sure, dramatically different concerns from those of the nuclear family inform the demands of these new kinship structures. We now have a whole new set of political concerns and possibilities. The new politics of filiation address differently issues of reproduction, parental rights, adoption, custody, inheritance, education, parenting, home ownership, etc., etc.

When I became active, the relationship of the CLA to the new family was one of the central aspects of our organizing. The lesbian baby boom in particular had transformed the quotidian existence of many key members of the CLA. Realistically, many new parents could form a stroller contingent at marches and rallies but had little time to debate strategy during evening hours that coincided with feedings, homework, bedtime, and so on. It therefore became important to formulate the agenda of the CLA in a way that would incorporate this experience and create new structures germane to queer families.

We organized public forums on lesbian and gay families. At our Pride Brunch in 1996 we honored an innovative structure that involved a lesbian and a gay couple all coparenting—"Heather" had two mommies *and* two daddies. We also formed a Parent Teachers and Allies subcommittee (CLA-PTA), which began work in the school system to improve responsiveness to gay and lesbian parents *and* youth. As one of its initial activities, this group organized a photo exhibit at an elementary school that displayed images from a wide variety of family structures, including lesbian and gay families. The exhibit brought much-needed visibility into the schools and, more important I would say, it set up lasting formal relations with key members of the school committee and the bureaucracy.

Amidst these general activities, I would like to focus on two aspects of our organizing in 1995/1996 in order to examine how inclusion and transformation played out in our political organizing as it targeted the state or civil society. In 1995 the membership of the CLA set out an agenda that concentrated on (1) the promotion of gay marriage, and (2) a response to a violent murder in the queer community.

In the midst of these activities, gay marriage might have been dismissed as an initiative too divisive for the CLA, given that a general section of the core group was hesitant to undertake what was understood as a purely inclusionary agenda item. Also many understood the gay-marriage initiative as being inclusionary only for a small group of lesbians and gays who fit a specific "moral" model, i.e., those who approximated the bourgeois nuclear family. Four factors helped overcome this objection and led to our decision to address this question. Chief among these factors was of course the then-pending court case in Hawaii that seemed to make gay marriage an imminent reality, granting the issue a certain sense of historical urgency. Further, a stance on gay marriage was seen as allowing us to adopt an offensive posture vis-à-vis the newly organized Cambridge chapter of the Christian Coalition. Third, the core group of the CLA contained a number of advocates of the Freedom to Marry Coalition (FMC). The FMC recognized in Cambridge the potential for a successful test case of its resolution initiative. Finally, the careful wording of the resolution convinced any opposition within the CLA to work to organize a vote in the city council. It is important that we dwell for a moment on the language of the resolution.

The wording of the resolution was crucial: "The state shall enact no legislation to interfere with the ability of lesbians and gays to marry." Such wording removed any "moral" imperatives from the argument for gay marriage. In fact, the resolution made no argument for gay marriage at all; rather, it attempted to promote state moral minimalism. It required of the state that it withdraw from the regulation of marriage, thereby allowing for a de facto expansion of the parameters of civil society. Through such wording we were able to form a unique lobbying group that united religious and moral conservatives with lesbian and gay leftists. In lobbying city councillors, we repeatedly stressed a division between the benefits granted to married couples by the state versus the moral/religious aspects of marriage. The questions of morality and religion, we argued, were the domain of the various churches and not the state. The resolution passed in city council, interestingly without opposition. The five-member progressive majority on the council voted in favor and the four conservative members abstained.

When addressing our second agenda item, we experienced a vastly different set of challenges. Where gay marriage represented new challenges in filiative politics, the response to the brutal murder of Chanelle Pickett, a transgendered woman, represented new challenges in affiliative politics. The rage over the murder, the media coverage, the police inactivity, and the proffered defense[15] brought hundreds of people from the gay and lesbian community out to a memorial service to show solidarity with the transgendered community for the first time. For many transgendered individuals attendance at the service amounted to their first experience of social and political community. This common rage empowered a group of activists, Transsexual Menace (TM), to expand their organizing efforts. I approached the Cambridge organizer of TM, Nancy Nangeroni, to offer the CLA's support.[16] We agreed to work on adding language to the Cambridge Human Rights Ordinance that would allow such violence to be prosecuted as a hate crime.

Given that much of the violence the queer community experiences results from hatred, hate crime statutes provide a further tool in prosecuting violence. Without such statutes there is no mechanism to examine the specific motivation behind this violence, and bashings get categorized as robbery, assaults, or vandalism. To change the language of the Human Rights Ordinance, however, required a public hearing, and we felt it necessary to work against potential attacks. We used the political clout of the CLA to lobby the city council and we increased the visibility of the transgendered community. For instance, we opened up the annual Pride Brunch to cosponsorship. Every year this event serves to kick off our Gay Pride Celebration. It takes place in city hall, is attended by hundreds—including politi-

cians and business leaders—and is accompanied by the reading of a proclamation from the city council. Cosponsorship made TM immediately visible
to a large group of influential figures. Our efforts were again successful. The
vote to open initial hearings on the Human Rights Ordinance passed in city
council. Interestingly, this time the initiative passed with more support and
real opposition than the marriage resolution: seven members voting for and
two opposing.

As we formed the coalitions for these initiatives, various rifts in the
community evidenced themselves, threatening the projects from the outset.
The work on the marriage resolution required a coalition between two fac-
tions. One faction promoted a moral inclusionary paradigm for gay liberation that directly attacked the "unhealthy instability" of "most" gay relationships. In general this group desired an expansion of state authority. A
second faction consisted of members who advocated that queer relationships not be based on bourgeois paradigms. This faction desired a transformation of existing social forms and was ambivalent in its assessment of the
state.

The work on the inclusion of transgendered language in the Human
Rights Ordinance resulted in a break with a different sector. The coalition,
affiliative politics at its best, required the uniting of two communities under
the common rubric of queer: the lesbigay and the transgendered. To be sure,
questioning coalition links and connections of shared interest is a necessary
part of affiliative politics. However, portions of the lesbigay community
responded to the transgendered community much as the lesbian and gay
rights movements of the '70s and '80s had responded to bisexuals—fearing
a "watering down" of the community, or a "muddying of the waters." I will
confess that I was not prepared when members of the CLA challenged the
wisdom of cosponsoring the Pride Brunch. The most succinct reason I was
given for the challenge was the simple question during the brunch, "What
do I have to do with them?" Such questioning came from multiple directions in the group and was based primarily on the confusion of categories
caused by the appearance of the transgendered activists.

Because gay and lesbian identity is defined through same-sex object
desire, the transgendered desire to expand and transform gender categories
might not be immediately comprehensible. While one might hope for a certain empathy, the transgendered experience calls attention to an area of
identity construction that remains unexplored for most lesbians and gays,
and they approach this area with the same sense of "naturalness" with which
heterosexuals approach homosexuality. Instead of seeing the members of

TM as bravely opening up possibilities for all of us, many of the members of CLA feared that they (respectable gays and lesbians) might be perceived as being just like them ("unrespectable," "confused" transgendered people) and that we would thereby lose political clout. Many of the members of TM appeared at the brunch, engaging in gender transgression—for example, wearing dresses and beards. Perhaps if the members of TM had appeared seeking to pass in one of the two ideal categories—that is, in "straight drag"—challenges would not have been raised. But they showed up seeking to confuse established categories and in doing so made visual and explicit the transformative intent of their demands.

In assessing the success of the two agenda items, the organizing around marriage had the effect of strengthening community ties and increasing the future potential for coalition building. However, although I believe that our efforts were based in strategically significant arguments, ultimately gay marriage threatens to replace affiliative with filiative structures: structures based on individual freedom and choice with structures determined separate from individual control by birth and legal ordinance. For instance, it threatens to undermine domestic-partner regulations arrived at in local governments and businesses. Usually directed solely at gay and lesbian couples because such regulations are generally premised on the inability to marry, there are a number of instances in which benefits have been extended to unmarried heterosexual couples as well.[17] Such regulations make a variety of domestic arrangements possible. Granted, domestic partnership has its own limitations; however, gay marriage only allows one form of domestic arrangement, binding sexuality, property, and power arrangements more firmly to a single institution: marriage.

In terms of the work with the transgendered community, I would not dismiss the concerns voiced at the Pride Brunch. Instead, I would simply respond by suggesting that the willingness of two of the conservative city councillors (but not only the conservatives) to actively vote to change the ordinance resulted precisely from the point of anxiety expressed around the confusion of categories. For those conservative councillors gay, lesbian, and transgendered people all *equally* confused established categories. "Given that they are all a bunch of queers, why withhold protection from one group?" Indeed, while personally lobbying one of the progressive councillors, I was told that the transgendered language should be easier to pass than the marriage resolution, because "after all, they can't help being that way." This council member appeared willing to "excuse" transgendereds in the same way she would "excuse" gays and lesbians. In this agenda item we can ultimately recognize an expansion of affiliative politics that does not take place at the expense of filiative politics. Unlike the potential restrictions that haunt marriage legislation, hate-crimes legislation in no way restricts or limits the possibility of family/relational forms.

As a concluding point, however, I would like to invite us to examine the question of address that was at the center of our organizing efforts in Cambridge. The same positions on civil society tend to form political work in the lesbigay movement in general. In Hegel's description of ethics, he clearly described how the modern state assumed the role of last ethical instance, the "actuality of the ethical Idea." Clearly we see echoes of this position from the Family Research Council. As last ethical instance, the state acts as ultimate arbiter of the parameters of civil society. The truth of society does not lie with a homogeneous heterosexual desire. The state that presumes this heterosexual desire as ethical instance must either repress heterogeneous expressions of desire or transform its own ethical presumptions. Civil rights legislation, of course, bases itself on the latter action, pushing the state to recognize the freedoms of real members of civil society. The Family Research Council, the group Save Traditional Marriage, the Defense of Marriage Act, and so on, resist such political activity, seeking to hold onto heterosexuality as ethical instance. Neither direction questions the presumption of the state to act as last ethical instance.

It is possible, however, to understand civil society as providing a sphere of filiation and affiliation that is distinct from the state and requires no intervention from the state.[18] The separation of church and state removed issues of religion from the purview of the state. Religious difference, thus, ceased to have political importance and such difference became a purely secular issue, played out in civil society. Religious affiliation became a matter of individual freedom experienced in civil society. Likewise, when the state withdrew from regulating race relations, antimiscegenation laws were not replaced with promiscegenation laws. Rather, the state simply withdrew from claiming legitimacy in determining who could or could not marry on the basis of race. In such cases the state adopts an ethically neutral position.

The marriage resolution in Cambridge sought to follow the same strategy. We did not ask the state to pass civil rights legislation but to adopt a position of moral minimalism, to refuse to regulate the lives of lesbian and gay people. In the Defense of Marriage Act, the federal government denied this emancipation and reasserted its position as last ethical instance. Our second agenda item, the attempt to change the Human Rights Ordinance, addresses and relies on the state. While significant, the passage of hate-crimes legislation such as that on which we worked in Cambridge not only does not stop the violence, it ultimately reasserts the role of the state as last ethical instance.

Advocating a radical moral minimalism does not mean that we have to give up a relationship to the state. It does not mean that we have to give up on ethical social demands such as freedom, equality, solidarity, a violence-free existence. Likewise, radical moral minimalism should not be understood as a call to give up work on civil rights. It does mean, however, that we should rethink the way we conceive of civil rights.

Advocating a radical moral minimalism on the part of the state means that we become more attentive to how we frame our demands on the state. Such demands must seek to transform the state, to put an end to its role in minoritizing and stigmatizing portions of its citizenry while granting special rights to other portions. In the face of the Christian states in Europe, Jews and Muslims were permanently doomed to an existence as a religious minority. Secularization overcame stigmatization at the level of state, removing the special rights of the Christian citizens. Similar transformations of the state in the area of sexuality should be our goal. We must end the special rights afforded by the state to reproductive heterosexuality. But such goals should be only one portion of an overall strategy. By advocating state moral minimalism, we also come to face more fully our position in civil society.

Civil rights protections as currently framed direct people to "do the right thing." They lead many citizens to think twice about discriminating *openly* in matters such as housing and employment. However, such protections do not stop discrimination. We turn to hate-crimes statutes *after* sad and violent events. While this ineffectual quality of the state might disturb at a certain level, we should be happy that total control of civil society eludes the state.

Political emancipation before the state is not complete human emancipation. Equality or protected status before the state can never guarantee equality or protection in civil society. Political emancipation before the state did not remove anti-Semitism, racism, or misogyny from civil society. Gains in political emancipation by lesbian, gay, bisexual, and transgendered individuals have not ended heterosexism, discrimination, and violence. In October 1998 the brutal murder of Matthew Shepard drew national attention to antigay violence. In November of the same year violence struck once again in the Boston area, taking from us Rita Hester, a transwoman. This murder did not receive the same attention as that of Matthew Shepard. Their brutal deaths diminish us all. No easy answers are available to us. However, as we develop strategies to protect our queer family, such violence must draw our attention to other, non-state oriented activities that are available to us.

NOTES

1. For a quick overview of various positions, review the website of the Family Research Council at http://www.frc.org/insight/is96c2hs.html, the American Family Association at http://www.afa.net, or Reverend Fred Phelps's Westboro Baptist Church at http://www.godhatesfags.com.

2. A transcript of this broadcast is available at http://www.frc.org/net/st96d2.html.

3. For an extensive discussion of "drawing the line," see Rubin 1993.

4. It may be important to recall at this moment that this political form, the nation-state, that came to dominate geopolitical form after World War II has a history of its own. It replaced kingdoms, realms, empires, city-states, and other political structures, for a state form that makes a claim to legitimacy based on a concept of natural mass belonging and coherence: the nation.

5. By "bourgeois nuclear family," I refer to a particular kinship structure that emerged in the nineteenth century based on certain class and social exigencies. This household—based on immediate family with two parents of the opposite sex, the female of which stays at home with a limited number of offspring—has always been in competition with other family forms. However, it came to pervade our understanding of what is ideal, successful, healthy, natural, etc. so that individuals outside this form were represented as, and often came to understand themselves as, outside the possibility of happiness.

6. The historical and sociological work on family and kinship transformations during this period is enormous. Although somewhat dated, Laslett (1972) continues to be a standard text in the history of the family, and is, as well, a good read. See also Anderson (1980) or Mitterauer (1982). For more recent work see Sheehan et al. (1996), Crossick (1995), or Hunter and Mason (1991).

7. For ease in referencing, I will cite Hegel by paragraph rather than page number.

8. "Filiation" refers here to relationships that are predetermined by birth. Individuals have no choice over the family into which they are born, nor do they have immediate choice regarding the relationships that result from the par-

ticular type of family or kinship structure into which they are born. Many times the filiative relationships are described as the natural relationships, mistaking accidents of birth and preexistent structures for nature. Or worse, often the filiative relationships will be put forward as the only significant type of relationships. Affiliation is the process whereby the individual begins to confront preexistent structures, make choices, and develop rational processes—all in order to establish relationships beyond the moment of filiation.

9. Kant, only a few decades earlier, had used the term "house" (*Haus*) in his discussion of the family, designating the family as a larger production unit than found in Hegel's parameters.

10. "Natural" heterosexuality is not synonymous with coitus. Men and women "naturally" enjoy many forms of mutual pleasuring that have nothing to do with coitus. However, proceeding from the "naturalness" of this union, Hegel went on to identify the "natural" essential traits of the gendered partners of this form of marriage. The well-known litany ensued: passivity versus activity, internal versus external, intuition versus reason, etc. These oppositions in turn established the "naturalness" of the well-known division between the private (familial) sphere and the public sphere. The ethical union of marriage as site of heterocoital sexuality is thus the ethical center of "natural" concentric spheres that comprise the various levels of the nation. From this ethical union emerges the (male) individual who occupies a productive public position and further recognizes his role as citizen and member of the nation-state. See especially paragraphs 164–167. Alternative to the assertions of "nature" here, one way of explaining the urgency with which Hegel aligned marriage and racial reproductive capabilities is in the recognition that where the modern state bases its legitimacy on a claim of lineage to territory, the regulation of marriage becomes one of its chief concerns as the site of the perpetuation of the nation.

11. Hegel writes, "When women are in charge of government, the state is in danger, for their actions are based not on the demands of universality but on contingent inclination and opinion" (*PR* 166).

12. The term Hegel deployed, translated here as "civil society," is *bürgerliche Gesellschaft*. The *Bürger* is both citizen and bourgeois. Thus the common translation of the term as "civil society" masks its class character made explicit by the alternate and equally valid translation, "bourgeois society."

13. See Knight (1996). In this essay Knight, in a catechism-style question-and-answer section provided an answer that evidenced clearly his dread of the expansion of civil rights. No vision of socially negotiated consent underlies

his answer. He turns his back on questions of individual autonomy, freedom, and the pursuit of happiness. Instead, he raises a specter of social dissolution. He clings to the sanctity of established institutions, requiring that they remain always and forever as they are now.

Q   But if two people—any two people—love each other, why not let them marry?

A   Marriage is not just a matter of feelings. It is the specifically defined legal, social, economic and spiritual union of a man and a woman. The two sexes must be present for it to be marriage. If that definition is radically altered based on the "feelings" of those in other relationships, then the sky is the limit. There is no logical reason for not letting several people marry, or for gutting other requirements, such as minimum age, blood relative status or even the limitation of the relationship to human beings.

14.   By "queer families," I do not mean simply families that include lesbian and/or gay parents. I would hope we could think beyond Heather's two mommies and think about little Sarah with two mommies, two daddies, and a number of other significant caregivers, or little Sam with only one mommy. We could think of relations that are distinct from children and parenting. Or, as Foucault once enjoined us to do, we could think about families that might undo notions of age and power, e.g., in which younger people adopt older people. Thus the term "queer families" should designate any families deviating from the kinship structure of the bourgeois nuclear family.

15.   The lawyer defending Ms. Pickett's murderer was trying to craft an argument akin to the "homosexual panic" argument that had been used successfully to acquit gay-bashers.

16.   For those interested in questions of gender transgression, Ms. Nangeroni runs a radio program, "Gender Talk," and has an excellent website at www.gendertalk.com.

17.   For media discussions of varying domestic-partner agreements and legislation see Richardson, Ames, Sulavik, Joseph, Beachy, and Park (1993) or "Domesticated Bliss" (1992). Further The Human Rights Campaign Fund maintains a list of cities, colleges, and private employers with domestic partner laws; see http://www.hrc.org/issues/workplac/dp/dplist.html.

18.   One of the major critiques of the modern state came from a theorist whose name is currently out of fashion. In his critiques of Hegel, Karl Marx sought to identify the limits of a political emancipation vis-à-vis the modern state. For an excellent edited collection see McLellan (1977).

REFERENCES

Anderson, Michael. 1980. *Approaches to the History of the Western Family, 1500–1914.* London: MacMillan.

Crossick, Geoffrey. 1995. *The Petite Bourgeoisie in Europe, 1780–1914: Enterprise, Family, And Independence.* London: Routledge.

"Domesticated Bliss: New Laws Are Making It Official for Gay Or Live-In Straight Couples." 1992. *Newsweek*, March 23, pp. 62–63.

Hegel, Georg Wilhelm Friederich. *Elements of the Philosophy of Right.* 1821. Reprint, Cambridge: Cambridge University Press, 1995.

Hunter, Jean E. and Paul T. Mason, eds. 1991. *The American Family: Historical Perspectives.* Pittsburgh: Duquesne University Press.

Knight, Richard. 1996. "Answers to Questions About the Defense of Marriage." Family Research Council publication IS96C2HS.

Laslett, Peter. 1972. *Household and Family in Past Time.* Cambridge: Cambridge University Press.

McLellan, David, ed. 1977. *Karl Marx: Selected Writings.* Oxford: Oxford University Press.

Mitterauer, Michael. 1982. *The European Family: Patriarchy to Partnership from the Middle Ages to the Present.* Chicago: University of Chicago Press.

Richardson, Lynda, Katrine Ames, Christopher Sulavik, Nadine Joseph, Lucille Beachy, and Todd Park. 1993. "Proud, Official Partners: Gay and Other New Yorkers Using Law." *New York Times,* August 1, sec. 4, p. 1+.

Rubin, Gayle. 1993. "Thinking Sex: Notes for a Radical Theory of the Politics of Sexuality." In Henry Abelove, Michèle Aina Barale, and David M. Halperin, eds., *The Lesbian and Gay Studies Reader,* pp. 3–44. New York: Routledge.

"Same-Sex Marriage? Straight Talk from the Family Research Council." Radio discussion between Kristi Hamrick, Gary Bauer, Robert Knight, Anthony Falzarano. Family Research Council. WAVA, Washington D.C., 10 April, 1996.

Sheehan, Michael, with James K. Farge, ed. 1996. *Marriage, Family, and Law in Medieval Europe: Collected Studies.* Toronto: University of Toronto Press.

23

Transgenderism and Sexual Orientation: More Than a Marriage of Convenience?

Mary Coombs[1]

A hot topic in the gay and lesbian community these days is "same-sex marriage": Can we get it? Do we want it? How can we keep it? Apparently, from the flurry of activity in Hawaii and Vermont, and in the United States Congress and various other state legislatures, the religious right is equally agitated about making sure we don't have marriages they have to recognize. Curiously, however, very little attention has been paid to "same-sex marriages" that have existed for some time, in which one of the partners has undergone sexual reassignment surgery. Both gays and lesbians, on the one hand, and opponents, on the other, have settled attitudes and legal positions regarding gay and lesbian same-sex marriages between John and Sam or Susan and Lisa. But the terms of the debate also affect the transgendered "same-sex marriages" between John and "Sam, formerly known as Susie" or between John and "Susie, born as Sam."

In this essay, I want to examine the relationships—both theoretical and political—between transgenderism and homosexuality. I suggest that the two characteristics, and the communities of those whose identities are significantly formed by those characteristics, are related in complex ways. They are deeply linked politically, because they are seen as linked and treated as aspects of a similar deviance by the dominant straight community. Largely because of these perceptions, they often share common battles and thus can benefit from strategic cooperation and alliances. The questions of same-sex marriage and the related litigation that will follow the passage of the Defense of Marriage Act (DOMA)[2] provide one useful lens to examine this politics.

Conceptually, the two categories are quite distinct. Homosexuality is defined by one's sexual orientation: one is erotically attracted to people of one's own sex. Transsexualism is defined by one's gender identity: transsexuals experience a disjuncture between their anatomical sex at birth and their gender identity (a disjuncture termed by the medical profession as "gender dysphoria"). They frequently seek to change the anatomy to match the gender identity (since it appears impossible to change the gender identity to match the anatomy). Those who have completed sexual-reassignment surgery are sometimes referred to as postoperative transsexuals; one can also be considered a transsexual before surgery and some transsexuals never undergo surgery, though they consider themselves members of the "opposite" sex and often dress and act in ways that persuade most observers to agree with that assessment (see, e.g., Bolin 1995:447; Rothblatt 1995). A transsexual can be heterosexual or homosexual.[3] For example, a male-to-female transsexual who is attracted to women would define herself as a lesbian.

There is thus no logical connection between one's gender identity and one's sexual orientation. Historically, however, being attracted to women has been part of the definition of what it meant to be masculine (and being attracted to men part of the definition of femininity). Homosexuality was thus viewed as a kind of gender disorder: gay men were seen as naturally effeminate and lesbians as mannish. Part of the struggle for gay liberation has been a rejection of this medicalized view of homosexuality and an insistence on a conceptual separation between "homosexuality" and "gender disorder." This necessary movement has succeeded in many ways, including having homosexuality removed from the American Psychological Association's list of psychological disorders (although "gender disorder of childhood" has remained to haunt both gay and lesbian and transsexual youngsters, see Minter and Frye 1996; Sedgwick 1994). For many transsexuals, by contrast, the diagnosis of gender dysphoria is necessary to get the medical approval needed for the desired sex-reassignment surgery.

One, perhaps unintended, consequence of this divergence has been to create complex and sometimes troubled relationships between the gay/lesbian and the transsexual communities. We fight over history and heroes: were cross-dressing, unmarried historical figures such as jazz trumpeter Billy Tipton or the eighteenth-century aristocrat the Chevalier D'Eon unrecognized gay men or were they unrecognized transsexuals? The relationships are further complicated by the uneasy relationship between the leadership of gay/lesbian groups and the flamboyant drag queens (who cross-dress but are not, typically, transsexual) who were among the heroes of the Stonewall riots but who are sometimes treated as a political embarrassment (Arriola 1995).

On the one hand, the two communities have not been consistently politically allied. For a long period, the gay/lesbian community ignored the still nascent transgender community. This neglect was perhaps understandable; in the struggle to form a community, what appeared to be marginal issues, such as the inclusion or exclusion of groups like the transgendered, were neglected. The neglect has reflected primarily sins of omission, although in some contexts, such as the fight for protection against employment discrimination, many gay/lesbian political leaders have adopted a strategy that ignored the interests of transgender people in the hope of developing legislation that could be passed.[4] The results of a recent poll in a leading gay magazine, indicating that 64 percent of respondents felt that "gay and lesbian civil rights groups [should] make an effort to support the cause of transgender rights," is heartening (*The Advocate* 1997:8).

On the other hand, the transsexual and the gay/lesbian communities have common political interests, in large part because they have common enemies. Those enemies—the defenders of "traditional family values," who understand little about traditions, less about families, and nothing about any values worth protecting—see gays and lesbians as dangerous and disgusting in part because we, our love, and our relationships threaten their views of what men and women are. Transgendered people, their love and marriages, can and do evoke much the same fear and loathing and for much the same reasons. For example, Robert H. Knight, the "director of cultural studies" for the Family Research Council, who regularly denounces gay marriage, described transgenderism as "yet another social pathology" that "is part of a larger cultural movement to confuse the sexual roles and to usher in a relativistic mind-set concerning sexuality itself" (Knight quoted in Lembrorse 1997:13). And our common opponents often treat sexual orientation and gender-identity nonconformity as two aspects of the same "pathology." They "identify" gay men—so they can target them for discrimination—as much by their limp wrists and lack of interest in sports as by their lack of sexual interest in women.

The dominant ideology perceives sex, gender, and sexual orientation as inherently and essentially linked together in very specific patterns. These patterns are seen as natural, biological, and God-given—though simultaneously so fragile that they need the strong hand of the law to protect them. As Mary Anne Case, Katherine Franke, and Frank Valdes have all explained, that conflation of sex, gender, and sexual orientation is both powerful and powerfully dangerous (Case 1995; Franke 1995; Valdes 1995).

In the rest of this essay I focus on the way that conflation has been played out in the particular context of marriage. I begin with an examination of the cases involving marriage and transsexuals to see what they reveal about the images of sex and gender, of marriage and intimacy, embedded in the law of domestic relations, including the implications of those rules and images for the legal control of the relationships of gays and lesbians. I then consider the law and politics embedded in the challenges to restrictions on same-sex marriage that we can expect to contrive to arise over the next few years and consider how those challenges will be facilitated if the gay and lesbian community and the transgendered community work together.

SAME-SEX(?) MARRIAGES

CHALLENGES TO THE DOMINANT vision of marriage have been brought both in the context of gay or lesbian would-be spouses and of transsexual marriages. In the former context, the challenges have always been brought before any marriage; gay or lesbian couples sought to compel public officials to grant them marriage licenses. In all the cases until recently the judges rejected the challenges, often with a breathtaking dismissiveness, based on the dictionary definition of marriage[5] or a barely veiled religious view of what marriage must be.[6] Two more recent challenges have had more impact. The courts in Hawaii found that the refusal to permit same-sex marriages violated the state constitutional ban on sex discrimination since a woman could marry John, a man, but would be forbidden from marrying Susan, solely because Susan was a woman.[7] More recently, the Vermont Supreme Court found that the "common benefits" clause of the state constitution obligated Vermont to provide same-sex couples with all the legal benefits of marriage.[8]

Some of the most revealing discussions of same-sex marriages, however, occur in cases involving transsexuals. In these cases, typically, there *was* a marriage. Thereafter, the husband sought an annulment on the grounds that he could not have been married to the defendant since she was also a man (or, conversely, a wife claimed that the defendant-husband was really also a woman). In order to decide if there was a valid marriage, the court was forced to decide what it thought a marriage was and—insofar as it assumed a marriage is by definition a relationship between a "man" and a "woman"— how it defined those latter terms.

The best-known and most extensive discussion is in the British case of *Corbett v. Corbett.*[9] The petitioner-husband, Arthur Corbett, a transvestite who was married to a genetic woman, had associated with a "deviant" sub-culture and engaged in homosexual encounters before he met April Ashley. April, who was born as George Jamieson, a former merchant seaman, had joined a troupe of female impersonators and had later undergone sexual-reassignment surgery. Arthur fell in love with April and asked her to marry him, though he also testified that he was jealous of her success at feminin-ity. Just a few months after the wedding, Arthur successfully sought an annul-ment on two grounds: April was a man and (s)he had refused to consum-mate the marriage.

In the course of his decision, Lord Ormrod, who was a physician as well as a judge, discoursed at length on the sexual peculiarities of the parties and on transsexualism in general (as cited in Smith 1971:963, 1005 n. 277). He set out several potential criteria for determining an individual's sex, including (1) chromosomal factors; (2) gonadal factors (i.e., the presence or absence of testes or ovaries); (3) genital factors (including internal sex organs); (4) psy-chological factors; and (5) hormonal factors or secondary sexual character-istics (such as distribution of hair, breast development, physique, etc., which are thought to reflect the balance between the male and female sex hor-mones in the body). He concluded that the most significant were chromo-somes, gonads, and genitals, which together constituted "biological sex," or "true sex." These—or at least the first two—were fixed at birth and thus nothing afterwards, including sexual-reassignment surgery, could change an individual's true sex.

Lord Ormrod explained as follows why these criteria appropriately determined sex for purposes of marriage:

> sex is clearly an essential determinant of the relationship called marriage, because it is and always has been recognised as the union of man and woman. It is the institution on which the family is built, and in which the capacity for natural heterosexual intercourse is an essential element. . . . Since marriage is essentially a relationship between man and woman, the validity of the marriage in this case depends, in my judgment, on whether the respondent is or is not a woman. . . . The question then becomes what is meant by the word "woman" in the context of a mar-

riage. . . . Having regard to the *essentially heterosexual character of the relationship which is called marriage*, the criteria must, in my judgment, be biological, for even the most extreme degree of transsexualism in a male or the most severe hormonal imbalance which can exist in a person with male chromosomes, male gonads and male genitalia cannot reproduce a person who is naturally capable of performing the essential role of a woman in marriage.[10]

The judge simply assumed, without any felt need for argument or explanation, that the essence of marriage is a legal relationship within which heterosexuals can carry out heterosexual sexual relations. This worldview, in which heterosexuality is simply assumed as the only proper form of sexuality, is often referred to as "heterocentrism" (Franke 1995; Valdes 1995). Since marriage is essentially a heterosexual institution, it requires a man and a woman to be the "husband" and the "wife" respectively. But what exactly is the "essential role of a woman in marriage" that makes April ineligible? Perhaps it is that which April concededly could not do—procreate. Indeed, some opponents of recognizing gay marriage have argued that the core reason for legally recognizing and protecting marriage is to provide an institution in which procreation can occur. For example, conservative gay rights opponent Hadley Arkes has said that " '[s]exuality' refers to that part of our nature that has as its end the purpose of begetting . . . other forms of 'sexuality' may be taken as minor burlesques or even mockeries of the true thing" (Arkes 1995:321, 323).[11]

The logical flaws in such an argument are perhaps too obvious to mention, but I cannot resist. First, no state has ever required proof of capacity to procreate before issuing a marriage license to a different-sex couple, as the regular weddings at Century Village retirement community attest. Second, procreation does not need marriage. Third, procreation does not, in the late twentieth century, even need intercourse; assisted reproduction is a booming business. Fourth, parenting does not require procreation: singles and couples, married and unmarried, straight, gay, and transgendered can successfully raise children (if the state will let them). Finally, even if we thought marriage was a good thing for those who were going to rear children, providing a stable home and more than one adult deeply committed to the child's day-to-day welfare, it is unclear how the children reared in such homes would be harmed if Uncle Ted and Uncle George were also married.

Alternatively, Lord Ormrod may have meant that the essential role of a woman in marriage is providing a vagina as a penis receptacle. April, however, was a postoperative male-to-female transsexual; she *had* a vagina. Furthermore, an earlier English case had held that a husband was not entitled to an annulment because his wife had a physical defect that rendered intercourse impossible, since an operation was available that could adequately enlarge her vaginal cavity.[12] Lord Ormrod, however, in allowing Corbett's claim based on April's alleged refusal to consummate, stated:

> In any event, however, I would, if necessary, be prepared to hold that the respondent was physically incapable of consummating a marriage because I do not think that sexual intercourse, using the completely artificial cavity constructed by Dr. Burou, can possibly be described as "ordinary and complete intercourse" or as "vera copula"—of the natural. When such a cavity has been constructed in a male, the difference between sexual intercourse using it, and anal or intra-crural intercourse is, in my judgment, to be measured in centimetres.[13]

The syllogism seems to be: (1) April was born male; (2) therefore April is still male; (3) therefore intercourse between a man and April is inherently sodomy. For the judge to hold this marriage legitimate would be to break down the wall—perhaps stretched to mere centimeters—between "normal" heterosexual sexual relationships and gay ones.

Most American cases involving actual or contemplated transsexual marriages follow a similar, though more abbreviated, logic. In *Anonymous v. Anonymous*,[14] a New York court granted an annulment. It could have done so solely on the grounds of the wife's fraud—or perhaps the husband's incompetence—since he alleged that he was unaware until his wedding night that his bride had male sex organs. This aspect of the decision seems unexceptional: concealing the fact that one lacks the expected sexual equipment clearly fits the legal ground of fraud going to the "essentials of the marriage." The *Anonymous* court also held, however, that the marriage was void because the defendant was a man. Not only was he a man at the time of the marriage, with male genitalia, but, the court asserted, even sexual-reassignment surgery would not make him the requisite "true female." Marriage required a true male and a true female, since its purpose was procreation.[15]

Not long after *Anonymous*, the New York courts in *B. v. B.*[16] faced a challenge by a wife to the validity of a transsexual marriage. During their courtship, Frances B. explained, she had assumed Mark was a man, relying on his words, dress, and appearance. Upon marriage she discovered he was incapable of normal sexual intercourse, since he "does not possess a normal penis, and in fact does not have a Penis."[17] Mark answered that he was a female-to-male transsexual in transition. The court first held, citing both *Anonymous* and the gay marriage cases of *Baker v. Nelson*[18] and *Jones v. Hallahan*,[19] that marriage required one male and one female since "the marriage relationship exists with the results and for the purpose of begetting offspring."[20] "While it is possible that defendant may function as a male in other situations and in other relationships, defendant cannot function as a husband by assuming male duties and obligations inherent in the marriage relationship."[21] While one might think from the language above that these male duties involved impregnating one's wife, the court, confusingly, also cited cases granting annulments in cases of physical incapacity for intercourse.

B. v. B. had suggested that categorization of a person's sex is a functional question and that Mark might be legally male in other contexts. Other courts, however, have been reluctant to recognize a sex change in other legal contexts for fear that it will facilitate the petitioner's ability then to marry in his new sex. For example, the immediate issue before the court in *In re Ladrach*[22] was whether Ladrach, a postoperative male-to-female transsexual, could obtain a new birth certificate, reflecting her current sex and name. The court refused to order the bureaucracy to issue such a certificate precisely because Ladrach might then use that birth-certificate sex to marry "another" man.

More recently, a Texas court in *Littleton v Prange*[23] had to determine if Christie Littleton had been validly married and was thus a "surviving spouse" who could bring a medical malpractice action. Littleton was a postoperative male-to-female transsexual when she married. Her husband knew of her status and they were married for seven years before his death. Nonetheless, the court held that, since she was born with male biology and "a person's gender [is] immutably fixed by our Creator at birth,"[24] she remained legally male. The marriage was thus void.

One should highlight the irony of such rulings. A male-to-female transsexual cannot legally marry a genetic man. Since she is still legally a man, then, she could marry a woman. In effect, the legal rule, designed to prevent same-sex marriages, would forbid postoperative transsexuals from entering into what appear to be opposite-sex, heterosexual marriages but permit them to enter into what would appear to be, and what the person and his/her partner would understand to be, marriages between two women or two men.

The most disturbing aspect of these cases is the normative imposition of a particular state-sanctioned view of marriage. Even where the parties are aware of the sexual identity of their partners, the marriage is void because it is not within the legally cognizable bounds of marriage. This conception of marriage, like the one underlying the Defense of Marriage Act, and the debate preceding it, treats the desires of the parties to the marriage as irrelevant. Marriage between any couple except a "real" man and a "real" woman is void. These holdings permit one of the parties to such a marriage to use the law strategically to avoid marital obligations they willingly and knowingly accepted, just as some lesbian biological mothers have sought to deny the legitimacy of their relationships in order to block their comother from continued access to their child.[25] They would also apparently permit such a marriage to be ignored or challenged by third parties, such as parents, children of a prior marriage, insurance companies, or tortfeasors, who would benefit legally if the marriage did not exist, just as people in those categories benefit by the legal invisibility of lesbian and gay relationships.[26]

Just as *Baehr* and *Baker* reversed a consistent pattern of losses in gay and lesbian marriage cases,[27] one of the transsexual marriage cases got its result right and its analysis at least partially right. *M. T. v. J. T.*[28] involved a marriage between a man and a wife whom the husband knew had undergone male-to-female sexual-reassignment surgery before the marriage; indeed they began living together before the operation and J.T. had helped pay for M.T.'s surgery. They married and lived as husband and wife for two years, regularly engaging in penile-vaginal intercourse. Nonetheless, when M.T. sued for divorce, J.T. countered that she was a man and that the marriage was therefore void. M.T., with the equities clearly in her favor, prevailed. The court assumed that marriages are heterosexual unions, between differently sexed persons.[29] But it concluded that M.T. was a woman. It held, unlike Corbett or Littleton, that the most important criteria for classifying a person as male or female is core gender identity, at least where contemporaneous anatomy was consistent with it, not chromosomes. "[T]he dual test of anatomy and gender" determined sexual capacity, which was defined as "the coalescence of both the physical ability and the psychological and emotional orientation to engage in sexual intercourse as either a male or a female."[30] Under this test, M.T. was a female and her marriage to a male was therefore valid.

In one sense, *M. T.* splits the interests of gays and lesbians from those of heterosexual transsexuals, since it assumes that heterosexual sexual intercourse is the defining marital act. Its analysis, however, provides a step forward from *Corbett* and *Anonymous* in advancing the mutual interest of all sexual minorities in de-heterosexualizing marriage and in exploding the conflation of sex, gender, and sexual orientation. *M. T.* rejects procreation as the necessary purpose of marriage; instead, it views the core meaning of the marital relationship as intercourse and intimacy. Procreation excludes non-heterosexual relationships by definition. While gays and lesbians can and do procreate, neither marriage nor sexual intimacy advances their capacity to do so. Intimacy and intercourse, however—at least if the latter is not narrowly limited to penile-vaginal forms of erotic intimacy—are as descriptive of gay relationships as of heterosexual ones.

The legal responses to transsexual marriages reveal the insistence, often in the face of contrary evidence, that society and law can and must divide people into two genders (masculine and feminine), which precisely map onto two sexes (male and female). Yet it is readily apparent that gender is neither inherent in the biology of sex differences nor naturally divided into two distinct and internally coherent categories. As a friend put it, "knowing who is the butch doesn't tell you who changes the tires." Less obviously, biological sex is also more complex than the dichotomous model,[31] as the transsexual case law described above demonstrates. There are numerous criteria for classifying people as male or female (Smith 1971:965). Many of these criteria themselves do not divide people into two distinct groups. Intersexed people may have ambiguous genitalia or gonads that are male on one side and female on the other (Lorber 1994). Secondary sex characteristics are even more variable; there are women with more facial hair than some men and men with more developed breasts than some women. Even if an individual could be easily classified on each individual criterion, he or she might have "male" genitalia but "female" secondary sex characteristics as a result of a lack of testosterone. *Corbett* and *M. T.* provide only two of numerous possible formulae to apply in such cases.

The difficulty of classification by gender or sex might make us consider whether and when society or the legal system really needs to classify individuals by sex at all (Rothblatt 1995). And, of course, if the state did not engage in such classification, it would not and could not limit the right to marry based on that no-longer-legally available information. Same-sex marriage would be achieved as a political matter because the state would have no way of knowing as a legal matter the sex of the two parties to the ceremony. As one commentator notes, "it is only by virtue of having limited the marital partnership to two persons of opposite sexes that courts find themselves in the uncomfortable position of having to define explicitly what those opposite sexes are" (Franke 1995).

The challenge to prescriptive-sex classification might extend beyond the law itself. In a range of areas, the social demand for conformity to one of two (the right one of two) gender models disadvantages people who cannot or will not conform: transgendered people, as well as masculine women and effeminate men who don't self-identify as transgendered. Many of these gender nonconformists are in fact gay or lesbian. Others are assumed to be, because, as one commentator put it: "popular opinion agrees with medical science: a 'sissy' should, must, and does inhabit every 'queer,' and a 'tomboy' every 'dyke,' and vice versa" (Valdes 1995).

A challenge to the coherence of sex as a conceptual and not merely a legal category, however, is problematic for the gay/lesbian community. It would require that gays and lesbians "question their definition of their sexual identity, which is currently based solely on the [sex] of their desired partners" (Signorile 1996). If this description is correct, gay/lesbian identity rests on a coherent and stable sense of the partners' sex (Whittle 1996:196, 202). If I am a lesbian, then I am a woman who is attracted to women, rather than men. But how do I respond to someone whose sex is unclear or inconsistent?

One might restate the dilemma by asking whether what attracts one person to another person is their sex, or their gender, or some complex interaction of the two. Is sexual orientation about attraction to organs and what we do with them or to feminine or masculine persons? The latter are clearly cultural constructs, though statistically highly linked to sex, i.e., female and male anatomies. Like most interesting questions, the answer, I suspect, is a form of "it depends." Some people, both gay and straight, are primarily erotically attracted to particular bodies; others have a sexual orientation rooted more in a desired intimacy with people of a particular gender. For example the protagonist in Leslie Feinberg's *Stone Butch Blues* is attracted at different points in the novel to femme lesbians and to a male-to-female transsexual. She explains: "It doesn't matter whether it's women or men—it's always high femme that pulls me by the waist and makes me sweat" (1993:274). Other people are erotically attracted only to certain combinations of sex and gender, as with femmes who desire butches, but not masculine males.

Because sex and gender are so conflated, we have only the merest fragments of data from which to theorize about what sexual orientation might mean in a world where gender either became disassociated from anatomical sex or disappeared as a coherent category. One source of knowledge may develop from erotic uses of the World Wide Web, in which people can and do take on gender identities distinct from their anatomy and engage in virtual sex with people whose "real world" sexuality and gender they cannot know (Turkle 1995). Another is an examination of the responses of people whose sexual partners announce their transsexualism and their intent to change their anatomical sex. Some partners leave, while others maintain the relationship (thus creating some of the marriages discussed above, which are arguably "same-sex"). Perhaps those with sexual orientations are more likely to leave; those with gender orientations more willing to stay (Bolin 1995:483–84).

In any event, transsexuals are not simply interesting data points for sociological analysis, but real people with real relationships and real political interests. In the remainder of this chapter, I examine the ways in which DOMA may affect such marriages and the questions that impact raises for political and legal strategies by the gay/lesbian and the transsexual communities.

TRANSGENDERS, QUEERS, AND DOMA

ONE ASPECT OF THE prejudice against gays, lesbians, and other sexual minorities has always been the restriction on the right to marry. The issues involved in determining who may marry were immediately and concretely crucial for such transgendered people as M.T. and Ashley Corbett. Until recently, however, marriage seemed so unlikely that it was not a major focus of the political agenda of the gay/lesbian community. Recent events, however, have changed the political landscape. A constitutional referendum eliminated the practical effect of the court victory in Hawaii, and the Vermont legislature chose to grant gays and lesbians the benefits, but not the status, of marriage, in response to that state's constitutional challenge. The picture overall is somewhat muddy, but the likelihood that same-sex marriage will become a reality somewhere in the United States is substantially higher than anyone would have predicted ten years ago.

Meanwhile, political forces, largely fueled by the religious right, have rallied throughout the United States to derail gay marriage. Note that I say gay marriage here, though the Hawaii and Vermont litigation and the various marriage-restricting bills are articulated in terms of same-sex marriage. The opponents' rhetoric makes clear that they have conflated the two; the focus of the opposition is on two gay men or two lesbians celebrating and legitimating their love in a process that both recognizes that union with symbolic public approbation and provides the concrete economic benefits that accrue to those who are married. (One might note the irony that groups that once excoriated gays and lesbians for their alleged wild and promiscuous sexuality now work to deny gays and lesbians access to the most traditional, monogamous sexual outlet.)

The conflation of "gay" and "same-sex" assumes what is generally, but not necessarily, true: that a "man" who wants to marry another "man" is erotically attracted to the sex of his chosen partner. First, this assumes that marriage is always about sexual attraction and never about companionable but nonerotic couplings (as has occurred not infrequently in situations where one or both partners is gay/lesbian). It also assumes that sex and sexual orientation are stable. But consider the marriage of a couple who were male and female when married. Afterward, the wife recognizes herself as a transsexual and undergoes sex-reassignment surgery. Adam and Eve have now become Adam and Steve. If Adam chooses to remain married because he still loves the person he married, though he is more sexually attracted to women, we would have a same-sex marriage but not a gay marriage.

Thus, when legislation uses "same-sex" language it in fact forbids more than homosexual marriages; it forbids some existing marriages. This overinclusiveness may provide a means by which gay/lesbian and transgender lawyers and activists can cooperate and organize together to fight such laws. If the gay leadership ignores its transgender compatriots, however, it may instead facilitate an undesirable resolution of the gay/same-sex disjuncture. Legislators and courts may shift their focus from marriage and intimacy and gender equality—grounds on which the gay/lesbian community has the moral high ground—to a more problematic focus on homosexual sodomy.

Those lawyers and activists who are working to make same-sex marriage rights available recognize that much of the political and strategic work must focus on various new and old state laws that restrict marriage licenses to applicant couples in which "one party is a male and the other party is a female," or that refuse to recognize out-of-state same-sex marriages. In planning legal strategy, however, they have focused in significant part on DOMA, while recognizing how these state laws will frame litigation options. I shall take the same focus in this chapter.

DOMA, the extraordinarily ill-named Defense of Marriage Act, was passed by Congress and signed by President Clinton in late 1996. The statute has two parts. The first, in effect, authorizes states to ignore same-sex marriages entered into in other states. This is extraordinary, because one of the basic understandings of our federal system, built into the Constitution and implementing legislation, is what is known as "full faith and credit." It means that each state must recognize the legitimacy of legal proceedings in other states. For example, if I sue you in North Dakota and win a judgment that you owe me five thousand dollars, I can move to collect that judgment against you in Ohio, and Ohio must recognize the judgment; they cannot let you reargue the case in the Ohio courts. DOMA changes this fundamental rule for same-sex marriages. It says that no state "shall be required to give effect to any public act, record, or judicial proceeding" of any other state "respecting a relationship between persons of the same sex that is treated as a marriage under the laws of such other State . . . or a right or claim arising from such relationship."[32]

The second substantive section of the statute requires the federal government to ignore such marriages. "In determining the meaning of any Act of Congress, or of any ruling, regulation, or interpretation of the various administrative bureaus and agencies of the United States, the word 'marriage' means only a legal union between one man and one woman." It further, if somewhat ungrammatically, states that in such federal statutes, regulations, etc., "the word 'spouse' refers only to a person of the opposite sex who is a husband or wife."[33]

This statute has a wide range of implications, some of which are more readily challengeable than others. Lawyers and activists seeking to overturn the statute must strategize carefully to consider how best to structure challenges to the statute to maximize the chances of winning and to maximize what will be won.

How can a case arise under DOMA? First, there must be a same-sex marriage that has occurred and is valid under the laws of the state where it was celebrated. The second part of DOMA will create cognizable harm when someone in such a marriage is denied some federal benefit to which he or she would otherwise be entitled, such as spousal benefits under Social Security or rights to visit a spouse in a Veterans' Administration hospital. The first part will be challengeable when a case arises in, say, Florida, in which part of the issue is whether the Florida courts must recognize the validity of a same-sex marriage celebrated in Vermont. Thus, no DOMA challenge involving a gay or lesbian marriage can occur until some state finally decides that such marriages are legal there. This is at least months, perhaps years, away.

Meanwhile, arguably same-sex marriages already exist. The most likely of these to lead to legal problems under DOMA involve transsexuals. The transsexual marriages that might lead to DOMA-based harms and thus to challenges to DOMA, come in two forms. First, a challenge may arise in cases such as *M.T.* or *Corbett*, involving a marriage between a person of one sex and a person who had already transitioned to the other sex—for example, a genetic man marrying a male-to-female transsexual. Licenses for such marriages may have been obtained either because the documentation of the transsexual partner had been changed to reflect her new sex or because the bureaucrats in the state where the marriage was performed, seeing what appeared to be an ordinary male-female couple, never asked for documentary proof of sex. Since the then-married couple does not appear to raise any same-sex marriage issues, the challenge to the validity of the marriage will likely arise as a litigation tactic by the nontranssexual spouse, as it did in *Corbett* and *M.T.*, or by some other party with knowledge of the transsexualism who would benefit by having the marriage declared void, as happened in *Littleton.* Imagine a divorce case or an inheritance case in which the issue of transsexualism is raised and in which the marriage was celebrated in New Jersey, between New Jersey residents, and litigation later arises in Florida. Ordinarily, the Florida court would look to the law of New Jersey to decide the validity of the marriage. Thus, a marriage that was valid when performed in New Jersey, remains valid even after the spouses move to Florida. One of the spouses in Florida can sue and get spousal support or a portion of the marital property. Similarly, the surviving partner will be deemed a widow(er) entitled to inherit in preference to, say, the deceased partner's parents. Either spouse will be entitled to bring a loss-of-consortium claim if the other spouse is injured during their vacation in Florida.

These obligations of one state to recognize an out-of-state marriage are not absolute, however. Even among opposite-sex marriages, states can apparently refuse to recognize an out-of-state marriage in certain narrow circumstances, such as when they deem it incestuous. The interplay of these fuzzy rules, state laws about who can marry, and the complexity of DOMA itself will make any litigation over the duty to recognize an out-of-state same-sex marriage complicated. If the court needs to reach the question, however, there are a number of arguments that might be available to hold that DOMA is unconstitutional and thus that the marriage—or an alimony award or inheritance claim that flow from the marriage—is valid.

A transsexual and his/her partner might also provide the test case to challenge DOMA and other limitations on the recognition of same-sex marriage via a different route. Begin with a traditional mainstream couple: he is genetically, anatomically, and chromosomally male and dresses and acts in a masculine fashion; she is similarly female and feminine. One of them, after the marriage, recognizes that he or she is a transsexual. Assume, for example, that the wife comes to understand himself to be a man, although born with female anatomy. He then begins to dress and act as a man, takes male hormones, and ultimately undergoes sexual-reassignment surgery. The husband may, of course, decide that this was not part of his expectations at marriage and seek a divorce. But not all partners of transsexuals are, in effect, so committed to sex and sexual orientation as central to their intimate lives, or their marriages. The husband may decide that he still loves and wishes to remain married to the person whom he married, although that person is now a man. Meanwhile, the transsexual spouse may also want to remain in the marriage, whether because he understands himself to be a gay man or because, whatever his erotic interests, he still loves his husband. We now have, for all intents and purposes, a same-sex marriage. It may or may not be a "gay marriage," depending on how the spouses understand themselves. In effect, this is the situation that *Baehr* makes doctrinally central: it is about gender/sex, not necessarily about sexual orientation.

Of course, one could argue that this is not a same-sex marriage. If *Corbett* and *Littleton* were right, and sex is defined by chromosomes, the wife is still a woman, though he is now a woman with a penis. And, as a woman, he is entitled to marry a man or, certainly, remain married to a man. He is, in the language of DOMA, a "person of the opposite sex who is a wife." Nonetheless, by external appearances and by the self-understanding of the spouses, this has become a same-sex marriage. Such a couple might present the same problems of interstate recognition of marriages and of their legal consequences as were described above in the context of a marriage that follows the sexual-reassignment surgery of one of the spouses.

The challenge to traditional notions of marriage as being limited to opposite-sex couples can also arise in a slightly different context—one in which the couple are genetically and anatomically opposite sex at the time they marry, but one of them intends to have sex-reassignment surgery. In effect, the marriage is formally quite traditional, but the intent of the parties is to have a same-sex marriage. As the legal rules are currently designed, such couples can marry. For example, an Ohio judge held he was legally required to issue a marriage license to Debi Easterly and Paul Smith, since Paul still had male sex organs, although Paul was in transition to becoming a woman and described himself as a lesbian.[34] The same situation occurred in Oregon where the Associated Press reported that Lori Buckwalter had been taking hormones and planned surgery to complete her male-to-female transformation, but "since he legally remains a man until then, Buckwalter is free to marry Sharon Contreras today."[35] (In effect, a gay man can marry another gay man today—but only if one of them is a female-to-male transsexual!)

In either of these latter situations, we have a couple, legally married, who appear to be of the same sex. Because they present a *visual* challenge to the notion that marriage is limited to opposite-sex partners, they are more likely to face the denial of any of a range of federal benefits contingent on marriage.[36] A Social Security agency may be unwilling to grant a surviving spouse's benefit, upon the death of a male worker, to a person who looks like a man and says he is a man. The Immigration and Naturalization Service might be unwilling to grant the spousal immigration preference to a female United States citizen's apparently female spouse. An Internal Revenue Service auditor may challenge a joint tax return signed by Anne and Linda Smith. In such cases, the spouse/couple will presumably seek to protect their continued access to the benefits associated with their marriage by raising all possible arguments, including constitutional arguments.

As a matter of formalist legal doctrine, these transsexual same-sex marriage situations are analogous to the cases that might later be presented by gay or lesbian couples who will be married in the first state to explicitly permit same-sex marriage. Because these marriages already exist, however, the first cases challenging DOMA may arise before gay/lesbian same-sex marriages even occur. Whether transsexuals end up litigating the validity of their marriage under DOMA depends on the actions of both the federal authorities and of the parties to such marriages. Activists and scholars can carefully design the "perfect lawsuit" with the "perfect plaintiffs," but real people whose real interests are at stake will not await the convenience of the activists. (It is worth noting, in this regard, that the landmark Hawaii litigation challenging marriage restrictions originally arose from the actions of the plaintiffs themselves and only later became a test case for Lambda Legal Defense Fund and other legal-activist organizations.) The course of such litigation, however, and the strategic decision-making surrounding it, can be influenced by activists and community leaders, if they maintain trust and lines of communication with the population that may end up as the actual parties to such litigation.

In considering how to deal with the strong possibility that these first challenges will involve people from the transgender community, those whose primary concern is the validity of gay and lesbian marriages, must examine both the legal and the political commonalities and differences between gay/lesbian marriages and transgender marriages, between our political interests and the political interests of the transgender community. In trying to imagine how a court will respond to a transgender marriage case, one must recognize the various ways in which a court could distinguish it from a gay or lesbian marriage. In some ways, transgender marriages may appear even more problematic; public understanding and support of transsexuals is probably still at a more primitive stage than that for gays and lesbians, especially gays and lesbians who seek the relatively traditional lifestyle defined by marriage.

Similarly, the equal-protection argument may be harder for a court to understand in a transgender context. In any equal-protection case the plaintiff has to argue, in effect, "You are treating me differently than some other group of persons, and you don't have a sufficiently good justification for doing so." The argument is very difficult to make unless one can claim that you are being treated differently based on some characteristic that the courts have already recognized as particularly troubling, such as race or gender. The gay/lesbian plaintiffs would argue, as they did in the Hawaii litigation: "I am being discriminated against because of my sex. If I were a woman, you would let me marry Sam. The only reason you are preventing me from doing so is because I am a man." The transsexual's equal-protection argument is more difficult. In any particular lawsuit, the court might say: "We find that you are a man; therefore you can't marry [or be married to] this other man." One response is precisely the gay/lesbian argument; if there were no sex-based limitation on who could marry whom, it wouldn't matter what sex we decided this transsexual person was. Alternatively, the transsexual plaintiff would have to argue that he or she had an equal-protection right to be treated the same as nontranssexuals who had the same chromosomes, or who had the same gender identity. But this is not readily described as discrimination based on sex. Thus, it would seem that transsexual plaintiffs would have a harder time than gay or lesbian plaintiffs challenging marriage restrictions.

On the other hand, as Phyllis Randolph Frye, a leading transgender activist, has argued, there is a factually appealing case for finding against DOMA and thus in favor of the marriage, when the nontransgendered partner to a "postwedding transsexual marriage" case is the litigant.[37] Imagine that John marries Susan. Susan then comes out as a transsexual, undergoes sex-reassignment surgery, and now presents himself as Sam. John chooses not to divorce. Imagine further that the government now refuses to allow

John to file his income tax returns jointly with Sam or to obtain Social Security benefits as Sam's spouse. Or imagine that Sam dies and his parents claim that they are the next of kin because John can't be Sam's spouse, since both are men. Here is a person who has chosen to "stand by his man" and to maintain a marriage, while the state is seeking to deny the legitimacy of that marriage or to deny him benefits he was already entitled to obtain. Family values are about encouraging and stabilizing marriage, not punishing marital fidelity. The nontranssexual spouse as plaintiff presents perhaps the most appealing challenger to DOMA.

The different potential litigation structures present cases of differing strengths, whether the litigants are a transgendered person and spouse or a gay or lesbian couple. For example, the traditional structures of full faith and credit doctrine indicate that it will be much harder to argue that DOMA is unconstitutional when applied to the recognition of a marriage than when applied to the recognition of a judgment, such as a divorce decree or a judgment in a wrongful death claim against the killer of one's same-sex spouse, which "aris[es] from [a same-sex marital] relationship." On the other hand, winning the easier case may result in a judgment of limited effect. If our divorces are recognizable everywhere, but our marriages are not, we can, for example, go to Hawaii to marry, but we can't safely leave. There are similarly complex judgments involved in strategizing over which cases to bring, which arguments to raise, and in which states to litigate, and in picking the cases with the best facts and the most attractive plaintiffs. Deciding whether the "best" plaintiffs for a particular challenge are a gay couple, a heterosexual transsexual couple, or even a gay transsexual couple would be part of that strategizing.

Strategy involves not just picking which cases to bring (especially since no one can prevent others from bringing other cases) but also working in an engaged and respectful way in providing litigation advice, political and financial support, and amicus briefing to help shape the litigation. It also involves understanding that litigation itself is only likely to be effective as part of broader strategies of influencing legislation, raising consciousness, organizing communities, and educating the public. In these wider contexts, as well as in litigation, the question of community definition and group alliances are crucial. The goals of gay and lesbian activists, both lawyers and others, are most likely to be met if they work with their transsexual counterparts, while recognizing that the concerns of the two communities are not identical.

The marriages of transsexuals and their partners are the ones first at risk.

Those of us in the gay/lesbian community cannot ask them to wait for us to litigate our cases, especially if and when they suffer concrete harm, merely because DOMA was designed only to harm gays and lesbians. The legislators who passed that statute, had they thought of transsexuals, would surely have discriminated against them as well. Here, as elsewhere, different minorities share common enemies and therefore common concerns. We need, at least, to overcome distrust and difference and create strategic alliances in order to serve our common interest in opposing discrimination. If and when that discrimination ends, we can decide what else binds us together and whether we are part of a larger queer community.

NOTES

1. Thanks to my colleague Clark Freshman and to Mary Bernstein for their suggestions, only some of which I was wise enough to adopt here.
2. The Defense of Marriage Act, PL 1–4–199 (Sept. 21, 1996), codified at 28 U.S.C. 1738C [Section 2] and 1 U.S.C. 7 [Section 3].
3. See Ross 1986, noting that there is no necessary link between transsexualism and sexual orientation and citing one study that showed that postoperative transsexuals were disproportionately homosexually oriented.
4. The text of the *Employment Non-Discrimination Act* (ENDA), as submitted in Congress and lobbied for by the Human Rights Campaign and other gay/lesbian leaders, provided protection on the basis of sexual orientation but not on the basis of gender nonconformity.
5. *Jones v. Hallahan*, 501 S.W.2d 588, 589 (Ky. Ct. App. 1978).
6. *Baker v. Nelson*, 191 N.W.2d 185, 186 (Minn. 1971). Other early cases include *Singer v. Hara*, 11 Wash. App. 247, 522 P. 2d 1187, rev. denied, 84 Wash 2d 1008 (Wash. Ct. App. 1974) and *Dean v. District of Columbia*, 653 A. 2d 307 (D.C. 1995).
7. See, e.g., *Baehr v. Lewin*, 852 P. 2d 44 (Haw. S. Ct. 1993) finding that the State could only win if it could show that the ban was needed to further a compelling state interest and *Baehr v. Miike*, 1996 WL694235 (Haw. Cir. Ct. 1996) trial court's decision that the state had been unable to do so. The legal effect, if not the logical persuasiveness, of those decisions has since been eviscerated, since the voters in Hawaii in November 1998 approved an amendment to the state constitution banning same-sex marriage.
8. *Baker v. Vermont*, 744 A. 2d 864 (Vt. S. Ct. 1999). In response, the Vermont legislature chose not to extend marriage per se but to give same-sex couples the

opportunity to enter "civil unions," which have essentially all the practical characteristics of marriages. See Vt. H.B. 847 (enacted 2000).

9. [1971] P. 83, [1970] 2 All E.R. 33, [1970] 2 WLR 1306.

10. [1970] 2 All ER at 48 (emphasis added).

11. See Arkes 1995. See also *Adams v. Howerton*, 673 F. 2d 1036. 1042–43 (9th Cir.), *cert. denied*, 458 U.S. 1111 (1982), indicating that refusal to grant preferential immigration status to same-sex spouses might be justified by the fact that "homosexual marriages never produce offspring."

12. *S. v. S.* (otherwise W.), [1962] 3 All ER 55, sub nom S.Y. v. S.Y., [1963] P 37, [1962] 3 WLR. 526.

13. [1970] 2 All E.R. at 49. The term "intra-crural" refers to a form of intercourse in which the penis of one partner moves back and forth between the thighs of the other.

14. 67 Misc. 2d 982; 325 N.Y.S. 2d 499 (1971).

15. 325 N.Y.S. 2d at 501.

16. *B. v. B.*, 78 Misc. 2d 112, 255 N.Y.S. 2d 712 (1974).

17. 255 N.Y.S. 2d at 715.

18. 291 Minn. 310, 191 N.W. 2d 185 (1971), *appeal dismissed*, 409 U.S. 810 (1972).

19. 501 S.W.2d 588 (Ky. Ct. App. 1973).

20. 255 N.Y.S. 2d at 717.

21. 255 N.Y.S. 2d at 718.

22. 32 Ohio Misc. 2d 6, 513 N.E. 828 (1987).

23. 9 S.W. 3d 223 (Tex. Ct. App. 1999).

24. 9 S.W. 3d at 224.

25. See, e.g., In re Alison D. v. Virginia M., 77 N.Y. 2d 651, 569 N.Y.S. 2d 586, 572 N.E. 2d 27 (N.Y. Ct. App. 1991); T.B. v. L.R.M., 753 A. 2d 873 (Pa. Super. Ct. 2000); V.C. v. M.J.B., 748 A. 2d 539 (N.J. Sup. Ct. 2000).

26. This has already occurred in Littleton (challenge by tort-feasor) and, more recently, in a case brought by the child of a prior marriage, challenging the inheritance rights of his father's transsexual widow. As of this date, the trial court, in an unreported opinion, had followed the "once-a-man-always-a-man" approach. *Wall Street Journal*, July 7, 2000, p. A1.

27. See Franke 1995, at 42 n.165 (collecting cases). So far, however, no state has actually permitted same-sex marriage. The significance of Vermont civil union status for couples not residing in Vermont is entirely unclear at this time.

28. 140 NJ Super. 77, 355 A. 2d 204 (1976). More recently, in the unreported case of *Vecchione v. Vecchione*, the California trial judge recognized that Joshua, a postoperative female-to-male transsexual was a man and thus legally entitled

to be treated as the father of the child Kristi bore as the result of assisted reproduction during the marriage.

29. "[A] lawful marriage requires . . . two persons of the opposite sex. . . . In the matrimonial field the heterosexual union is usually regarded as the only one entitled to legal recognition and public sanction" 355 A. 2d at 207.

30. 355 A. 2d at 209.

31. See generally Burke 1996 and Lorber 1994, both analyzing the cultural construction of gender and its coercive effects.

32. 28 U.S.C. 1738C.

33. 1 U.S.C. 7.

34. *New Times* [Miami], January 8–15, 1997, p. 11.

35. Associated Press, December 14, 1996 (quoted in posting to Queerlaw listserv, December 16, 1996).

36. If the courts had a single, consistent definition of who is male and who is female for purposes of marriage, then either these couples would be deemed opposite sex (since they are chromosomally still one XX and one XY) or the post–sex-change married couples would be deemed opposite sex (since they currently have, between them, one set of male genitalia and one set of female genitalia). Doctrinal and logical consistency, however, have not been the hallmarks of case law involving transgendered people, gays and lesbians.

37. Comment during presentation on DOMA, National Gay & Lesbian Lawyers Association Conference, New Orleans, October 25, 1996.

REFERENCES

The Advocate. 1997. February 4, p. 8.

Arkes, Hadley. 1995. "Questions of Principle, Not Predictions: A Reply to Macedo." *Georgetown Law Journal* 84 (2): 321–28.

Arriola, Elvia R. 1995. "Faeries, Marimachas, Queens, and Lezzies: The Construction of Homosexuality Before the 1969 Stonewall Riots." *Columbia Journal of Gender and Law* 5: 33–77.

Bolin, Anne. 1994. "Transcending and Transgendering: Male-to-Female Transsexuals, Dichotomy, and Diversity." In Gilbert Herdt, ed., *Third Sex, Third Gender: Beyond Sexual Dimorphism in Culture and History*, pp. 447–86. New York: Zone Books.

Burke, Phyllis. 1996. *Gender Shock: Exploding the Myths of Male and Female.* New York: Anchor Books.

Case, Mary Anne. 1995. "Disaggregating Gender from Sex and Orientation: The Effeminate Man in the Law and Feminist Jurisprudence." *Yale Law Journal* 105: 1–106.

Feinberg, Leslie. 1993. *Stone Butch Blues: A Novel.* Ithaca, N.Y.: Firebrand Books.

Franke, Katherine M. 1995. "The Central Mistake of Sex Discrimination Law: The Disaggregation of Sex from Gender." *University of Pennsylvania Law Review* 144: 1–99.

Lambrose, R. J. 1997. "Career Opportunities." *Lingua Franca* 7, no. 10 (December/January): 13.

Lorber, Judith. 1994. *Paradoxes of Gender.* New Haven: Yale University Press.

Minter, Shannon and Phyllis Randolph Frye. 1996. "GID and the Transgender Movement: A Joint Statement by the International Conference on Transgender Law and Employment Policy (ICTLEP) and the National Center for Lesbian Rights (NCLR)." Unpub. ms. on file with author.

Ross, Michael W. 1986. "Gender Identity: Male, Female, or a Third Gender?" In William Walters and Michael Ross, eds., *Transsexualism and Sex Reassignment*, pp. 1–8. New York: Oxford University Press.

Rothblatt, Martine. 1995. *The Apartheid of Sex: A Manifesto on the Freedom of Gender.* New York: Crown.

Sedgwick, Eve Kosofsky. 1994. "How to Bring Your Kids Up Gay." In Michael Warner, ed., *Fear of a Queer Planet: Queer Politics and Social Theory*, pp. 69–81. Minneapolis: University of Minnesota Press.

Signorile, Michelangelo. 1996. "Transgender Nation," *OUT* 40 (June): 40–42.

Smith, Douglas K. 1971. "Comment, Transsexualism, Sex Reassignment Surgery, and the Law." *Cornell Law Review* 56: 963–1009.

Turkle, Sherry. 1995. *Life on the Screen: Identity in the Age of the Internet.* New York: Simon & Schuster.

Valdes, Francisco. 1995. "Queers, Sissies, Dykes, and Tomboys: Deconstructing the Conflation of 'Sex,' 'Gender,' and 'Sexual Orientation' in Euro-American Law and Culture." *California Law Review* 83: 1–377.

Whittle, Stephen. 1996. "Gender Fucking or Fucking Gender?" In Richard Ekins and Dave King, eds., *Blending Genders: Social Aspects of Cross-Dressing and Sex-Changing*, pp. 196–214. New York: Routledge.

24

Gender, Queer Family Policies, and the Limits of Law

Mary Bernstein

The interrelated purposes of this chapter are to understand shifts in lesbian- and gay-family policies, including domestic partnership, adoption, and marriage, and to situate these outcomes within the broader historical framework of lesbian and gay law in the United States. To understand the success of disparate laws regarding sexual orientation, I will first examine the nature of the challenge to dominant cultural norms about gender and sexuality presented by three areas of lesbian and gay law—sodomy statutes, discrimination, and family law—that "represent the central areas of the struggle for lesbian/gay equality" (Rubenstein 1993:xvi). For each area, I will argue that the political "bargains" made by activists in fighting for these laws circumvent rather than embrace the challenge to heteronormativity, thus leaving dominant norms intact. In the long run, incremental legal change may provide the space for more lesbians and gay men to come out, which could challenge heteronormativity. But the likelihood of legal change is determined by the ability of lesbian and gay activists to frame issues in such a fashion that dominant norms are no longer threatened as well as by the type of state action required.

The lesbian and gay movement has never been unified in its goals. While some claim that homosexuality is a trait as neutral as left-handedness (Cruikshank 1992), a trait that in the absence of discrimination would be inconsequential, others argue that by its very nature, homosexuality presents a script for relationships not based on gender hierarchies, and for sexual liberation more generally (Adam 1987; Weeks 1989). Thus lesbian and gay activists pursue disparate goals or at times even the same goals for vastly different reasons. While acceptance is the goal of some, transformation of dominant cultural norms is the goal of others.

Because the law has been used to circumscribe the lives of lesbians and gay men, legal change is an important end in itself. For example, prohibitions that criminalize private, consensual sodomy between adults have been, and continue to be used to justify legal discrimination against lesbians and gay men (Copelon 1990; Cain 1993).[1] Historically, these statutes have been used to deny basic rights of association to lesbians and gay men, making, for example, lesbian and gay bars illegal and banning lesbian and gay student groups (Boggan, Haft, Lister, and Rupp 1975). By effectively equating lesbians and gay men with the commission of illegal acts, the sodomy statutes continue to be used to justify denying employment to lesbians and gay men, removing children from lesbian mothers, and a host of other injustices (Rubenstein 1993). Although few people are actually arrested under the sodomy statutes, the collateral damage remains great. In many states that have repealed their sodomy statutes, the law still provides no protection for lesbians and gay men from discrimination in housing, employment, or public accommodations. Other forms of antigay discrimination occur when the law grants benefits to opposite-sex spouses that it denies to same-sex couples (see Chambers, chapter 19) or when lesbians and gay men are either barred from adopting children or are disadvantaged in custody cases simply because of their sexual orientation. In short, lesbians and gay men need legal grounds for redress.

In addition to material ramifications, the law also has a symbolic function. By privileging certain family forms and prescribing gender behavior, the law helps construct some identities, persons, and families as "normal" while others are deemed "deviant." Those who do not conform to cultural norms are denied basic rights to which others are entitled. Activists often turn to the law for validation and acceptance or as a way to gain recognition for new identities.

Legal scholars recognize that the structure of legal discourse transforms everyday problems into its own terms (Merry 1990; Smart 1989). Interactions with legal institutions (and with the state more generally) have a conservatizing effect on social movements (Naples 1998; Rosenberg 1991), leading to cooptation of activists (Piven and Cloward 1977), to the abandonment of principles, or to reframing discourse and claims (Katzenstein 1990, 1995) so that the movement's transformative potential is lost. Scholars of so-called new social movements argue that the radical potential of social movements lies in their ability to create new values and recognition for new identities (Cohen 1985; Melucci 1985, 1989; Touraine 1981). Engagement with the state, then, may subvert the transformative potential of the lesbian and gay movement. Therefore it is important to understand why laws change, first because they provide limited protection from harm and often grant certain benefits, and second, to understand whether and how legal change will help lesbians and gay men either to gain acceptance on the one hand or to transform dominant cultural norms on the other.

This chapter will contend that the extent to which the state is asked to abstain from judgment and punishment or to actively acknowledge and endorse gender nonconformity and nontraditional family forms will significantly affect the likelihood of change. In other words, if the nonnormative behavior can remain hidden, or lesbians and gay men can be constructed as subjects separate from their gender and sexual object choice, or their relationships can be unequivocally classified as less than the dominant hetero- and gendernormative models, change may occur. The venue for change, whether through the courts or legislatures, is also affected by the nature of the "gender dissent" (Hunter 1991). The rule of *stare decisis* often makes the courts more amenable to change than the legislatures. Precedent, such as the right to privacy, lets litigants avoid making the gender- or sexual-object choice of lesbians and gays subject to debate.

This tension between obtaining legal change in order to gain acceptance for lesbians and gay men in the mainstream and refashioning dominant cultural norms creates a fundamental paradox. Although legal change is crucial to ending state interference in lesbian and gay lives as well as granting benefits and protection, the law does little to alter dominant norms, particularly when compromise is used to further legal change, as I will demonstrate. Those who turn to law and policy as a means to gain social acceptance will also be sorely disappointed, because the bargains they must make with lawmakers ensure that dominant norms underlying the opprobrium associated with homosexuality remain unchanged. In the battle over discourse and norms about gender and sexuality, legal change marks one step in the battle, not an endpoint.

DON'T PUNISH US: SODOMY STATUTES

OPPOSITION TO SODOMY STEMS initially from objections to nonprocreative sex; sodomy statutes initially condemned such acts between opposite-sex as well as same-sex partners (Greenberg 1988). During the twentieth century, sodomy has become increasingly linked to inappropriate sexual-object choice and to gender dissent. For example, in the early 1900s a "fairy" (i.e., a man who let himself be penetrated by other men) was considered abnormal, while the men who penetrated the fairy were considered appropriately masculine (Chauncey 1994). Similarly, "mannish" (Newton 1984) or "butch" lesbians were considered the *true* lesbians because of their (presumed) active-sexual role, which was an indicator of their inappropriate gender behavior. Experts suspected that conventionally feminine lesbians had been duped into lesbianism by their mannish counterparts, and even lesbians feared that "femmes" were most likely to "revert" to heterosexuality (Kennedy and Davis 1993). Eventually, the inappropriate gendered nature of the sexual-object choice embedded in the act of sodomy, more than its lack of connection to procreation, accounted for sodomy's continued criminal classification. Legally, the shift in thinking was codified by eight states in the 1970s that decriminalized sodomy between opposite-sex partners, while "specifying" homosexual sodomy for punishment (Bernstein 1997b; Hunter 1992).

Thus laws against sodomy signify state disapproval of sexual conduct considered by many to be sinful, sick, or morally repugnant, giving the state's official stamp of approval to heterosexual behavior. Even more profoundly, such laws signify support for a heteronormative order that posits distinct gender roles for men and women and thus supports a strict sex/gender system (Rubin 1984). This hegemonic masculinity equates penetration with femininity and hence with emasculation; men should be the agents of sexual encounters, not their object (Connell 1995). So why, then, have thirty-three states (ACLU 1999) overturned their sodomy laws?

A precise explanation of the pattern and timing of legal change would require an examination of variables such as the strength of the lesbian and gay movement, the type of state party system, and the size of the fundamentalist opposition (Bernstein 1997b; Button, Rienzo, and Wald 1996; Haider-Markel and Meier 1996; Nice 1988), but the purpose of this chapter is to create a more heuristic explanation of why such changes were possible at all, and why such changes vary across different areas of lesbian and gay law.

Sodomy laws not only condemned same-sex sexual behavior but also, theoretically at least, required the state actively to enforce those statutes. Repealing the sodomy statutes would not require the state to revoke its condemnation of sodomy, but only its responsibility for eradicating such behavior. In short, legal change could take place in the absence of condoning gender and sexual behavior considered "inappropriate." No state endorsement of gender dissent was necessary.

Second, the notion of a "right to privacy" could be used to justify removal of sanctions on the basis that no one would have to know about the gender/sexual transgressions taking place. Thus the price for an uneasy liberal tolerance is the closet. As Backer (1993) argues, "In return for removing the formal threat of severe criminal sanction for *hidden and discrete* acts (which society had rarely enforced in any case), dominant heterosexual society has sought the quiescence of sexual nonconformists—their tacit agreement to hide themselves from view and spare the beneficent dominant culture the disgust of any type of public presence" (759). Evidence that secrecy was the price of legal change is apparent in both judicial and legislative decision-making.

Legislative repeal of the sodomy statutes was based on an emerging legal trend toward eliminating "victimless" crime statutes. The stage for the repeal of the sodomy statutes was set in 1955 when the American Law Institute (ALI) set out to rationalize this country's laws, publishing a Model Penal Code for states to adopt, in whole or in part.[2] Among other changes, the revised code omitted penalties for private, consensual sodomy with another adult (whether same-sex or opposite-sex). The ALI's rationale was repeated in state legislatures across the country. In all, thirty-three states have decriminalized sodomy. Of the twenty-five states (twenty-six if you count Washington, D.C.) that decriminalized sodomy legislatively, twenty-one did so as part of overhauling their penal codes (Apasu-Gbotsu et al. 1986; Hunter 1992).

The drafters of the Model Penal Code were primarily concerned with practical issues of law enforcement. Embedded in the growing debate among scholars and lawyers over victimless crimes, the ALI wanted to eliminate crimes that lacked a complainant and from which no quantifiable harm resulted (Geis 1972). From a practical standpoint, the lack of a complainant (most arrests were for solicitation of sexual acts, not for commission of the acts themselves) made enforcement difficult. In order to catch people "in the act," potentially unconstitutional methods such as drilling holes in public toilets in city parks were used, turning the police into "Peeping Toms." Such methods were "unseemly," and entrapment and voyeurism could well be illegal. Evidence also suggested that such laws led to police corruption, as officers would blackmail fearful homosexuals in exchange for dropping all charges. Finally, lack of enforceability would lead to general disrespect for the law (Model Penal Code 1980).

None of the ALI's justifications for decriminalization challenged the normative status of homosexuality or allowed space for public approval or exposure to lesbians and gay men. Concerns over both victimless crimes and practical issues of law enforcement revolved around the private nature of the acts. No public harm occurred because the acts were consensual and discreet. Police became Peeping Toms because the acts were hidden. By contrast, the Model Penal Code maintained provisions for solicitation of "deviate" sexual contact because of the presumed public nature of the act. Later efforts to justify removal of solicitation statutes revolved around privacy as well, since it was argued that gay men (lesbians were generally not arrested for solicitation, since they do not have the same patterns of cruising as gay men) only solicited those they thought were also gay (UCLA 1966), leaving homosexuality with its attendant challenge to the sex/gender system below the public radar. In short, the reduction in state regulation was predicated on the private nature of the acts in question.

In order to repeal the sodomy statutes, the state also had to sidestep the issue of morality. Whether arguing that strict gender roles were divinely or biologically ordained, they were constructed as the foundation on which the family and ultimately society rested. Reporters for the ALI feared that homosexual "conduct threaten[ed] the moral fabric of society by undermining the viability of the family or on the supposition that permitting such behavior between consenting adults leads inevitably to the corruption of youth" (Model Penal Code 1980:90). But other provisions of the penal code prohibited nonconsensual sodomy and included age-of-consent laws so toleration rested on issues of consent and privacy. If homosexuality was indeed amoral behavior, the question still remained as to whether or not the law should or could punish all forms of amoral behavior.

A survey of legislative reference librarians (Apasu-Gbotsu et al. 1986) shows that states that decriminalized separated morality from law, arguing that law did not signify moral countenance or approval of sexual conduct, that immorality was not the same as criminality, that law should not be used to enforce purely religious or moral standards, or that these laws had no relationship to "family values." For example, in 1985, when Wisconsin, by special legislative bill omitted sanctions for private, consensual sex acts between adults, it stated explicitly that the state did not encourage sex outside marriage and supported the institution of marriage (Apasu-Gbotsu et al. 1986).

In short, the dominant sex/gender system was left intact, despite the decriminalization of sodomy.

In the 1986 *Bowers v. Hardwick* decision, the U.S. Supreme Court ruled that no right to engage in homosexual sodomy could be found in the constitution. This decision was part of a general erosion of the right-to-privacy doctrine (Tribe 1990) and was also based on misinformation and homophobia (Copelon 1990; Rubenstein 1993). The *Hardwick* defeat does not negate the idea that secrecy is the price lesbians and gay men must pay not to be branded criminal; rather, it shows that the state does not always accept the bargain of privacy.

When activists violated the bargain of liberal tolerance, no sodomy laws were overturned. For example, soon after *Hardwick*, the National Gay and Lesbian Task Force (NGLTF) issued a call to arms, appointing Sue Hyde director of its newly formed Privacy Project. Under the auspices of the NGLTF, Hyde was sent to the sodomy states to help organize repeal efforts (Hyde 1987). The Privacy Project coincided with a resurgence of radical tactics among lesbian and gay organizations that had been sparked by radical AIDS activism (Shilts 1987). In Georgia, for example, a demonstration in early 1990 "included gay couples lying down together in the road and embracing" (Walston and Usdansky 1990). According to the *Atlanta Journal and Constitution*, Rep. Cynthia McKinney, one of the bill's sponsors, "thought some House members were frightened off by mentions of homosexuality associated with the bill and that others harbored resentment stemming from a demonstration against the state sodomy law" (Walston and Usdansky 1990). The price for coming out of the closet was defeat.

State courts, similarly, required a secrecy-for-repeal bargain. Where discourse remained close to hegemonic values and argued for change based on privacy, state courts unflinchingly took on the consensual-sex statutes. So, for example, in *Commonwealth v. Wasson*, the Kentucky Supreme Court upheld the trial and Court of Appeals ruling that the statute violated the Kentucky state constitutional right to privacy and federal guarantees of equal protection. The Court, citing Kentucky's history of protecting the civil rights of its citizens, upheld the lower court decisions (Harlow 1992/93). Similarly, the Massachusetts Supreme Court ruled that the oral-sex statute violated the right to privacy (Rubenstein 1993).[3] More recently, the high court in Georgia overturned its sodomy statute based on state constitutional rights to privacy (*Powell v. State* 1998).

After *Hardwick*, privacy arguments were avoided in federal courts and litigators worked toward dissolving the equation of lesbian and gay status with commission of sexual acts. By separating identity from conduct, litigators could claim that discrimination against lesbians and gay men was unwarranted, because such decisions were based on status not behavior. In most court cases, it was never shown that those discriminated against actually engaged in prohibited sexual acts (Cain 1993). So litigators moved beyond simply arguing that unconventional sexuality was tolerable behind closed doors, to argue that such sexual activity might not be taking place at all. By stressing the independence of identity (being gay or lesbian) from behavior (committing sodomy), litigators abandoned any challenge to dominant cultural norms around sexuality.[4] Thus lesbian and gay activists placed themselves in the potentially dubious position of arguing that homosexuality has nothing to do with sexual acts.

Where novel claims demanded recognition of the morality of sodomy or of homosexuality, challenges generally failed. For example, the Texas Human Rights Fund (THRF) began a civil challenge to the Texas statute, with named plaintiffs seeking a civil declaratory judgment (*Texas v. Morales*). The THRF argued that the stigma that accrued to lesbians and gay men as a result of the mere existence of the sodomy statute, as well as the real danger of loss of housing or employment, entitled them to standing. By incorporating the idea of stigma into their argument, the THRF recognized the symbolic significance of the sodomy laws. By underscoring the collateral damage caused by the sodomy statute, the THRF was forcing the court to acknowledge that one should be allowed to have the public identity of being lesbian or gay (status) *even* if that implied certain expressions of sexuality (behavior). The trial judge found the statute unconstitutional (Wolfson and Mower 1994).

Faced with these novel claims, the Texas high court avoided ruling directly on sodomy. The Texas Supreme Court ultimately reversed the Court of Appeals decision that ruled the sodomy statute unconstitutional in *Morales*, claiming that Texas's bifurcated judicial system (between civil and criminal) meant that it lacked jurisdiction and thus the decision did not hold. A similar case in Louisiana that moved beyond simple issues of privacy also met with failure. Like *Texas v. Morales*, *People v. Baxley* argued that the stigma of the mere existence of the law should give the plaintiff standing. The Louisiana Supreme Court ultimately ruled that Baxley lacked standing because he had only been charged with solicitation and found the statute facially neutral, seeing no evidence of selective enforcement (Wolfson and Mower 1994). Thus in states where arguments moved beyond issues of privacy, challenges either failed or were the result of judicial legerdemain.

Eventually in *Lawrence and Garner v. Texas* (2000), a case where two men were arrested for having consensual sodomy in one of their homes, the Texas Court of Appeals found the sodomy law to be an unconstitutional violation of the state Equal Rights Amendment. The Court declared, "Our Constitution does not protect morality; it does, however, guarantee equality to all persons under the law" (cited in Lambda 2000).

The sodomy statutes support heteronormativity. Sexual contact between persons of the same sex fundamentally challenges hegemonic views of masculinity and femininity with their attendant views of sexuality. The rubric of the right to privacy allows laws to change while leaving dominant norms unchallenged. The importance of precedent for determining legal outcomes makes the courts amenable to change, because sexuality, gender, and morality never have to be discussed. However, when activists argue that the *public* stigma associated with sodomy and codified by the law is wrong, court challenges usually fail or are decided based on privacy.[5] Similarly, when the sodomy statutes are explicitly linked to lesbians and gay men, as in legislative debates, they are less likely to pass.

PROTECT US FROM HARM: HUMAN RIGHTS LAW

FIGHTING FOR THE INCLUSION of sexual orientation in human rights laws has occupied the lion's share of lesbian and gay activism[6] (Bernstein 1997b) and requires state intervention on behalf of lesbians and gay men. Such laws provide protection from discrimination based on categories such as race, sex, and national origin in a number of areas including employment, housing, and public accommodations (Bernstein 1997b, Button, Rienzo and Wald 1996, Haider-Markel and Meier 1996). So-called lesbian- and gay-rights ordinances add "sexual orientation" to the list of protected categories, granting basic protection enjoyed by other citizens to lesbians and gay men. Inasmuch as these laws protect people considered gender and sexual nonconformists from discrimination, they challenge gender stereotypes. Lesbian and gay activists have been quite successful in the area of human rights, passing such laws in 165 cities and counties, ten states, and Washington, D.C. (ACLU 1998).

In order to frame lesbian- and gay-rights ordinances so that gender norms were left unchallenged, activists had only to portray these laws in terms of basic rights to be protected from discrimination. In and of themselves, human-rights ordinances do not conceptualize lesbians and gay men as sexual or gendered beings, only as abstract citizens deserving of protection. Lesbians and gay men as commercial subjects (e.g., as employees, renters, and so on) do not, by definition, pose a challenge to dominant notions of gender and sexuality. Passing such laws, as it has turned out, does not involve any state endorsement of the morality or normalcy of homosexuality. Although lesbian- and gay-rights ordinances required more effort on the part of the state than repealing sodomy statutes (because many states provided some form of redress for those discriminated against [Button, Rienzo, and Wald 1996, 1997]), these laws do not require the creation of new state agencies, since lesbians and gay men could be incorporated into existing human-rights commissions designed to address issues of discrimination. Thus neither endorsement of homosexuality and gender dissent nor the equation of lesbian and gay relationships with heterosexual relationships was required for lesbian and gay rights ordinances to be passed.

Historically, activists have at times used campaigns for lesbian- and gay-rights ordinances as a way to challenge dominant views of gender and sexuality. At other times, the campaigns were attempts to obtain narrow legal protection from harm (Bernstein 1997a, 1997b). During the early 1970s heyday of gay liberation, activists in New York City used the struggle for lesbian and gay rights as a chance to gain a public forum from which to make a symbolic and cultural statement and to pursue the goals of politicization, mobilization, and visibility. Political reformists viewed mobilizing a lesbian and gay constituency in order to gain access to the polity as the primary goal of activism (Bernstein 1997a, 1997b). Cultural activists,[7] on the other hand, used the rights campaigns as a theater from which to stage a cultural critique. In line with the liberation movement's focus on challenging gender roles and the naturalness of heterosexuality (Adam 1987), the cultural leaders demanded open acknowledgment and representation of transvestites. New York City Council members ultimately used the confusion between homosexuality and transvestism to defeat the antidiscrimination bill, expressing fear that fair employment for homosexuals would require hiring transvestites (Marotta 1981:226).

Similarly, in Minneapolis in the early 1970s, cultural activists engaged in "a conscious struggle to redefine the social relations of gender and sexuality at the level of everyday life and experience" (Knopp 1987:247). Cultural strategies included a parade of drag queens testifying at committee hearings to underscore the social construction of gender and sexuality. As in New York, Minnesota political reformists sought access to the polity on its own terms, emphasizing similarities to the majority and thus neglecting the critique of hetero- and gendernormativity (Knopp 1987). Similar divisions over goals have occurred in other political campaigns (see for example, Halle chapter 22). Although battles for human-rights ordinances are often used as a vehicle for challenging gender- and heteronormativity, activists can choose to divorce these issues from political campaigns, as they alternately deploy identity to stress similarities to or differences from the majority (Bernstein 1997a, 1997b).

Although opponents often try to make lesbian- and gay-rights ordinances about sexuality and gender, there is nothing about antidiscrimination laws that inherently challenges the construction of gender. To counter such claims, activists in many states reframed their rhetoric and shifted strategies so that the passage of antidiscrimination laws was separated from issues of gender and sexuality. For example, on billboards and radio announcements, activists in Eugene, Oregon, simply insisted, "Discrimination, that's the issue" (Gay Writer's Group 1983). Similarly, in 1983 the Massachusetts Gay and Lesbian Political Caucus, which had worked unsuccessfully for ten years to pass a statewide lesbian and gay rights bill, hired a full-time professional lobbyist to pursue "what might be termed a quintessential 'insider' strategy" (Cicchino, Deming, and Nicholson 1991:567). According to Cicchino et al. (1991), the strategy was to emphasize that lesbians and gay men are ordinary people, just like everyone else; to maintain a nonconfrontational style, requesting only protection from certain harms; to minimize publicity; and to foster personal contacts with legislators (1991:567).

Unlike the early activists who embraced the unconventional, lesbian and gay activists in Massachusetts dodged the issue of morality, claiming that, moral or not, being lesbian or gay does not warrant discrimination. Over time, opponents capitalized on the publicity surrounding gay foster parents, in order to exploit misguided fears that gays are pederasts and thus to defeat the bill. Fear that AIDS was a "gay disease" was also used to defeat the bill. Advocates, instead of dispelling unfounded myths about lesbians and gay men, accepted amendments that pandered to the opposition: sexual orientation was defined as excluding relations between adults and minor children; the bill cannot be used to force the placement of children in lesbian or gay foster homes, to recognize same-sex marriage, or to endorse a "gay lifestyle."[8]

Acceptance of limiting amendments shows that it was not difficult to separate antidiscrimination measures from gender and sexual dissent. In the fight to include sexual orientation in civil rights laws, lesbians and gay men could be constructed abstractly as employees, renters, or citizens deserving protection from discrimination in such a fashion that dominant norms remained intact. Because the state could, in effect, separate the details of homosexuality from the idea of protection from discrimination, the passage of lesbian and gay rights ordinances could be viewed as a narrow political reform rather than as an endorsement or acceptance of gender and sexual dissent.

The public, as well as the state, seems largely to have embraced the disapproval of discrimination based on sexual orientation, while abhorring the sexuality and gender dissent (real or imagined) of those they would protect from such discrimination. Numerous opinion polls show that a majority of the public feel simultaneously that lesbians and gay men should not be discriminated against and that homosexuality is wrong and even disgusting (Herek 1991). The inclusion of sexual orientation in hate-crimes legislation (Jenness and Grattet 1996), similarly, need not be interpreted to condone gender or sexual dissent, but only to signify that lesbians and gay men should not be physically assaulted because of that dissent. The ability to separate the details of homosexuality from the desire for protection explain why legislative change has been possible.

ACCEPT US: FAMILY LAW

DOROTHY SMITH (1999) DESCRIBES the Standard North American Family (or SNAF) as an ideological code that, much as the genetic code does, "replicates its organization in multiple and various sites." According to Smith,

> [SNAF] is a conception of The Family as a legally married couple sharing a household. The adult male is in paid employment; his earnings provide the economic basis of the family-household. The adult female may also earn an income, but her primary responsibility is to the care of husband, household, and children. The adult male and female may be parents (in whatever legal sense) of children also resident in the household. . . . The nuclear family is a theorized version of SNAF. (159)

Families that deviate from SNAF are considered defective (see Bennett and Battle, chapter 4; Bernstein and Reimann, chapter 1; see also Smith 1999). SNAF is also predicated on a heteronormative order.

The religious right is motivated by a desire to return to a traditionally defined version of the nuclear family. The right views the "lavender menace," followed closely by feminists, as public enemy number one (Liebman and Wuthnow 1983). Although the right has a wide-ranging political agenda (Diamond 1989), it is marked by three dominant themes: anti-Communism and economic and social conservatism (Himmelstein 1983). Falling into the latter category, the campaign for "family values" has included attacks on abortion rights (Luker 1984), lobbying against the *Equal Rights Amendment*, as well as attacks on lesbian and gay rights (e.g., Bull and Gallagher 1996; Herman 1994; Liebman and Wuthnow 1983). In the early 1980s conservative activists lobbied for passage of a federal *Family Protection Act* whose provisions included "withdrawal of Federal support for child and spouse abuse programs, bilingual educational programs, voluntary prayer in the schools . . . [and] would bar Federal funds from being made available to any individual or organization 'for the purpose of advocating, promoting, or suggesting homosexuality, male or female, as a lifestyle' " (National Gay and Lesbian Task Force 1982). A decade later, Vice President Dan Quayle assailed fictional character Murphy Brown for being a single mother; and conservatives attacked women on welfare for allegedly producing inadequate families (Naples 1997). These are but a few examples of the right's attempt to influence culture and the state so that the United States may "return" to a (mythical) time of traditional, peaceful, gendered, family existence. At the center of the maelstrom over family values sit lesbian and gay families. Arguing from God and nature, lesbians and gay men are constructed as threats to civilization itself (Bull and Gallagher 1996; Herman 1994).

Adding sexual orientation to human rights laws does not require the state to view lesbians and gay men as gendered or sexual beings, whereas sodomy statutes acknowledge lesbians and gay men as sexual beings. Nonetheless, repeal of sodomy statutes says, at most, that the law does not have to enforce morality and that in any event no one has to know what goes on behind closed doors. Family policies that include same-sex partners must not only acknowledge lesbians and gay men as sexual beings but also mark such unions official and confer a host of benefits on the blessed (see Chambers, chapter 19).

Family law, by definition, defines individuals in relationship to one another. In order to subsume lesbians and gay men into family law, the state must recognize the (sexually and emotionally) intimate relationships constructed by lesbians and gay men as valid. Lesbians and gay men as parents imply the separation of sexuality from procreation and raise questions about how, without both a mother and a father, boys and girls will grow up to be "normal" (read appropriately gendered and sexually inclined toward the opposite sex) men and women.

Demanding access to policies based on intimate familial relations challenges the gendered basis of the heterosexual nuclear family (Hunter 1991; see Walters, chapter 20). Domestic partner benefits that permit same-sex domestic partners to receive benefits (such as health insurance and bereavement leave to which a legally married spouse would be entitled), marriage, and inheritance rights are predicated on two-person monogamous relationships that are presumably sexual in nature, fulfilling both economic and emotional needs. When the relationships in question are between persons of the same sex, the ideological justification for the gendered nuclear family breaks down. No predefined hierarchical relationship exists between persons of the same sex (class and racial/ethnic differences notwithstanding), leaving heterosexuals to question their own gendered division of labor. State recognition of same-sex relationships, then, would undermine the belief that such relations between opposite-sex partners, based on a gendered division of social traits, are divinely or biologically ordained.

Adoption and insemination policies separate children from procreation, once again challenging hegemonic notions of family. Second-parent adoption (see Dalton, chapter 13) and alternative insemination (see Murphy, chapter 12) fly in the face of the notion that children are the property of their biological (read natural) parents. Such changes in law and policy pose the ultimate threat to conservatively defined "family values" that view two parents of the opposite sex as necessary for a child's proper gender and sexual development. Just as single mothers have been attacked for raising children without a male role model, and the allegedly matriarchal structure of African American families has been blamed for black poverty and crime (see Bennett and Battle, chapter 4), gays and lesbians who choose to parent, either solely or with a partner of the same sex, are open to similar charges. Even worse, lesbian and gay parents are presumed to create inappropriate gender behavior and potentially inappropriate sexual-object choice in their children, if it is not assumed that they will outright molest their children (Herek 1991; Rivera 1991). Of course hegemonic notions of masculinity (Connell 1995) make it almost incomprehensible why gay men would want to parent.

Different areas of lesbian and gay family law require different levels of state intervention. Laws relating to children do not require the state actually to sanction lesbian and gay relationships, although state officials must abandon their myths about lesbians and gay men as child molesters (Herek 1991).

In the context of children, activists and the state have found a way to elide the association of lesbians and gay men with "inappropriate" sexual-object choice and "unconventional" gender. The fear, after all, where children are concerned, is that sexual and gender dissent, like a disease, is communicable. If activists can show that lesbian and gay parents present no threat to their children's sexual and gender development, then such parents no longer pose a threat to heteronormativity. Recognition of actual relationships between adult partners of the same sex requires active state endorsement of those relationships. Nonetheless, the state is free to *define* those relationships in such as way as to acknowledge the sexual and gendered aspects of the relationship or to define them in ways that avoid challenges to heteronormativity, much in the way lesbian and gay identities are defined in antidiscrimination legislation. Given the historical compromises needed to create changes in sodomy law and human rights laws, how have lesbian and gay family policies fared, and what are the prospects for continued change?

Whether the issue regarding children is custody after divorce, second-parent adoption, or foster parenting, the fear is that lesbian and gay parents will be (unwilling to or) incapable of producing appropriately masculine boys and feminine girls, and that their offspring will grow up to be lesbian or gay. The majority of social science research has found this not to be the case (see also Wright, chapter 17); in fact, children raised by lesbians and gay men are no different in terms of their gender and sexual-object choice than their counterparts raised in heterosexual families.[9] Evidence that lesbian and gay parents do no harm to their children (by subverting the heteronormative order) is trotted out in custody and adoption cases to show that lesbians and gay men pose no threat (Little 1994). In court, social workers attest to the "proper" gender development of children. Such evidence is deemed proof that lesbians and gay men can be fit parents, because in the end, the dominant culture wins out. Radical arguments that being raised by lesbians and gay men could lead to a subversion of gender that would benefit the child and society are rarely adduced.

Custody decisions are mostly judge-made law. The current legal standard is "the best interest of the child." Maintaining contact with a primary caretaker, or ensuring a child's financial future are taken into consideration when determining/constructing what is in a child's "best interest" (Connolly 1998). Given that women's financial status usually deteriorates after divorce (Weitzman 1985), ensuring the child's economic interest would tend to favor granting custody to the father, potentially disadvantaging lesbians in white families. However favoring the mother in custody decisions would work to the advantage of lesbians. Couples of color are more likely to be poor before divorce, and so the financial interest of the child would not be the determining factor. Class issues, similarly, played out in a Virginia case (*Bottoms v. Bottoms*) where working-class lesbian Sharon Bottoms lost custody of her daughter to her own mother. Virginia's sodomy statute was invoked to brand Sharon Bottoms a criminal for being a lesbian and thus an unfit mother.

Yet capitalism can work to the advantage of economically privileged lesbian and gay families, as class serves as a countervailing pressure to traditional gender and sexual norms. For example, in granting the first known second-parent adoption to a lesbian, the Court reasoned that because the "second parent" was a wealthy woman who could, if allowed, contribute financially to her adoptive daughter's education and other economic needs, the adoption was in the child's best interest. Because second-parent adoption is an extremely expensive process (see Dalton, chapter 13), it is a middle- and upper-class phenomenon, beyond the reach of working-class and poor lesbian and gay couples. Economic concerns become important determinants of outcome. The lesbian and gay parenting movement, thus, is largely middle-class, reflecting the concerns of those with economic resources (see Boggis, chapter 11). When juxtaposed with arguments that neutralize the perceived (negative) effect of a parent's sexual orientation, best-interest standards can be met without acknowledging or sanctioning lesbian and gay relationships or challenging dominant gender norms.

Nonetheless, obtaining access to second-parent adoption has met with mixed success. Supreme Courts in Vermont, Massachusetts, and New York, as well as Appellate Courts in Illinois, New Jersey, Oregon, and the District of Columbia have ruled that lesbian and gay parents have a right to pursue second-parent adoptions; and an additional fourteen states have granted at least one second-parent adoption. Higher courts in Wisconsin, Ohio, Colorado, and Connecticut have ruled against second-parent adoptions. Florida (1977), New Hampshire (late 1980s), and Arkansas (1999) have gone so far as to legislate against allowing adoptions by lesbian and gay adults (ACLU 1997; Connolly 1998; see Dalton, chapter 13; NGLTF 1999). Significantly, no state has legislated that lesbians and gay men have a right to second-parent adoption, leaving such decisions below the public radar (Connolly 1998).

If legislation were ever proposed to allow lesbians and gay men uniformly to adopt or become foster parents, and if it were to have a hope of passing in a public forum, activists and lawyers would have to concede that neither children's gender roles nor their sexual orientation are affected by their parents' sexual orientation. Such proactive legislation would enable working-class lesbians and gays to form families, despite their lack of financial resources. But once again, in order to legally create and preserve their families, activists would have to acquiesce to heteronormativity when making claims on the state.

During the 1990s domestic-partner benefits have proliferated. In 1990 only 9 employers provided benefits for domestic partners (including medical benefits). By 1995 the number had jumped to over 270. Some estimate that between 1 and 3 new employers per week are adding some form of domestic-partner benefits (Winfield and Spielman 1995). Nationwide, more than 400 employers provide domestic-partner benefits for their employees (Curiel 1997). In 1997 employers doing business with the city of San Francisco were required to provide domestic-partner benefits for their employees (Curiel 1997). Similar legislation is being considered in cities including New York, Boston, Seattle, Philadelphia, Cleveland, and Minneapolis (ACLU 1998b; Baker 1998; Horne 1994). Just as second-parent adoption policies favor the middle and upper classes, domestic-partner policies only serve those with jobs that have benefits such as health insurance, leaving the status of less privileged lesbians and gays unaffected.

Compare these trends in domestic-partnership policies and laws to the fate of same-sex marriage. Congress overwhelmingly (342 to 67 in the House, and 84 to 14 in the Senate) passed the Defense of Marriage Act (DOMA) in 1996, which permits states and the federal government *not to recognize* same-sex marriages performed in another state (Baker 1998; Coombs chapter 23; Wolfson and Melcher 1996). As an impending court decision made it more and more likely that same-sex marriage would become legal in Hawaii, the citizens of that state added an amendment to the Hawaii constitution allowing the state to legislate against same-sex marriages, thus potentially rendering the court's deliberations moot. In the meantime, fearing that courts across the country would follow the Hawaii example, antigay and antilesbian activists quickly succeeded in passing at least twenty-five state-level anti–same-sex marriage bills across the country (ACLU 1998a). The Vermont Supreme Court recently surprised the country in *Baker v. State* by ruling that the Vermont legislature must grant the same benefits to lesbian and gay couples that married heterosexual couples receive. The legislature responded by creating "civil unions" for lesbians and gay men, a structure meant to parallel marriage. Reminiscent of the notorious "separate but equal" doctrine that mandated segregation for African Americans, the Vermont legislature discursively marked lesbian and gay unions as less than heterosexual marriages.

The discussion of sodomy and human rights laws suggests that the disparate success of same-sex marriage and domestic-partner benefits can be explained by the challenge they present to heteronormativity and the extent to which that challenge can be circumvented. Despite the fact that domestic-partner benefits assume an intimate relation between persons of the same sex (although some policies cover unmarried opposite-sex partners as well), the nature of this relationship is constructed in fiducial terms. Although requirements for proof of partnership vary considerably, to avail themselves of these benefits, partners must usually show that they are financially dependent on one another, have a shared residence, be over 18 years of age and not currently married (Blum 1998; Rutherford 1997). Financial requirements often include joint bank accounts, wills naming each partner as the other's heir, something that married opposite-sex partners are not required to do, and terms that working-class and poor queers are often unable to meet. Thus even among those lesbians and gays with jobs that give benefits, further class distinctions are made. No assumptions are made about the emotional or sexual aspects (such as "consummation") of the relationship, although the propertied nature of the relationship, as a monogamous possession remains. For example, in *Braschi v. Stahl*, exclusiveness of the relationship was considered salient by the court when it ruled that a gay man was entitled to take over the lease of the apartment where he lived, which had been in the name of his deceased partner. Thus middle- and upper-class gays and lesbians, who by creating more conventional family structures pose the least threat to heteronormativity (see Gamson, chapter 5; see also Ringer, chapter 9), gain the most from domestic partner policies.

Second, claims for domestic-partnership benefits can easily be framed in terms of equal pay for equal work. By denying benefits to employees' same-sex partners, employers discriminate on the basis of marital status and sexual orientation, something that the public has deemed unjust. Additionally, economically conservative arguments based on market logic of doing what's best for business can also be adduced. For example, in a recent debate in Arizona, openly gay Republican state representative Steve May joined Democratic colleague Ken Chevrount in claiming that the proposed ban on domestic-partner benefits would discriminate by denying equal pay for equal work. The proposed ban was also criticized for closing off an entire pool of applicants, running the risk of failing to hire the best person for the job, contrary to sound business practices. So just as in human rights laws, domestic-partnership benefits can be framed in antidiscrimination terms that fit within a conservative rhetoric of market logic (see also Raeburn

2000).Validation of intimate relationships need not be part of the equation. Thus capitalism is justified rhetorically by leaving benefits linked to occupation, while the cultural meaning of homosexuality is left unchallenged.

Unlike same-sex marriage, the state need not comment on the morality of same-sex relations in domestic partner laws. And in fact, the vast majority of domestic-partner policies have been implemented by private-sector employers (Horne 1994). The state has not taken a leadership role (Baker 1998). Same-sex marriage, on the other hand, demands not only that the benefits of marriage be given to same-sex couples who choose to marry but also that the terms of the marital contract be equivalent. Marriage, of course, lies at the heart of the conservative notion of "family values," with its attendant notions of who should marry (opposite-sex couples) and how familial responsibilities should be allocated—based on some gendered division of labor that gives the husband primary responsibility for breadwinning (even if his wife works) and the wife primary responsibility for childrearing (even if her husband "helps" with the childcare)—and what form families should take (self-sufficient, nuclear, and privatized with husband, wife, and children). This entire gendered division of labor breaks down when the partners are of the same sex.

Marriage is also supposed to determine who can and cannot have sexual relations. Sex is an expectation of and is assumed by marriage (and has historically been a legal obligation [Freeman 1995; Mansbridge 1986]) in a way that it is not for domestic partners. Although such laws have been removed from the books in many states, in others, such as Arizona, prohibitions against fornication, adultery, and cohabitation remain on the books. Failure to consummate a marriage, of course, can lead to annulment.

Finally, paternity is also determined by the marriage contract (see Dalton, chapter 13). The husband of a woman who becomes pregnant by another man or through alternative insemination automatically has paternity rights to the child. Same-sex marriage undermines the gendered edifice upon which the Standard North American Family is built and is therefore intolerable even to those who otherwise support gay rights.

Advocates of same-sex marriage have often framed the issue as one of choice (see Javors, chapter 18). But such a frame has little "resonance" (Snow and Benford 1988) with wider cultural values. If advocates of same-sex marriage are ever to pass legislation making same-sex marriage legal or, even more modestly, to stem the tide of antimarriage bills, they will need to find a way to circumvent the challenge to heteronormativity. Activists in Vermont and Hawaii successfully framed the denial of same-sex marriage in terms of sex discrimination, and Vermont's creation of civil unions provides a way to avoid the challenge to heteronormativity posed by same-sex marriage. By segregating lesbian and gay "marriages" under the rubric "civil unions," heterosexual marriage remains the cultural norm distinct (and safe) from lesbian and gay civil unions. Nonetheless, the Vermont Court has set the stage for lesbians and gay men to challenge their "separate but equal" status in court. While the legal change does not transform dominant cultural norms or create acceptance, it has sparked nationwide discussion and debate that may ultimately challenge hetero- and gendernormativity or create more acceptance for lesbians and gay men. Yet, as the case in Hawaii and the current backlash in Vermont illustrate, court decisions can be mooted in a variety of ways, and the law is unlikely to be far ahead of pubic opinion.

This chapter has argued that resistance to changes in laws regarding sexual orientation derives from an adherence to hegemonic conceptions of masculinity and femininity, with their attendant notions of appropriate sexual behavior and a traditional view of the nuclear family.

Changes in laws regarding sexual orientation are dependent on the ability to frame the challenge in a way that leaves heteronormativity untroubled. Sodomy has been decriminalized in more than half the American states, because it was framed as an issue of privacy or as a victimless crime. Such a framing has helped in gaining a narrow legal victory but has neither challenged the underlying opprobrium associated with homosexuality nor helped in the quest for acceptance. Even the symbolic victory of decriminalization is mooted by the insistence on privacy. Lesbian- and gay-rights ordinances have passed because lesbians and gay men were constructed as commercial subjects, abstracted from their sexuality, leaving dominant gender norms intact. Because they deal with lesbians and gay men in public settings, however, such ordinances potentially have an impact on cultural norms, although in all likelihood, cross-dressers and other gender radicals could still be fired or denied housing.

Changes in laws regarding children, similarly, are important for economically privileged lesbian and gay parents but, once again, leave heteronormativity intact. The paradox of same-sex marriage is that those who are pushing for it most strenuously are those most desirous of acceptance (see for example, Javors chapter 18; Eskridge 1993 and 1996; Sullivan 1995) and those who are least likely actively to challenge gender norms or the privatized nuclear family (see Walters, chapter 20). But as this chapter has shown, legal change is usually achieved by circumventing the challenge to heteronormativity that underlies disapproval of homosexuality. Legal change may reduce the costs of coming out and transform public consciousness in the long run, but it is unlikely that by itself legal change will create acceptance or transform dominant cultural values.

NOTES

1. Throughout this chapter, the sodomy statutes discussed prohibit private, consensual sodomy between adults. Depending on the state, this prohibition may apply to both heterosexual (with exemptions for married couples in some states) and homosexual sodomy. Through case law or through express statutory language, "sodomy" also includes any oral-genital contact.

2. In revising sex laws, the reporters of the Model Penal Code also relied on the latest scientific evidence regarding homosexuality. Medical opinion was divided over the causes of homosexuality (whether genetic or psychological) and the prospects for a cure. Because sexual-psychopath laws provided neither therapy nor other forms of treatment, and supported by assertions that those engaging in such behavior were not a homogenous group of dangerous sex criminals, little justification remained for criminal enforcement. As a medical condition, homosexuality was better treated by medical authorities than by the criminal justice system (Model Penal Code 1980).

3. Massachusetts had separate statutes for oral and anal sex. The law prohibiting anal sex remains on the books. According to Rubenstein (1993), the precedent set would probably render the other law invalid, but the ACLU still counts Massachusetts among the "unreformed" states (ACLU 1999).

4. There was disagreement among litigators over appropriate tactics, but separating status from conduct became the primary strategy (Cain 1993).

5. For example, in both *Gryzcan v. Montana* and *Campbell v. Sundquist* (in Tennessee), two proactive challenges brought on behalf of several lesbians and gay men, the courts ruled that these states' laws that applied only to same-sex partners violated state constitutional rights to privacy.

6. I am considering the AIDS movement to be a separate, albeit related, movement.

7. I borrow the terms "cultural" and "political" reformists from Marotta (1981) to distinguish among activists with different goals.

8. In 1989 the bill, with its homophobic amendments intact, passed both houses of the Massachusetts legislature and was signed by the governor into law. Ironically, the religious opposition was proscribed from seeking a referendum

to repeal the new law because religious institutions were exempted from the bill's employment clause. In Massachusetts, laws about religion cannot be subject to a referendum (Cicchino, Deming, and Nicholson 1991).

9. The only difference found consistently is that children raised in lesbian and gay families are more tolerant of differences than children raised by heterosexuals.

REFERENCES

ACLU. 1997. "Lesbian & Gay Rights: ACLU Fact Sheet: Overview on Lesbian and Gay Parenting." Internet release date: May 1997, http://www.aclu.org/issues/gay/sodomy.html.

——. 1998a. "Statewide Anti-Gay Marriage Laws." Internet release date: January 1998, http://www.aclu.org/issues/gay/gaymar.html.

——. 1998b. "Lesbian & Gay Rights: State and Local Laws Protecting Lesbians and Gay Men Against Workplace Discrimination." Internet release date: October 1998, http://www.aclu.org/issues/gay/gaylaws.html.

——. 1999. "Lesbian & Gay Rights: Status of U.S. Sodomy Laws." Internet release date: January 1999, http://www.aclu.org/issues/gay/sodomy.html.

Adam, Barry D. 1987. *The Rise of a Gay and Lesbian Movement.* Boston: Twayne.

Apasu-Gbotsu, Yao, Robert J. Arnold, Paul DiBella, Kevin Dorse, Elisa L. Fuller, Steven H. Naturman, Dung Hong Pham, and James B. Putney. 1986. "Survey on the Constitutional Right to Privacy in the Context of Homosexual Activity." *University of Miami Law Review* 40 (1): 521–657.

Arizona Republic. 1999. "Sodomy Law Tossed Out for Invasion of Privacy." *Arizona Republic,* p. A5.

Backer, Larry Cata. 1993. "Exposing the Perversions of Toleration: The Decriminalization of Private Sexual Conduct, the Model Penal Code, and the Oxymoron of Liberal Toleration." *Florida Law Review* 45 (5): 755–802.

Baker, James P. 1998. "Equal Benefits for Equal Work? The Law of Domestic Partner Benefits. *The Labor Lawyer* 14, no. 1 (Summer): 23–52.

Bernstein, Mary. 1997a. "Celebration and Suppression: The Strategic Uses of Identity by the Lesbian and Gay Movement." *American Journal of Sociology* 103 (3): 531–65.

——. 1997b. "Sexual Orientation Policy, Protest, and the State." Ph.D. diss., New York University.

Blum, Robert A. 1998. "Domestic Partner Benefits: Issues and Planning." ALI-ABA course material journal, no. 22 (April 2): 5–14.

Boggan, E. Carrington, Marilyn G. Haft, Charles Lister, and John P. Rupp. 1975. *The Rights of Gay People: The Basic ACLU Guide to a Gay Person's Rights* (An American Civil Liberties Union Handbook). Dutton.

Bull, Chris and John Gallagher. 1996. *Perfect Enemies: The Religious Right, the Gay Movement, and the Politics of the 1990s*. New York: Crown.

Button, James W., Barbara A. Rienzo, and Kenneth D. Wald. 1996. "The Politics of Gay Rights in American Communities: Explaining Antidiscrimination Ordinances and Policies." *American Journal of Political Science* 40 (4): 1152–1178.

——. 1997. *Private Lives, Public Conflicts: Battles over Gay Rights in American Communities*. Washington, D.C.: Congressional Quarterly Press.

Cain, Patricia A. 1993. "Litigating for Lesbian and Gay Rights: A Legal History." *Virginia Law Review* 79: 1551–1641.

Chauncey, George. 1994. *Gay New York: Gender, Urban Culture, and the Making of the Gay Male World 1890–1940*. New York: Basic Books.

Cicchino, Peter M., Bruce R. Deming, and Katherine M. Nicholson. 1991. "Sex, Lies, and Civil Rights: A Critical History of the Massachusetts Gay Civil Rights Bill." *Harvard Civil Rights-Civil Liberties Law Review* 26 (2): 549–631.

Cohen, Jean. 1985. "Strategy or Identity: New Theoretical Paradigms and Contemporary Social Movements." *Social Research* 52: 663–716.

Connell, R. W. 1995. *Masculinities*. Berkeley: University of California Press.

Connolly, Catherine. 1998. "The Description of Gay and Lesbian Families in Second-Parent Adoption Cases." *Behavioral Sciences and Law* 16, no. 2 (Spring): 225–36.

Copelon, Rhonda. 1990. "A Crime Not Fit to Be Named: Sex, Lies, and the Constitution." In David Kairys, ed., *The Politics of Law: A Progressive Critique* (rev. ed.), pp. 177–94. New York: Pantheon.

Cruikshank, Margaret. 1992. *The Gay and Lesbian Liberation Movement*. New York: Routledge.

Curiel, J. 1997. "The Little City That Could." *The Advocate*, March 18, pp. 28–34.

D'Emilio, John. 1983. "Capitalism and Gay Identity." In Ann Snitow, Christine Stansell, and Sharon Thompson, eds., *Powers of Desire: The Politics of Sexuality*, pp. 100–13. New York: Monthly Review Press.

Diamond, Sara. 1989. *Spiritual Warfare: The Politics of the Christian Right*. Boston: South End Press.

Eskridge Jr., William N. 1993. "A History of Same-Sex Marriage." *Virginia Law Review* 79: 1419–1514.

——. 1996. *The Case for Same-Sex Marriage*. New York: The Free Press.

Freeman, Jo. 1995. "The Revolution for Women in Law and Public Policy." In Jo Freeman, ed., *Women: A Feminist Perspective*, pp. 365–404. Mountain View, Cal.: Mayfield.

Gay Writer's Group. 1983. *It Could Happen to You: An Account of the Gay Civil Rights Campaign in Eugene, Oregon.* Boston: Alyson.

Geis, Gilbert. 1972. *Not The Law's Business? An Examination of Homosexuality, Abortion, Prostitution, Narcotics, and Gambling in the United States.* Washington, D.C.: US Government Printing Office.

Greenberg, David F. 1988. *The Construction of Homosexuality.* Chicago: University of Chicago Press.

Haider-Markel, Donald P. and Kenneth J. Meier 1996. "The Politics of Gay and Lesbian Rights: Expanding the Scope of Conflict." *Journal of Politics* 58 (2): 332–49.

Harlow, Ruth. 1992/93. "Kentucky Ruling a Milestone in Struggle for Gay Rights." *Civil Liberties: The National Newsletter of the ACLU* 378 (Winter): 1, 11.

Herek, Gregory M. 1991. "Myths About Sexual Orientation: A Lawyer's Guide to Social Science Research." *Law & Sexuality* 1: 133–72.

Herman, Didi. 1994. *Rights of Passage: Struggles for Lesbian and Gay Legal Equality.* Toronto: University of Toronto Press.

Himmelstein, Jerome L. 1983. "The New Right." In Robert C. Liebman and Robert Wuthnow, eds., *The New Christian Right: Mobilization and Legitimation,* pp. 13–30. New York: Aldine.

Homer, Steven K. 1994. "Against Marriage." *Harvard Civil Rights-Civil Liberties Law Review* 29, no. 2 (Summer): 505–30.

Horne, Philip S., 1994. "Challenging Public- and Private-Sector Benefit Schemes Which Discriminate Against Unmarried Opposite-Sex and Same-Sex Partners." *Law and Sexuality* 4: 35–52.

Hunter, Nan D. 1991. "Marriage, Law, and Gender: A Feminist Inquiry." *Law and Sexuality* 1: 9–30.

——. 1992. "Life After Hardwick." *Harvard Civil Rights-Civil Liberties Law Review* 27 (Summer): 531–54.

Hyde, Sue. 1987. "To: NGLTF Board of Directors." Memo over the signature of Sue Hyde, Director, Privacy Project. Collection 7301 (National Gay and Lesbian Task Force), box 130, folder "Privacy Project Program Review." Cornell University Library.

Jenness, Valerie and Ryken Grattet. 1996. "The Criminalization of Hate: A Comparison of Structural and Polity Influences on the Passage of 'Bias-Crime' Legislation in the United States." *Sociological Perspectives* 39 (1): 129–54.

Katzenstein, Mary Fainsod. 1990. "Feminism Within American Institutions: Unobtrusive Mobilization in the 1980s." *Signs: Journal of Women in Culture and Society* 16 (1): 27–54.

——. 1995. "Discursive Politics and Feminist Activism in the Catholic Church." In Myra Marx Ferree and Patricia Yancey Martin, eds., *Feminist Organizations: Harvest of the New Women's Movement,* pp. 35–52. Philadelphia: Temple University Press.

Kennedy, Elizabeth and Madeline D. Davis. 1993. *Boots of Leather, Slippers of Gold: The History of a Lesbian Community*. New York: Routledge.

Knopp, Lawrence. 1987. "Social Theory, Social Movements, and Public Policy: Recent Accomplishments of the Gay and Lesbian Movements in Minneapolis, Minnesota." *International Journal of Urban and Regional Research* 11 (2): 243–61.

Lambda 2000. "Texas Tosses 'Homosexual Conduct' Law, Clears Two Men Arrested in Home." Internet release date: June 8, 2000, http//www.lambdalegal.org/cgi-bin/pages/documents/record?record=641.

Liebman, Robert C. and Robert Wuthnow. 1983. "Introduction." In Robert C. Liebman and Robert Wuthnow, eds., *The New Christian Right: Mobilization and Legitimation*, pp. 1–9. New York: Aldine.

Little, Christine. 1994. "Adoption: Parent Versus Parent Custody Battles When a Parent Is Gay or Lesbian: Is the Oklahoma Standard in the Best Interest of the Child?" *Oklahoma Law Review* 47, no. 4 (Winter): 695–710.

Luker, Kristin. 1984. *Abortion and the Politics of Motherhood*. Berkeley: University of California Press.

Mansbridge, Jane. 1986. *Why We Lost the ERA*. Chicago: University of Chicago Press.

Marotta, Toby. 1981. *The Politics of Homosexuality*. Boston: Houghton Mifflin.

Melucci, Alberto. 1985. "The Symbolic Challenge of Contemporary Movements." *Social Research* 52: 789–816.

——. 1989. *Nomads of the Present*. London: Hutchinson Radius.

Merry, Sally Engle. 1990. *Getting Justice and Getting Even: Legal Consciousness among Working-Class Americans*. Chicago: University of Chicago Press.

Model Penal Code and Commentaries. 1980. "213.2 Deviate Sexual Intercourse by Force or Imposition, Comment," pp. 357–76. Philadelphia: American Law Institute.

Naples, Nancy A. 1998. *Grassroots Warriors: Activist Mothering, Community Work, and the War on Poverty*. New York: Routledge.

——. 1997. "The 'New Consensus' on the Gendered 'Social Contract': The 1987–1988 U.S. Congressional Hearings on Welfare Reform." *Signs: Journal of Women in Culture and Society* 22 (4): 907–45.

NGLTF. 1999. "Press Release: Task Force Denounces Arkansas Foster Care Ban." Internet release date: January 7, 1999, http://www.ngltf.org/press/arfoster.html.

National Gay and Lesbian Task Force. 1982. "Apuzzo Debates F.P.A. Advocates in Boston Appearance." *News From NGLTF* Press Release January 22. Files "NGLTF." Lesbian Herstory Archives, Brooklyn New York.

Newton, Esther. 1984. "The Mythic Mannish Lesbian: Radclyffe Hall and the New Woman." In Estelle B. Freedman, Barbara C. Gelpi, Susan L. Johnson, and Kathleen M. Weston, eds., *The Lesbian Issues: Essays from SIGNS*, pp. 7–25. Chicago: University of Chicago Press.

Nice, David C. 1988. "State Deregulation of Intimate Behavior." *Social Science Quarterly* 69 (1): 203–11.

Piven, Frances Fox and Richard A. Cloward. 1977. *Poor Peoples Movements: Why They Succeed, How They Fail.* New York: Vintage Books.

Polikoff, Nancy D. 1993. "We Will Get What We Ask For: Why Legalizing Gay and Lesbian Marriage Will Not 'Dismantle' the Legal Structure of Gender in Every Marriage." *Virginia Law Review* 79 (7): 1535–1550.

Raeburn, Nicole C. 2000. "The Rise of Lesbian, Gay, and Bisexual Rights in the Workplace." Ph.D. diss., Ohio State University.

Rivera, Rhonda R. 1991. "Sexual Orientation and the Law." In John C. Gonsiorek and James D. Weinrich, eds., *Homosexuality: Research Implications for Public Policy*, pp. 81–100. Newbury Park, Cal.: Sage.

Rosenberg, Gerald. 1991. *The Hollow Hope: Can Courts Bring about Social Change?* Chicago: University of Chicago Press.

Rubenstein, William B. 1993. *Lesbians, Gay Men, and the Law.* New York: New Press.

Rubin, Gayle. 1984. "The Traffic in Women." In Alison Jaggar and Paula Rothenberg, eds., *Feminist Frameworks: Alternative Theoretical Accounts of the Relations Between Women and Men*, pp. 155–71. New York: McGraw-Hill.

Rutherfold, Elizabeth A. 1997. "Domestic Partner Benefits: Are You Doing It Right?" *Employee Relations Law Journal* 23, no. 1 (Summer): 125–32.

Shilts, Randy. 1987. *And the Band Played On: Politics, People, and the AIDS Epidemic.* New York: Penguin.

Smart, Carol. 1989. *Feminism and the Power of Law.* London: Routledge.

Smith, Dorothy E. 1999. *Writing the Social: Critique, Theory, and Investigations.* Toronto: University of Toronto Press.

Snow, David A. and Robert D. Benford. 1988. "Ideology, Frame Resonance, and Participant Mobilization." In Bert Klandermans, Hanspeter Kriesi, and Sidney Tarrow, eds., *International Social Movement Research: From Structure to Action.* Greenwich, Conn.: JAI Press.

Sullivan, Andrew. 1995. *Virtually Normal: An Argument About Homosexuality.* New York: Knopf.

Touraine, Alain. 1981. *The Voice and the Eye: An Analysis of Social Movements.* Cambridge: Cambridge University Press.

Tribe, Laurence H. 1990. *Abortion: The Clash of Absolutes.* New York: Norton.

UCLA. 1966. "Project–The Consenting Adult Homosexual and the Law: An Empirical Study of Enforcement and Administration in Los Angeles County." *UCLA Law Review* 13: 643–707.

Walston, Charles and Margaret L. Usdansky. 1990. "House Vote Kills Sodomy Issue for Session." *The Atlanta Journal and Constitution*. Collection 7301 (National Gay and Lesbian Task Force), box 126, folder "90GA." Cornell University Library.

Weeks, Jeffrey. 1989. "Movements of Affirmation: Sexual Meanings and Homosexual Identities." In Kathy Peiss and Christina Simmons with Robert A. Padgug, eds., *Passion and Power: Sexuality in History*, pp. 70–86. Philadelphia: Temple University Press.

Weitzman, Lenore J. 1985. *The Divorce Revolution: The Unexpected Social and Economic Consequences for Women in America*. New York: The Free Press.

Winfield, L. and S. Spielman. 1995. *Straight Talk About Gays in the Workplace*. New York: Amacom.

Wolfson, Evan and Michael F. Melcher. 1996. "Constitutional and Legal Defects in the 'Defense of Marriage' Act." *QLR* 16, nos. 1/2 (Spring): 221–29.

Wolfson, Evan and Robert S. Mower. 1994. "When the Police are in Our Bedrooms, Shouldn't the Courts Go In After Them?: An Update on the Fight Against 'Sodomy' Laws." *Fordham Urban Law Journal* 21 (4): 997–1055.

Contributors

ASSOCIATE PROFESSOR JUAN BATTLE holds a joint position at Hunter College and the Graduate Center of the City University of New York (CUNY). His fields include sexuality, race, social problems, and quantitative research methods. His primary research agenda examines the impact of homophobia within the African American community. His other research agenda, with a particular emphasis on families of color, examines the effects of family structure on children's educational outcomes.

MICHAEL BENNETT is associate professor of English at Long Island University, Brooklyn. He is the coeditor of *The Nature of Cities* and *Recovering the Black Female Body* and the author of the forthcoming *Democratic Discourses: Antebellum American Literature and the Abolition Movement*.

MARY BERNSTEIN is assistant professor of justice studies at Arizona State University. Her research, which has appeared in the *American Journal of Sociology* and the *American Sociological Review*, focuses on sexuality, social movements, and the law. Currently, she is writing a book on lesbian, gay, bisexual, and transgender political strategies and legal change.

In 1988 (the year her son was born) TERRY BOGGIS helped found Center Kids. She now directs that organization, which has become the largest regional alternative families program in the country. Before directing Center Kids, Terry was the New York City Lesbian and Gay Community Center's director of communications.

LIONEL CANTÚ is assistant professor of sociology at the University of California, Santa Cruz. He is currently working on a manuscript of his dissertation research, entitled *Border Crossings: Mexican Men and the Sexuality of Migration*, examining how sexuality influences migratory processes.

DAVID L. CHAMBERS is the Wade H. McCree Jr. Collegiate Professor of Law at the University of Michigan. He works principally in the area of family law.

MARY COOMBS is professor of law at the University of Miami School of Law. She teaches and writes in the areas of criminal law, family law, and legal issues of gender and sexual orientation.

SUSAN E. DALTON is visiting assistant professor in the law and society and women's studies programs at the University of California, Santa Barbara. As a lesbian feminist activist and scholar, she writes and teaches in the area of lesbian and gay families, sexual politics, and the law.

JOSHUA GAMSON is associate professor of sociology at Yale University, and author of *Claims to Fame* and *Freaks Talk Back*. He has written about television, popular culture, and lesbian/gay politics for numerous academic journals, as well as *The Nation, The American Prospect, Brill's Content, Tikkun*, and the *Utne Reader*.

DONALD P. HAIDER-MARKEL is assistant professor of political science at the University of Kansas. He has authored and coauthored several articles and book chapters on gay and lesbian politics, some of which have appeared in the *Journal of Politics, Political Research Quarterly, Policy Studies Journal*, and *State Politics and Policy Quarterly*.

RANDALL HALLE is currently assistant professor in the department of modern languages and cultures at the University of Rochester. He has published on topics ranging from antihomosexuality in the Frankfurt School to analyses of contemporary queer film. He is currently completing *Queer Readings in Social Philosophy from Kant to Adorno*.

PHILIP C. HO is a graduate student in speech and communication studies at San Francisco State University. He teaches an introductory speech course and is active in academic conferences.

IRENE JAVORS, is a psychotherapist in private practice in New York City. She teaches women's studies at New Jersey City University, New Jersey. Since the debacle of United for the Freedom To Marry, Inc. she has moved on to found Links, Inc., an organization dedicated to mentoring gay, lesbian, bisexual, and transgendered youth in Queens, New York.

ELLEN LEWIN is professor of women's studies and anthropology at the University of Iowa. Her work on lesbian and gay family issues includes *Lesbian Mothers: Accounts of Gender in American Culture* and *Recognizing Ourselves: Lesbian and Gay Ceremonies of Commitment*. Her current research examines gay fatherhood in the United States.

KAREN E. LOVAAS earned her Ph.D. from the University of Hawaii in 1993. She currently lectures in the department of speech and communication studies at San Francisco State University. Her teaching, research, and consulting work are in the areas of sexuality, culture, gender, conflict, and communication.

JOHN C. MILLER, father of three daughters, Marialisa, Amanda, and Rachel, and gay rights activist (plaintiff in the successful challenge to Colorado's Amendment 2) lives with his life partner, Robert E. Bixler. He is professor of Spanish at the University of Colorado, Colorado Springs, and specializes in U.S. Latino writings.

JULIEN S. MURPHY is professor of philosophy at the University of Southern Maine, Portland. She is the author of *The Constructed Body: AIDS, Reproductive Technology and Ethics*, a feminist book in bioethics, and editor of *ReReading the Canon: Feminist Interpretations of Jean-Paul Sartre*. Her work has appeared in numerous collections on bioethics and continental philosophy.

NANCY A. NAPLES is associate professor of sociology and women's studies at the University of California, Irvine. She is author of *Grassroots Warriors: Activist Mothering, Community Work, and the War on Poverty* and editor of *Community Activism and Feminist Politics: Organizing Across Race, Class, and Gender*. Her scholarship includes exploring the state's role in reproducing or challenging inequality and analyzing how differing community contexts influence women's political activism.

ELIZABETH RANDOLPH is a poet and writer of short fiction and nonfiction, as well as a screenwriter. Her work has appeared in *The Key to Everything: Classic Lesbian Love Poems, Contemporary Lesbian Writers of the United States*, and *ColorLife Magazine*. She lives in New York City and is currently writing her first stage play.

RENATE REIMANN received a Master of Divinity from Hamburg University (Germany) and earned her Ph.D. in sociology from the Graduate Center of the City University of New York (CUNY). Her graduate work focused on queer families. She currently is conducting a cross-cultural study of dance and club cultures and the popular music industry in Europe and North America.

R. JEFFREY RINGER is currently a visiting professor at Akita University in Japan, teaching English conversation. He is on a leave of absence from and will eventually return to his regular position at St. Cloud State University, Minnesota, where he is professor of speech communication and teaches courses in interpersonal and organizational communication.

MAUREEN SULLIVAN completed her Ph.D in sociology at the University of California, Davis, where her dissertation project focused on lesbian coparent families living in the San Francisco Bay Area. The longer work from which the chapter in this book is taken will be published as a book by the University of California Press. She is assistant professor of sociology at Northern Illinois University.

ROLAND MCALLEN-WALKER is a member of the Navajo Nation. He grew up in a reservation community in the Southwest region of the Navajo Nation. He was raised to navigate within the dominant culture while continuing to cherish and observe the essence of traditional Navajo cultural values and practices. He is a first-generation high school and college graduate and the first person in his community to earn a law degree. He is professor of legal studies and federal Indian law.

MARGARET ANN WALLER is associate professor in the School of Social Work at Arizona State University. She teaches human development, cultural diversity, and direct practice, and has been a family therapist for fifteen years. Her primary research interest is resilience, particularly in individuals, families, and communities from diverse cultural contexts.

SUZANNA DANUTA WALTERS is associate professor of sociology and director of the women's studies program at Georgetown University. She is the author of several books on feminist cultural studies and has recently completed a manuscript entitled *All the Rage: The Story of Gay Visibility in America*. She has written and lectured widely on queer theory, gay and lesbian representation, popular culture, and feminist theory.

JANET M. WRIGHT, chair of the department of social work at the University of Wisconsin-Whitewater, and mother of five children, is the author of several articles as well as *Lesbian Step Families: An Ethnography of Love*. She lives in rural Wisconsin with her partner, children, and many animals.

GUST A. YEP is professor of speech and communication studies and human sexuality studies at San Francisco State University. He is the recipient of several research grants, as well as teaching and community service awards, and his work has appeared in numerous interdisciplinary journals and anthologies.

Index

BETWEEN MEN ~ BETWEEN WOMEN
Lesbian and Gay Studies
Lillian Faderman and Larry Gross, Editors

Richard D. Mohr, *Gays/Justice: A Study of Ethics, Society, and Law*

Gary David Comstock, *Violence Against Lesbians and Gay Men*

Kath Weston, *Families We Choose: Lesbians, Gays, Kinship*

Lillian Faderman, *Odd Girls and Twilight Lovers: A History of Lesbian Life in Twentieth-Century America*

Judith Roof, *A Lure of Knowledge: Lesbian Sexuality and Theory*

John Clum, *Acting Gay: Male Homosexuality in Modern Drama*

Allen Ellenzweig, *The Homoerotic Photograph: Male Images from Durieu/Delacroix to Mapplethorpe*

Sally Munt, editor, *New Lesbian Criticism: Literary and Cultural Readings*

Timothy F. Murphy and Suzanne Poirier, editors, *Writing AIDS: Gay Literature, Language, and Analysis*

Linda D. Garnets and Douglas C. Kimmel, editors, *Psychological Perspectives on Lesbian and Gay Male Experiences*

Laura Doan, editor, *The Lesbian Postmodern*

Noreen O'Connor and Joanna Ryan, *Wild Desires and Mistaken Identities: Lesbianism and Psychoanalysis*

Alan Sinfield, *The Wilde Century: Effeminacy, Oscar Wilde, and the Queer Moment*

Claudia Card, *Lesbian Choices*

Carter Wilson, *Hidden in the Blood: A Personal Investigation of AIDS in the Yucatán*

Alan Bray, *Homosexuality in Renaissance England*

Joseph Carrier, *De Los Otros: Intimacy and Homosexuality Among Mexican Men*

Joseph Bristow, *Effeminate England: Homoerotic Writing After 1885*

Corinne E. Blackmer and Patricia Juliana Smith, editors, *En Travesti: Women, Gender Subversion, Opera*

Don Paulson with Roger Simpson, *An Evening at The Garden of Allah: A Gay Cabaret in Seattle*

Claudia Schoppmann, *Days of Masquerade: Life Stories of Lesbians During the Third Reich*

Chris Straayer, *Deviant Eyes, Deviant Bodies: Sexual Re-Orientation in Film and Video*

Edward Alwood, *Straight News: Gays, Lesbians, and the News Media*

Thomas Waugh, *Hard to Imagine: Gay Male Eroticism in Photography and Film from Their Beginnings to Stonewall*

Judith Roof, *Come As You Are: Sexuality and Narrative*

Terry Castle, *Noel Coward and Radclyffe Hall: Kindred Spirits*

Kath Weston, *Render Me, Gender Me: Lesbians Talk Sex, Class, Color, Nation, Stud-muffins . . .*

Ruth Vanita, *Sappho and the Virgin Mary: Same-Sex Love and the English Literary Imagination*

Renée C. Hoogland, *Lesbian Configurations*

Beverly Burch, *Other Women: Lesbian Experience and Psychoanalytic Theory of Women*

Jane McIntosh Snyder, *Lesbian Desire in the Lyrics of Sappho*

Rebecca Alpert, *Like Bread on the Seder Plate: Jewish Lesbians and the Transformation of Tradition*

Emma Donoghue, editor, *Poems Between Women: Four Centuries of Love, Romantic Friendship, and Desire*

James T. Sears and Walter L. Williams, editors, *Overcoming Heterosexism and Homophobia: Strategies That Work*

Patricia Juliana Smith, *Lesbian Panic: Homoeroticism in Modern British Women's Fiction*

Dwayne C. Turner, *Risky Sex: Gay Men and HIV Prevention*

Timothy F. Murphy, *Gay Science: The Ethics of Sexual Orientation Research*

Cameron McFarlane, *The Sodomite in Fiction and Satire, 1660–1750*

Lynda Hart, *Between the Body and the Flesh: Performing Sadomasochism*

Byrne R. S. Fone, editor, *The Columbia Anthology of Gay Literature: Readings from Western Antiquity to the Present Day*

Ellen Lewin, *Recognizing Ourselves: Ceremonies of Lesbian and Gay Commitment*

Ruthann Robson, *Sappho Goes to Law School: Fragments in Lesbian Legal Theory*

Jacquelyn Zita, *Body Talk: Philosophical Reflections on Sex and Gender*

Evelyn Blackwood and Saskia Wieringa, *Female Desires: Same-Sex Relations and Transgender Practices Across Cultures*

William L. Leap, ed., *Public Sex/Gay Space*

Larry Gross and James D. Woods, eds., *The Columbia Reader on Lesbians and Gay Men in Media, Society, and Politics*

Marilee Lindemann, *Willa Cather: Queering America*

George E. Haggerty, *Men in Love: Masculinity and Sexuality in the Eighteenth Century*
Andrew Elfenbein, *Romantic Genius: The Prehistory of a Homosexual Role*
Gilbert Herdt and Bruce Koff, *Something to Tell You: The Road Families Travel When a Child Is Gay*
Richard Canning, *Gay Fiction Speaks: Conversations with Gay Novelists*
Laura Doan, *Fashioning Sapphism: The Origins of a Modern English Lesbian Culture*